La ville promenade

1670 Les desseins de Louis XIV

1667
1677

1670
1672
1674
1675

1680
1682

1724
1728
1731

1752
1770
175

170
17
17

A DESIGN MANUAL

Museum Buildings

Paul von Naredi-Rainer

Contributions by

Oliver Hilger

Gerhard Kahlert

Helmut F. O. Müller

Herbert Pfeiffer

Hans Jürgen Schmitz

Birkhäuser – Publishers for Architecture
Basel · Berlin · Boston

Editor: Angelika Schnell, Berlin

Layout and cover design: buero kleinschmidt, Berlin

Cover photograph: Hélène Binet, © Kunsthaus Bregenz

Frontispiece: Paris, Pavillon de l'Arsenal, new exhibition architecture
(Finn Geipel LIN, 2004), © Georges Fessy

Translation: Fiona Greenwood, Pacifica / California, USA
edited by Christian Rochow, Berlin

Lithography: Licht & Tiefe, Berlin

Printing: Medialis, Berlin

This book is also available in a German language edition (ISBN 3-7643-6579-X)

A CIP catalogue record for this book is available from the Library of Congress,
Washington D.C., USA

Bibliographic information published by Die Deutsche Bibliothek
Die Deutsche Bibliothek lists this publication in the Deutsche Nationalbibliografie;
detailed bibliographic data is available in the Internet at http://dnb.ddb.de

© 2004 Birkhäuser – Publishers for Architecture, P.O.Box 133, CH-4010 Basel, Switzerland
Part of Springer Science + Business Media

Printed on acid-free paper produced from chlorine-free pulp. TCF ∞

Printed in Germany
ISBN 3-7643-6580-3

9 8 7 6 5 4 3 2 1
www.birkhauser.ch

Principles of the Museum as a Building

10672   C (NAR)

Selection of Projects

Open Plans

Free-form Spaces

Conversions and Extensions of Architectural Monuments

Appendix

Münchenstein/Basel, Schaulager, entrance area
(Herzog & de Meuron, 2003)

Foreword

Designing a museum is currently regarded as a particularly attractive and desirable building commission. Arising out of the Renaissance and Baroque architecture of secular power, maturing into an autonomous building type in the age of Enlightenment, vehicle of self-representation in the nineteenth century, the museum increasingly became a mirror of architectural possibilities in the second half of the twentieth century. The connection between the 'museumization' of our society, which has become a topic of discussion everywhere, and the dynamics of the civilization process generates that field of tension in which museums as the showplace of cultural development turn into the identifying locale by which towns and regions define themselves. Not only increasing globalization but also the claims to qualitative sophistication associated precisely with the museum and its architecture have long since led to the museum-building becoming an issue of not only public interest, but also international sophistication, against the standards of which the local intentions must compete.

From all this it appears that in the end, there can be no generally applicable rules for the architecture of the museum, which of course must meet a series of functional requirements. The claim on the one hand to represent a place in which special things from the past will be shown and conserved for the future, and on the other hand, to adequately represent the present in an ambience unique in each case requires a specific amount of inventiveness per se, one that goes beyond the limits of that which can be regulated. These limits are formed more by the specific position of the respective museums within the wide range of museum concepts and the history of the building task itself, within which museum buildings, in order to position themselves, are allowed to become an expression of architectural self-referentiality to a special extent. Therefore neither can this book be, nor does it seek to be a handbook of rules for building a museum, but instead, by selecting and commenting on a wide variety of examples – each pithy in one way or another – and their embedding in a multilayered context, it seeks to fulfil the function of an atlas, a "hefty tome with charts from a field of knowledge." Just as an historical atlas cannot determine the further course of history, this Design Manual of Museum Buildings cannot determine in advance how museums will look in the future. But it can stimulate ideas and help one to plot one's own position. The saying "If one does not know where one comes from, then one cannot know where one is going" holds true particularly for building museums.

Out of the virtually innumerable new museum buildings that in the last decades have come into being primarily in Europe, in the United States and in Japan, more than six dozen museum buildings were chosen. These offer exemplary solutions for important aspects of the museum-building task and/or distinguish themselves by their unusual formal qualities. As there is no indubitably objective standard for the last-mentioned criterion in particular, the responsibility for the selection is borne to the largest extent by the author, who takes this opportunity to express his gratitude for the friendly support from the majority of the architectural offices contacted and only seldom encountered so little readiness to cooperate that the planned inclusion in the selection of one museum or another could not be carried through due to a lack of supporting documentation.

This book, born of many years of involvement with its subject, would not have come into being without help and a variety of stimuli, which are much too long to list here and in any case, I would run the risk of forgetting someone who did not merit being forgotten. However, I would like to explicitly thank Angelika Schnell, Andreas Müller and Oliver Kleinschmidt in Berlin, Petra Braselmann in Innsbruck, Franz Ebner in Bunzlau, my brother Hermann in Munich and above all, Dagmar, my wife, who was the standard of reference not only in some of the museum rooms illustratively documented here, but has always been the standard of reference everywhere. This book, the fruit of innumerable museum trips together, is dedicated to her.

Paul von Naredi-Rainer   Matrei, August 2003

Principles of the Museum as a Building

The Museum as Institution

Museums presuppose collecting, an activity that is a universal phenomenon as old as mankind itself. As a particular kind of collection, the museum is a compilation of natural objects or art objects – the latter term understood in the widest sense – that have been taken out of economic circulation, either temporarily or permanently, are carefully protected and exhibited in a self-contained place specially furnished for that purpose.[1]

The term 'museum' – from the Greek μουσεῖον (= place of the muses; place and dance floor of the muses and their mother Mnemosyne, the Greek goddess of memory) – was initially used in the ancient world to designate the schools of poetry and philosophy that came to be attached to the shrines of the muses. Later the term came to refer to the research facilities that were attached to collections such as the museum in Alexandria,[2] the most famous example which was equipped with a great library. Until the early eighteenth century, the term 'museum' referred primarily to an academy of scholars and only secondarily to a place that housed a collection. Only since the nineteenth century has 'museum' meant a building for the safekeeping and presentation of actual collections as well as the research facility attached to it.[3]

Treasure Chamber, Workplace, Collection Room

At the beginning of museum development we find the Greek treasure chambers, the Thesauroi (*fig. 1*), in which were exhibited statues of the victors of battles, booty, weapons and other gifts of all sorts dedicated to the gods,[4] objects whose iconic value was more important than their material or artistic value. However, the Romans were already filling their villas with statues and paintings which they esteemed primarily for their artistic value.[5]

The mediaeval collections held in secular treasure chambers and above all the valuable ecclesiastical collections held in church treasuries[6] were compiled similarly to the temple treasures of the ancient world: head-shaped reliquaries, jewellery, curiosities of nature, and exotica. One of Albrecht Dürer's woodcuts, whose accompanying text speaks of "Silver, gold and precious stones, of little pearls" as well as of "costly robing" (*fig. 2*), shows a treasure chamber like those found not only north of the Alps, but also at the court of Mantua, for example. There, immediately above this room described as a *grotta* was located what was called a studiolo – a type of room verifiably existing since the fourteenth century, more typical for Italy and France, which not only served as a place of safekeeping for collections of objects, but was also and above all a place for studying, a room to which one could withdraw into secluded creativity (*fig. 3*).[7] In the course of the cinquecento, the studiolo gradually lost the character of a workplace and developed into a room exclusively for a collection, in particular at the courts of the Humanist princes. Eventually, in the studiolo of Francesco I, the Grand Duke of Tuscany, the ambition manifest by the collection room was elevated to the point where the aim was to attain universality (*fig. 4*): that studiolo's picture program, which served more or less as a painted inventory of the objects in the collection (which were kept in cabinets), integrates the macrocosm of nature and the microcosm of mankind into a complex system which in the end becomes a metaphor for the duke and the splendour of the state he reigns over as well.[8]

The desire to grasp – or capture – the world scientifically and the interest in history were the prerequisites for the development of the museum. Its real history begins in Italy in the fifteenth century. In addition to contemporary art, relics of classical antiquity were also collected, and a new meaning was conferred on these objects when they were removed from their original context.[9] The new context – legitimated essentially by the concept of art – of these collections, which for the most part belonged to royalty, also implied the question as to whether classical and contemporary art could be equivalent in value. It thereby established not least that principle of the comparative regard which is still the key characteristic of art museums today. In the age of Humanism it was with no less enthusiasm that people dedicated themselves to the exploration of nature, surrounding themselves with minerals, plants, animalia and curiosities of all kinds. In the sixteenth century, the interest in both art works and the peculiarities of nature led – in Germany above all – to the emergence of those chambers of wonders and art whose combination of *artificialia* and *naturalia* was to form the core of many subsequent museum collections.[10] In addition to the royal chambers of artworks and rarities, the most famous of which were probably those of Archduke Ferdinand II in Ambras Castle in the Tyrol and Emperor Rudolf II in Prague,[11] there were also the encyclopaedically-conceived collections of nobles and scholars, arranged as *theatrum mundi*. Their intention was not to satisfy the lust for sensation but to educate and cultivate their observers – in whatever special sense. A well-known example

1 Delphi, Athenian Treasure Chamber after 490 BC (rebuilt in 1906)

2 Albrecht Dürer: Treasure vault from the "Triumphal arch of Emperor Maximilian I", Woodcut, 1515

3 Vittore Carpaccio: Vision of Saint Augustine, 1502; Venice, Scuola S. Giorgio degli Schiavoni

4 Studiolo of Grand Duke Francesco I. de Medici, 1570-72; Florence, Palazzo Vecchio

5 Museo Cospiano, Bologna: copperplate engraving for a title page, 1677

6+7 Daniel Mytens: Thomas Howard, 2ⁿᵈ Earl of Arundel and Surrey, in his gallery of antiquities | Alathea, Countess of Arundel and Surrey, in her picture gallery, circa 1618; London, National Portrait Gallery

8 David Teniers the Younger: Archduke Leopold Wilhelm in his picture gallery in Brussels, circa 1651; Vienna, Kunsthistorisches Museum

9 Picture gallery in Schloß Weissenstein ob Pommersfelden, built for the Duke of Schönborn; copperplate engraving by Salomon Kleiner, 1728

10 Hubert Robert: Grande Galerie in the Louvre, 1794/96; Paris, Louvre

of this is the Museum Kircherianum in Rome, which was founded by the German Jesuit and polymath Athanasius Kircher, and whose catalogue, published in Amsterdam in 1678, included objects from almost all subject areas, from optics through physiology to philology, from musical instruments to geography.[12] In the collection of the Bolognese nobleman Fernando Cospi (*fig. 5*), a clear distinction was made between specimens of natural history and *artificialia*[13] – a trend toward increasingly methodologically-determined collecting, which eventually led to collections being separated out into collections of antiquities, picture galleries, cabinets of coins, natural history museums, etc.

Art Galleries and the Public

The interest in classical antiquity that had arisen since the early Renaissance led to the development of collections of ancient works of art, at first in Italy, but soon in other European countries as well,[14] not least in England. There, in about 1615, Lord Arundel had a gallery constructed in his London residence (*fig. 6*)[15] especially for his collection of classical sculptures, which at the time was considered the most important one outside Italy. A complement to the duke's picture gallery, the sculpture gallery was placed opposite it (*fig. 7*). Picture galleries came into being in many courts at the same time; in them, monuments were established to taste and patronage and to satisfy the princes' need for representation.[16] A prominent example is the collection of paintings that belonged to the Archduke Leopold Wilhelm, the Hapsburg governor of the Netherlands. The collection he built up still forms the basis of the picture gallery in the Vienna Kunsthistorisches Museum, and it was recorded at his request several times by his court painter and gallery director, David Teniers the Younger (*fig. 8*).[17]

In the eighteenth century, as collections of antiquities (promoted by systematic excavations and the first scientific studies)[18] had become established in most European countries,[19] and art galleries in many seats of royal power (*fig. 9*) had replaced the old ideal of the chamber of art by limiting the area of collecting, a heightened historical consciousness combined with normative thinking began to prevail. It was this consciousness that created a new context legitimated by the conception of art,[20] and upon which the modern museum is based.

The replacement of representation by connoisseurship, which also found expression in the publication of systematic collection catalogues, led not least to the demand, associated with the emancipation of the bourgeoisie, for the royal collections to be generally accessible. In 1750, at the Palais Luxembourg in Paris, an exhibition of paintings selected from the royal possessions was mounted especially for the purpose of opening to the general public two days a week. When the Luxembourg gallery was closed again in 1779, there were already plans in the works for a larger museum in the Louvre that was to be publicly accessible. In 1759, the British Museum in London was opened. At first it contained only a library and natural history collections.[21] It was not until the nineteenth century that art collections were added, among them the Parthenon sculptures acquired by Lord Elgin.[22] Although complicated regulations regarding visitors made the British Museum accessible only with difficulty at first, the decisive point was that what was at issue in this testamentary endowment was the foundation of a museum decreed by an Act of Parliament and thereby declared an issue of public interest.

Now, according to Johann Georg Sulzer's influential *Allgemeine Theorie der schönen Künste*, first published in 1771, the word 'museum' – significantly – referred exclusively to art collections. They were supposed to be "permanently open for study to artists and connoisseurs," because they served the purpose of the "development of taste." It was with this argument so typical of the Enlightenment that the opening of the royal art collections was pursued, and in the aftermath of the French Revolution, it led eventually to the royal art collection, which had previously been nationalized, being installed in the Musée Français in the Louvre in 1793 and made accessible to all (*fig. 10*).[23] Since 1802, this museum has had the administrative structure which is still typical today: a chairman, three curators for painting, antiques, and prints and drawings, as well as administrative staff and guards. It was open to the public free of charge three days out of ten, and for the rest of the time reserved for artists for the purposes of studying and copying. Inexpensive catalogues, labels for the pictures – which were hung in a chronological system – and guided tours underlined the character of the museum as a state educational institution that had established the idea that art works were the property of the nation, to be protected by the institution of the museum and at the same time, to be presented. Another event crucial for the idea of the museum was the simultaneous establishment of the Musée des Monuments Français in a former monastery in Paris, where the painter Alexandre

11 Munich, Glyptothek (Leo von Klenze, 1816-30)

Lenoir catalogued confiscated ecclesiastical art works that were initially supposed to be destroyed, and in the end, exhibited them. Wilhelm von Humboldt, who was deeply impressed by this museum that showed mediaeval art works for the first time, recognized that Lenoir had only been able to save the objects entrusted to him from the revolutionary iconoclasm by converting what had formerly been historic monuments and objects of religious veneration into works of art.[24] For the development of the concept of the museum[25] in the nineteenth century, this occurrence was of no lesser consequence than the multitude of architectural designs by French revolutionary architects was for the development of museum architecture, which will be the subject of the next chapter.

Art and Cultural History Museums
The Romantic reverence for art and the spirit of national identity allowed the existing collections of whatever sort to appear in a new light at the beginning of the nineteenth century. The constitution and development of the individual areas of knowledge ensured that the collections were held in high esteem and, at the same time, promoted the development of the different types of museums. Particular interest was devoted to the art museums, for which the first great independent museum buildings came into existence, initially in Germany. Their design, oriented on the baroque palace as well as on the architecture of the temples of classical times, underlined the status of the museum as a place of national representation and a shrine to art (*fig. 11*).

In addition to the great German art museums of the first half of the nineteenth century in Berlin, Munich, Dresden and Stuttgart – whose buildings commissioned by sovereigns could be interpreted as the monumental correspondence to the history of art– a series of regional museums came into being, particularly in the Austro-Hungarian monarchy. These museums started ethnic and regional, historical and art-historical collections, but also collections of technology and libraries; they were supposed to awaken not least a consciousness of national identity:[26] in 1802, the Hungarian National Museum was established in Budapest,[27] in 1803, the Brukenthal National Museum for Transylvania, in 1811, the Joanneum in Graz was established as a "national museum ... for everything which Nature, the changing times, human endeavour and perseverance had brought forth in Inner Austria,"[28] in 1817, the regional museum for Bohemia and Moravia in Brno, in 1818, a museum of the fatherland in Prague, in 1823, the Tyrolean regional museum, the Ferdinandeum in Innsbruck.[29] Even the Germanische Nationalmuseum founded in 1852 in Nuremberg[30] still understood the collecting of German works of art and consumer goods as a contribution to the cultural identity of the nation. Significantly, these museums of cultural history – in which the Romantic longing for the past,

12 Berlin, Neues Museum, Roman hall; overcrowding at the end of the 19th century

13 Berlin, Kaiser-Friedrich-Museum, cabinet of Venetian painting and sculpture from the late quattrocento in the arrangement by Wilhelm von Bode, 1904

14 Berlin, Kaiser-Friedrich-Museum, the same room after rearrangement by Karl Koetschau with paintings on white walls, 1933

focused primarily on the people's own mediaeval past, played an important role – were almost exclusively creations of the middle classes. Since the middle of the nineteenth century they had begun to erect art museums for their collections – funded mostly by private patrons – such as that of the canon of Cologne, Ferdinand Franz Wallraf,[31] modelled on the royal museum buildings.[32]

As the place in which the treasures of the past were conserved and protected, the museum of the nineteenth century had become the protector of traditional values and a facility for scholarly research – both elementary functions in an age that was convinced the knowledge of the past was indispensable for coping with a present characterized by constant change. The omnipresent significance of history in the culture of the nineteenth century endowed the art museum with the charge not only of preserving the artistic inheritance of the past, but also of making it fruitful for the present. On one hand, art was to serve for pleasure and edification, but on the other hand, for developing aesthetic taste and educating too. Out of this a distinction gradually developed between the intentions of a relatively small upper class interested in culture, which still strived for a classical aesthetic education, and a significantly larger group of all those who were 'engaged in trade,' so to speak, who were creative or who appreciated, bought and used the products of 'applied art.' The distinction between the supposedly functionless 'fine arts' (painting, sculpture, etc.) and the 'applied arts' – which resulted from the association of artistic production with technology – led to the establishment of museums of applied arts (arts and crafts), of which the first, the South Kensington Museum (now the Victoria and Albert Museum) occasioned by the first World Exposition in 1851,[33] was opened the following year in London.[34] In 1864, the Österreichisches Museum für Kunst und Industrie (today the Museum of Applied Arts / Contemporary Art) was founded in Vienna, in order to render the aesthetic perception of the present a salutary experience through an exemplary collection of older works of art, and in order to promote the contemporary creation of works of applied art.[35] In the succeeding years, museums of arts and crafts were established in Berlin, Leipzig, Nuremberg, Hamburg and other German cities too,[36] but with the demise of historicism only a quarter of a century later, they lost their importance as collections of teaching aids for technology and aesthetics and went over to organizing their stocks chronologically and topographically on one hand and on the other, granting increasing attention to contemporary artistic creation and – this still holds true in many cases – continuing their collections up to the present day.

Strategies of Aesthetic Effect

Toward the end of the century, the assumption – self-evident in the early nineteenth century – that art needs to be seen historically, and that both moral instruction and civic virtues are to be derived from the history of art was increasingly thrown into question, as evidenced by the tension between historical consciousness and cultural creativity. This led to museums being increasingly seen as tired memories of the heavy weight of history burdening the present, even as mausoleums of art.[37] Moreover, the advancing 'museumization' of cultural assets had allowed the scale of museums to expand to such an extent that the normal museum visitor was hardly in a position any more "to find out what is important in the endless abundance and to concentrate on the individual work of art, undisturbed by that which hangs or stands next to it or above it," in the words of a contemporary critic.[38] A way out of this dilemma was seen on one hand in a reunion of arts and crafts as in the aesthetic movement of Art Nouveau, and on the other hand, in new collection and exhibition strategies that were no longer oriented encyclopaedically, but instead, aesthetically: the intent was no longer to be to gather specimens of every school and every master artist, but instead to buy as many masterworks by the most highly regarded artists as possible – the standard of quality for which was the degree of individuality and originality they possessed.

Established by Wilhelm von Bode and later named after him as well, the Kaiser-Friedrich-Museum in Berlin, opened in 1904[39] was epoch-making for this museological striving toward reform, in which the exhibition rooms were no longer crammed with a plethora of objects (*fig. 12*), but instead, carefully composed arrangements of the different genres – painting, sculpture and crafts – were integrated into a joint production, wherein aesthetic effect was given priority over didactic intention (*fig. 13*). As a result, the exact stylistic reproduction of the milieu where the objects originated (as it was practised in the so-called basilica of the same museum or in general in the Bayerisches Nationalmuseum[40] and recommended in the *Handbuch der Architektur* of 1906 as well) became outmoded.[41] The avant-garde of museum specialists, first and foremost the director of the Hamburger Kunsthalle, Alfred Lichtwark, eventually arrived at the idea that the art

15 Cologne, Kunstgewerbemuseum, exhibition room in 1925 (arrangement by Karl Schäfer)

16 Cologne, Kunstgewerbemuseum, exhibition room in 1932 (arrangement by Karl With)

17 Cologne, Kunstgewerbemuseum, exhibition room in 1935 (arrangement by Rudolf Verres)

museum should evoke the neutral mood of an atelier.[42] Trusting in the aesthetic power of the art work, one reduced the museum staging to a minimum and hung the pictures on a white wall in a single row, with as much space as possible between them (*fig. 14*). This development could be particularly clearly followed in the installation of the Cologne Kunstgewerbemuseum: while in 1925 a Meissen porcelain cabinet was arranged in the style of a milieu reconstruction (*fig. 15*), it was only a few years later that a presentation which at the time won much acclaim (*fig. 16*) was organized in accordance with criteria such as material and workmanship, purpose and form, as well as colour and ornament, "so as to master the unlimited abundance of materials by organizing it, without reducing individual pieces to an illustrative purpose."[43] Significantly, although this form of exhibition oriented on the principles of the Bauhaus and the artistic avant-garde was revised again soon after the Nazis seized power (*fig. 17*), the ideal of the 'modern museum' developed at the beginning of the twentieth century eventually prevailed worldwide in the end; it has dominated museum practice to a large extent until now, even if the ideological premises upon which the museum reformers used to base themselves have long since ceased to be accepted, or at most are accepted only in part.

Educational Institution or Theme Park?

Not only in those countries that only paid relatively little attention to museums in the years of reconstruction following the Second World War, erecting only limited quantities of new museum buildings, but also more or less worldwide, in the eyes of the public at the time, museums were considered to be boring or elite and were poorly visited. The accusation that the museums had cut themselves off from their own present time was coupled with the opposing assessments of museums as either temples to art or prisons thereof, but in both cases, the accusations targeted their exclusivity. The demand that was already being made by forward-looking museum experts at the end of the fifties, to transform museums and in particular, museums of modern art, into trading centres for new ideas and centres for the exchange of ideas[44] a decade later met the objectives aspired to by the protest movement triggered off by the student revolts beginning in 1968, which sought to transform the ivory towers of scholarly work into places of social discourse and to convert the museums from temples of the muses into places of learning.[45] The result is well known: the "museum for tomorrow's society,"[46] without which museum pedagogy is unimaginable,[47] and whose future in 1970 generated reflections oscillating between scepticism and optimism,[48] experienced a 'Gründerzeit'[49] whose end is not in view, despite disappearing financial resources. The paucity of public funds led to financing shifting into the private sphere in Europe, following the American model. This entails both opportunity and risk at one and the same time, allowing museums more autonomy and flexibility, but forcing them to submit to the laws of commercial efficiency. In the context of the tourist industry, it threatens to make them into art fairs[50] which will be judged on the extent to which they turn out to be successful in drawing in the public, and, moreover, this success is evaluated as evidence of the democratisation of culture. The public role of the museum is thus changing, and not insignificantly so. In the end, it raises the question as to whether the museum is a "theme park or [an] educational institution."[51]

The Museum in Media Society: Responsibilities and Opportunities

Even if today people sometimes flirt with the idea of throwing the museum into question[52] following the tradition of avant-garde front-liners like the Futurists,[53] as institutions, they are more successful than ever before. Never before have more people visited museums,[54] and never before have so many museum buildings been erected in such a short time. Never before has there been such a variety of museums; they range from museums of art and architecture to science and technology museums, from museums of natural history of all sorts to the most varied of historical, cultural history or ethnological museums. The "'museumization' of our cultural environment,"[55] which has reached an unprecedented extent in the meantime,[56] carries with it the danger of using history to compensate for the rapid developments of the present time and in so doing, obstructing the view of our own time.[57] On the other hand, that is precisely where the museum's opportunity lies, as an "island in time" to be a place for those things "that remain after time's flight in pursuit of progress, in which they are not replaced by something new."[58] As a living form of memory, the museum should not simply content itself with just archiving these things, however; it must instead address the question as to how the experiences contained in them can be made useable for us, and even more, how the present can be measured against that which is timeless. In these formulations of the museum's functions, two different conceptions of the museum can be detected: a more recent one, currently in vogue, in which the museum is an archive for objects, and an older one in which it is the *Mouseion*, the place of the muses.[59] By contrasting a collection of things once wakened to life, then abandoned by it, subsequently selected from a meaningless quantity of similar objects, and thereby elevated to lastingness – the selection assigning meaning by the very act of being included in a collection – the museum acquires a social authority that fundamentally distinguishes it from the mass media's ephemeral and often arbitrary-seeming plethora of information. However, because people approach the museum from the perspective of consumers, seeking sensory experiences and amusement and with the need to stroll, saunter or windowshop instilled by the experiences of everyday life – attitudes cultivated by the mass media – the museum is obliged to combine knowledge value, entertainment value and consumer value.[60] This is a dilemma that must be solved not least by the museum's architecture – or which leads to there being two types of museum in future: one, "the place, where inheritance and history have to be conserved and the [other, the] place that one seeks out in order to stroll about, to entertain oneself, to play, to enjoy oneself."[61]

A further consequence of the changed situation of the museum in the media and consumer world is the blurring of the boundary-line that used to be located between the profane market where art was traded and the temple dedicated to art. The museum is unavoidably tied to the art market – and in consequence to the rapid rhythm of event culture – by contemporary art, which, as it finds its stage there, is increasingly produced directly for the museum. It is therefore menaced with losing its status precisely as a space outside of the present. Transformed thus into a medium, the museum can only legitimate itself as the antithesis of the mass media, the instance that invites one to remember time and to experience space and things.[62] This applies in particular when one takes into account the 'imaginary museum' that has long been available in databases, which the French writer André Malraux once described as the boundless and spatially unbounded collection of the art works of all epochs and cultures.[63] The real museum is distinguished from that not only by its unique collection, to be found in no other place in this combination, but above all by the fact that it is originals that are at issue. In contrast to Walter Benjamin's fear, expressed in 1936, that the work of art's technical reproducibility would steal its aura from it[64] we are now finding out that precisely the reverse is true: the omnipresence of reproduction underlines the uniqueness of the original and thereby actually lends it an aesthetic cult value. In a world "in which the surrogate appears to be everything in the meantime, the real strength of the museum emanates from the original; for in the original, people encounter the unique."[65] If its aura stimulates the imagination and promotes the development of a visual culture[66] that can at least oppose the transformation of our built environment into wasteland, and if critical reflection can be stimulated by the presentation of these originals, then the museum can now contribute more than ever to the conservation of the humane by fulfilling its classical responsibility of "collecting, conserving, and exhibiting" in a manner adapted to the changed conditions.

The Museum as a Building Type –
a Historical Survey

19 Mantua, Galleria della Mostra in the Palazzo Ducale (Giuseppe Dattaro and Anto Maria Viani, circa 1590)

20 Munich, Antiquarium (cabinet of antiquities) in the royal residence (Wilhelm Egkl and Friedrich Sustris, 1568-71 and after 1580)

21 Rome, Galleria in the Palazzo Colonna (Antonio del Grande and Girolamo Fontana, 1675-78)

22 Florence, the Tribuna of the Uffizi (Bernardo Buontalenti, 1581-84)

The history of the museum as a building type begins in the Renaissance.[67] The courtyard of statues in the belvedere of the Vatican, which was designed in 1508 by the most important architect of the time, Donato Bramante, for Pope Julius II, is considered to be the first architectural work created especially for exhibiting works of art. The most prominent classical sculptures still stand in the niches developed out of the corners of this courtyard, which, significantly, was called the Atrio del Piacere by contemporaries (*fig. 18*), although it was later altered.[68] Subsequently, similar courtyards of statues were built in various Roman palaces and villas, and their ground plans, which have been square for the most part since the museum projects of the French Revolution, have advanced to become one of the fundamental components of the museum.

Gallery and Central Hall

It was in the sixteenth century too that a particular type of room – the gallery – was already coming into being, one that initially developed out of the context as a whole of the castle or palace in France and Italy[69] – and which in the final analysis was rooted in classical times. It was an extended interior room mostly lighted by windows placed along the long sides and suitable both for the emplacement of sculptures and hanging paintings. A lavish decorative program, exemplarily embodied in the gallery of the French King François I erected in Fontainebleau in 1533-40, served both representation and recreation, which is fitting for the works of art shown there. A two-storey gallery commissioned by Vespasiano Gonzaga in Sabbioneta built in 1583-84,[70] forms an open corridor with arcades on both sides on the ground floor. The upper storey designed with niches for busts and painted walls served for exhibiting antique sculptures just as did the similarly designed Galleria della Mostra in the Palazzo Ducale of Mantua, commissioned somewhat later by Duke Vincenzo I Gonzaga (*fig. 19*). However, the most ambitious example is the Antiquarium of the Munich Residenz, founded under Duke Albrecht V of Bavaria,[71] a combination of gallery and treasure chamber, above which the ducal library was housed on the upper floor. This most outstanding secular Renaissance room of the sixteenth century north of the Alps was executed between the years 1568 and 1571 by Wilhelm Egkl and shortly afterward converted into a banquet hall by Friedrich Sustris. The 66-meter-long room does not have a flat ceiling like the other galleries mentioned above, but instead is roofed over by a relatively low, broad barrel vault, into which seventeen groins are cut into each of the two long sides. It is lit by windows placed high up in the walls in such a way that the three-dimensional qualities of the sculptures exhibited there are shown off to advantage in a specific way (*fig. 20*).

As an almost indispensable constituent of palace building, galleries are found in the seventeenth and eighteenth centuries both in the city palaces of Rome and, with very varied furnishings, in the different German seats of princely power. A particularly magnificent gallery that served both for the exhibition of sculptures and the presentation of paintings, and whose ceiling frescoes glorified the owner is the Galleria in the Palazzo Colonna in Rome, designed in 1675-78 by Antonio del Grande and Girolamo Fontana (*fig. 21*). In 1733, in one wing of the Munich Residenz, François Cuvilliés the Elder erected a picture gallery with seven axes (the Grüne Galerie), which – evidently following the design of the gallery of mirrors in the Palace of Versailles – only had window openings on one of the long sides, and across from it, alternating room-high mirrors and doors. Finally, in England, we often find galleries combined with a central room – an architectural motif that is much favoured in museum buildings in recent times and whose origins go back to long before the beginnings of real museum architecture.

After 1581, Bernardo Buontalenti adapted the upper storey of the Uffizi in Florence – initially designed in 1560 by Giorgio Vasari as offices – to house the Medici art collection. However, for the main works of the collection, he was commissioned by the Grand Duke Francesco I to create the famous Tribuna in the east wing, an octagonal room roofed over by a cupola and conceived as an allegory of the universe with its four elements (*fig. 22*).[72] In addition to the universal ambition of this spatial creation, brought to expression by the decoration as well as by the statues exhibited there in such a manner as to emphasize their significance, it was certainly also the lighting by means of a central skylight, favourable from a museum technology perspective, which made the Tribuna of the Uffizi a milestone in the history of museum architecture. Sebastiano Serlio had already pointed out the quality of the incidence of light from above in the third book of his treatise on architecture published for the first time in 1540, and had therein praised the classical Pantheon in Rome – whose original purpose was for displaying statues of the gods – for the way it directed light and also for its spatial design as an exemplary collection room.[73] Thus it is not by chance that Peter Paul Rubens had a multi-storey rotunda lit only from above built for his art collection in his city palace in

18 The Vatican, courtyard of statues in the belvedere and the Museo Pio-Clementino, ground plan; engraving in the manner of Paul Letarouilly: Le Vatican, Paris 1882

24 The Vatican, rotunda of the Museo Pio-Clementino (Michelangelo Simonetti, 1773-80); engraving in the manner of Paul Letarouilly: Le Vatican, Paris 1882

23 Robert Adam: Newby Hall, Yorkshire: Section through the sculpture gallery, circa 1767

30 Kassel, Museum Fridericianum (Simon Louis du Ryl, 1769- 77)

31 Dulwich Picture Gallery (Sir John Soane, 1811-14)

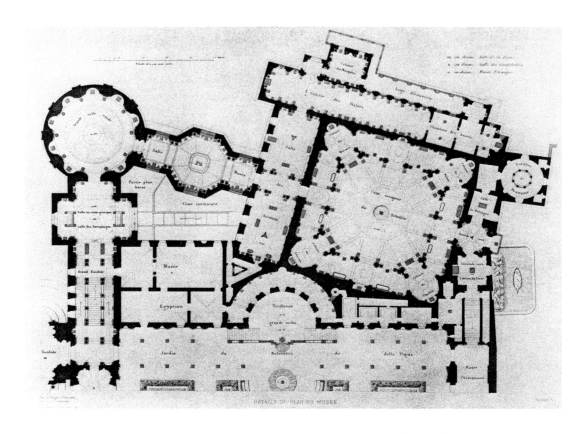

Antwerp; contemporaries compared it with the Pantheon.[74] A century later the motif, inspired by the Pantheon, of a dome-vaulted room accessed by a portico was found in the program for a generously proportioned, four-wing museum in Dresden, in which both the Tribuna of the Uffizi and Rubens' antique room were cited as models.[75] Finally, since the second half of the eighteenth century domed rotundas – as a rule combined in one way or another with a gallery – belong to the fixed repertoire of museum buildings.

A typical example of this motif especially adequate to English classicism is the gallery erected by Robert Adam for the sculpture collection of a Yorkshire nobleman around 1767 as the showpiece of his house Newby Hall: two rectangular rooms with low ceilings and windows only on one side, combined with a rotunda lighted from above in between them (*fig. 23*).[76] More prominent and thus also more influential than the English private museums, which came into being mostly as the result of the Grand Tour to Italy that nobles were expected to undertake to round out their education[77] was the Museo Pio-Clementino in the Vatican, built around 1773-80 following Bramante's octagonal courtyard mentioned at the beginning, and named after the Popes Clement XIV and Pius VI.[78] The real significance of this architectural monument, designed by Michelangelo Simonetti, Gaetano Marini and Guiseppe Camporesi, lies in the number of magnificent individual rooms, whose pivotal point is the Sala Rotunda (*fig. 24*), which consciously reminds one of the Pantheon, the only classical space in Rome that was conserved in its entirety.

Museums as Public Buildings

As if summarizing the architectural motifs described until now, the numerous museum designs of the revolutionary epoch in France almost always provide for a rotunda at the centre of a generously proportioned four-wing arrangement, its square ground plan usually divided into four courtyards by four inner wings – like the outer wings, developed as galleries – in the form of a Greek cross. This is shown in an exemplary fashion by the museum design of Jacques-Nicolas-Louis Durand, considered by his contemporaries as a textbook example (*fig. 25*).[79] Between 1778 and 1814, the Parisian Académie d'Architecture, a centre of Neoclassicism along with Rome and England, several times offered the renowned Grand Prix de Rome for the design of a museum. It is true that these designs, which released the museum from the old architectural obligations and made it into an autonomous building, were not executed, but some were published. In this way, they exerted a significant influence on the subsequent development of museum architecture. The 1783 museum design by Etienne-Louis Boullée (*figs. 26-29*) is particularly spectacular:[80] it is a square building accentuated by four victory columns, with four cloverleaf-like extended colonnades and Greek cross included on the ground plan. Surrounded by columns, an enormous round central room at the ele-

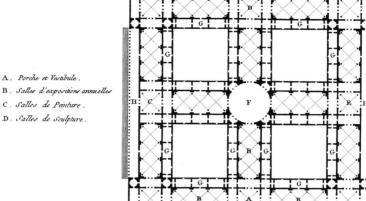

A . *Porche et Vestibule*.
B . *Salles d'expositions annuelles*
C . *Salles de Peinture*.
D . *Salles de Sculpture*.

E .. *Salles d'Architecture*.
F . *Salle de Réunion*
G . *Cabinets des Artistes*.
H . *Entrées particulieres*.

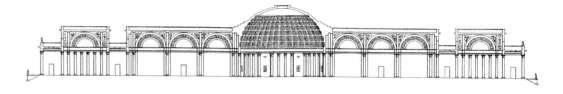

vated intersection of the arms of the cross, themselves developed as stairways roofed over with huge barrel vaults, takes the form of an entirely bare hemisphere – outwardly not apparent – with a round central opening. Although the gigantic dimensions of this ideal design are not calculated with a view to being executed, the intention of this museum project – which was called the "Temple of Glory," seeking to be both the shrine of the muses and a memorial to great men at one and the same time and thereby, in the end, a symbolic monument for the universality of the spirit of man – nonetheless went far beyond the intention of a largely royal art collection and lent the task of building a museum a status that was reflected, at least to some extent, by the first museum buildings of the nineteenth century and is given more weight than ever in the museum architecture of our time.

Only a few years previously, between 1769 and 1777, Simon Louis Du Ry had erected a strictly symmetrical, two-storey three-wing building in Kassel. The client who commissioned it, Friedrich II, the Landgrave of Hessen, called it the "Museum Fridericianum," according to the inscription on the gable of the six-columned portico that distinguishes the nineteen-axed main façade structured by colossal Ionic pillars (*fig. 30*).[81] Uncoupled from the castle complex, the building, whose architectural form combines baroque castle tradition and early neoclassicism, was from the beginning planned exclusively as a publicly accessible (!) link between library and museum and thus can be regarded as Europe's first autonomous museum building. It is not without reason that the classical-style portico – an architectural symbol of dignity which in this case was certainly linked to the educational ideal of the Enlightenment – was afterwards to be found on numerous nineteenth century museum buildings.

It was not until a generation later, in 1811-14, that another museum building, the Dulwich Picture Gallery designed by Sir John Soane, was erected on the outskirts of London. Although it is unconventionally attached to the mausoleum for the client, the building, originally consisting of a rhythmic sequence of five main rooms alternately square and rectangular and flanked by cabinets can claim to be the first picture gallery erected as an independent building.[82] What is remarkable about this building is not only the unpretentious exterior, but above all the skylight construction, which is still considered exemplary (*fig. 31*).

The task of building a museum was definitively established as a special category in architecture by the great museums erected at a significant cost in materials and planning in Berlin, Munich and London after the Napoleonic wars. For the Glyptothek in Munich, the building of which was initiated by the Bavarian crown prince who later became King Ludwig I for the exhibition of his important collection of antiques,[83] the architects Karl von Fischer, Karl Freiherr Haller von Hallerstein and Leo von Klenze delivered a series of designs. In different ways these processed the impulses of the French ideal designs, implementing the

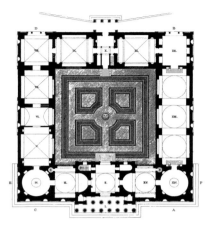

32 Munich, Glyptothek, ground plan
(Leo von Klenze, 1816-30)

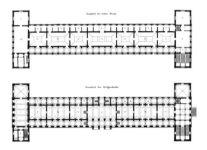

33 Munich, Alte Pinakothek, ground plan
(Leo von Klenze, 1822-36)

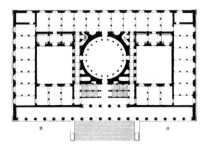

34 (bottom) + **35** (top) Berlin, Altes Museum
(Karl Friedrich Schinkel, 1823-30), ground floor
plan | rotunda; from: K.F. Schinkel: Sammlung
architektonischer Entwürfe, 1831

motifs of the rotunda and the portico. Klenze, who in the end was awarded the brief for the building, which was executed between 1816 and 1830, developed the Glyptothek from inside out – in contrast to his competitors – by coordinating the number, form, decoration, and lighting of the rooms with the objects of the collection, which were arranged chronologically for the first time. Combined with the banquet halls and vestibules that the client demanded, a four-winged building resulted; it had a square interior courtyard (*fig. 32*) and thus provided the opportunity for a circular tour leading through differently shaped and furnished rooms, during which "the observer clearly sees the course of art, its rise and fall" to use the words of the architect. Both the frescoes by Peter von Cornelius, now destroyed, and the ornaments and sculptural reliefs in the individual rooms related directly to the art works exhibited therein. The main façade, an eight-columned ionic portico between lower wings, was designed in the 'Greek style' analogous to the content of the collection in accordance with the explicit desire of the client, to whom Klenze had also presented variations in the 'Roman style' as well as in the 'style of the Renaissance.' The fact that the empty aedicula niches in the windowless walls are more reminiscent of the Renaissance than of models from classical times shows that for Klenze, it was definitely a matter of creating a new type of building.

The architectural features borrowed from the Italian architecture of the sixteenth century that Klenze chose for the building of the Alte Pinakothek in Munich were to refer programmatically to the painting of the Renaissance, esteemed as the high point of art historical development and represented in particular by Raphael's paintings.[84] In 1822, while the building work on the Glyptothek was still going on, Klenze, commissioned to design a building for the Wittelsbach collection of paintings, planned a long building for the optimal arrangement and lighting of the collection; on the upper storey there was a series of seven rooms of different sizes lit by skylights. On the north side of them, there were twenty-five cabinets laterally lit by northern light, interconnected with each other and connected to the larger rooms at short intervals. Their counterpart on the south side was a gallery that enabled all of the main rooms to be accessed directly. This was destroyed during the Second World War and replaced by Hans Döllgast's grand stairway. The short lateral wings contained the stairwell and some special rooms, the ground floor, storerooms, and offices (*fig. 33*). With this arrangement, Klenze pointed the way to the type of the modern picture gallery and, at the same time, turned away from the French museum designs canonized particularly by Durand, whose influence was still clearly perceptible not only in Klenze's design for the Glyptothek, but also in the design for the Altes Museum in Berlin that Karl Friedrich Schinkel was drafting at that time.

By the age of nineteen, and without having been commissioned, Schinkel had already delivered the design of a museum building with a portico and two domed rooms set in an idealized classical landscape.[85] With the Altes Museum in the Berlin Lustgarten, erected in 1823-30, he created a building on a par with the palace and the cathedral, the two most important building projects of the preceding century – that was supposed to not only house the works of art, but also – as a building dedicated to art in accordance with the programmatic motto "First give pleasure, then edify" – embody the idea of beauty and enable art to carry out its educational mission.[86] A show side developed as a colossal colonnade over a raised ground floor pierced by a straight-flight stairway elevated the building – destined both for the presentation of sculptures and a collection of paintings – above the level of everyday architecture. Although otherwise appearing as a solid, two-storey block, it also emphasized its public character by adhering to the tradition of using the roofed-over columned hall of classical times. The two storeys each contain laterally lit exhibition rooms, those in the lower storey supported by two rows of columns. These exhibition rooms form four wings surrounding a rectangle; the latter is divided into two small courtyards by a cubic central building extending above eaves height and surrounding a central rotunda. In the stairwell, which provides the central access to the museum and which is transversely placed in the row of exhibition rooms between the columned hall and the rotunda, the one-storey representation area and the two-storey usable area interpenetrate in a very artistic fashion (*fig. 34*). In spite of certain difficulties of use caused especially by the lack of lighting from above in the picture gallery, Schinkel's Altes Museum is considered to be the building that definitively ennobled the task of museum-building because of its clear and memorable architecture that linked the functional with the sublime and permanently established the domed rotunda (*fig. 35*) as a motif of museum architecture.

These early royal museum buildings in Berlin and Munich, which could be described as prototypes of the 'representative museum,' exerted an extraordinarily great influence on the numerous museum projects of subsequent years both in Germany and abroad, and as they were considered exemplary, the solutions that

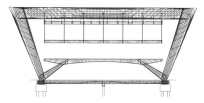

52 Rio de Janeiro, Museum of Modern Art, section through the gallery wing (Affonso Eduardo Reidy, 1954)

53 London, Crystal Palace (Joseph Paxton, 1850-51)

54 Norwich, Sainsbury Centre for the Visual Arts, University of East Anglia (Norman Foster, 1974-77)

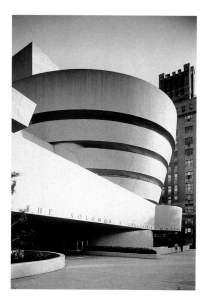

55 New York, Solomon R. Guggenheim Museum (Frank Lloyd Wright, 1943-59)

being made between permanent, more or less completed collections and temporary exhibitions. The Wilhelm-Lehmbruck-Museum in Duisburg, built in 1959-64, is considered to be a classic example of the combination of a static and a dynamic museum area. Manfred Lehmbruck, who had already grouped disparate museum areas and other cultural facilities such as a pavilion around a central entrance hall in the Reuchlinhaus in Pforzheim (*fig. 51*),[122] used a glazed entrance wing here to link the static museum part dedicated to his father's sculptural works and formed of concrete slabs, to a glazed hall, conceived as a large display case for temporary exhibitions and which allowed all manner of spatial development with the aid of standardized installation assembly elements. By transferring the supporting structural elements to the exterior, it allowed all types of light incidence. Affonso Eduardo Reidy had already effected a comparable construction in the gallery wing of his museum for modern art in Rio de Janeiro, completed in 1955 (*fig. 52*).[123]

The concept of the 'living museum,' the prerequisite for which is a variable spatial design, had been developed in the early post-war years by the Hanover museum director Alexander Dorner, who later became a university lecturer in the United States. He does not consider the museum a "temple of eternal values" but as a "place in which the evolutionary growth of our cultural strengths" should become apparent.[124] It was not least the recognition that the criteria for evaluating preservation and exhibition value are subject to continuous change that led to a rejection of mono-functional buildings and to the demand, voiced by Walter Gropius among others, for the greatest possible flexibility in the interior of the museum through the avoidance of a rigid arrangement of walls.[125] The first spatial constructions that a century previously had already essentially fulfilled these conditions were the neutral and flexible buildings of iron and glass. The most spectacular of these, Joseph Paxton's Crystal Palace, erected within the space of nine months (*fig. 53*), achieved wide renown through World Exposition in London in 1851[126] and within a short time, had numerous successors.[127] The fact that the glass palace erected in Munich in 1853-54 for an industry and trade exhibition[128] was designed by August von Voit is interesting, for he is the architect who had built the Neue Pinakothek shortly before. Nonetheless, at first a strict distinction was made between museum buildings and the buildings constructed with iron. These latter were by their very nature anti-museums; they "were presentation buildings, without being at the same time representation buildings."[129] Although this type of exhibition architecture was used in isolated cases for American museums in the succeeding decades, it was not until more than a century had passed that it came into use in museum buildings, for example, in Norman Foster's Sainsbury Centre for the Visual Arts at the University of East Anglia in Norwich, designed in 1974 (*fig. 54*)[130] or in the American Wing of the Metropolitan Museum in New York, built in 1980 by Kevin Roche and John Dinkeloo.[131] Although the Neue Nationalgalerie in Berlin (cf. pp. 198-199) is usually interpreted as a temple metaphor because of its formal perfection, as the design for a large column-free space that Mies van der Rohe had initially intended to be an administrative building,[132] it is situated in the tradition of the glass palaces of the nineteenth century. The Centre Pompidou in Paris, built between 1972 and 1977, is the building that must be considered their real successor (cf. pp. 174-177); its architects, Renzo Piano and Richard Rogers, planned it as a "flexible container and dynamic communication machine" and thus as a counterweight to the design of the museum as a sacred place (p. 38, *fig. 99*). It seems paradoxical that the interior space of the Centre Pompidou, intended to be entirely open, was in the end subdivided into small spaces by other architects and thereby lost much of its dynamism and flexibility, while the undivided spatial container of the Neue Nationalgalerie in Berlin, built a decade previously by Mies van der Rohe (cf. pp. 198-199), functions only to a limited extent as a flexible exhibition space, although as an architectural monument, it carries on directly where Schinkel's Altes Museum left off. From this discrepancy, which comes to light particularly clearly in the disputes over the building of the Neue Staatsgalerie in Stuttgart (cf. pp. 70-73), it becomes clear that since the seventies at the latest, there has not been any unilinear evolution in museum building. The reasons for this are complex and contradictory.[133] Although the increasing density and networking of information and the enormous intensification of cultural and economic interrelations that has enabled American architects to build in Europe, Austrians in France, Italians in the Netherlands, Japanese in Spain, and Germans in America would lead one to expect a similar assimilation in architectural expression, the diversification of the spectrum of museum buildings, the transgression of the boundaries between genres that resulted out of an expanded conception of art, but above all, the widening of the museum's functional scope, transforming it into an experiential space, a new public space and not least, into an identity-generating factor for a location have, in actual fact, led to great variety in architectural design, which it is hardly possible to systematize.

56 Mönchengladbach, Museum Abteiberg
(Hans Hollein, 1972-82)

57 Groningen, Museum, Gallery of Old Masters
(Coop Himmelb(l)au, 1992-94)

58 Munich, Goetz collection
(Jacques Herzog & Pierre de Meuron, 1989-92)

The task of building museums has certainly been considered particularly attractive in the last decades not only because of the oft-cited fact that "the planning of museums represents something like the last free space for the exercise of designing with artistic ambitions, which is because it is one of the few tasks for which no special guidelines, building codes or standardized expectations have been developed until now, luckily"[135] – which, at best, only partially still holds true – but instead and above all, probably because hardly any other building task is more suitable for representing the self-image of architecture oscillating between fiction and function. In this regard, the possibilities of architectural design range from extreme dynamic force and formal opulence to extreme reduction. As an incunabulum of the belief that architecture does not have to serve art, but instead to challenge it,[136] the Solomon R. Guggenheim Museum in New York (p. 27, *fig. 55*), on which Frank Lloyd Wright worked since 1943 and whose opening in 1959 he did not live to enjoy, very soon found its established place in the history of architecture.[137] Although the large sculptural form of the rising, funnel-shaped spiral, sharply criticized for its very limited functionality, but undisputed as an architectural work of art, did not have any direct successors, it has established the importance of the museum as an architectural work of art so successfully that the museum building in Bilbao, commissioned half a century later by the Guggenheim Foundation (cf. pp. 218-221) was obliged to measure itself against the inimitable conciseness of Wright's building and to counter it with a contemporary equivalent.

The task of building a museum finally became the focus of public interest at the beginning of the eighties with Hans Hollein's Abteiberg Museum in Mönchengladbach (cf. pp. 138-141; *fig. 56*), which won several rewards. It united the traits of heterogeneous museum types into an effectively staged architectural landscape that met a variety of functional requirements, without ever giving up its artistic claims. The museum in Mönchengladbach is at the beginning of a continuing wave of new museum buildings whose stylistic labelling, which ranges from the Postmodernism of the eighties[138] via Deconstruction (*fig. 57*) to the Minimalism of the nineties (*fig. 58*), says little, of course, about the respectively specific characteristics or typological categorization of these buildings.[139] Despite their very divergent formal language, what almost all these buildings have in common is their architectural ambition:[140] while many of the museums apostrophized as Postmodern replace the awe-inspiring gesture of the nineteenth century by generating a curious, often ironically staged attitude of expectation, the museums reduced to the simplest volumes, whose prototype is considered to be the small Goetz collection in Munich (Jacques Herzog & Pierre de Meuron, 1989-92)[141] are determined by an aesthetic as rigorous as it is refined. The Kunsthaus Bregenz (cf. pp. 196-197), for example, is hardly any more neutral in relation to the works of art than the bulky architecture of the extension pavilion of the Groninger Museum (p. 42, *fig. 118*),[142] whose architects are proud that no-one has yet succeeded in designing a good exhibition in it.[143]

Although the functional requirements of visitor circulation, lighting, etc. in cultural history museums or museums of technology are basically the same as those in art museums, the opportunities and problems of contemporary museum architecture are particularly evident there, because the confrontation with the works of fine art directly challenges architecture – either to create an envelope whose purpose is to serve or to produce the self-projection of an artistic genre on a par with the works of art. Therefore, in this account we shall deal primarily with art museums, and for these it is true that the variable – and at the same time, critical – point is the view of art, which for some is something exciting, occasionally moving or even amusing, but always something consumable, while for others it is a way to understanding. For architecture, particularly because it understands itself to be art, the great challenge is still to design museums "that are neither dormitories nor entertainment centres, but instead laboratories for sensory appreciation and unrelenting rational, critical reflection."[144]

The Semantics of the New Museum Architecture

59 Munich, Pinakothek der Moderne, exhibition hall on the upper floor (Stephan Braunfels, 1992-2002)

60 Weil am Rhein, Vitra Design Museum (Frank O. Gehry, 1987-89)

61 Vaduz, Kunstmuseum Liechtenstein (Arbeitsgemeinschaft Morger, Degelo und Kerez, 1997-2000)

The comparison between artistic and religious experience as it became a conventional formula above all in the German Romantic movement,[145] and the conception of the museum as a pedagogic facility are the two poles of the museum concept[146] that have decisively marked the appearance of museum architecture all along. The duality of edification and education, which found expression in the museum buildings of the nineteenth century in a finely-grained hierarchy of architectural formulae for dignity, now characterises more than ever the different views of the relationship between that which is exhibited and the architecture that houses it. If the historical consciousness of the nineteenth century – and of the early twentieth century as well – required that works of art be presented in a stylistically appropriate architecture in chronological order – such as in the Bavarian National Museum in Munich – now the so-called 'neutral' case or envelope is considered the ideal, at least among museum experts (*fig. 59*). The 'white museum' first realized in 1950-51 by Franco Albini in the Palazzo Bianco in Genoa[147] reflects on one hand the post-war notions of a new beginning and, on the other hand, is a construction – seen as inimical to history – of the purist modernism that stages itself. However, the supposedly neutral envelope does not result in the oft-proclaimed 'democratic' proximity at all, but instead isolates the art works and in so doing, distances or alienates the observer.[148] As an aesthetic principle, the isolation is an achievement of the last hundred years and therefore anything but timeless, emphasizing the unique aura of the work of art and elevating it to a "zone of unquestioningness ..., which is the secular correspondent of worship."[149] As far as that is concerned, the neutrality of the white cube[150] is a stubborn myth aptly apostrophized as "pride of asceticism,"[151] which conceals a specific attitude to the function of art that cannot claim universal applicability at all. Rather, it raises the question as to whether in our own time – in which the real is increasingly superseded by a virtual world – in addition to the aura of the original work of art, the aura of the space of the museum too will become increasingly significant and anthropologically important, because it offers spatial experiences (*fig. 60*) that are becoming increasingly rare in view of the developments in media society.[152] Seen from this perspective, the controversy about whether architecture should serve art or art architecture turns out to be obsolete in the end – not least because in the transformation of culture by mass civilization, art, like architecture, has long since been subsumed by that event culture in which the museum is also part of the tourist industry and art too a form of entertainment.[153] In this connection, the polarity between edification and education, supplemented by the factor of the experiential character, broadens into a three-way relationship in which the museum – in addition to being an 'aesthetic church' dedicated to contemplation as well as a place of teaching and learning, in the end, as an 'entertaining museum' – also functions as a sort of art fair. The architectural conceptions of the museum, ranging from the elite treasure house (*fig. 61*), via the reduction to the functional container of a factory hall, to the ambitious work of art (*figs. 62-64*), are correspondingly varied. It is self-evident that this categorization is itself only a construct whose boundaries can hardly be sharply drawn in view of built reality, in particular because of the high value that the aesthetic criterion of originality was accorded in the twentieth century. Although the ambiguity of the concept of the museum on one hand and the stylistic variety of contemporary architecture on the other hand renders it difficult to attempt to discern something like a semantics of museum architecture, in view of the ambition common to almost all museum buildings, it appears justified.

65 Berlin, Bauhaus Archive
(Walter Gropius / Walter Ceijanovic, 1963 / 1976-78)

66 Appenzell, Museum Liner
(Annette Gigon and Mike Guyer, 1996-98)

67 St. Pölten, Niederösterreichisches Landesmuseum, (Hans Hollein, 1992-2002)

68 Krems, Karikaturmuseum
(Gustav Peichl, 2001-02)

73 Saint-Ours-les-Roches near Clermont-Ferrand,
"Vulcania" (Hans Hollein, 1994-2002)

Function and Symbol

In modern museum-building, the search for a symbolic architectural language characterizing the task of building a museum[154] led initially to the sawtooth roof construction, which, as a relatively conspicuous architectural characteristic, resolves one of the most important technical museum problems, at least for picture galleries, which is to say the right lighting – and at the same time, brings it into focus. Thus the sawtooth roof construction is implemented as a design feature by architects who are hardly comparable otherwise, such as Walter Gropius (Bauhaus Archive in Berlin; *fig. 65*),[155] Gigon & Guyer (Museum Liner in Appenzell; *fig. 66*)[156] or Hans Hollein (Niederösterreichisches Landesmuseum in St. Pölten; (*fig. 67*)[157] – even, in the last case, to purposely differentiate between the picture gallery and the natural history wing across from it, whose telescoped volumes appear almost zoomorphic.

While in these cases the choice of the sawtooth roof has primarily a functional justification, it is also used in Gustav Peichl's small caricature museum in Krems[158] (*fig. 68*) as an *architecture parlante* to transform the façade into a wavy roof landscape, whose silhouette fits together with the pointed structural elements of the upper storey to suggest a clown's mask – an unmistakable reference to the purpose of the building.[159] The fact that the implementation of anthropomorphic elements in architecture has a long history[160] does not change the semantic effect of this façade at all. Shanghai's art museum appears in its design to be incomparably more lavish, but in its immediate architectural reference to the content of the museum, it is entirely comparable (*fig. 69*).[161] This museum's exterior is oriented on one of China's oldest vessels, the bronze 'thing,' several examples of which are contained in the precious collection of the museum, whose interior has a largely conventional design. In a similar way, the parabolic cupola in Friedrich Kiesler's Shrine of the Book in Jerusalem (cf. pp. 210-211) has an illustrative character, in that it is supposed to be reminiscent of the cover of that vessel in which the Qumran scripture rolls that are now exhibited there survived the centuries. Yet such examples of direct architectural illustration – to which one could add the design of the Keramion in Frechen (*fig. 70*)[162] which is supposed to remind one of a potter's wheel – remain isolated and can certainly not claim to express the meaning 'museum' clearly and in a universally valid fashion. The Evoluon technology museum in Eindhoven (*fig. 71*) gives evidence of the ephemeral character of architectural connotations of forms adopted from the domain of technology in particular. Opened in 1966, the museum is supposed to represent a flying saucer. At first it was a magnet for the public, but with the victorious advent of virtual worlds, it lost its futuristic attraction and was closed in 1989, since then serving primarily as a conference centre. It is true that the design of a rotating body such as Oscar Niemeyer's museum of contemporary art, opened in 1996 in Niterói in Brazil (*fig. 72*)[164] is able to evoke fascination as always, but it is here chosen primarily because of its unusual location on a cliff jutting out over the ocean, and thus has more to do with a concern with the surroundings than with illustrative symbolism.

The design of the Vulcania museum, opened in 2002 in the Auvergne in France, with which Hans Hollein attempted to represent the subject of volcanism through architecture, is inspired by the unusual landscape to the same degree that it is marked by archetypical symbolism. In dialectic correspondence to a deep artificial crater, a truncated cone rises 28 meters into the air; it is split in half, with the two halves telescoped against each other, its interior panelled with golden titanium screens: it is a paraphrase of the volcanic cones in the surrounding area, just as it symbolizes the eruptive force of red-hot magma (*fig. 73*).[165]

It is clear that such a graphic illustrative form relatively independent of function but deeply symbolic remains the exception. Let us therefore turn back once again to the the sawtooth roof design, whose form, doubtless primarily functionally determined, can also be used to adapt to the topographic context, as the museum complex at the foot of Cologne Cathedral shows (cf. pp. 108-109). It is above all in some smaller interior rooms that are almost literally crushed by the form of these sawteeth, equally-dimensioned throughout, where it becomes evident to what a large extent the formative influence of the sawtooth roof structure reacts primarily to the dominant architecture of the Gothic cathedral, and not to functional considerations. Thus we must remember that a motif like the sawtooth roof – resulting out of the function of optimum lighting – is only relatively seldom used in a form-determining way, and that non-functional limitations such as taking account of the surroundings further relativise its semantic connotation to the museum concept. For the most part, the sawtooth roof – de facto quite often used – is concealed, as it is, for example, in the Kunstsammlung Nordrhein-Westfalen building in Düsseldorf (cf. pp. 116-117), whose elegant curved façade of granite polished as smooth as glass suggests refinement and value, and with which this motif derived from factory architecture does not appear compatible.

72 Niterói, Museum of Contemporary Art
(Oscar Niemeyer, 1991-96)

71 Eindhoven, "Evoluon"
(L. C. Kalff and L.L.J. de Bever, 1962-66)

70 Frechen, "Keramion"
(Peter Neufert, 1971)

69 Shanghai, Shanghai Museum
(Xing Tonghe, 1992-95)

77 Liège, Mont de Bueren

75 Maastricht, Bonnefantenmuseum, stairway
(Aldo Rossi, 1990-95)

76 Munich, Alte Pinakothek, stairway
(Hans Döllgast, 1956-57)

In addition to the right lighting, visitor circulation is a central problem for museums. Although the quality of the routes and spatial connections, extremely important for conditioning visitors' attitudes, by its very nature manifests itself only in a limited fashion in architectural motifs that can be classified as a language and interpreted as signs, it is precisely here that it becomes evident that the symbolic language of architectural postmodernism, admittedly able to generate semantic categories in a special way, can also be developed without using motifs that are associated with certain historical connotations.

The access at the entrance area very often proves to be a place where heightened design aspirations aim well beyond simply fulfilling functional requirements. Thus the enormous dramatic stairway in the Ludwig Museum (p. 40, *fig. 105*; p. 109) presents an unexpected contrast to the modesty of the entrance. In the end, however, the almost baroque gesture of this cascade of steps is unproductive, because it opens into a room that feels much too low-ceilinged under the omnipresent sawtooth roof. This would indicate that a solution that is formally unsatisfactory cannot produce convincing iconological content either, yet nonetheless this content is recognizable and proves itself to be entirely acceptable.

In Aldo Rossi's Bonnefantenmuseum in Maastricht (cf. pp. 78-79; *fig. 75*), a stairway placed exactly in the axis of the symmetric, three-winged building extends across the whole depth of the space. It leads into a domed room, whose purist coldness presents a peculiar contrast to the metal-clad exterior of this most striking part of the building. This stairway cannot deny its origin in palace architecture; there is a hint of it in the ground plan of the Bonnefantenmuseum as well and one is thereby reminded of one of the roots of museum architecture per se. It is above all the communicative component of the museum – which is set against the moment of meditative concentration in the almost bodiless space under the cupola – that is manifested in the stairway, interrupted by several landings and in which something of the ceremonial character of baroque stairways becomes perceptible. While in Maastricht this antagonism of mutual encounter and immersion is designed as a sequence of route and goal, in the concentrated architecture of the Kunstmuseum in Bonn (cf. p. 130-133), it is astoundingly summarized in a central rotunda which is nothing more than a stairwell from which all views and routes depart – a motif that in Munich's Pinakothek der Moderne (cf. p. 128-129) eventually broadens out into an enormous, funnel-shaped stairway which, in a single gesture, links the three main levels of the museum and with its two wedges opens into a multi-storey rotunda dominated by an enormous domed skylight.

In the combination of rotunda plus stairway, we encounter a motif that is used remarkably often in museum architecture. Its careful staging usually goes far beyond the necessity of simply fulfilling functional requirements; it consists in the use of certain forms aiming at a statement about the content, forms to which particular meanings have accrued because of particular historical constellations.[166] Karl Friedrich Schinkel, for whom 'the architectural ideal' was only fully attained when "a building fulfills its purpose entirely, in all its parts and as a whole, intellectually and physically,"[167] called the rotunda vaulted over by a coffered dome in the centre of his Altes Museum in Berlin (p. 22, *fig. 35*) a "shrine in which the most precious objects will be conserved."[168] Without doubt, Schinkel is alluding here to the Pantheon in Rome and in so doing, following the classical tradition of evoking the character of a sanctuary. This is just as well known as the fact that the rotunda of the Museo Pio-Clementino in the Vatican (p. 20, *fig. 24*) and many museum designs by French architects during the Revolutionary era (p. 21, *fig. 25-29*) have also played their part in securing this form its place in the vocabulary of architecture as a museum characteristic.

This link to the past, repeatedly taken up in the new museum architecture, becomes very clear in the architecture of Mario Botta, who, in the centre of his Museum of Modern Art in San Francisco (cf. pp. 86-87) places a rotunda in the form of a cylinder with a slanting cap – the same form that he also (and certainly not by chance) used for a sacred building built at the same time, Evry Cathedral near Paris.[169] Botta again chose the motif of a central rotunda for the Museum of Rovereto, opened in 2002 (*fig. 74*).[170] A dome of steel and glass with a round roof opening, it is not only reminiscent of the Pantheon model, but also matches its absolute dimensions to a large extent. The crucial difference from the unmistakably quoted model consists – despite the different styles and materials – in Botta's rotunda being a publicly accessible external space, a piazza, from which the interior of the museum is accessed.

In this way, a further level of meaning is added to the link between museum and sanctuary, which has become a topos since Schinkel, namely the linking of the museum with public space. This means nothing other than the architectural concretization of the ambiguity of the term museum outlined at the beginning, which oscillates between edification and entertainment, contemplation and communication.

78 Hanover, Sprengel Museum, museum passage (Peter and Ursula Trint, Dieter Quast, 1973-92)
81 Frankfurt on Main, Museum für Kunsthandwerk, circulation (Richard Meier, 1980-85)

79 Ludwigshafen, Wilhelm-Hack-Museum, Great Hall (Walter and Susanne Hagstotz, Peter Kraft, 1972-79)

80 Rotterdam, Kunsthal, exhibition ramp (Rem Koolhaas, 1987-92)

82 Nijmegen, Museum Het Valkhof (Ben van Berkel, UN studio, 1996-99)

If we look at Aldo Rossi's Bonnefantenmuseum once again under this aspect, then the fact that its stairway is bounded by raw brick walls (p. 32, *fig. 75*) proves to be meaningful and informative. For the time being, it can be understood as a clear allusion to the grand, long stairway in unplastered brickwork that Hans Döllgast inserted into Munich's Alte Pinakothek (p. 32, *fig. 76*)[171] in place of Klenze's loggia, which was destroyed during the Second World War – a homage to a double incunabulum as it were, of museum architecture. In addition, however, because the brickwork is used nowhere else in the interior, the walls of the staircase become exterior walls so to speak. These exterior walls now give the stairway running between them the character of a public route – somewhat like the one to be found in the magnificent Mont de Bueren complex in Liège, only 30 kilometres from Maastricht (p. 32, *fig. 77*).

We encounter this phenomenon of a public route bounded by exterior walls inside a building in a series of other museums, for example, in the Sprengel Museum in Hanover (cf. pp. 106-107), through which runs an angled 'museum passage,' which, like a ravine bridged over several times and with a variety of views of all the levels, forms the backbone and the access route of the museum bursting forth from its external bounds. The street character of the Hanover Museum's passage is clearly represented both by the materials and by the very sophisticated detail design (*fig.78*). A wide, bridged-over ramp, which enables views into almost all the areas of the buildings, informs the interior of the Wilhelm-Hack-Museum in Ludwigshafen, completed in 1979 (*fig. 79*)[172] and brings its access system into focus. Finally, in the spindle-formed convolutions of the Kunsthal in Rotterdam (cf. pp. 162-163), whose ramps appear to be permeable in all directions in different ways and with differing intensity (*fig. 80*), the routing goes far beyond simply the fulfilment of functional requirements and in itself, represents to a certain extent the concept of this museum.

The staging of the routing often leads to a picture puzzle interplay between inside and outside that brings the communicative aspect directly into view, as it does, for example, in Frankfurt's Museum für Kunsthandwerk (cf. pp. 154-155) and in the stairway in the Sainsbury Wing of the National Gallery in London (cf. pp. 112-113). This interpenetration of exterior and interior space (*figs. 81 and 82*) shows that here, architecture wants to be more than an elementary envelope. It thematizes itself and in so doing, becomes the object of observation. In that it frequently does not content itself with an abstract representation of its basic possibilities, however, but has recourse to certain motifs and examples from its own history, it not only emphasizes its historical dimension, but also its participation in modern art, which is characterized not least by its self-referentiality.

In exemplary clarity, but at the same time with playful lightness too, all these aspects are united in James Stirling's Neue Stuttgarter Staatsgalerie (cf. pp. 70-73), which is considered to be the incunabulum of new museum architecture, probably not unjustifiably. Stirling has designed the generally accessible connection required by the property developer between the two streets running along the sides of the museum as an exciting route through a dynamic architectural landscape, which leads eventually through a central rotunda and in so doing, makes it into an external space (*fig. 83*). In contrast to Schinkel's Altes Museum, whose ground plan disposition (p. 22, *fig. 34*) is intentionally quoted here as one of the prototypes of this architectural endeavour, Stirling's rotunda is designed not as a dome-vaulted 'Pantheon of the arts,' but in ironic reversal of this neoclassicist formula for pathos, as a hollow cylinder open to the sky, whose walls are overgrown with vegetation like those of a ruin (*fig. 84*). The fact that the spiral-form route leading along the high wall of the rotunda additionally quotes the twisting exhibition ramp in Frank Lloyd Wright's Guggenheim Museum in New York (and with this allusion also reverses inside and outside) is further proof of the intentional ambiguity of this architecture, which in any case can claim to express the meaning 'museum' and to continue in the tradition that refers to the sanctuary too. Perhaps it is due not only to Stirling's memorable knotting together of these lines of tradition, but also to the incredible response from the media that accompanied the erection of the Neue Stuttgarter Staatsgalerie, that the motif of a central rotunda, and also the staging of the circulation inevitably awakens these associations.

The semantic field 'sanctuary' that evokes the museum concept linked to the 'temple of the muses' does not limit itself at all, however, to the motif of the rotunda, however it may be quoted or alienated, but is also linked to the temple metaphor,[173] which is also based on Schinkel's Altes Museum in Berlin, although its façade lacks one of the temple's essential traits, the front gable. Perhaps it is precisely this combination of typological difference and aesthetic affinity to the classical temple that makes the Schinkelian motif into the progenitor of such varied architectural adaptations of this formula of dignity as the Neue Nationalgalerie in Berlin (cf. pp. 198-199; *fig. 85*), the Sheldon Memorial Art Gallery in Lincoln, Nebraska (*fig. 86*),[174] and the Carré d'Art in Nîmes (cf. pp. 82-83; *fig. 87*).

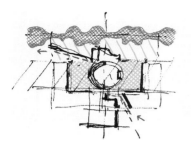

83 James Stirling: sketch of the ground plan of the Neue Staatsgalerie Stuttgart, 1977

84 Stuttgart, Neue Staatsgalerie, rotunda (James Stirling, 1977-84)

86 Lincoln/Nebraska, Sheldon Memorial Art Gallery (Philip Johnson, 1961-63)

87 Nîmes, Carré d'Art (Norman Foster, 1984-92)

85 Berlin, Neue Nationalgalerie (Ludwig Mies van der Rohe, 1962-68)

The Museum as City

Can the motifs we have considered be grouped together under a common denominator? With the aid of the examples shown, it was recognizable that the phenomena marking the different museum positions, i.e. of walking, of lingering, of communication, and of concentration, have found their architectural expression in the motif of a central rotunda – however modified – and in the theme of more or less lavishly designed visitor circulation. In both cases, one could allude to models, which, because of the historical distance and particular constellations, not only had come to convey the aforementioned meanings, but with which we have also learnt to associate the concept of the museum.

However, the overarching context of this motif is nothing other than the city.[175] The most exposed expression of architectural environmental design, the city is one of the oldest utopias of mankind apart from Paradise, the imagined happy place of primeval times and the end of time in the form of a garden with a fence around it. As the focus of social life-processes, the city is the venue for social and political developments and controversies, economic processes and cultural stimulation. From the outset, the characteristic features of its architecture have been the walled enclosure, the street, the block of houses, the market, the shrine, and the citadel.

Until well into the nineteenth century, the city wall was one of its most striking distinguishing features. Its dual function – protection against attacks from outside and demarcation of the system of order enclosed by it – corresponds to a double origin, one technical and practical, one ritual. The latter means the conception of the city as temenos, as a clearly defined, inviolable district.[176] After what we have said, it is not in the least surprising that we also encounter the motif of the city wall in the museum buildings of recent decades as a metaphor for the city – again, of course, in partially fragmented reflections. Thus the apparently genuine part of a city wall in the Abteiberg Museum in Mönchengladbach (p. 36, *fig. 88*) turns out in the end to be the continuation of that brickwork that Hollein describes as "rice terraces" (p. 36, *fig. 89*), which still belongs as much to nature as to architecture. In this way, the demarcating function of the city wall is thrown into question there just as it is in the Sprengel Museum in Hanover, where the protecting wall at the back of the museum *(p. 36, fig. 90)* turns into a hill on the entrance side that can be climbed by means of steps set into it and whose surface structure, transgressing the boundaries of the building, continues into the interior of the museum. In both cases, the antagonism fundamental to the museum – between conserving (objects) and welcoming (visitors) – is brought to expression and simultaneously cancelled out by the motif of the city wall modified like this, its metaphoric significance remaining entirely recognizable. Primarily justified by the topographical situation, but as far as its effect is concerned, also implying the aforementioned aspects, a high wall shields the Kunstmuseum in Bonn (cf. pp. 130-133) from the outside, but through carefully selected openings allows the interior to be experienced as a form suggestive of the city. The Deutsches Architekturmuseum on the Museumsufer in Frankfurt (cf. pp. 236-237) once more brings into view not only the city wall motif in a different form, but also simultaneously thematises the idea of the congruence between building and city, through the 'house in the house' that develops out of a four-columned space, which as the primeval hut or canopy is of both archetypical and religious significance. This building reduced to its simplest form is enveloped by the cored villa, which is not only supported by the differently-coloured plinth, but is also circumscribed, as if by a city wall. A cult metaphor and a city metaphor as the image of the museum simultaneously conserving and presenting the works of art give access to each other and embrace each other.

In the first architectural treatise of the modern era, Leon Battista Alberti already demanded that the house be a small city. "For that reason, in building it, one will have to take into account almost everything that relates to the construction of a city."[177] Hans Hollein's variously composed building complex, the Museum Abteiberg in Mönchengladbach (cf. pp. 138-141) appears to be an implementation of this idea and can be interpreted as an abbreviation of a city and its building types.[178] The interrelations of its individual parts are no more rigidly fixed than those of the buildings of the Acropolis in Athens, in the history of modern architecture repeatedly praised as being of model character. (p. 36, *fig. 91*) The comparison between the Nike temple on the Acropolis and the temple-like entrance pavilion, also pushed right up against the cliff edge is immediately evident. At the same time, though, the conversion of the Tempietto into a simple entrance – the museum as the real shrine is in the interior of the mountain – signalizes a degree of reflecting distancing that is no less ironic than Stirling's transforming the rotunda by making it a ruinous exterior space. In comparison with Aldo Rossi's museum in Maastricht, in which one reaches the sanctuary in the

88 Mönchengladbach, Museum Abteiberg,
"city wall"

89 Mönchengladbach, Museum Abteiberg,
"rice terraces"

90 Hanover, Sprengel Museum, entrance side

91 Athens, Acropolis

usual hierarchy via a stairway leading upwards, Hollein's reversal of this arrangement and order of precedence does not mean that the semantic fields sketched out are removed, but as in every mannerism, their evidence is presupposed. Hollein underlines the relative importance of the extremely condensed access system in the Museum für Moderne Kunst in Frankfurt (cf. pp. 136-137), which culminates in a turning point situated at the heart of the museum, by making it not only usable but also exposing it to view again and again, even exhibiting it demonstratively. Richard Meier, who was given the unique opportunity to design an art museum, the Getty Center, high over Santa Monica as a modern acropolis (figs. 92-96),[179] uses the street motif in the Museum für Kunsthandwerk in Frankfurt (cf. pp. 154-155) in an entirely different form, but undoubtedly with metaphoric intention too; its carefully executed axial cross evokes not only the structure of towns and field camps based on the right-angled intersection of two main streets, a structure introduced by the Roman agrimensors and their successors in the Middle Ages and still surviving in the term [city] quarter, but also goes all the way back to ritual beginnings when the augurs divided the horizon by marking the four cardinal directions.[180]

The network of streets and paths first acquired the structure that we experience as urban through having squares as their goal and point of departure. As markets, squares were always the focus of social and economic activities. Since antiquity people have gathered there and it is there that we usually find particularly important buildings. Surrounded by the clear and yet sophisticatedly arranged volumes of the museum spaces and the semi-circular classical theatre, the centre of the Museo d'Arte contemporanea in Prato[181] forms an irregularly shaped piazza, which creates an urban effect precisely through this irregularity. Ieoh Ming Pei's light-flooded atrium crisscrossed by catwalks and bridges, around which he grouped the East Wing of the National Gallery in Washington also creates the impression of an urban meeting point (cf. pp. 134-135). Covering almost as much area as the exhibition rooms around it and being the place to which all the routes in the museum repeatedly return, this space brings to expression communicative qualities as a significant – and genuinely urban – aspect of today's museum's concept.

The structure of the museum wing designed by Pei, although geometrically severe and justified from the perspective of urban planning, but because of its triangular module not congruent with the model of a classical city, alerts us to the fact that the majority of the motifs discussed until now correspond to the ideal of a pre-industrial city, and in that regard represent a projection. It is not by chance that it is above all Postmodernism that likes to avail itself of this projection. If 'the museum as city' metaphor is to attain more far-reaching validity, one has to ask whether the interpenetration, the density and the transgression of the boundaries of the modern city, in which the order contained and constituted by the city walls is cancelled out and reversed, have also manifested themselves in today's museum architecture. One will have to answer this question affirmatively, as one will be able to recognize traits of the modern city in the complicated interlocking access system of the Kunsthal in Rotterdam (cf. p. 162-163) just as in the broken-open structure of deconstructivist architectures (p. 28, fig. 57). Yet the affinities between the modern museum and the city lie less on the level of figuration than in their fundamental reaction to the mechanisms of today's consumer society, which threatens to lead if not to the "de-auratizing of Van Gogh," then certainly to an "auratization of McDonald's."[182] One does not have to go as far as to consider the goal of visiting a museum to be the arrival at the museum shop (after the spiritual experience of the untouchable and unpurchasable in the museum, the museum shop leads back again like a sluice into the customary consumer world)[183] to concede that economic necessity has long since become unavoidably prevalent in the domain of art, and the museum as well. This finds very varied expression in museum architecture; the so-called "dark museum" was already developed in the sixties, first in the Völkerkunde Museum in Berlin-Dahlem,[184] in whose interior the architecture takes a back seat to a presentation of the exhibits oriented on the department store's display of its wares. An excellent example for this is the Römisch-Germanische Museum in Cologne,[185] which does not celebrate individual pieces as a rule, but instead is counting quite consciously on massing its exhibition objects in shelves or on pedestal islands (p. 38, fig. 97). There, if the architecture comes to the fore at all, it does so as it would on the sales floors of department stores. Precisely the other way round, the showplace of economic transactions is effectively staged architecturally in the Stuttgart Staatsgalerie: the ticket window and the museum shop are located in a rotunda – this time vaulted over by a glass dome – whose semantic spectrum thereby once again comes into allusive use, and not without sarcasm. And Alessandro Mendini, the colourful figure who created the design for the spectacular museum in Groningen,[186] has again and again thematized a culture of the trivial and declared the

92-96 Santa Monica near Los Angeles, Getty Center
(Richard Meier, 1984-97)

97 Cologne, Römisch-Germanisches Museum, isolated plinth "Goods handling in the Rhine harbour" (Heinz Röcke and Klaus Renner, 1963-74)

99 Paris, Centre Pompidou, side façade (Renzo Piano and Richard Rogers, 1971-77)

98 Groningen, Museum (Alessandro Mendini, 1990-94)

100 Bilbao, Guggenheim Museum (Frank O. Gehry, 1991-97)

museum the "department store of knowledge,"[187] a "supermarket with a collection of objects that are capable of generating human pleasure and craving, even if it is through false functionality, by suggestion, by appealing to the desire to play, neo-kitsch or fashion." Thus the tower of the museum, covered with golden laminate, (*fig. 98*) evokes a fantasy world – somewhere between the Kaaba and Dagobert Duck's treasure house of gold – that the philosopher Jean Baudrillard sees already realized in Disneyland, a social microcosm exalted almost religiously as the "imaginative exchange" of the city.[188]

Cities today define themselves not least through their museums. In 1961, the American cultural historian Lewis Mumford had already described the museum as the "metropole's most typical institution" because it represents complexity and variety in concentrated form, but has also taken over many negative characteristics of today's big cities: "the indiscriminate craving for acquisition, the tendency to exaggerated expansion and disorganization, and the habit of measuring its success by the number of people who enter it."[189] Movement, dynamism, and flexibility are some of the positive characteristics of the city that can also be described as characteristics of the new museum architecture. Two museum buildings, whose appearance can hardly be more different, both of which are, however, considered to be milestones of contemporary museum architecture, might substantiate my necessarily fragmentary concluding remarks with which I have tried to hint at the spectrum of architectural possibilities of expression in museum building, a spectrum that since the Second World War has been not only stylistic, but also semantically broad – and for this reason, usually ambiguous. On one hand, we have the Centre Pompidou in Paris, opened in 1977 (cf. pp. 174-177), which the clients wanted to "mark our century" as a cultural centre in the form of an architectural and urban complex, but which was understood by its architects, in contrast, as an "event venue with information and entertainment." On the other hand, two decades later, we have the Guggenheim Museum in Bilbao, which has become the new emblem of the Basque metropole (cf. p. 218-221; *fig. 100*), and which is extolled as "one of the most complex formal creations of our time."[190]

As the most important access ways circumnavigating all the floors, caterpillar-like tubular escalators mark the technoid Centre Pompidou, conceived as "flexible container and dynamic communication machine made of prefabricated parts," and decisively determine not only its appearance (*fig. 99*), but also bring into clear focus the myth of movement and mobility that has become a leitmotif of the modern age. The bright colours of the exposed supply lines – blue ventilation shafts, green water pipes, yellow electrical installations – display elementary structural functions in pithy symbolism. It is not without reason that this building – in which not only are the boundaries between technology and architectural form suspended, but also the plaza in front of the building is allowed to become its foyer through the reversal of inside and outside – has become the epitome of a conception of culture provocatively transgressing the boundaries, representing as it does a counterweight to the design of the museum as temple. In contrast, the museum building in Bilbao, covered with titanium plates and executed with the help of a computer program borrowed from aircraft construction, appears to be a built sculpture, its effect emphasized even more by effective mirroring in the water. The architect says: "I have always thought 'city' in sculptural, three-dimensional categories ... The city itself is a sculpture that one can form and in which certain relationships can be created."[191] In actual fact, Gehry's building is able to focus its heterogeneous surroundings apparently without difficulty, without giving up its aesthetic distance. Its biomorphic forms generate associations that range from an enormous animal to a ship, and in any case, embody movement, dynamic force, and growth – principles that characterize the essence of the urban. However, the enormously increased rhetoric and the concomitant loss of semantic clarity also allow one to interpret the complexity of this building and its illusionary effects – hardly less plausibly – as an expression of the omnipresent dominance of capital, that measures aesthetic sensation by its economic success.[192] This too belongs to the reality of the urban – and thereby to the essence of today's museum architecture.

Form and Function

Inside and Outside

101 Innsbruck, Museum Ferdinandeum, entrance
(Anton Mutschlechner, 1842-45; Natale Tommasi
1882-87)

102 Mönchengladbach, Museum Abteiberg,
entrance

The function of the museum as a place in which the special is conserved and at the same time exhibited
has certain consequences, firstly for the design of the entrance area. In the representative museums of the
nineteenth century, more or less distinctive formulae of dignity from architectural history's canon distinguish the entrance, which almost always lies in the building axis, and in that way indicates that the interior
contains something extraordinary (*fig. 101*). The stairway leading up to the entrance, usually above street
level, brings the distinguishing aspect immediately into view. In contrast to this, in today's museums that
strive more to be places of learning or fairs than to be temples of the muses, architects go to much trouble
to reduce the fear of the unknown and even prevent it from arising in the first place. The first new museum
building in post-war Germany, the former Wallraf-Richartz-Museum in Cologne (cf. pp. 88-89), although it
took up the basic structure of the previous nineteenth century building (p. 23, *fig. 39*), did without its projecting centre, and shifted the ground-level entrance noticeably away from the middle, making it recognizable only by means of a discreet bronze roof (which was not originally planned). Since then only seldom has
an attempt been made to stage an entrance situation that allows the entrance into the museum to become
a ceremonious act. Even in the entrance of the Neue Pinakothek in Munich, whose design is not without
pathos (cf. pp. 94-95), the suction effect overcomes the fear of the unknown and the gloomy ceremonious-
ness created by the entrance hall is mitigated by the use of room-height glazing creating transparency.
The entrance is usually designed in a consciously unpretentious manner, as it is in the Fondation Beyeler in
Basel (cf. 118-121) for example, and in the Kunsthaus Bregenz (cf. pp. 196-197) and in the Neues Museum
in Nuremberg (cf. pp. 124-125). From time to time it is displaced with ironic casualness as it is in the
Stuttgart Staatsgalerie (cf. pp. 70-73), reduced to a meagre hatch as it is in the Museum La Gongiunta in
Giornico (cf. pp. 84-85), or almost hidden, as in the Kunstsammlung Nordrhein-Westfalen in Düsseldorf
(cf. pp. 116-117). In contrast to this, the entrance to the Abteiberg Museum in Mönchengladbach (cf. pp.
138-141) is in an affected Tempietto very obviously placed (*fig. 102*), from which the way leads down into
the museum, partially hidden in the mountain, so that it becomes a ritual cave, thus reversing the temple
metaphor. Although this staging says a great deal about a certain facet of today's museum concept, it
nonetheless remains as much an exception as the building task resolved by Ieoh Ming Pei in the form of
a glass pyramid, to create a new central main entrance in the Cour Napoléon of the Louvre for the largest
museum in the world (*fig. 103*).[193] What is remarkable about this creation primarily determined by urban
planning is not least the fact that due to its weightlessness and transparence, the pyramid, lighted from inside at night, and under which an enormous hall distributes the public, does not evoke funereal symbolism,

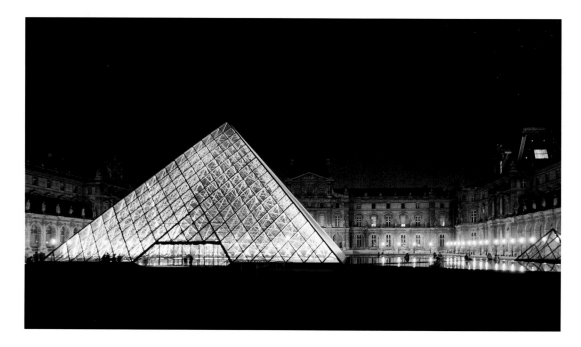

103 Paris, Grand Louvre, Cour Napóleon, entrance pyramid (Ieoh Ming Pei, 1983-89)

104 Cologne, old Wallraf-Richartz-Museum, stairway with frescoes by Edward von Steinle, 1861-64

105 Cologne, Museum Ludwig, stairway (Peter Busmann and Godfried Haberer, 1976-86)

107 Barcelona, Museu d'Art Contemporani, access ramp (Richard Meier, 1987-95)
106 Poissy, Villa Savoye, ramp (Le Corbusier, 1928-31)

108 Porto, Museu de Serralves, entrance situation (Álvaro Siza Vieira, 1996-99)

but on the contrary, evokes openness and clarity: an indication of an understanding of the museum that was significantly marked by the establishment of the Musée Français two centuries previously at this very spot.

The entrance to the museum, which as the seam between inside and outside in a way represents the architectural interface between the public and the content of the collection, triggers in the visitor a certain attitude of expectation, which is confirmed, modified or corrected by the foyer or the entrance hall. While the visitor to a nineteenth-century museum – almost always two storeys or more – will usually be received by a representative stairway designed as a Gesamtkunstwerk that continues the contents expressed in the architectural forms and sculptural programs of the exterior[194] and provides edification as well as instruction through referential frescoes (*fig. 104*),[195] the design spectrum for the entrance area in the museums of the late twentieth century includes a multiplicity of possibilities, whose common denominator is most likely to be that there are no more fixed relations between inside and outside. "The unpredictability of the architectural experience has virtually become a program."[196] Thus the sluice-like entrance and the low reception area behind it in Cologne's Ludwig Museum (cf. p. 108-109) present an unexpected contrast to the almost baroque drama of the stairway connected to it, positioned perpendicularly to the entrance (*fig. 105*) – an effect which, although formally more logical, also characterises the entrance situation of the Het Valkof Museum in Nijmegen (cf. p. 122-123) while on the other hand, the stairway of the Bonnefantenmuseum in Maastricht, which lies along the axis of the building (cf. p. 78-79; p. 32, *fig. 75*) fulfills with logical consequence that expectation triggered off by the emphasized projecting main entrance. In Munich's Pinakothek der Moderne (cf. pp. 128-129), the antagonism between the portal and the staircase is cancelled out in the end, because the building-high glazed entrance and its mirrored correspondent, the Wintergarden, appear to be only imaginary boundaries of the enormous diagonal stairway, already visible from outside. In other cases, the stairway is reduced entirely to its function of connecting the different floors, as is the case, for example, in the Kunsthalle in Hamburg (cf. pp. 74-77) or, in reaction to the origin of its space-determining role in the baroque architecture of power, replaced by the ramp (*fig. 106*), which is considered to be a genuine motif of classical modernism. In addition, it offers the advantage of being suitable for wheelchair access. Examples for this can be found not only in Richard Meier's museum buildings indebted to this modernism (cf. pp. 102-103 and 154-155; *fig. 107*), but also in the Stuttgart Staatsgalerie, regarded as the incunabulum of the postmodern. However, portals and entrance halls or stairways in most cases no longer play a significant role as classical key features of the antagonism between interior and exterior. As a further consequence, the entrance is not located in the façade, but inside the envelope, and in the Kunsthal in Rotterdam (cf. pp. 162-163), for example, it is situated at the interface between the public ramp and the slanted floor of the interior opposite, thus leaving the boundaries between exterior and interior blurred. At times, the ambivalence between exterior and interior space serves less for the dismantling of barriers than for the thematization of architectural possibilities per se, as we have already pointed out in the chapter on the semantics of museum architecture (p. 34, *fig. 81*). The tendency to lead visitors into the museum so that on one hand they do not experience thresholds, and on the other, they are granted an exciting architectural experience can be particularly clearly observed in the entrance scenario of the Museu de Serralves in Porto, meticulously but playfully laid out (cf. pp. 90-93), so that visitors reach the interior of the building by means of a succession of comparatively long hallways alternately broad and narrow (*fig. 108*). Finally, in the Centre Pompidou in Paris (cf. pp. 174-177), the situation is completely reversed, in that the escalator by which the building is accessed is shifted to the exterior and thereby determines the appearance of the façade: thus the plaza in front of the museum becomes the real foyer.

Circulation

Inside the museum, the circulation generated by the arrangement and linking of the individual spaces[197] determines the quality of the museum experience to at least as great an extent as the form or character of the individual spaces. In assuming that awareness of one's location and continuity of movement are some of the elements people are conditioned to expect, and that in addition, however, their rhythmically composed nature either consciously or unconsciously resists all stereotypes and unmodified repetitions of the same elements, one is bringing to mind crucial criteria for the structuring of sequences of spaces in museums.[198] Although on these physiological and psychological aspects are superimposed to a greater or lesser extent a series of additional factors such as operational sequences and urban planning dependencies etc., nonetheless they obviously already played an important part in the first rooms designed for exhibition purposes like the Antiquarium in the Munich Residenz (p. 19, *fig. 20*) or the galleries in Sabbioneta and Mantua (p. 19, *fig. 19*): the long halls enable and even force the visitor walking along them to observe the immobile objects in a sequence – a process of successive perception which is similar to experiencing a city and which fundamentally differs from the virtuality of a monitor. The inherent laws of consecutive perception are taken into account by all spatial layouts that correspond to the principles of continuity and linearity. Rigid spatial sequences arranged in enfilade (*fig. 109*) are sufficient to meet the exigencies of this aspect, as are corridor-like rooms joined together (*fig. 110*), and even – as here it is less a matter of concrete geometric form than one of spatial interrelations – spiral arrangements, the most well-known of which, the Guggenheim Museum in New York,[199] for its part goes back not only to Frank Lloyd Wright's earlier parking structure design, but above all, to Le Corbusier's 1931 design for a "museum of unlimited growth" (p. 25, *fig. 111*). According to Le Corbusier's concept, its square spiral, whose archetypal symbolic meaning related to growth and continual return he undoubtedly was aware of, was supposed to be extended continuously as the collection grew.[200]

Open space stands in fundamental opposition to the last-mentioned design – never executed – which drives the principle of linearity to extremes, and which, although guaranteeing continuity of movement and also enabling didactic efficiency in the presentation of collection objects, limits visitors' freedom significantly, however. Without further adaptation, open space is only in rare cases suitable for the presentation of exhibition objects, and for this reason it can only form the architectural frame for an exhibition facility that is flexible and variable. The sketch of an exhibition staging by the museum architect Manfred Lehmbruck shows how such a staging could be structured, taking into account the physiological and psychological dependencies of the museum visitors mentioned above (*fig. 112*).[201] The way the visitor routing unfolds is crucial: although in principle continuous, backward loops and cross-connections are not ruled out.

Most of the new museum buildings assembled in this publication offer the possibility of choosing between several paths, a possibility that was already a given as an idea of civil freedom in Schinkel's Altes Museum in Berlin, in spite of the rigid structure of its ground plan (p. 22, *fig. 34*). The range extends from the extension of the main route through a straight sequence of rooms by means of accessory paths that always come back to this main route, to the complexity of the room layouts referred to here as 'matrix-like,' which do not allow a dominant direction to come to the fore, but instead leave the visitor several different ways to go that appear equally good. The grid-like connections placed in the corners of the exhibition rooms (p. 61, *fig. 146*) are paradigmatic examples of this. In addition to the advantage of offering the greatest possible amount of space for hanging pictures and the suspense of diagonal views each offers three different possibilities for continuing the tour. However, the suspense engendered by the possibility of choosing leads to helplessness, and sooner or later the pleasure of discovery turns into confusion when visitors become disoriented, losing track of where they are. Therefore orientation should be enabled at calculated intervals, by means of periodic retracing of the multifarious routes through to unambiguous sequences of rooms, as in the Kunstmuseum in Bonn (cf. pp. 130-133), for example, or in the Pinakothek der Moderne in Munich (cf. pp. 128-129), or by means of obvious orientation points that provide an overview of the spatial interconnections, like those we find in Mönchengladbach (cf. pp. 138-141), where counterpoised exhibition levels are staggered at half-storey intervals, on one hand opening surprising perspectives, while on the other, also facilitating orientation. Here it becomes clear, too, that linearity or complexity in circulation design does not have to be limited to a single level; instead differences in level can contribute significantly to avoiding monotony. In this way the route in Munich's Neue Pinakothek, accompanied by several accessory routes, but in principal clearly recognizable (cf. pp. 94-95) purposefully overcomes step by step the difference in level of one floor to the next before it leads back again to the exit level. In Mönchengladbach, richly varied stairway forms characterize not only the appearance of diverse counterpoised and staggered exhibition rooms, but also become the architectural expression of a three-dimensional route – a trend that leads finally to Alessandro Mendini's stairway sculpture clad with coloured mosaic tiles in the Groninger Museum, which itself becomes an exhibition object.

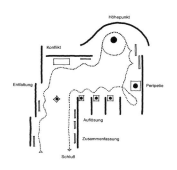

109 Stuttgart, Neue Staatsgalerie, exhibition rooms

110 Humlebæk, Louisiana Museum (Jørgen Bo and Vilhelm Wohlert, 1956-98)

112 Manfred Lehmbruck, 'staging' of an exhibition in chronological and spatial succession, 1979

115 Paris, Musée d'Orsay
(Gae Aulenti and Italo Rota, 1980-86)

117 Berlin, Gemäldegalerie
(Heinz Hilmer and Christoph Sattler, 1991-98)

118 Groningen, Gallery of Old Masters
(Coop Himmelb(l)au, 1990-94)

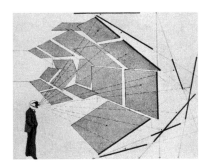

119 Herbert Bayer: design for the architecture
photo show of the Deutscher Werkbund in Paris,
1930

Spatial Experience and Object Presentation

However, despite the weight of meanings that have devolved upon the architecture of the museum, going beyond this primary function, the real purpose of the museum continues to lie, as it always has done, in the presentation of objects, among which a special status accrues to works of art, because their reception not only conveys knowledge to the observer, but should also engender an aesthetic experience. Out of this results the fundamental question of the connection between space and object, which in turn implies the problem of perception.

The experience of space is one of mankind's elementary experiences.[202] We experience spatial impressions expansively, with the body, whereby the relation between one's own body size and the size of the building and its dimensions forms an essential component of this experience. The route that one takes through the architectural space is essential to grasping it. On the other hand, though, we grasp the spatial quality visually by means of geometric abstraction, by dividing the built space in the areas surrounding it that are revealed principally by their outlines.[203]

The object in space, which we initially capture in its total spatial context, achieves a particular value through its placing within this context. When the spatial conditions (size and proportions, lighting, materials, colours, etc.) change, the effect that the object has on the observer changes too. Conversely, different objects are able to transform one and the same space entirely, as is shown by an exhibition room in the Abteiberg Museum in Mönchengladbach that was created for a particular work of art (*fig. 113*): it is hardly able to offer an adequate frame for another one (*fig. 114*). The contrast between the Musee d'Orsay in Paris – converted with great creative effort from a nineteenth century railway station into a museum for objects from that period (*fig. 115*)[204] – and a video installation in a low-key, but definitely not neutrally-designed room in the Museu de Serralves in Porto (cf. pp. 90-93; *fig. 116*) may demonstrate the sheer unbounded variety of possible relations between space and object.

The person-object-space constellation may occur in accordance with a variety of design principles:[205] as correspondence or harmonious connection, as contrast or conscious antithesis, or as adaptation or association, in which the imaginative aura of the object finds a more or less adequate correspondence in the building. While the latter relation between object and exhibition space corresponds essentially to the milieu reconstruction favoured around 1900, the two remaining possibilities mark in a fairly wide range of variation the appearance of museum rooms today. If one takes picture galleries as an example, the scope of this ranges from supposedly neutral prism-formed white space (p. 29, *fig. 59*) to those gallery rooms considered classic, with coloured wall covering, skirting boards, moulding and ceiling vaults (*fig. 117*), to the deconstructivists' exploded spatial forms in which hanging wall panels have to be used as aids in order to achieve the optic isolation required by conventional panel painting, which cannot be provided entirely by picture frames alone (*fig. 118*).

The "withdrawal out of the picture" propagated since the late fifties of the twentieth century – which on one hand sought to lead art, which had arrived at the limit of its exhibitability, out of the museum, but on the other hand made the museum the place where the now stageable art could be shown and thereby into the fulcrum of the avant-garde[206] – demanded from museum spaces, however, qualities that strived to dissolve the classical static relationship between object and observer in favour of one understood to be dynamic. This had already been the intention of the Bauhaus artist Herbert Bayer in 1930, in his design for the architectural photo show of the Deutscher Werkbund in Paris, in which he tried to expand the experience of the observer by not limiting himself to the usual perpendicularly arranged wall areas, but activating other spatial areas (*fig. 119*).[207] Man's basic orientation to what is perceived as vertical, however, let spatial experiments of this type remain the exception and helped museum designs such as Carlo Scarpa's, for example, to achieve the widest acceptance. Scarpa's Museo Castelvecchio in Verona, whose staging is still considered exemplary even half a century after it was built,[208] shows, for instance, just how much orthogonally arranged areas adapted in colour and dimension to the objects and the space can intensify the effect of exhibition objects[209] without dominating them (*fig. 120*).

The interrelationship between object and space and above all, the relations between the observer and the object are significantly marked by lighting.[210] Without going into the technical aspects of the lighting of museum spaces here – that has its own section – let me point out at least the basic differences between natural and artificial light on one hand, and between light from above and lateral lighting on the other

Similarly, building simulation is appropriate for determining the optimum constitution of building component materials with regard to their heat and humidity storage capacity. The heating and cooling requirements of a museum building and the total energy requirement determined on the basis of an energy balance sheet offer both the client and the occupant a high degree of planning security for construction and operation.

The projection of the running costs taking into account rising energy costs is an important tool for establishing the economic efficiency of regenerative measures in building planning, for example, the increase of the energy storing masses, solar protection measures, the direction the building faces, intermediate climatic zones inside the building, using natural light, regulating the amount of artificial lighting, geothermics, photovoltaics, geothermal energy exchangers for pre-heating fresh air, etc. Involving experts and ensuring that they play a part in the decision-making in the competition process in order to make the participating architects and the jury aware of the specification of the climatic requirements is another important step toward improving museum and conservational climate when planning new museums. The need for extensive renovation in modern museums – which often becomes apparent when they go into operation for the first time – does enormous damage both to the cultural and artistic property on display, and the reputations of these museums. The politico-economic loss is substantial and usually, the museum operators cannot finance the repairs.

Stringent limitations are placed on the implementation of conservational standards by museum architecture concentrating primarily on the exterior to the detriment of the interior – and thereby violating elementary laws of physics regarding buildings – and, as well, by the transformation of our museums into highly technicized "conservation machines" maintained at comfortable room temperatures and flooded with light. We will only be able to reduce the risk for the cultural assets entrusted to us if we abandon this concept – from an ecological perspective now outmoded – and recall passive preservation mechanisms. Experience has shown, however, that it is only with difficulty that such concepts can gain acceptance when they come up against the interests of the architects, planners and experts involved in competitions and planning practice; the latter will continue to be particularly problematic as long as their fees are calculated according to the amount of technology that is built in.

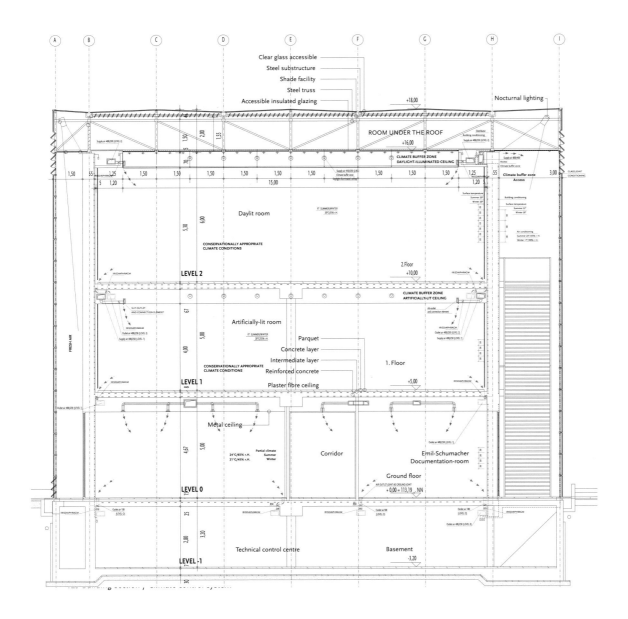

Climate control system for the new building of the Emil-Schumacher-Museum, Hagen, Germany

Architects: Lindemann Architekten, Mannheim
Climate control system: Ingenieurbüro Kahlert, Haltern

A three-storey reinforced concrete structure forms the core zone for the museum's exhibition rooms. A supporting structure of steel trusses spans the entire museum and supports the glass roof as well as the accessible daylight-illuminating ceiling. A glass façade stiffened by steel cables on all sides forms an intermediate climatic zone between the outside skin and the museum itself. The southwest and the east zones serve exclusively as a climatic buffering zone to the exterior climate. The north façade forms the central access space.

Building component conditioning is installed in all of the concrete components as a passive basis for the climate control system. In order to avoid condensation of the secondary air humidity on the north façade, glass joint conditioning has been provided. For secondary air conditioning, an air distribution system has been installed in the peripheries of the daylight ceilings and artificial light-illuminating ceilings. The supply air flows into the exhibition rooms vertically via a surrounding wall/ceiling joint and is drawn off via a wall/floor joint. In combination with a foil dust ceiling, the daylight-illuminating ceilings and the artificial light illuminating-ceilings form their own air space, independent from the secondary air. The cooling burden arising from the lighting is drawn off directly in this intermediate climatic zone.

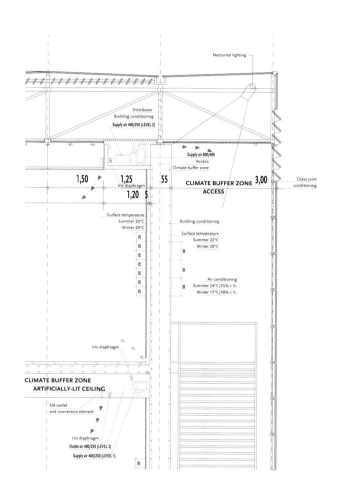

124 Detail of the glass façade (connection with the roof)

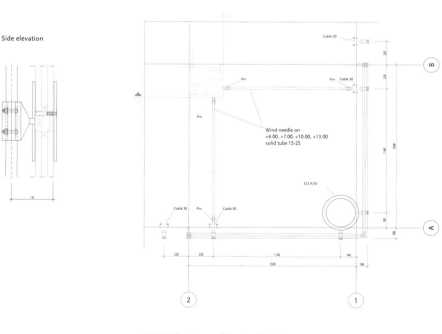

125 Detail of the steel cables (connection with the floor) / Glass façade

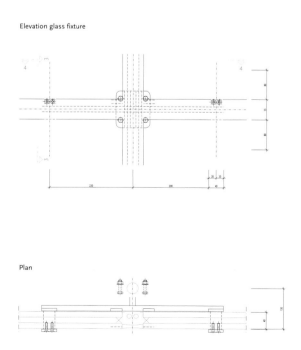

Elevation glass fixture

Side elevation

Plan

126 Detail – Glass joint conditioning

127 Detail – Corner of the glass façade

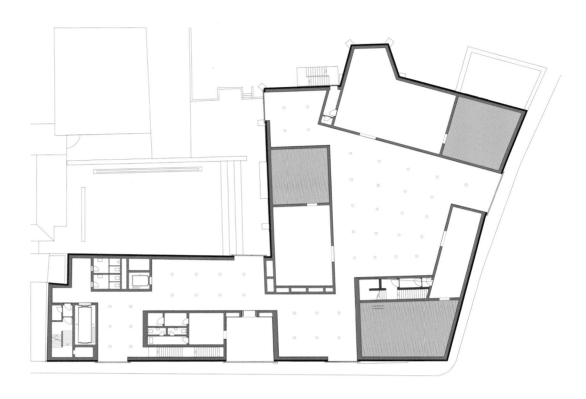

128 Ground plan of the exhibition floor

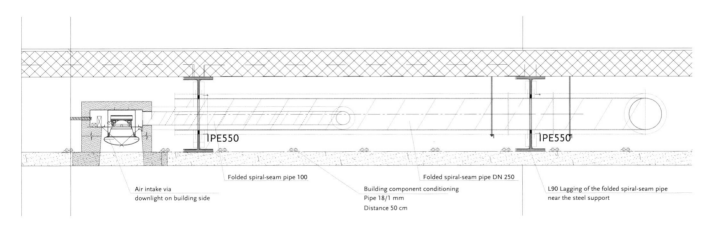

Air intake via
downlight on building side

Folded spiral-seam pipe 100

Building component conditioning
Pipe 18/1 mm
Distance 50 cm

Folded spiral-seam pipe DN 250

L90 Lagging of the folded spiral-seam pipe
near the steel support

IPE550

IPE550

129 System section – Steel lattice ceiling structure

Climate control system – new building of the Kolumba Diocesan Museum in Cologne

Architect: Peter Zumthor, Haldenstein, Switzerland
Climate control system: Ingenieurbüro Kahlert, Haltern

Together with the building component conditioning, the massive, monolithic brickwork and reinforced concrete ceilings form the passive basis for the climate control system. An air distribution system for secondary air conditioning is built into the steel lattice structure of the ceilings of each storey. The supply air flows vertically via the ceiling downlights through the exhibition rooms and is drawn off as waste air via a wall/floor joint.

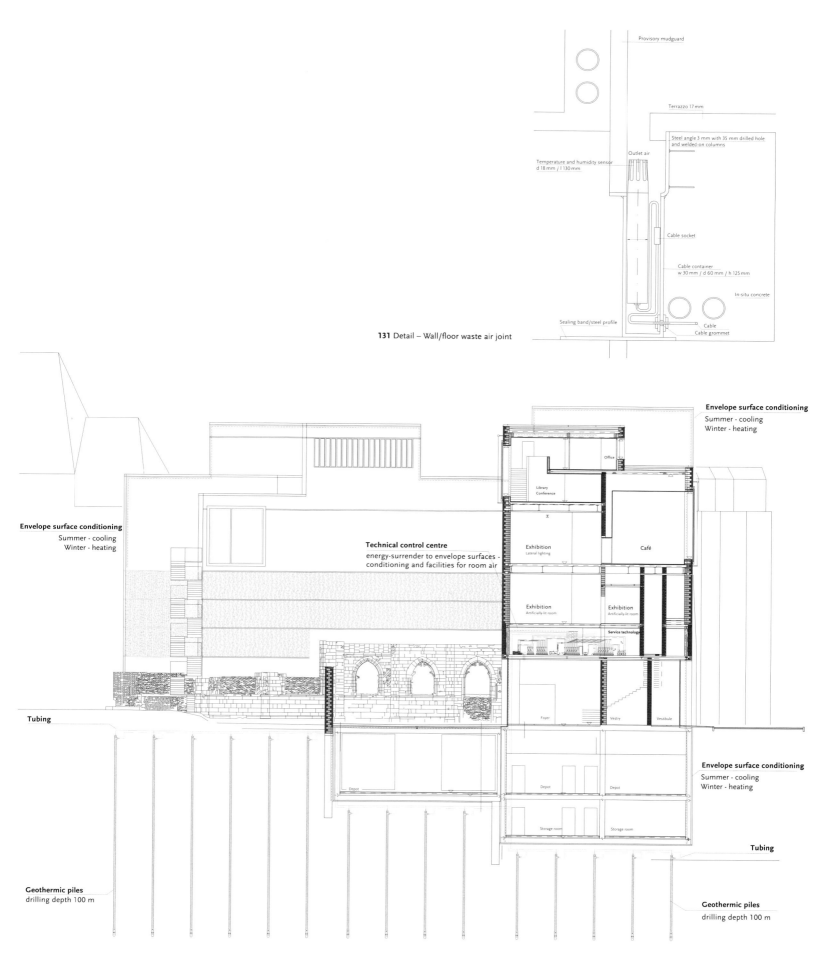

131 Detail – Wall/floor waste air joint

Provisory mudguard

Terrazzo 17 mm

Steel angle 3 mm with 35 mm drilled hole and welded-on columns

Outlet air

Temperature and humidity sensor
d 18 mm / l 130 mm

Cable socket

Cable container
w 30 mm / d 60 mm / h 125 mm

In-situ concrete

Sealing band/steel profile

Cable
Cable grommet

Envelope surface conditioning
Summer - cooling
Winter - heating

Envelope surface conditioning
Summer - cooling
Winter - heating

Technical control centre
energy-surrender to envelope surfaces -
conditioning and facilities for room air

Office

Library
Conference

Exhibition
Lateral lighting

Café

Exhibition
Artificially-lit room

Exhibition
Artificially-lit room

Service technology

Foyer

Vestry

Vestibule

Envelope surface conditioning
Summer - cooling
Winter - heating

Depot

Depot

Depot

Storage room

Storage room

Tubing

Tubing

Geothermic piles
drilling depth 100 m

Geothermic piles
drilling depth 100 m

130 Building section – Exhibition rooms above
the excavations and the Kolumba chapel

HELMUT F.O. MÜLLER (DAYLIGHT)
HANS JÜRGEN SCHMITZ (ARTIFICIAL LIGHT)

Lighting Design in Museums

1. Requirements

Planning the lighting design for a museum requires that a huge number of factors be taken into account, some of which are mutually contradictory. Not only should exhibits be visible, but they also need to be protected against light. The architectural aspects of general lighting, spatial orientation, and view of the outside are indispensable components of lighting design for museums.

1.1 Visibility

Visibility requires a minimum level of illumination, good contrast without shadows, good colour rendering, and avoidance of glare. The requirements vary enormously depending on the type of exhibit. The three-dimensional microstructure of the surface of a two-dimensional painting needs lighting conditions quite different from those required by a three-dimensional object such as a sculpture that needs to be viewed from all sides. Objects made of light or video installations must be shielded from light that would distract the observer, while large objects such as monuments or excavation sites should be shown in as natural a light as possible, without, however, being exposed to damaging weather conditions. There is no magic formula for these different museum lighting tasks, so that the requirements always have to be determined in accordance with the type of exhibit. Lighting should, moreover, be variable to a certain extent so that exhibitions of different kinds of objects can be presented.

1.2 Protection of objects

Protecting objects is often inconsistent with lighting them to achieve good visibility, which increases with light intensity, for light energy damages objects through absorption of radiation. Signs of aging appear, such as colours bleaching out, discolourings, and destruction of substance. Because the energy intensity of radiation increases as the wavelength diminishes, the ultraviolet or blue spectrum is more damaging than the red or infrared spectrum (see Table 1).

Table 1: Damage factors in dependence on wavelength[1,2]

Spectrum wavelength [nm]	Description	Relative Damage Factor
546	yellow-green	1
436	blue	22
405	blue-violet	60
389	violet	90
365	ultraviolet	135

In principle, the damaging absorption of radiation depends on the degree of absorption or reflection of the material and its spectral classification. This means that the damage to a dark surface will be greater than to a light surface, and a reddish surface will be more damaged than a blue one. In addition, sensitivity to radiation depends to a great extent on the type of material. Art works on paper are much more sensitive than ceramic or metal artworks, for example. Finally, damage is dependent on the duration of the radiation. Illuminating an object at 1000 lux for an hour has the same damaging effect as illuminating it for 1000 hours at one lux (assuming the same light composition). Corresponding to the light sensitivity of materials, effective threshold loads according to Günter Hilbert[1] have been established to determine the critical value of the light energy radiation for visible discolorations (for example newsprint 5 Wh/m² or watercolours on paper 175 Wh/m²).

For these reasons, maximum illuminance intensities are frequently set for objects of a specific light sensitivity. As 50 lux is considered to be the lowest level for good visibility, illuminances of 50 lux for paper and textiles, and 150 lux for paintings on canvas have been established. This guideline is not scientifically well-founded, because it does not take into account the spectral composition of light and the radiation energy. For this reason, many museums attempt to protect their objects by requiring the following:

138 Bregenz, Kunsthaus (Architect: Peter Zumthor)

132 Arrangement of windows and its influence on shadowing or lighting of walls

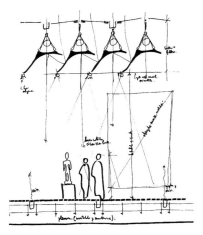

133 Daylighting through the roof, solar protection, and light distribution by lamella-shaped roof elements; Menil Collection, Houston, Texas (USA); rough sketch by Renzo Piano

- *determination of different maximum values of luminous intensity in dependence on the source of light*
- *limitation of the maximum duration of exposure*
- *complete ultraviolet protection and dimming of light outside visiting hours*
- *classification of the individual artworks according to categories of light-sensitivity.*

Karen Colby has worked out a detailed proposal for the classification of artworks on paper and recommended annual lighting limits. The Victoria & Albert Museum has developed simplified rules, according to which light-sensitive objects may be exhibited for 20 percent of the base lifespan of 500 years at 50 lux, while exhibits from the more durable category can be displayed in permanent exhibitions at 200 lux.

Such exigencies for object protection require absolute UV protection, the facility to dim lights, and precise adjustability of luminous intensity with minimum radiation energy. Finally, the potential damage to objects from the thermal effects of lighting should be taken into account (tension, stretching, crack formation). Heating of objects due to heat radiation that can lead to damage must be avoided,[3] so 'cold' light without infrared is recommended.

1.3 Room lighting, orientation, view of the outside world

For the orientation of staff and visitors and for sensory perception of the space, general lighting of the interior is useful as a rule. Special exhibitions in darkened rooms where only the objects are lighted are the exception. General lighting can also serve to light objects as well, but this can also be done independently. Frequently, additional object lighting is provided. If the protection of light-sensitive objects requires limited luminous intensities, the general lighting has to be adjusted correspondingly. For this reason, it is advisable to implement zoning with different illuminances and darkening possibilities when planning buildings

135 Brussels, Musée des Beaux Arts, daylighting through the atrium

and their illumination. In general, it should be borne in mind that light-coloured room surfaces favour even light distribution for room lighting and object lighting.

Visual connection with the outside is indispensable for the well-being and orientation of staff and visitors. Correspondingly, sufficient numbers of view windows should be arranged in such a way that it is possible to see the exterior surroundings including the horizon.

2 Daylighting

Daylight has a special role as a natural light source for many exhibition purposes, because of its spectral composition for colour rendering of objects or because of the characteristic change of intensity and the colour of the light depending on the sky and the time of year and time of day.

2.1 External conditions

In our latitudes, illuminances can amount to up to 100,000 lux outside when the sun is shining, while when the sky is overcast, it reaches at most 18,000 lux and on average, 10,000 lux (cf. DIN 5034). With direct sunlight, the colour composition of daylight is not the same as it is with a blue sky or when it is overcast; and it changes with the time of day and the season. People are familiar with the resulting interplay of light and shadow, and daylight can therefore be advantageously implemented in museum architecture for general lighting and/or object lighting. This is particularly true when an exhibition is to be displayed under lighting conditions that resemble exterior conditions, but the object requires a display case to protect it.

141 Interference in spatial perception with spotlighting alone

144 Spotlighting can become a space-forming element

Light direction and shadow formation

The light direction determines how an exhibit appears to observers. When using directional light, care should be taken first and foremost to avoid observers casting shadows on the exhibit. With reflecting surfaces (for example pictures under glass or display cases), it is necessary to ensure that light sources cannot reflect in them.[7] Bright window surfaces too can lead to reflections that make observation difficult (*cf. fig. 143*). For the illumination of three-dimensional exhibits, a combination of direct and diffuse light is ideal. The proportion of diffuse light can also result from the reflection of direct light on the surfaces in the room, otherwise illumination from several sides and of varying intensity is to be provided.

An object's own shadow engenders plasticity and there, it is a sign of the quality of good museum lighting. However, deep shadows have to be avoided as far as possible. They can be moderated by diffuse light, but remain nonetheless disturbingly evident. Particularly disturbing shadows are caused when stripes of sunlight fall directly on the exhibits, for example. Window frames can cause striping patterns totally overlaying exhibits. Also, badly positioned lights may cast the edges of rooms into shadow or cause shadows to be cast at the edges of deep picture frames.

3.2 Lights and luminaires

As industrially manufactured products, the lamps for museum lighting are to be selected from the range on offer. In this regard, the type of room lighting determines the category of lighting methods.

- *Light bulbs:* spot-shaped light sources, directional lighting possible, good colour rendering, warm light colour, small models available, wide performance spectrum.
- *Discharge lamps:* spot-shaped or linear, limited colour rendering, high performance, models more suitable for general lighting.
- *Special case:* fibre-optics, very small models available, especially suitable for accent lighting, low proportion of ultraviolet and infrared minimizes the damage potential.
- *LED:* very low illuminating power and limited wavelength spectrum with correspondingly bad colour rendering limits the use in museum lighting to special cases.

Luminaires can be manufactured for the special requirements of the respective lighting tasks and particularly in museums, the proportion of special lights is very high. In this regard, the lighting geometry can be adjusted precisely to the requirements. The largest market segment for variable spotlights is in museum lighting.

3.3 Conventional lighting systems

The two most important lighting systems for museums with their advantages and some potential problems are only introduced as examples here. Because of the usability of daylight, the illuminated ceiling is a widespread form of museum lighting. Illuminated ceilings offer the possibility of eliminating reflections on exhibits to a large extent and thus enable perception of the space and of the objects. Important conditions for the implementation of an illuminated ceiling suitable for a museum are the height of the room and the type of glazing; with daylight-illuminated ceilings, the type of solar protection and the distribution of light, and with artificially-illuminated ceilings, the lighting power installed and the colour of the light. In low-ceilinged rooms, the use of an illuminated ceiling leads to a large differential between horizontal and vertical luminous intensities. Because the eye first adapts to the brightest area in the field of vision, exhibits on the walls appear dark. With an illuminated ceiling, the choice of glazing is particularly important, as on one hand high transmission is necessary, but on the other hand, with illuminated ceilings that are too transparent, the patterns of the lights or the daylight openings above them can be seen and thus impair perception of the room. With artificially-illuminated ceilings it must be borne in mind that observers tend to associate an illuminated ceiling with daylight. This means that a corresponding lighting power will be expected and illuminated ceilings that do not give enough light are perceived as dim and uncomfortable. As illuminated ceilings give diffuse light, supplementing them with spotlights at least optionally has to be provided for, for example by inserting contact rails in the grid or at the edge of the illuminated ceiling.

Spotlighting is particularly suitable for creating a very sophisticated lighting situation. The spectrum in the lighting power and distribution of light enables very small objects to be lit up, for example with track lighting, and even outside areas can be spotlighted. When lighting with spotlights, the risk of glare from reflection and the formation of shadows has to be taken into account. When spotlights alone are implemented, there is the danger that spatial perception is only possible with difficulty, and visitors will be disoriented. In arranging spotlights or rather when establishing possible spotlight positions, it absolutely has to be taken into account that they have to be spatially integrated, as otherwise the spotlights themselves are turned into space-forming elements.

145/146 Basel, Museum für Gegenwartskunst
(architects: Wilfried and Katharina Steib, 1979-80) |
Munich, Pinakothek der Moderne (architect:
Stephan Braunfels, 1992-2002)

3.4 Light and energy

Museum lighting usually gives rise to complex lighting installations requiring high numbers of unit watts per square metre that cannot be compared with other uses. With pictures, for example, it has to be borne in mind that here the wall surface has to be lighted and the specific connected value based on the floor area can be very high. In particular, with high-ceilinged galleries, connected values may rise to 100 W/m². The lighting causes a significant heating load for HVAC systems, and it has to be drawn off in order to avoid the rooms being overheated. The solution often arrived at, of installing additional spotlights for special exhibitions, makes designing the HVAC system for the lighting conditions problematic in general.

The consumption of expensive electrical energy for artificial light can amount to a significant proportion of the operating costs of a museum. In addition to that there is the cost of maintenance and the changing of light bulbs – usually short-lived – of the luminaires. Taking into account ecological and economic factors, optimizing the lighting requirements and choosing the optimum illumination source should therefore be a fixed component of the planning process, also when exhibition plans are changed.

Notes

1
Krzysztof Pomian, Der Ursprung des Museums. Vom Sammeln, Berlin, 1986; Pomian, "Das Museum: Die Quintessenz Europas," in: Wunderkammer des Abendlandes. Museum und Sammlung im Spiegel der Zeit, exhibition catalogue, Kunst- und Ausstellungshalle der Bundesrepublik Deutschland, Bonn, 1994, 112-119.

2
Gustav Parthey, Das alexandrinische Museum, Berlin, 1838; Kenneth Hamma (ed.) Alexandria and Alexandrianism, Malibu, California, 1996.

3
Melanie Blank/Julia Debelts, Was ist ein Museum? "... eine metaphorische Komplikation... ", Vienna, 2002.

4
R.E. Wycherley (ed.), Pausanias, Description of Greece (Loeb Classical Library), Cambridge, Mass., 1935.

5
Adolf Furtwängler, "Ueber Kunstsammlungen in alter und neuer Zeit," keynote speech given on 11th March 1899 at the public meeting of the Royal Bavarian Academy of Sciences in Munich on the occasion of the 140th anniversary of its foundation, Munich, 1899, 9 ff.

6
Klaus Minges, Das Sammlungswesen der frühen Neuzeit, Münster, 1998, 11 ff.

7
Wolfgang Liebenwein, Studiolo. Die Entstehung eines Raumtyps und seine Entwicklung bis um 1600. Berlin, 1977; Heike Frosien-Leinz, "Das Studiolo und seine Ausstattung," in: Natur und Antike in der Renaissance, exhibition catalogue, Frankfurt on Main, 1985, 258-281.

8
Liebenwein, op. cit. (note 7), 154 ff.

9
Germain Bazin, Le Temps des musées, Liège, 1967; Ingo Herklotz, "Neue Literatur zur Sammlungsgeschichte," in: Kunstchronik 47/1997, 117-135.

10
Julius von Schlosser, Die Kunst- und Wunderkammern der Spätrenaissance, 2nd ed., Braunschweig, 1978 (Leipzig 1908); Horst Bredekamp, Antikensehnsucht und Maschinenglauben. Die Geschichte der Kunstkammer und die Zukunft der Kunstgeschichte, Berlin, 1993.

11
Elisabeth Scheicher, Die Kunst- und Wunderkammern der Habsburger, Vienna/Munich/Zurich, 1979; however, the electors of Saxony, Bavaria, Brandenburg and a whole series of other princes such as Ferdinand Albrecht zu Braunschweig-Lüneburg also possessed chambers of art and curiosities. Cf. Die Brandenburgisch-preussische Kunstkammer, exhibition catalogue, Berlin 1981; Barocke Sammellust. Die Bibliothek und Kunstkammer des Herzogs Ferdinand Albrecht zu Braunschweig Lüneburg (1636-1687), exhibition catalogue, Wolfenbüttel, 1988; Géza von Habsburg, Fürstliche Kunstkammern in Europa, Stuttgart/Berlin/Cologne, 1997.

12
Schlosser, op. cit. (note 10), 201 f.

13
Ibid. (note 10), 204 ff.

14
Renate von Busch, Studien zu deutschen Antikensammlungen des 16. Jahrhunderts, Dissertation. Tübingen, 1973.

15
Alma S. Wittlin, Museums. In Search of a Usable Future, Cambridge, Mass., 1970, 31 ff.

16
Scherer, op. cit. (note 38), 43 ff.; Minges, op. cit. (note 6), 143 ff.

17
Klara Garas, "Die Entstehung der Galerie des Erzherzogs Leopold Wilhelm," in: Jahrbuch der kunsthistorischen Sammlungen in Wien 63/1967, 39-80; Garas, "Das Schicksal der Sammlung des Erzherzogs Leopold Wilhelm," in: ibid. 64/1968, 181-278; David Teniers, Jan Brueghel y los gabinetes de pinturas, exhibition catalogue, ed. Matías Díaz Padrón and Mercedes Royo-Villanova, Madrid, 1992.

18
Above all, the works of Johann Joachim Winckelmann, Gedanken über die Nachahmung der griechischen Werke in der Malerei und Bildhauerkunst, 1755; Beschreibung des Torso im Belvedere zu Rom, 1759; Geschichte der Kunst des Altertums, 1764; cf. Thomas W. Gaethgens (ed.), Johann Joachim Winckelmann 1717-1768, Hamburg, 1986; Bredekamp, op. cit. (note 10), 86 ff.

19
Antikensammlungen im 18. Jahrhundert, ed. Herbert Beck, Peter C. Bol, Wolfram Prinz and Hans v. Steuben, Berlin, 1981.

20
Minges, op. cit. (note 6), 182 ff.

21
Marjorie Caygill, The Story of the British Museum, 3rd ed., London, 2002.

22
B. F. Cook, The Elgin Marbles. 2nd ed., London, 1997.

23
Elke Harten, Museen und Museumsprojekte der französischen Revolution, Münster, 1989, 157 ff.

24
James J. Sheehan, Museums in the German Art World from the End of the Old Regime to the Rise of Modernism, Oxford, 2000.

25
Gottfried Fliedl (ed.), Die Erfindung des Museums. Anfänge der bürgerlichen Museumsidee in der französischen Revolution, Vienna, 1996.

26
Walter Wagner, "Die frühen Museumsgründungen in der Donaumonarchie," in: Das kunst- und kulturgeschichtliche Museum im 19. Jahrhundert, ed. Bernward Deneke/Rainer Kahsnitz, Munich, 1977, 11-18.

27
József Korek, "Der Museumsgedanke und die Sammlungsmethoden in Ungarn. Die ersten fünfzig Jahre des Ungarischen Nationalmuseums (1802-1852)," in: Das kunst- und kulturgeschichtliche Museum im 19. Jahrhundert, 19-28 (note 26).

28
Zwischen Himmel und Erde. Allumfassend – Das Joanneum, exhibition catalogue, Graz, 1996, 6.

29
Bettina Schlorhaufer, Das Tiroler Landesmuseum Ferdinandeum, Dissertation, Innsbruck, 1988.

30
Das Germanische Nationalmuseum Nürnberg 1852-1977, ed. Bernward Deneke/Rainer Kahsnitz, Munich/Berlin, 1978.

31
Rainer Budde, "Das Wallraf-Richartz-Museum und seine Sammlungen," in: Wallraf-Richartz-Museum Köln. Von Stefan Lochner bis Paul Cézanne. 120 Meisterwerke der Gemäldesammlung, Cologne, 1986, 9-30.

32
Volker Plagemann, Das deutsche Kunstmuseum 1790-1870, Munich, 1967, 150 ff.

33
Winfried Kretschmer, Geschichte der Weltausstellungen, Frankfurt on Main, 1999.

34
Gert Reising, Das Museum als Öffentlichkeitsform und Bildungsträger bürgerlicher Kultur. Unter besonderer Berücksichtigung der Entwicklungsgeschichte des South Kensington Museums in London, Darmstadt, 1985.

35
Hanna Egger/Edwin Lachnit, "Ein Museum für die Zukunft," in: Österreichisches Museum für angewandte Kunst, ed. Peter Noever, Vienna, 1986, 11 ff.

36
Barbara Mundt, Die deutschen Kunstgewerbemuseen im 19. Jahrhundert, Munich, 1974.

37
Sheehan, op. cit. (note 24), 213 ff. of the German edition.

38
Valentin Scherer, Deutsche Museen. Entstehung und kulturgeschichtliche Bedeutung unserer öffentlichen Kunstsammlungen, Jena, 1913, 246.

39
Alexis Joachimides, "Die Schule des Geschmacks. Das Kaiser-Friedrich-Museum als Reformprojekt," in: Museumsinszenierungen. Zur Geschichte der Institution des Kunstmuseums. Die Berliner Museumslandschaft 1830-1990, ed. Alexis Joachimides, Sven Kuhrau, Viola Vahrson and Nikolaus Bernau, Dresden/Basel, 1995, 142-156.

40
Cf. footnote 98.

41
Heinrich Wagner, "Museen. Neu bearbeitet von Heinrich Wagner jun.," in: Handbuch der Architektur, Part 4, 6th Half-volume, No. 4, 2nd ed., Stuttgart, 1906, 272 ff.

42
On the various aspects of this museum reform in Germany, which has been repeatedly undertaken since 1870, see Alexis Joachimides, Die Museumsreformbewegung in Deutschland und die Entstehung des modernen Museums 1880-1940. Dresden, 2001.

43
Das Kunstgewerbemuseum der Stadt Köln, Cologne, 1971, 62.

44
Werner Hofmann, "Funktionswandel des Museums," in: Jahresring 1959/60, 99-109.

45
Ellen Spickernagel/Brigitte Walbe (eds.), Das Museum. Lernort contra Musentempel, Gießen, 1976.

46
Gert von der Osten, Museum für eine Gesellschaft von morgen. Cologne, 1971.

47
Wolfgang Klausewitz, Museumspädagogik, Frankfurt on Main, 1975; Heidi Heinse, Das Museum als gesellschaftlicher Lernort. Aspekte einer pädagogischen Neubestimmung, Frankfurt on Main, 1985; Museumspädagogik in neuer Sicht, ed. Hildegard Vieregg, Marie-Louise Schmeer-Sturm, Jutta Thinesse-Demel and others, Baltmannsweiler, 1994.

48
Das Museum der Zukunft. 43 Beiträge zur Diskussion über eine Zukunft des Museums, ed. Gerhard Bott, Cologne, 1970.

49
Monika Zimmermann, "Museum heute: Musentempel, Lernort oder Jahrmarkt? Ein Bericht von den Dortmunder Architekturtagen," in: Museumskunde 44/1979, 98-99. [Translator's note: the term 'Gründerzeit' designates the period immediately following the Franco-German war of 1870/71, when the economy underwent a boom and the industrialization of Germany, which until then had lagged behind the other industrialized countries, made a great leap forward. It was accompanied by a generalized feeling of great optimism.]

50
For an early example of that which has now become everyday, see Rudolph Ganz, "Die Kunsthalle als Bankschalter," in: Notizbuch 3. Kunst – Gesellschaft – Museum, ed. Horst Kunitzky, Berlin, 1980, 171 f.

51
Uwe M. Schneede, Museum 2000 – Erlebnispark oder Bildungsstätte?, Cologne, 2000.

52
For example, Beat Wyss, in: Denkraum Museum, ed. Moritz Küng, Baden, Switzerland, 1992, 69 ff.

53
Walter Grasskamp, Museumsgründer und Museumsstürmer. Zur Sozialgeschichte des Kunstmuseums, Munich, 1981, 42 ff.

54
Hans-Joachim Klein/Monika Bachmayer, Museum und Öffentlichkeit. Fakten und Daten – Motive und Barrieren, Berlin, 1981.

55
Hermann Lübbe, Die Aufdringlichkeit der Geschichte, Graz/Vienna/Cologne, 1989, 13.

56
Wolfgang Zacharias (ed.), Zeitphänomen Musealisierung. Das Verschwinden der Gegenwart und die Konstruktion der Erinnerung, Essen, 1990.

57
Nicola Borger-Keweloh, "Das totale Museum," in: Das Museum. Die Entwicklung in den 80er Jahren. Festschrift für Hugo Borger zum 65. Geburtstag, ed. Achim Preiß/Karl Stamm/Frank Günther Zehnder, Munich, 1990, 129-140.

58
Hans Belting, "Orte der Reflexion oder Orte der Sensation?," in: das diskursive museum, ed. Peter Noever/MAK, Vienna, 2001, 82-94, quotation p. 89.

59
Michael Fehr, "Das Museum – Ort des Vergessens," in: Zacharias (note 56), 220-223.

60
Petra Schuck-Wersig, Die Lust am Schauen oder Müssen Museen langweilig sein? Plädoyer für eine neue Sehkultur, Berlin, 1986.

61
Peter Gorsen, in: Christian Reder, Wiener Museums-gespräche. Über den Umgang mit Kunst und Museen, Vienna, 1988, 193.

62
Hans Belting, "Das Museum als Medium," in: Die Zukunft der alten Meister. Perspektiven und Konzepte für das Kunstmuseum von heute, ed. Ekkehard Mai, Cologne/Vienna/Weimar, 2001, 31-43.

63
André Malraux, Le musée imaginaire, Genève 1947

64
Walter Benjamin, Das Kunstwerk im Zeitalter seiner technischen Reproduzierbarkeit, Frankfort on the Main, 1963 (first published in: Zeitschrift für Sozialforschung 1/1936). (English edition, "The Work of Art in the Age of Mechanical Reproduction," included in: Walter Benjamin, Illuminations: Essays and Reflections, ed. Hannah Arendt. New York, 1968 and 1969.)

65
Hugo Borger, Die Kölner Museen, Cologne, 1990, 11.

66
Helmut Börsch-Supan, Kunstmuseen in der Krise. Chancen, Gefährdungen, Aufgaben in mageren Jahren, Munich, 1993, 97.

67
Fundamental publications with comprehensive bibliographies: Helmut Seling, Die Entstehung des Kunstmuseums als Aufgabe der Architektur, Unpublished dissertation, Freiburg, 1952; Seling, "The Genius of the Museum," in: The Architectural Review 141/1967, 103-111; Nikolaus Pevsner, A History of Building Types, London, 1976.

68
James S. Ackerman, The Cortile del Belvedere, Vatican City, 1954, 18 and 32 ff.

69
Wolfram Prinz, Die Entstehung der Galerie in Frankreich und Italien, Berlin, 1970; on this, see the comprehensive review by Volker Hoffmann in: architectura 1/1971, 102-112, as well as Frank Büttner, "Zur Frage der Entstehung der Galerie," in: architectura 2/1972, 75-80.

70
Gerrit Confurius, Sabbioneta oder die schöne Kunst der Stadtgründung, Munich, 1984, 175 ff.

71
Heike Frosien-Leinz, "Das Antiquarium der Residenz: erstes Antikenmuseum Münchens," in: Glyptothek München 1830-1980, exhibition catalogue, ed. Klaus Vierneisel and Gottlieb Leinz, Munich, 1980, 310-321.

72
Detlef Heikamp, "Zur Geschichte der Uffizien-Tribuna," in: Zeitschrift für Kunstgeschichte 26/1963, 193-268, in particular 198-209; Amelio Fara, Bernardo Buontalenti, Basel, 1990, 196 f.

73
Sebastiano Serlio, Tutte l'opere di architettura et prospettiva, ed. Giovanni Domenico Scamozzi, Venice, 1619 (Reprint 1964), III, fol. 50 r.

74
Max Rooses, Rubens, Philadelphia/London, 1904, 150 f.

75
Pevsner, op. cit. (note 67), 114 f.

76
Joseph and Anne Rykwert, Robert und James Adam, Stuttgart, The Men and the Style (Architectural Documents), London, 1985, 139 ff.

77
John Kenworthy-Browne, "Private Skulpturen-Galerien in England 1730-1830," in: Glyptothek (note 71), 334-353.

78
Bartolomeo Nogara, Origine e Sviluppo dei Musei e Gallerie Pontifiche, Rome, 1948; Seling, op. cit. (note 67), 101 ff.; Gottlieb Leinz, "Das Museo Pio-Clementino und der Braccio Nuovo im Vatikan," in: Glyptothek (note 71), 604-609.

79
Seling 1952 (note 67), 234-277; Seling, "Das Museum als Aufgabe der Architektur im Frankreich der Revolutionszeit," in: Glyptothek (note 71), 328-333; Elke Harten, Museen und Museumsprojekte der französischen Revolution, Münster, 1989.

80
Adolf Max Vogt, Boullées Newton-Denkmal. Sakralbau und Kugelidee, Basel/Stuttgart, 1969, 216 ff.; Gottfried Fliedl/Karl-Josef Pazzini, "Museum – Opfer – Blick. Zu Etienne Louis Boullées Museumsphantasie von 1783," in: Fliedl (note 25), 131-158.

81
Hans-Kurt Boehlke, "Das Museum Fridericianum, eine Beschreibung ihrer Architektur und ihrer Verwendung durch seinen Baumeister Simon Louis du Ry," in: Zeitschrift für hessische Geschichte und Landeskunde 74/1963, 91-107.

82
Giles Waterfield, Soane and After: The Architecture of Dulwich Picture Gallery, London, 1987.

83
Volker Plagemann, 1967 (note 32), 43-64; Glyptothek (note 71); Britta-R. Schwahn, Die Glyptothek in München. Baugeschichte und Ikonologie, Munich, 1983; Leo von Klenze. Architekt zwischen Kunst und Hof 1784-1864, exhibition catalogue, ed. Winfried Nerdinger, Munich, 2000, 238-249 (= cat. no. 34).

84
Plagemann 1967 (note 32), 82-89; Peter Böttger, Die Alte Pinakothek in München, Munich, 1972; Leo von Klenze 2000 (note 83), 282-290 (= cat. no. 46).

85
Plagemann 1967 (note 32), 42.

86
Hans Kauffmann, "Zweckbau und Monument: Zu Friedrich Schinkels Museum am Berliner Lustgarten," in: Eine Freundesgabe der Wissenschaft für Ernst Hellmut Vits zur Vollendung seines 60. Lebensjahres am 19. September 1963, ed. Gerhard Hess, Frankfort, 1963, 135-166; Plagemann 1967 (note 32), 66-81; Goerd Peschken, "Schinkels Museum am Berliner Lustgarten," in: Glyptothek (note 71), 360-371; Renate Petras, Die Bauten der Berliner Museumsinsel, Berlin, 1987, 37-52; Gian Paolo Semino, Karl Friedrich Schinkel, Zurich/Munich/London 1993, 71-81; Andreas Haus, Karl Friedrich Schinkel als Künstler, Munich/Berlin, 2001, 216-242.

87
Plagemann 1967 (note 32), 127-131; Werner Mittlmeier, Die Neue Pinakothek in München 1843-1854, Munich, 1977.

88
Plagemann 1967 (note 32), 131-144; Harald Marx/Heinrich Magirius, Gemäldegalerie Dresden, Leipzig, 1992.

89
Herbert Haupt, Das Kunsthistorische Museum. Die Geschichte des Hauses am Ring, Vienna, 1991, in particular. 19 ff.; Beatrix Kriller/Georg Kugler, Das Kunsthistorische Museum. Die Architektur und Ausstattung, Vienna, 1991; Gottfried Semper 1803-1879, exhibition catalogue, ed. Winfried Nerdinger and Werner Oechslin, Munich/Zurich, 2003, 430 ff.

90
These were the words of Carl von Lützow, Professor at the Vienna Academy, at the opening of the Kunsthistorisches Museum in 1891, quoted from Haupt 1991 (note 89), 29.

91
Jörn Bahns, "Kunst- und kulturgeschichtliche Museen als Bauaufgabe des späten 19. Jahrhunderts," in: Das kunst- und kulturgeschichtliche Museum im 19. Jahrhundert, ed. Bernward Deneke and Rainer Kahsnitz, Munich, 1977, 176-192; Volker Plagemann, "Zur Museumsarchitektur im 19. Jahrhundert," in: Dortmunder Architekturausstellung 1979: Museumsbauten: Musentempel, Lernorte, Jahrmärkte (= 15th Dortmunder Architekturheft), Dortmund, 1979, appendix (n. pag.).

92
Plagemann 1967 (note 32), 93-101; Uta Hassler, Die Kunsthalle als Kunstwerk, Karlsruhe, 1993.

93
Plagemann 1967 (note 32), 160-164.

94
Albert Verbeek, "Das erste Wallraf-Richartz-Museum in Köln," in: Wallraf-Richartz-Jahrbuch 23/1961, 7-36; Plagemann 1967 (note 32), 169-175.

95
Plagemann 1967 (note 32), 117-126.

96
Plagemann 1967 (note 83), 145-149.

97
Wagner (note 41), 273 f.

98
Georg Himmelheber, "Gabriel Seidls Bau des Bayerischen Nationalmuseums," in: Münchner Jahrbuch der bildenden Kunst. 3rd series, vol. 23/1972, 187-212.

99
Jörg Bahns, "Die Museumsbauten von der Übernahme der Kartause im Jahre 1857 bis gegen 1910," in: Das Germanische Nationalmuseum Nürnberg 1852-1977, ed. Bernward Deneke and Rainer Kahsnitz, Munich/Berlin, 1978, 357 ff.

100
Wagner 1906 (note 41), 272-277; significantly, this chapter, "Museen nach dem Angliederungs-system" is missing in the first edition of the Handbuch der Architektur published in 1893.

101
Joseph Mordaunt Crook, The British Museum, London, 1972.

102
Philip Hendy, The National Gallery of London, London, 1960; Palaces of Art. Art Galleries in Britain 1790-1990, exhibition catalogue, London, 1992, 100 ff.

103
William James Williams, "John Russell Pope. The Building of the National Gallery of Art, Washington," in: Apollo 349/1991, 166-170.

104
Neues Bauen in Wiesbaden 1900-1914, exhibition catalogue, Wiesbaden, 1984, 157-180; Winfried Nerdinger, Theodor Fischer. Architekt und Städtebauer 1862-1938, exhibition catalogue, Munich, 1988, 69 ff. and 264 ff.

105
Wagner 1906 (note 41), 257.

106
On the various aspects of this museum reform in Germany between 1870 and 1914, see Achim Preiß, Das Museum und seine Architektur. Wilhelm Kreis und der Museumsbau in der ersten Hälfte des 20. Jahrhunderts, Alfter, 1993, 51 ff.; Alexis Joachimides, Die Museumsreformbewegung in Deutschland und die Entstehung des modernen Museums 1880-1940, Dresden, 2001, 99 ff.

107
Achim Preiß, "Nazikunst und Kunstmuseum," in: Kritische Berichte 2/1989, 76-90.

108
Karl Arndt, "Das 'Haus der Deutschen Kunst' – ein Symbol der neuen Machtverhältnisse," in: Die "Kunststadt" München 1937. Nationalsozialismus und "Entartete Kunst," ed. Peter-Klaus Schuster, Munich, 1987, 61-82; Preiß 1993 (note 106), 296 ff.

109
Preiß 1993 (note 106), 337 ff.

110
Cf. A&U 171/1984, 31-66; Baumeister 8/1984, 74-77.

111
Helen Searing, "The Development of a Museum Typology," in: Building the New Museum, ed. Suzanne Stephens, New York, 1986, 14 ff.

112
Het Haags Gemeentemuseum. Het museumgebouw van H.P.Berlage, Den Haag, 1982; Preiß 1993 (note 106), 355 ff.

113
Kröller-Müller-Museum, ed. staff of the museum, Otterloo, 1977; Preiß 1993 (note 106), 353 ff.

114
Herta Hesse-Frielinghaus, "Die Museumsbauten Henry van de Veldes und ihre Vorgeschichte," in: Museumskunde 33/1964, 1-23, in particular 16 ff.

115
Roberto Aloi, Musei. Architettura – Tecnica, Milan, 1962 offers a comprehensive documentation of museum architecture, primarily of the 1950s, with particular attention paid to Italian museums.

116
Izzika Gaon, "Un museo in crescita: I primi 25 anni 1963-88. Israel Museum, Jerusalem," in: Architettura cronache e storia 437/1992, 190-200; Martin Weyl, "The Creation of the Israel Museum," in: The Israel Museum. Jerusalem, 1995, 8-21; David Simon Morton, "In expansion, Freed gives the Israel Museum a little Louvre," in: Architectural Record 186.3/1998, 39.

117
On German museum architecture in the first decades of the postwar era in general, see Peter J. Tange, "Museologie und Architektur. 'Neuer' Museumsbau in Deutschland," in: Dortmunder Architekturausstellung 1979 (note 91), appendix (n. pag.); Hannelore Schubert, Moderner Museumsbau. Stuttgart, 1986 offers a catalogue-like portrayal of the most important museum buildings in German-speaking countries since the Second World War.

Notes

118
Schubert (note 117), 182 f.

119
Museum Folkwang Essen. Das Museumsgebäude, ed. Museum Folkwang Essen, Essen, 1966; Schubert (note 117), 53 ff.

120
Built in 1963-74 by Heinz Röcke and Klaus Renner; Schubert (note 117), 94 ff.

121
Built in 1960 by Isoya Yoshida; Aloi (note 115), 44-52.

122
Manfred Lehmbruck, "Reuchlinhaus in Pforzheim," in: Architektur und Wohnform 70/1962, 152-165; Schubert (note 117), 56 f.

123
Aloi (note 115), 15-26.

124
Samuel Cauman, Das lebendige Museum. Erfahrungen eines Kunsthistorikers und Museumsdirektors, Alexander Dorner, Hanover, 1960 (first published in English in 1958), 180 f.

125
Walter Gropius, "Gestaltung von Museumsgebäuden," in: Jahresring 1955/56, 128-136, in particular 130 f.

126
Chup Friemert, Die gläserne Arche. Kristallpalast London 1851 und 1854, Dresden, 1984.

127
Erich Schild, Zwischen Glaspalast und Palais des Illusions. Form und Konstruktion im 19. Jahrhundert, (= Bauwelt Fundamente 20) Berlin/Frankfurt on Main/Vienna, 1967.

128
Volker Hütsch, Der Münchner Glaspalast. Geschichte und Bedeutung, Munich, 1980; Zwischen Glaspalast und Maximilianeum. Architektur in Bayern zur Zeit Maximilians II. 1848-1864, exhibition catalogue, ed. Winfried Nerdinger, Munich, 1997, 120-125 (cat. no. 1).

129
Tange (note 117).

130
The Architectural Review 982/1978, 345-362; François Chaslin/Frédérique Hervet/Armelle Lavalou, Norman Foster, Stuttgart, 1987, 72-85.

131
Helen Searing, New American Museums, New York, 1982, 61 ff.

132
Planned in 1957/58 as an office building for Bacardi in Santiago de Cuba, adapted in 1960/61 for the Georg-Schäfer-Museum in Schweinfurt, and finally realized in 1965-68 as the Neue Nationalgalerie in Berlin; Mies van der Rohes Neue Nationalgalerie in Berlin, ed. Gabriela Wachter, Berlin, 1995.

133
Cf. Das Museum der Zukunft. 43 Beiträge zur Diskussion über die Zukunft des Museums, ed. Gerhard Bott, Cologne, 1970.

134
Victoria Newhouse, Towards a New Museum, New York, 1998, attempts to organize this variety more associatively, alternatively in accordance with the aspect of ownership, the representative ambition and the position of the museum buildings in the development of architecture, etc.;

Stanislaus von Moos, "Museums-Explosion. Bruchstücke einer Bilanz," in: Vittorio Magnago Lampugnani/Angeli Sachs (eds.), Museums for a New Millennium, Munich/London/New York, 1999, 15-27, aware of the lack of systematics, proposes the following typology of the modern museum: the museum as renovated and adapted monument, the 'open' museum, the museum in the form of the traditional directed sequence of rooms, the museum as plastic architecture;' Arthur Rosenblatt, Building Type Basics for Museums. New York, 2001 organizes his selection – almost exclusively limited to American museums or those designed by American architects – simply according to functions: art museums, historical museums, etc.

135
Josef Paul Kleihues in the introduction to the catalogue of the Dortmunder Architekturausstellung 1979 (note 91).

136
Peter Eisenman, "Schwache Form," in: Architektur im Aufbruch. Neue Positionen zum Dekonstruktivismus, ed. Peter Noever, Munich, 1991, 39 ff.

137
Peter Blake, "The Guggenheim: museum or monument?," in: The Architectural Forum 12/1959, 86-92; Jack Quinan, "Frank Lloyd Wright's Guggenheim Museum: A Historian's Report," in: Journal of the Society of Architectural Historians 52/1993, 466-482; Das Solomon R. Guggenheim Museum, with a text by Bruce Brooks Pfeiffer, New York, 1995; Neil Levine (ed.), The Architecture of Frank Lloyd Wright, Princeton, 1996, 299-364.

138
Stephan Barthelmeß, Das postmoderne Museum als Erscheinungsform von Architektur, Munich, 1988.

139
Therefore, the selections for the numerous and usually opulent publications on contemporary museum architecture seem to have been made by chance, or are restricted to purely formal criteria such as temporal or regional categorization: Ingeborg Flagge (ed.), Museumsarchitektur 1985, Hamburg, 1985; Heinrich Klotz, Neue Museumsbauten in der Bundesrepublik Deutschland, Munich, 1985; Laurence Allégret, Musées. Vol. 2, Milan/Paris, 1987/1992; Josep Maria Montaner, Neue Museen. Räume für Kunst und Kultur, Stuttgart/Zurich, 1990; Vittorio Magnago Lampugnani (ed.), Museumsarchitektur in Frankfurt 1980-1990, Munich, 1990; Jost Schilgen, Neue Häuser für die Kunst. Museumsbauten in Deutschland, Dortmund, 1990; Luisa López Moreno and others (eds.), El arquitecto y el museo, Jerez, 1990; Museo d'arte e architettura, exhibition catalogue, Lugano, 1992; Räume für Kunst. Museumsmodelle. Europäische Museumsarchitektur der Gegenwart, exhibition catalogue, Graz-Groningen, 1993; James Steele (ed.), Museum Builders, London, 1994; Francisco Asensio Cerver, The Architecture of Museums, New York, 1997; Justin Henderson, Museum Architecture, Gloucester, Mass., 1998; Luca Basso Peressut, musei. architetture 1990-2000, Milan, 1999; France musées récents (le moniteur architecture amc), Paris, 1999; Gerhard Mack, Art Museums. Into the 21th century, Basel/Berlin/ Boston, 1999; Arian Mostaedi, Museums and Art Facilities, Barcelona, 2001; Frank Maier-Solgk, Die neuen Museen, Cologne, 2002; Josep Montaner, Jordi Oliveras, The Museums of the Last Generation, London, 1987; Joep Maria Montaner, Museums for a New Century, Barcelona, 1995; Josep M. Montaner, New Museums, New York, 1990.

140
Dieter Bartetzko, "Die reinste Verschwendung. Magie zwischen Minimalismus und Exzentrik: Tendenzen im Museumsbau der neunziger Jahre," in: Uwe M. Schneede (ed.), Museum 2000 – Erlebnispark oder Bildungsstätte?, Cologne, 2000, 129-141.

141
Herzog & de Meuron. Sammlung Goetz (= Kunsthaus Bregenz Werkdokumente), Stuttgart, 1995.

142
Coop Himmelb(l)au, 1992-94; Gerda Vrigteman/Steven Kolsteren, Groninger Museum, Groningen, 1996; Newhouse (note 134), 229-231.

143
This is what Wolf-Dieter Prix declared, according to Winfried Nerdinger in "Vom Kunsttempel zum Eventcenter – Kunstvermittlung durch Museumsarchitektur im Spiegel der Kunstrezeption," in: Die Zukunft der alten Meister, ed. Ekkehard Mai, Cologne/Weimar/Vienna, 2001, 57.

144
Vittorio Magnago Lampugnani, "The Architecture of Art", in: Museums for a New Millennium (note 134), 14.

145
In 1797, Wilhelm Heinrich Wackenroder demanded in his "Herzensergießungen eines kunstliebenden Klosterbruders" (ed. A. Langen, Kempen, 1948, 133) that museums "be temples where one would like to admire the great artists as the most elevated of earthly beings, in calm and silent humility and in the solitude that lifts up our hearts..."; Johann Wolfgang von Goethe wrote in "Dichtung und Wahrheit" (1811-14) about his visit to the Dresdner Schloßgalerie: "I stepped into this shrine and my astonishment was beyond expression... These... rooms gave a unique feeling of solemnity that resembled the feelings one has on entering a church all the more because the decorations of so many temples and so many objects of devotion appeared to be set up here once again only for the purposes of sacred art." [This translation by Fiona Greenwood] (Goethes sämtliche Werke. vol. 25, Propyläen edition, Munich, n.d., 11; English edition: From My Life: Poetry and Truth, Part 4 (Goethe: The Collected Works, vol. 5) Princeton, 1994).

146
Walter Hochreiter, Vom Musentempel zum Lernort. Zur Sozialgeschichte deutscher Museen 1800-1917, Darmstadt, 1994.

147
Aloi (note 115), 175-188; Michael Brawne, The New Museum, New York/Stuttgart, 1965, 32-35.

148
Nerdinger 2001 (note 143), 56 f.

149
Werner Hofmann, Museumsdämmerung? (= Schriften der Kurhessischen Gesellschaft für Kunst und Wissenschaft, Heft 1), Kassel, 1989, 14.

150
Brian O'Doherty, Inside the White Cube. The Ideology of the Gallery Space. 3rd edition, London, 1986; cf. Wolfgang Kemp (ed.), Der Betrachter ist im Bild. Cologne, 1985, 279-293; cf. Walter Grasskamp, "Die weiße Ausstellungswand. Zur Vorgeschichte des 'white cube'," in: Wolfgang Ullrich/Juliane Vogel (ed.), Weiß, Frankfurt on Main, 2003.

151
Wolfgang Pehnt, "Nicht nur das amerikanische Volk ist ein Volk von Museumsbesuchern geworden," in: Frankfurter Allgemeine Zeitung, 7th February 2000.

152
Belting 2001 (note 62), 40 f.

153
Peter Weibel, "Museen in der postindustriellen Massengesellschaft," in: kunst im bau, ed. Kunst- und Ausstellungshalle der Bundesrepublik Deutschland GmbH (Schriftenreihe Forum, vol. 1), Göttingen, 1994, 135-146.

154
Mieczyslav Wallis, "Semantic and Symbolic Elements in Architecture: Iconology as a First Step Towards an Architectural Semiotic," in: Semiotica 8/1973, 220-238; Adolf Reinle, Zeichensprache der Architektur. Symbol, Darstellung und Brauch in der Baukunst des Mittelalters und der Neuzeit. Zurich/Munich, 1976.

155
Bauhaus-Archiv, planned for Darmstadt in 1963/64, realized in Berlin in 1976-79; Ein Museum für das Bauhaus. Eröffnungsfestschrift. Berlin, 1979; Schubert (note 117), 118 f.;

156
Annette Gigon and Mike Guyer, 1996-98; Gigon + Guyer, Museum Liner Appenzell (Kunsthaus Bregenz Werkdokumente 18), Ostfildern-Ruit, 2000.

157
Realized in 1992-2002; Matthias Boeckl, "Welcome to the Club! St. Pölten hat sich auf die globale Kunstlandkarte gesetzt," in: Parnass 4/2002, 122-131.

158
Opened in 2001; Maribel Königer, "Zum Lachen ins Museum gehen. In Krems eröffnet Österreichs erstes Karikaturmuseum," in: Parnass 3/2001, 44-45.

159
Besides, contained therein is also an allusion to the architect's second profession; as the caricaturist Ironismus, he made fun of his colleagues' lack of imagination; Ironimus, Laßt Linien sprechen, Munich, 1982.

160
Daidalos 45/1992 is dedicated to the theme of bodies or volumes and buildings.

161
Xing Tonghe, design 1992, realization 1994-95; Jianzhu-xuebao 5/1994, 9-15.

162
Peter Neufert, 1971; Deutsche Bauzeitschrift 26/1978, 629-630.

163
L.C. Kalff and L.L.J. de Bever, 1962-66.

164
Realized in 1991-96; Oscar Niemeyer. Museu de Arte Contemporânea de Niterói. Revan, 1997; Oscar Niemeyer. A Legend of Modernism, exhibition catalogue, ed. Paul Andreas and Ingeborg Flagge, Frankfurt on Main/Basel, 2003,77 ff.

165
Realized in 1994-2002; Jean-Pierre Cousin, "Vulcania, parc europeen du volcanisme," in: Architecture d'aujourd'hui 343/2002, 114-117; Yehuda Safran, "Sotto il vulcano," in: Domus 852/2002, 88-99; Volcania, in: GA document 71/2002, 38-53.

166
For the basic fundamentals on this, see Günter Bandmann, "Ikonologie der Architektur," in: Jahrbuch für Ästhetik und allgemeine Kunstwissenschaft 1/1951, 67-109; reprinted in: Martin Warnke (ed.), Politische Architektur in Europa vom Mittelalter bis heute – Repräsentation und Gemeinschaft, Cologne, 1984, 19-71.

167
Alfred Freiherr von Wolzogen, Aus Schinkels Nachlaß, vol. 3, Berlin, 1863, 355.

168
Plagemann 1967 (note 32), 66-81.

169
Mario Botta. La cathédrale d'Evry, Milan, 1996.

170
MART (= Museo di arte moderna e contemporanea di Trento e Rovereto), planning begun in 1987, realized in 1997-2002; Rahel Hartmann, "Das 'Allerheiligste'," in: Bauwelt 86/1995, 1603.

171
Erich Altenhöfer, "Hans Döllgast und die Alte Pinakothek," in: Hans Döllgast 1891-1974. Munich, 1987, 45-91.

172
Walter and Susanne Hagstotz and Peter Kraft, 1972-79; Schubert (note 117), 122 f.

173
Michael D. Levin, The Modern Museum. Temple or Showroom, Jerusalem/Tel Aviv, 1983; Kurt W. Foster, "Temio? Emporio? Teatro? Riflessioni su due decenni di museografia americana / Shrine? Emporium? Theater? Reflections on Two Decades of American Museum," in: Zodiac 6/1991, 30-75.

174
Philip Johnson, 1961-63; Peter Blake, Philip Johnson, Basel/Berlin/Boston, 1996, 92 f.

175
Paul v. Naredi-Rainer, "Zwischen Stadt und Kult. Die Sprache moderner Museumsarchitektur (= Seventh Sigurd Greven lecture, held on 15th May 2003 in Museum Schnütgen, Cologne, 2003; Naredi-Rainer, "Der Traum von der Stadt. Zeitgenössische Museumsbauten als summa architectonica," in: Kunsthistoriker 13-14/1997-98 (= 9. Österreichischer Kunsthistorikertag, 16th-19th October 1997 in Vienna. Museumsquartier), 145-154; Naredi-Rainer,, "Zur Ikonologie moderner Museumsarchitektur," in: Wiener Jahrbuch für Kunstgeschichte 44/1991, 191-204, 291-302.

176
Paul v. Naredi-Rainer, "Die Stadtmauer in der Ikonographie der christlichen Kunst," in: Architektur Geschichten. Festschrift für Günther Binding zum 60. Geburtstag, ed. Udo Mainzer and Petra Leser, Cologne, 1996, 117-130.

177
Leon Battista Alberti, Zehn Bücher über die Baukunst, vol. 14, ed. Max Theuer (German edition), Vienna/Leipzig, 1912 (reprinted 1975), 262 (English edition: On the Art of Building in Ten Books, Cambridge, Mass., 1991).

178
Wolfgang Pehnt, Museum in Mönchengladbach. Architektur als Collage, Frankfurt on Main, 1986, 44 ff.

179
Planning begun in 1984, completed in 1997; Harold M. Williams/Bill Lacy/Stephen D. Rountree/Richard Meier, The Getty Center. Design Process, Los Angeles, 1991; Karen D. Stein/Robert Campbell, "The Getty Center," in: Architectural Record 11/1997, 72-107; Marco de Michelis, "Getty Center, Los Angeles," in: Domus 799/1997, 38-49; Wolfgang Bachmann, "The Getty Center in Los Angeles," in: Baumeister 2/1998, 16-27; Oliver Hamm, "Die Alte und die Neue Welt" in: Bauwelt 7/1998, 302-313.

180
Naredi-Rainer 1991 (note 175), 202 ff.

181
Italo Gamberini, opened in 1987; Domizia Mandolesi, "Centro per l'arte contemporanea a Prato," in: Industria delle costruzioni 208/1989, 22-29; Allégret 1992 (note 139), 62-65.

182
Hochreiter (note 146), 237.

183
Walter Grasskamp, "Unberührbar und unverkäuflich. Museen und Museumsshops," in: Museum und Kaufhaus. Warenwelten im Vergleich, ed. Bärbel Kleindörfer-Marx and Klara Löffler (= Regensburger Schriften zur Volkskunde, vol. 15), Regensburg, 2000, 107-117.

184
The "Erweiterungsbau Dahlem II" planned by Wils Ebert in 1962, begun in 1964 and opened in 1970 was converted into a "Dunkelmuseum" after 1965 by Fritz Bornemann; Schubert (note 117), 71 ff.

185
Heinz Röcke and Klaus Renner, competition won in 1963, realized in 1967-74; Hugo Borger, Das Römisch-Germanische Museum Köln. Munich, 1977, in particular 71 ff.

186
Design 1990, built in 1992-94; Vrigteman/Kolsteren, (note 142); Newhouse (note 134), 203-207.

187
documenta 8, Kassel, 1987, Vol. 2, 161.

188
Bart Lootsma, "Frans Haks und das Groninger Museum," in: Bauwelt 3/1995, 106-117.

189
Lewis Mumford, The City in History: Its Origins, Its Transformations, and Its Prospects, 1961.

190
Kurt W. Forster, in: Museums for a New Millennium (note 134), 130.

191
Coosje van Bruggen, Frank O. Gehry. Guggenheim Museum Bilbao, Ostfildern-Ruit, 1997, 72.

192
upw Nagel, "Die Basken fressen mir aus der Hand...," in: Der Architekt 9/1998, 508.

193
The Grand Louvre. A Museum transfigured 1981-1993, ed. Emile Biasini, Jean Lebrat, Dominique Bezombes and Jean-Michel Vincent, Milan/Paris, 1989; Carter Wiseman, I.M. Pei. A Profile in American Architecture, 2nd ed., New York, 2001, 228 ff.

194
Otto Martin, Zur Ikonologie der deutschen Museumsarchitektur zu Beginn des zweiten Kaiserreiches. Bauformen und Bildprogramme der kunst- und kulturgeschichtlichen Museen in den siebziger und achtziger Jahren des 19. Jahrhunderts, Dissertation, Mainz, 1983.

195
Paul v. Naredi-Rainer, "Die Fresken Edward von Steinles im Treppenhaus des ersten Wallraf-Richartz-Museums," in: Museen der Stadt Köln, Bulletin 5/1983, 50-54.

196
Wolfgang Pehnt, "Uferpromenaden – Kunstpfade – Gratwanderungen," in: Vittorio Magnago Lampugnani (ed.), Museumsarchitektur in Frankfurt 1980-1990. Munich, 1990, 25.

197
Michael Brawne, The Museum Interior: Temporary and Permanent Display Techniques, 1982.

198
On this subject, the most fundamental and unsurpassed article is Manfred Lehmbruck, "Freiraum Museumsbau," in: deutsche bauzeitung 8/1980, 9-13.

199
Cf. note 137.

200
Le Corbusier et Pierre Jeanneret, Œuvre complète 1929-34, ed. Willy Boesiger, 8th ed., Zurich, 1967; Moos (note 132), 23 f.

201
Lehmbruck (note 198), 12.

202
Herman Sörgel, Theorie der Baukunst, vol. 1: Architektur-Ästhetik. 3rd ed., Munich, 1921, 200 ff.; Alexander Gosztonyi, Der Raum. Geschichte seiner Probleme in Philosophie und Wissenschaften. vol. 2, Freiburg, 1976, 721 ff.; Herbert Muck, Der Raum. Baugefüge, Bild und Lebenswelt, Vienna, 1986; Franz Xaver Baier, Der Raum. Prolegomena zu einer Architektur des gelebten Raumes, Cologne, 2000, 25 ff. Ákos Moravánszky (ed.), Architekturtheorie im 20. Jahrhundert. Eine kritische Anthologie, Vienna/New York, 2003, 121 ff.

203
Wolfgang v. Wersin, Das Buch vom Rechteck. Gesetz und Gestik des Räumlichen, Ravensburg, 1956; Paul v. Naredi-Rainer, Architektur und Harmonie. Zahl, Maß und Proportion in der abendländischen Baukunst, 7th ed., Cologne, 2001, 140 ff.

204
Gae Aulenti and Italo Rota, 1980-86; Jean Jenger, Orsay, the metamorphosis of a monument, Paris, 1987.

205
Lehmbruck (note 198), 11.

206
Laszlo Glozer, Westkunst. Zeitgenössische Kunst seit 1939, Cologne, 1981, 284 ff.

207
Joan Ockman, "Pragmatist oder Pragmatiker. Alexander Dorner und Herbert Bayer," in: ARCH+ 156/2000, 90-97. (English edition: Joan Ockman, "The Road not Taken. Alexander Dorner's Way Beyond Art," in: Robert E. Somol (ed.), Autonomy and Ideology. Positioning an Avantgarde in America, New York, 1999, p. 80.)

208
Christine Hoh-Slodzyk, Carlo Scarpa und das Museum, Berlin, 1987; Bianca Albertini/Sandro Bagnoli, Scarpa. Museen und Ausstellungen. Tübingen/Berlin, 1992; "Paola Marini, Mostre e Musei 1944-1976," in: Carlo Scarpa, exhibition catalogue, Verona, 2000, 88-273.

209
Brawne 1982 (note 197), 38 ff.

210
Albert Erbe, Belichtung von Gemäldegalerien, Leipzig, 1923; Peter Balla/Christian Bartenbach, "Beleuchtung von Museumsräumen," in: Werk, Bauen und Wohnen 12/1980, 38-43; Harald Hofmann, "Licht im Museum," in: Bauwelt 20-21/1985, 804-806; Brawne 1982 (note 197), 102 ff.; Hanns Freymuth, "Tageslichttechnische Entwurfsunterstützung am Beispiel von Museumsräumen," in: Bauwelt 32/1989, 1485-1491; Stefan Trenkner, "Licht, Sinn und Wirkung – besonders für die Beleuchtung empfindlicher Objekte in Mu-

seen," in: AIT 7-8/1992, 78-79; John Darragh and James S. Snyder, Museum Design. Planning and Building for Art, New York/Oxford, 1993, 263 ff.

211
A summary of this discussion is to be found in Tange (note 117); cf. Stephan Waetzoldt, "Museumsarchitektur in der Bundesrepublik Deutschland nach 1945," in: Forma et subtilitas. Festschrift für Wolfgang Schöne zum 75. Geburtstag, ed. Wilhelm Schlink and Martin Sperlich, Berlin/New York, 1986, 290-299, in particular 295 ff.

212
Josep Lluís Sert, in collaboration with Bellini, Lizzero & Gozzi, 1961-64; Brawne 1965 (note 147), 99-102; Jaume Freixa, Josep Ll. Sert. 2nd ed., Zurich, 1984, 138-145.

213
Wilfried and Katharina Steib, 1978-80; Schubert (note 117), 127-129.

214
Lehmbruck (note 198), 13.

Lighting Design in Museums

1
Günter S. Hilbert, Sammlungsgut in Sicherheit, 2nd ed., Berlin, 1996

2
Gary Thomson, The Museum Environment, London, 1994

3
Matthias Stappel, Lecture notes for Light Protection Seminar, January 1999, Restaurierungszentrum Gelsenkirchen

4
Helmut F.O. Müller, "Dynamische Raumbeleuchtung," in: Danner/Dassler/Krause (eds.), Die klimaaktive Fassade, Leinfelden-Echterdingen, 1999

5
Carl Heinz Zieseniß, Beleuchtungstechnik für den Elektrofachmann, Hüthig Verlag, Heidelberg, 1989

6
Christoph Waller, Licht und Lichtschutz in Museen, http://www.cwaller.LichtBeleuchtung.htm

7
H. Lange, Handbuch für Beleuchtung, Landsberg, 2002

Directed Sequences of Rooms

Matrix-like Arrangement of Rooms

Spatial Interpenetration
and Spatial Isolation

Open Plans

Free-form Spaces

Conversions and Extensions
of Architectural Monuments

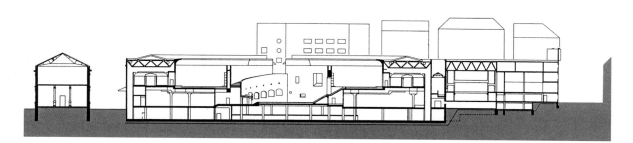

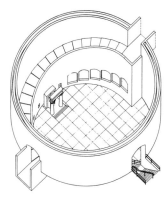

Longitudinal section of the rotunda

Axonometric projection of the rotunda

an enormous rotunda at the centre. Stirling contrasts this layout of rotunda and right-angled enfilade wings, which appears monumental in the ground plan but hardly so in built reality, with an almost extravagant abundance of very different motifs such as asymmetrically placed ramps with oversize railings in shocking pink and blue, Egyptian corbel cornices, and the concertina-like undulating glass wall of the entrance hall. This way, the regular forms of the basic structure are transformed into a dynamic architectural landscape that is inviting to walk through, in intentional contrast to the strict ground plan based on classical models, now hardly recognisable. The ensemble, separated from the road by two rows of trees, appears to be a

large-scale sculpture that can be walked through, its perspectives continually changing.

The main level, which is also the entrance level, is placed on a pedestal that hides the underground garage, and which can be accessed both by a ramp and a stairway opposite. Both of these start out underneath a steel case that simultaneously evokes both the primeval hut frequently invoked in architectural theory and that elementary dignity-evoking motif, the canopy. Here it shields an Egypticized wall-opening that leads directly into the underground garage, of all things. The real entrance to the museum is located on the main level, but shifted to the side and surprisingly, situated under-

neath a garishly painted cantilevered steel grille that forms a peculiar contrast to the apparent solidity of the stone walls. Upon closer examination, however, these latter turn out to be a thin cladding of alternating layers of sandstone and travertine slabs on the cast concrete building – and this too is carefully staged, in some places virtually put on display.

Like this, the tone for the basic attitude of this architecture is set almost as a leitmotif: historicising and contemporary motifs and the accompanying associations are not only set in relation to each other so as to fuse into a new synthesis, but also the associations that have accrued to them are at

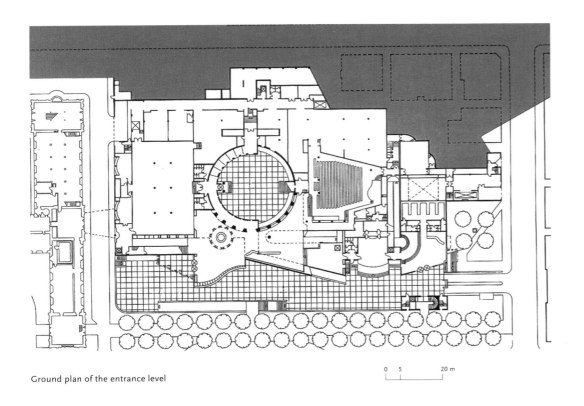

Ground plan of the entrance level

0   5   20 m

from left to right
The sales rotunda in the entrance area | The first gallery that
the ramp gives access to (in the middle of the room, Picasso's
Bathers, 1956) | The gallery rooms are connected by enfilade

the same time relativized in such a way that the
architecture appears to comment – occasionally
ironically – on them too. The aggregation of forms
and materials – almost always implemented skil-
fully and with a sure hand – that thus comes into
being is simultaneously the synthesis and the reflection of contradictory styles and contents, in this
way forming a new canon that unites the "monumental with the informal," as the architect puts it.

This attitude becomes particularly evident in the
form and function of the enormous central rotunda, a motif already found in earlier museum designs by Stirling that were not executed, a motif
that, like the whole ground plan of the Stuttgart

Staatsgalerie, quotes Schinkel's Altes Museum in
Berlin as one of the prototypes of this commission
and in so doing, follows an architectural tradition
that goes back to the Pantheon in Rome. In contrast to Schinkel's model, Stirling's rotunda is not
domed like a "pantheon of the arts," but designed
as a hollow cylinder open at the top, the walls of
which are overgrown with vegetation like a ruin, in
ironic reversal of the neoclassicist pathetic formula that reaches its logical conclusion in the foot-
path (required by the client as the link between the
streets on either side of the museum) that spirals
around the high wall of the rotunda and thus
transforms it into external space. As further evidence of the intentional multilayered quality and

the ambiguity of this architecture this twisted
ramp quotes Frank Lloyd Wright's Guggenheim
Museum in New York as one of the incunabula of
modern museum architecture (and also reverses
inside and outside with this allusion).

The rich variety of contradictions in this postmodern scenario continues through the spacious foyer,
a fluid space accentuated by a small rotunda lighted from above and visible from the outside as well
through the fluted glass wall. Here too, the dignity-
evoking tempietto motif – contrasting garishly with
the provocative pop-art-inspired bright green floor
– is meaningfully interpreted: it contains the ticket
window and the museum shop.

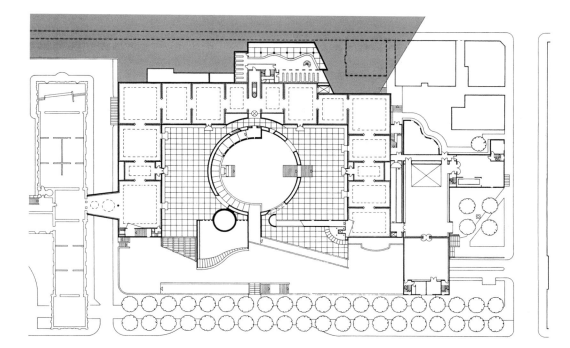

Ground plan of the gallery level

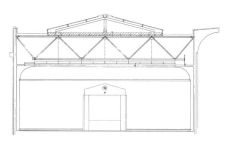

Cross section of a large gallery room

A ramp and a high-tech elevator give access to the classically proportioned, coved-ceilinged gallery rooms on the upper storey, arranged in enfilade fully in keeping with the tradition of the nineteenth-century museum buildings and their predecessors in baroque palace architecture. The entertaining scenario of the architecture of the exterior and the access area here gives way to a cool, quiet atmosphere in which at best the green-painted grids of the roof lights and isolated pieces of moulding detached from the wall and concealing high-wattage lights still remind one of the previous scenario.

wettbewerbe aktuell 12/1977, pp. 715-724 • *Deutsche Bauzeitung* 8/1980, pp. 22-24 (Falk Jaeger) and 9/1984, pp. 38-41 (Gerhard Ullmann) • *Der Architekt* 7-8/1984, pp. 343-348 (Christoph Hackelsberger) • *Architectural Design* 3-4/1984, pp. 48-55 (Charles Jencks) • *Bauwelt* 20/1084, pp. 832-851 (Jochen Bub) • *The Architectural Review* 1033/1983, pp. 31-41 (Peter Cook) and 1054/1984, pp. 18-47 • Neue Staatsgalerie und Kammertheater Stuttgart, edited by The Ministry of Finances for Baden-Württemberg, Stuttgart 1984 • Thorsten Rodiek, James Stirling. *Die Neue Staatsgalerie Stuttgart*, Stuttgart, 1984 • *L'architecture d'aujourd'hui* 235/1984, pp. 7-15 (Jean-Marc Ibos and Dominique Lyon) • *Baumeister* 8/1984, pp. 54-68 • *Casabella* 503/1984, pp. 38-41 (Giacomo Polin) • *Domus* 651/1984, pp. 2-15 • *Kunstchronik* 37/1984, pp. 369-377 (Wolfgang Pehnt) • *das kunstwerk* 3/1984, pp. 45-51 (Gunild Berg, Rolf-Gunter Dienst) • *Lotus international* 3/1984, pp. 23-46 (Frank Werner) • *Progressive Architecture* 10/1984, pp. 67-85 (Susan Doubilet) • *Architectural Record* 9/1985, pp. 140-149 (Martin Filler) • *Arquitectura* 5-6/1985, pp. 45-58 (Ignasi de Solá-Morales) • *Umbau* 8/1984, pp. 17-26

(Friedrich Achleitner) • James Stirling. Bauten und Projekte 1950-1983, Stuttgart 1984, pp. 252-260 • *Museumskunde* 50/1985, pp. 112-125 (Norbert Knopp) • *Techniques & Architecture* 368/1986, pp. 114-118 (142-146) • Francesco Dal Co / Tom Muirhead, I Musei di James Stirling, Michael Wilford and Associates, Milan, 1990, pp. 104-127 • Douglas Davis, The Museum Transformed, New York, 1990, pp. 114-121 • *Bauwelt* 38/1993, pp. 2049-2051 (Frank Werner) • James Stirling, Michael Wilford and Associates. Buildings and Projects 1975-1992, Stuttgart, 1994, pp. 54-63 • Robert Maxwell, James Stirling. Michael Wilford, Basel/Berlin/Boston, 1998, pp. 72-77

Allégret, vol. 2, pp. 66-71 • Jahrbuch für Architektur 1984, pp. 131-140 and 1985/86, pp. 131-140 (Heinrich Klotz) • Kähler, pp. 190-191 • Klotz 1984, pp. 340-341 • Klotz/Krase, pp. 20-22 and pp. 104-120 • Montaner/Oliveras, pp. 106-111 • Newhouse, pp. 179-181 • Schilgen, pp. 46-67 • Schubert, pp. 155-157 • Steele, pp. 234-239 • Tzonis/Lefaivre, pp. 126-131

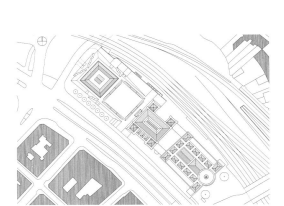

Site plan

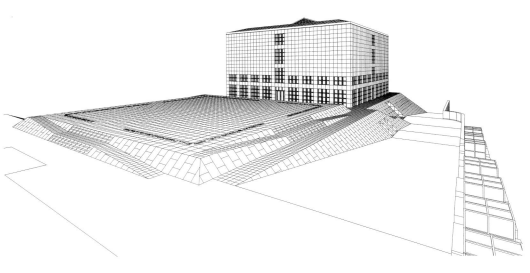

Perspective view (seen from the old building of the Kunsthalle)

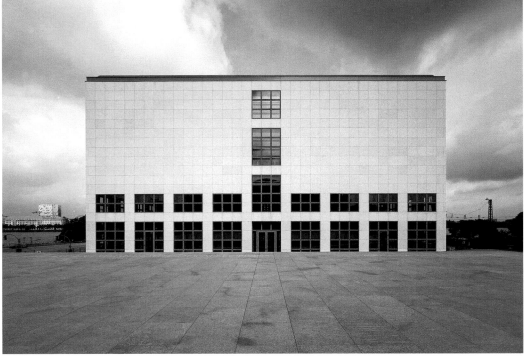

from left to right
View of the entire complex across the Alster | Galerie der Gegenwart seen from the old building | Central atrium

Galerie der Gegenwart

Hamburg, Germany

Client	Freie und Hansestadt Hamburg
Architects	Oswald Mathias Ungers, Cologne
Enclosed space	53,880 m³
Gross area	10,460 m²
Main net floor area	7,293 m²
Exhibition area	5,600 m²
Construction time	1992-1996 (Competition 1986)

The cubic solitaire is to be adjudged not only as an incarnation of the pronounced ideas on architectural theory that Oswald Mathias Ungers has long since developed, but to the same extent as the result of intensive analysis of the urban spatial conditions. It was the task of the architect to supplement the two existing parts of the Hamburger Kunsthalle with a Galerie der Gegenwart. The Kunsthalle was built of brick in 1863-69 by Georg Theodor Schirrmacher in Neo Renaissance forms; in 1912-19, Alfred Erben added to it a massive extension ending in a rotunda crowned by a cupola. In the northern extension of the axis of these two buildings, on a building site surrounded on three sides by streets and railways, Ungers shifts his

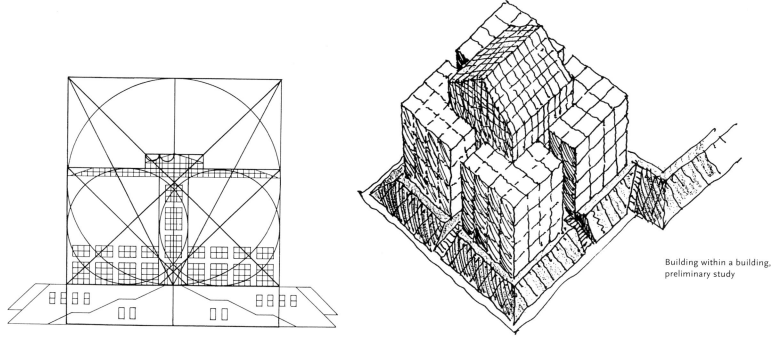

Sketch showing the proportions

Building within a building, preliminary study

new building to the outermost edge and puts it onto a bevelled plinth of red granite that raises the ensemble above the roar of traffic (thus reminding us of the city wall that once ran along there) and lends it the appearance of a museum island. The empty space – precisely calculated to correspond exactly to the quadratic ground plan of the new volume – between it and the old building allows not only the richly decorated façade of the old Kunsthalle to be shown off to good effect, but also the monumental impact and urban dominance of the Galerie der Gegenwart coated with white Muschelkalk. The archaic-seeming pyramid-shaped plinth lends the light-coloured cube (which grows out of it) calculated pathos – a deliberate reference both

to Schinkel's design for Schloss Orianda in the Crimea, which is crowned by a radiant museum temple above massive plinths, and to the visionary project of French revolutionary architecture operating with purely geometric volumes. The intention of aiming at the sublime also applies to Ungers' project, and the widespread dislike occasioned by this project is seen, evidently rightly, as evidence of the inability of our time to deal with the aesthetic category of the sublime.

Compositional laws of body and space contained in logical geometric systems – laws which Ungers, in his efforts to achieve a new abstraction and order in architecture, in the end traces back to the

square that he conceives of as an indicator of reason overstepping nature's ways of building – are demonstrated in an exemplary fashion in his museum in Hamburg. Both the relationship of the built volume to the undeveloped area and its spatial and façade articulation adopt a rhythm based on a square grid, each side 10 meters long. Through the windows, differentiated from storey to storey within this grid and ascending to the eaves line only in the central axis of all four similar façades, arises a balanced tension that is already set up in the proportioning of the volume itself. Starting with the idea of enclosing a central volume covered by a gable roof with four cubes separated from each other by an axial intersection, that which

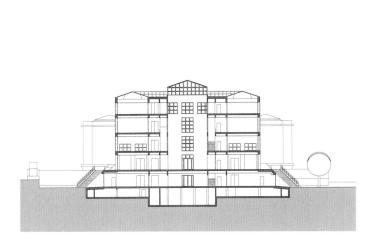

Cross section

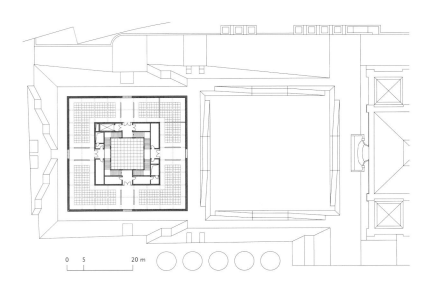

Ground plan of the plinth level

0   5   20 m

from left to right
Exhibition room on the first floor | Exhibition room on the
third floor | Exhibition rooms on the second floor

came into being in the end was a volume, 30 meters high and 36 meters long; although it deviates from the ideal cube form, it is nonetheless logically developed from the square, as the proportional sketch shows. (A pyramid that can be extrapolated by extending the edges of the pedestal can be exactly inscribed in this volume.)

The basic idea of the building within a building was conserved in the central atrium extending through all the storeys in the middle of the building and directing bright light through a glazed gable roof right down to the ground floor. It seems apparent that here what is evoked is not only the ground plan typology of Palladio's Villa Rotonda,

but above all, that of Schinkel's Altes Museum, whose central domed rotunda apostrophized as the "Holy of Holies" is here transformed into the "primeval hut" crowned with a gable roof.

By avoiding an accentuated entrance situation and leading visitors underground through exhibition rooms hidden in the granite plinth from the old building into the new building, Ungers enables the latter to be accessed concentrically from the interior to the exterior, allowing the tensional relation between the atrium and the four storeys stacked on top of each other that surround this vertical axis in several spatial envelopes to become directly perceptible. Two stairways running counter to each

other and winding in the form of a helix around the atrium each land on one arm of the view axis intersection that is formed by the vertical bands of windows on the outside of the building and in the atrium. This way, the spatial structure is emphasized and visitor orientation is facilitated.

The exhibition rooms in the three upper storeys (the ground floor contains a restaurant, a museum shop and event venues) linked in enfilade with each other – but also subdivisible at will by means of flexible partitions within the quadratic grid system – are lit on the first floor by lateral light, on the second by artificial light, and on the third, through the skylight (apart from the room-height

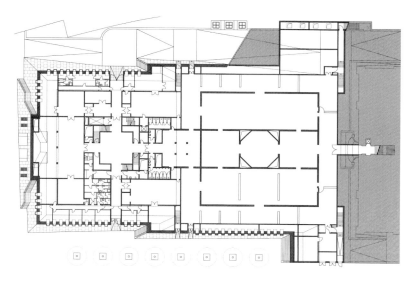

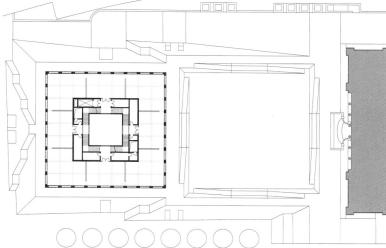

Ground plan of the first floor

Ground plan of the third floor

windows of the axis intersection) – thus showing, in a way, an encyclopaedia of museum presentation possibilities.

wettbewerbe aktuell 6/1986, pp. 351-362 and 12/1996, pp. 85-88 • *The Architectural Review* 1073/1986, pp. 37-42 (Peter Davey) • Oswald Mathias Ungers. Architektur 1951-1990, Stuttgart, 1991, pp. 176-179 • Martin Kieren, Oswald Mathias Ungers, Zurich/Munich/London, 1994, pp. 162-165 • *Bauwelt* 35/1996, pp. 1970-1977 (Peter Rumpf) • *Deutsche Bauzeitung* 9/1996, pp. 14-15 (Dirk Meyhöfer) • *Werk, Bauen und Wohnen* 7-8/1997, pp. 22-29 (Gert Kähler) • Uwe M. Schneede/Helmut R. Leppien (eds.), Die Hamburger Kunsthalle, Leipzig, 1997, pp. 189-201 (Manfred F. Fischer; Hartmut Frank) • Adolf Max Vogt, "Der weiße Kubus und der 'seltsam überanstrengte' Platz," in: Architektur in Hamburg, Jahrbuch 1997, pp. 8-15 • Jürgen Müller, "Die Heimat ist nicht der Ort," in: *Kunsthistoriker* 13-14 (9. Österreichischer Kunsthistoriker-

tag), 1997/98, pp. 156-161 • Oswald Mathias Ungers. Bauten und Projekte 1991-1998, Stuttgart, 1998, pp. 157-167

Lampugnani/Sachs, pp. 50-55 (Ulrich Maximilian Schumann) • Maier-Solgk, pp. 130-138 • Peressut, pp. 120-129

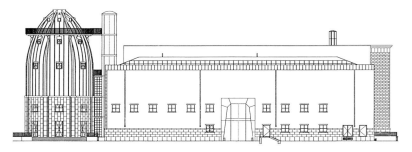

Elevation

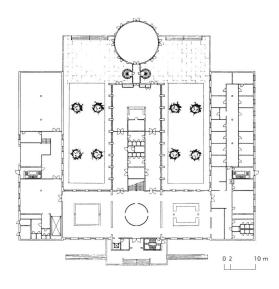

Ground floor plan

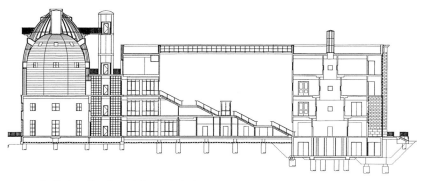

Longitudinal section through the central wing

Bonnefantenmuseum

Maastricht, Netherlands

Client	Provincial government of Limburg
Architect	Aldo Rossi, Milan
Enclosed space	94,000 m³
Total area	16,276 m²
Net floor area	13,154 m²
Exhibition area	8,000 m²
Construction time	1992-1994 (commissioned in 1990)

In what used to be an industrial estate on the banks of the Maas, across from the old town of Maastricht, the Bonnefanten Museum is the first identity-promoting building in the new city quarter planned by renowned architects. In strict typology, Aldo Rossi designed a symmetrical building on an E-shaped ground plan; its three wings include two rectangular courtyards that open toward the Maas as prescribed in the brief. The silhouette of the extended museum layout, visible from across the river and beyond, is dominated by a cupola-crowned tower which, being whitewashed on the bottom with its upper part clad in sheet zinc, not only builds material aesthetic suspense to the brickwork of the rest of the building, but also awakens associations

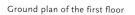

Ground plan of the first floor

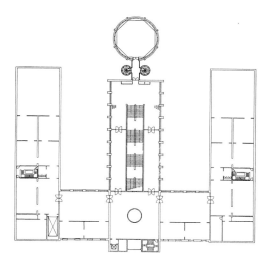

Ground plan of the second floor

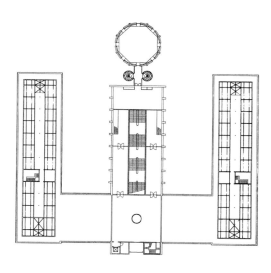

Ground plan of the third floor

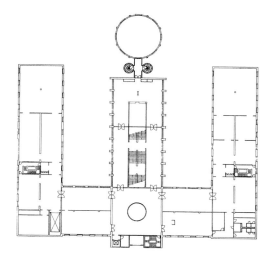

from left to right
General view across the Maas | Main entrance | Stairway |
Cupola | Exhibition room on the first floor

that range from homage to the erstwhile industrial site to a lighthouse. According to Rossi, it is to serve as "an identification signal and turning point in time."

However, the entrance to the museum lies in the massive central projection of the façade facing away from the river. A steel portal leads from there into the four-storey-high foyer into which daylight cascades through a round opening in the ceiling that has the appearance of an upturned funnel because of the recessing of the walls from one storey to the next. From the deepest-placed point of light incidence, the ascent begins via an enormous stairway, six metres wide and as long as the building is

deep, to the huge white domed room, its antipode in the striking round tower. (Rossi had actually intended to make the visitors themselves into the focus point of the light at the end of the ascent to the viewing terrace, no longer accessible today.) The ascent from the nadir to the zenith, canalized between brick walls the height of the building does not only effectively convey a sense of urgency, but also serves a practical purpose for access to the clearly organized exhibition rooms that form a very usable and unpretentious ambience for the large but disparate collection. On the second floor, these rooms are lit by natural light from above, while on the first floor, they have lateral lighting supplemented by artificial illuminated ceilings.

Domus 762/1994, pp. 7-22 (Aldo Rossi) • *Baumeister* 9/1994, pp. 34-39 (Arthur Wortmann) • *Bauwelt* 3/1995, pp. 118-125 (Carl Friedrich Schröer) • *Deutsche Bauzeitschrift* 8/1995, pp. 92-93 (W. Töpfer) • Alberto Ferlenga, Aldo Rossi. Opera completa 1993-1996, Milan, 1995, pp. 17-27 • Bonnefantenmuseum, Maastricht, 1996

Lampugnani/Sachs, pp. 108-115 • Maier-Solgk, pp. 166-173 • Museo d'arte e architettura, pp. 142-149 • Peressut, pp. 92-103

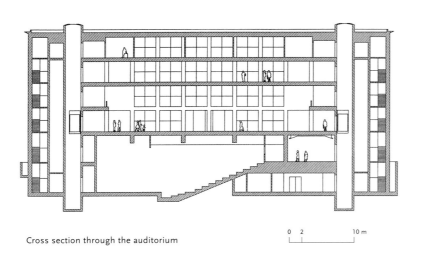

Cross section through the auditorium

0 2   10 m

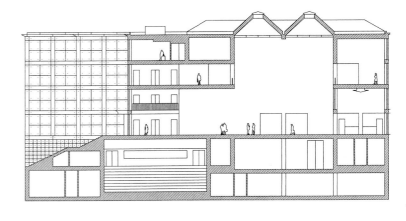

Longitudinal section through the atrium

Museum of Contemporary Art

Chicago / Illinois, USA

Client	Museum of Contemporary Art, Chicago
Architect	Josef Paul Kleihues, Berlin
Enclosed space	ca. 72,300 m³
Net floor area	ca. 13,000 m²
Exhibition area	ca. 3,600 m²
Construction time	1991-1996

The architect mentions both the location in a sky-scraper canyon running up to Lake Michigan and the reference to Chicago as architectural genius loci – strongly marked not least by Mies van der Rohe – as decisive factors in his design, modest and prag-matic in service to function without denying its theoretical basis. Chosen in an unusual selection procedure in which not the designs submitted, but all the works of each of the 226 applicants was examined, Kleihues demonstrates with this muse-um design his principles of a "poetic rationalism" that assumes the validity of universal laws without underestimating historical conditions or ignoring the suspenseful complexity of our lived reality.

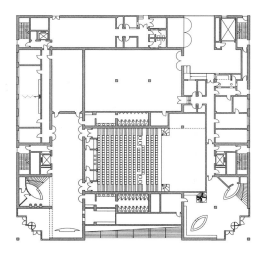 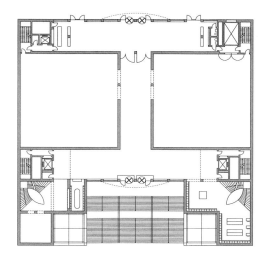 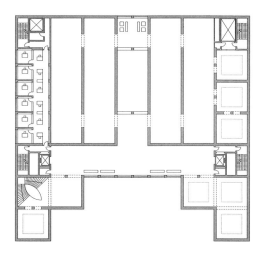

Ground floor plan

Ground plan of the first floor
(entrance level/temporary exhibitions)

Ground plan of the third floor (gallery level)

from left to right
The museum in its urban context | The entrance side developed
as a three-wing complex | The light-flooded atrium brings the
square interior structure directly into view | Gallery on the
upper floor | The stairway with its colliding, lense-shaped
landings placed discreetly in a corner of the foyer forms a
particularly poetic element, although nonetheless it follows
the square geometry

Clear proportions developed from the square characterize the building, which is supplemented by a
sculpture garden (also square), both in its spatial
structure and in its delicately-drawn surfaces. The
latticed windows, condensed into a glazed front on
the façade, and the cast iron slabs with which the
entire building is clad, iridescent with a brownish
patina, are subservient to the unifying formal strength
of geometry.

Both the façade – whose monumental open stairway framed by projecting bays intentionally reminds
one of the propylaea of the Athenian Acropolis and
Schinkel's Altes Museum in Berlin – and – notwith-
standing its great sophistication – the arrangement

of the interior, varying from one level to the next, are
symmetrically designed with the exception of the
ground floor which, containing an auditorium among
other things, is accessed by another entrance. On
the two upper main floors the exhibition rooms on
both sides of the building-high, light-flooded atrium
are wonderfully proportioned, but very different in
character and in their organisation. While on the
entrance level, accessible directly by the open stairway, enormous square rooms with artificial illuminated ceilings are intended to house temporary exhibitions, the permanent collection is displayed in
four parallel galleries whose elegant glazed barrel
vaults disseminate evenly distributed daylight coming in from the pyramid roofs above.

Architectural Record 5/1992, p. 23 (James Krohe Jr.) and
8/1996, pp. 80-87 (Cheryl Kent) • *Architecture (AIA)* 5/1992,
p. 23 (Blair Kamin) and 6/1996, pp. 38-39 (Franz Schulze) •
Progressive Architecture 5/1992, p. 27 (Cheryl Kent) and 12/-
1995, p. 30 (Cheryl Kent) • *Domus* 739/1992, pp. 48-53 and
XXII (Josef P. Kleihues) • *Architekt* 10/1996, p. 596 (Falk Jae-
ger) • *Building Design* 1274/1996, pp. 12-13 (Jeremy Melvin/
Nicola Martin) • *Deutsche Bauzeitschrift* 11/1996, pp. 91-94
(Falk Jaeger) and 3/1997, pp. 35-42 (Frank F. Drewes) •
Andrea Mesecke/Thorsten Scheer, Museum of Contemporary
Art. Josef Paul Kleihues, Berlin, 1996

Lampugnani/Sachs, pp. 132-139 (Franz Schulze)

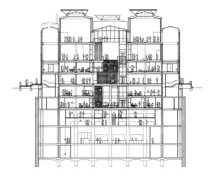

Cross section

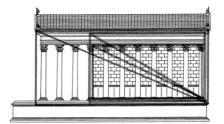 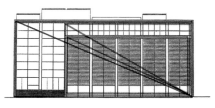

Proportional relations between the Maison Carrée and the Carré d'Art

Longitudinal section with surroundings

from left to right
The Maison Carrée and the Carré d'Art | Façade | Central
stairway | Exhibition room on the lower exhibition level

Carré d'Art

Nîmes, France

Client	City of Nîmes
Architects	Norman Foster and Partners, London
Enclosed space	90,000 m³
Net floor area	20,400 m²
Exhibition area	2,600 m²
Construction time	1987-1992 (invited international competition 1984)

The unusual urban context, a square directly opposite the Roman temple on a podium known as the Maison Carrée in the heart of Nîmes in southern France, was a decisive influence on Norman Foster's design, which he revised several times. In order to accommodate the enormous volume without disturbing the proportions of its surroundings, half of the nine-storey building – which in addition to an art museum also contains a library, a mediatheque, and other cultural facilities – was placed underground. The volume visible above a stone plinth, a transparent, modular, structured prism of light construction, turns its narrow side to face the ancient temple. The gracefully articulated, dazzling white steel scaffolding of the lamella canopy be-

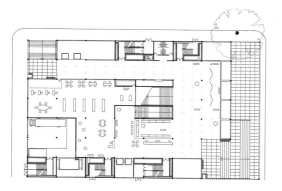
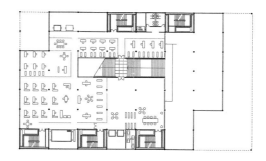
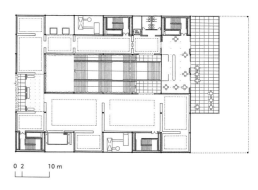

Ground floor plan

Ground plan of the mediatheque on the upper floor

Ground plan of the exhibition areas on the upper floor

hind which the actual building retreats in asymmetric gradation, paraphrases in a way as unmistakable as it is discreet the classical architecture of articulated building elements, whose structural proportions Foster's façade allusively picks up. The main entrance shifted to the corner and its counterpart, diagonally opposite on the rear façade, emphasize the function of the Carrée d'Art as an urban joint on an important urban connection axis.

The interior is laid out around a glass-roofed central courtyard that extends all the way to the library rooms on the lower storey and supplies the entire building with light. The individual floors are arranged like galleries around this atrium, in which

a broad stairway of semi-transparent greenish glass not only collects and distributes the stream of visitors, but also effectively fractures and modulates the incidence of light. From outside, the light is filtered through metal Venetian blinds, whose horizontal lines form an important design element. Glazed roofs with two fields of lamella allow the regulation of light intensity and light incidence in the high-ceiling exhibition rooms on the top floor. It is here too that we find the observation platform under the filigree canopy, from which one can see the classical temple set out on display like a costly jewel – in a way, the goal of the central stairway.

Techniques et Architecture 357/1984, pp. 10-15 (A. Pélissier) • *The Architectural Review* 1059/1985, pp. 31-43 (Jonathan Glancey) • François Chaslin/Frédérique Hervet/Armelle Lavalou, Norman Foster, Stuttgart, 1987, pp. 114-123 • *architektur aktuell* 159-160/1993, pp. 38-42 • *Baumeister* 8/1993, pp. 40-49 (Jonathan Glancey) • *Bauwelt* 19/1993, pp. 993-1000 (Sebastian Redecke) • *Deutsche Bauzeitschrift* 9/1993, pp. 1419-1423 (M. Helle) • *Werk, Bauen und Wohnen* 1-2/1994, pp. 12-15

Lampugnani/Sachs, pp. 34-41 (Kenneth Powell) • Räume für Kunst, pp. 24-25 (Josep M. Montaner) • Steele, pp. 58-63

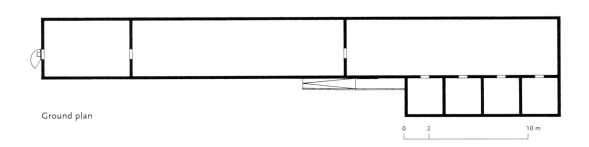

Longitudinal section

Ground plan

0   2   10 m

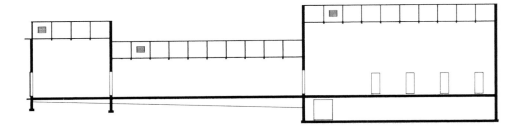

from left to right
View from the southwest | View from the northwest |
1. Interior space (from the entrance to the east) | 2. Interior
space (to the west) | 3. Interior space (to the west)

Museum
La Congiunta

Giornico, Switzerland

Client	Fondazione La Congiunta
Architects	Peter Märkli, Zurich
with Stefan Bellwalder, Naters
Exhibition area	225 m²
Construction time	1990-1992

This archaic-looking building, whose architect wants it to be understood not as a traditional museum building but rather as an "architectural essay on art," is situated in a narrow valley in the Alps, on the St Gotthard Pass, on the outskirts of Giornico in Ticino. Erected exclusively for the sculptures and reliefs of Hans Josephson (born 1920), not only does the building try to give an architectural response to the expressive sculptures and to bring them to the greatest possible degree of density and concentration, but also it gives the appearance of being itself a sculpture in the mountain landscape.

The long building, 42 metres in length, consists of three consecutive volumes of the same width, but

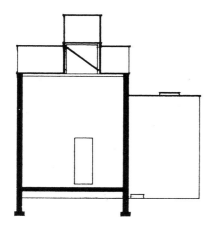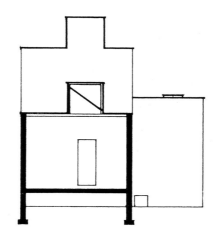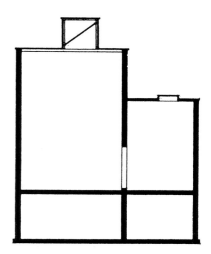

Cross sections

different heights. Along the top of each of them are set prisms, noticeably slightly off in their alignment with the axis. Light from above enters through them illuminating the otherwise entirely windowless building of cast concrete, whose unplastered, plinthless walls are marked by the pattern of formwork boarding and whose isolated ashlars are recognizably set apart from each other by the structure of the horizontal interstices precisely defined by the architect.

One accesses the interior from the narrow side facing away from the village. Visitors are thus forced to go around the building, experiencing it in its physicality and its attitude to the landscape. The three rooms lying one behind the other are linked in en-

filade but not quite in line with the axis; their mutual autonomy is emphasized by strikingly high door thresholds. The very different effect of these rooms arises exclusively out of the subtly pondered differentiation of their proportions owing nothing to any mechanical grid, and the resultant variety in the incidence of light. While the entrance room is only a little higher than it is wide and a little longer than it is high, and therefore more or less non-directional, the second room, which, like the third one, is two and a half times as long as the first, because of its significantly reduced height unfolds an effect of depth that is finally neutralized in the last and highest room. Four cabinets on the sides, which from the outside appear to be supplementary rectangular

parallelepipeds, horizontally placed, lend this room a more complex character, without cancelling out the impressive frugality of this architecture.

Faces. Journal d'architectures 26/1992, pp. 8-14 (Martin Steinmann/Beat Wismer) • *Werk, Bauen und Wohnen* 12/1992, pp. 30-35 • *Domus* 753/1993, pp. 4-5 (Luca Gazzaniga) • *Techniques et Architecture* 408/1993, pp. 70-73 • Stiftung La Congiunta. Peter Märkli – Haus für Reliefs und Halbfiguren des Bildhauers Hans Josephson, ed. Kunsthaus Bregenz. Werkdokumente, Stuttgart, 1994 • La Congiunta. Haus für Reliefs und Halbfiguren von Hans Josephson, ed. Fondazione La Congiunta, Zürich, 1996 • *Baumeister* 8/1996, pp. 35-39 (Marcel Meili)

Meseure/Tschanz/Wang, pp. 282-283 (Angeli Sachs) • Wang, pp. 242-243

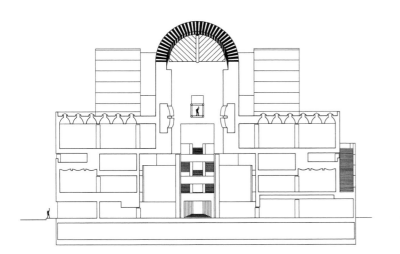

Cross section

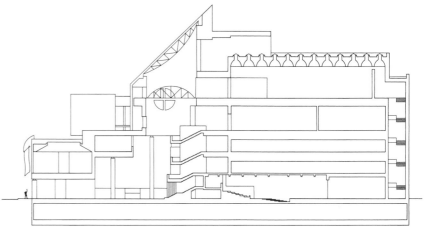

Longitudinal section

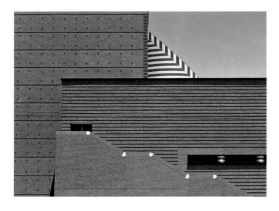

from left to right
Side façade, detail of the brick cladding | General view |
Main façade, middle part | Atrium | Gallery on the third floor

Museum of Modern Art

San Francisco/California, USA

Client	SFMOMA private foundation
Architect	Mario Botta, Lugano/Switzerland
Enclosed space	100,000 m³
Net floor area	18,580 m²
Exhibition area	4,645 m²
Construction time	1992-1995

The urban planning objective for the building that houses the San Francisco Museum of Modern Art was to mediate between a skyscraper canyon and a park with low perimeter development. In addition, the building was to be an important part of an urban revitalization project. Mario Botta, for whom this brief awarded in 1989 was his first in the United States, resolved the problem with a symmetrically composed building of stepped-back blocks stacked on top of each other, its centre formed by a diagonally capped cylinder. The black and silver-grey granite stripes on this cylindrical tower present a striking contrast to the red bricks that are not simply the cladding for the rest of the building (362 different brick sizes were used) but instead subtly structure

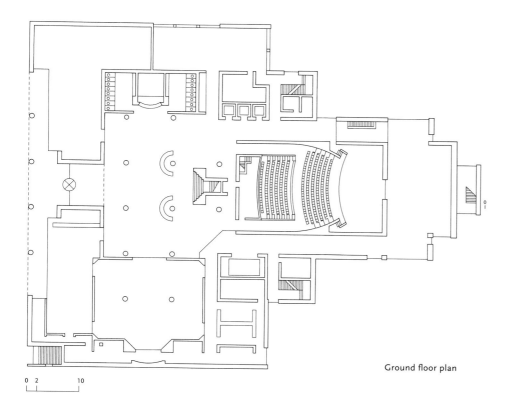

Ground floor plan

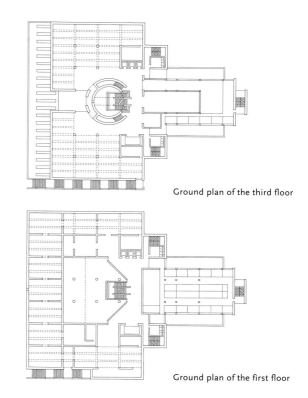

Ground plan of the third floor

Ground plan of the first floor

0 2 10

the surfaces of its stereometrically clear volumes and intensify the effect of plasticity. The brick façades, absolutely atypical for San Francisco, and their windowlessness point to this building's special meaning; indeed, it houses one of the most important collections of contemporary art on the west coast of the United States.

The dominant cylinder forms the centre of the museum in every respect. Its slant is not motivated just by urban planning concerns, but also and to the same extent by lighting technology and not least, iconology (it has been called a "seeing eye"). It is from there that the light falls through all the levels of the building into the atrium (whose design is highly

stylized, possibly too consistently) from which more than just the ground floor (with auditorium, multiple-use event space, seminar room, museum shop, cafe, etc.) is accessed. All the gallery levels above it can be accessed from it as well, via a staircase placed like a sculpture in this beam of light. Circulation through the galleries has been designed so that visitors always return to this centre point. The staggered stacking of the building volumes enables the majority of the galleries (with the sole exception of the second storey intended for the presentation of the photo collection), of varying heights and distributed over four storeys, to be naturally lighted via skylights whose form reminds one a little of the Kimbell Art Museum by Louis Kahn, one of Mario Botta's important teachers.

Pippo Ciorra, Botta, Eisenman, Gregotti, Hollein: musei, Milan, 1991, pp. 39-64 • The Making of a Modern Museum. San Francisco Museum of Modern Art, San Francisco, 1994 • achitektur aktuell 173-174/1994, pp. 54-61 (Georg Schrom) • Lotus international 86/1995, pp. 6-26 (Janet Abrams) • Emilio Pizzi, Mario Botta, Basel/Berlin/Boston, 1998, pp. 174-177 • Justin Henderson, San Francisco Museum of Modern Art, San Francisco, 2000

Cerver, pp. 20-31 • Henderson, pp. 46-53 • Lampugnani/ Sachs, pp. 76-83 (Kenneth Frampton) • Museo d'arte e architettura, pp. 150-155 • Newhouse, pp. 61-65

North-south section

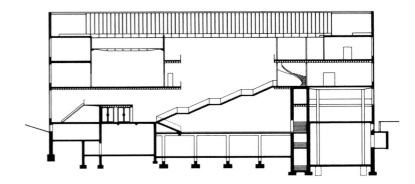

East-west section

from left to right
Bird's eye view from the northeast, 1957 | Southwest corner of the inner courtyard, 1957 | Hall with stairway | Top lighted exhibition room, 1972 | View through small exhibition rooms

Wallraf-Richartz-Museum

Cologne, Germany
now Museum of Applied Art

Client	City of Cologne
Architect	Rudolf Schwarz, Cologne with Josef Bernard
Enclosed space	47,000 m³
Net floor area	6,564 m²
Exhibition area	4,829 m²
Construction time	1953-1957 (restricted competition 1951) redesigned 1988-1989 Walter von Lom

The Wallraf-Richartz-Museum, Cologne's picture gallery, was the first large museum to be built in Germany after the Second World War. Rudolf Schwarz replaced the nineteenth century building that had been bombed out with a three-winged volume that traces the ground plan of the former Franciscan monastery and surrounds an inner courtyard where the fragmentarily conserved cloisters are located, and on whose south side rises the Gothic Minorite church, setting the proportions. The unpretentious brick architecture is characterized by its articulation in six bays running parallel to the Minorite church, each of them with a gable roof. Thus, the east and west sides resemble the fronts of narrow, gable-crowned houses set in a row – an allusion to the

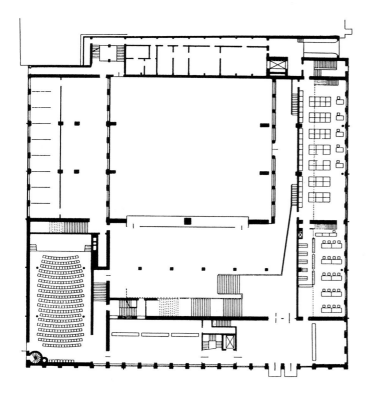

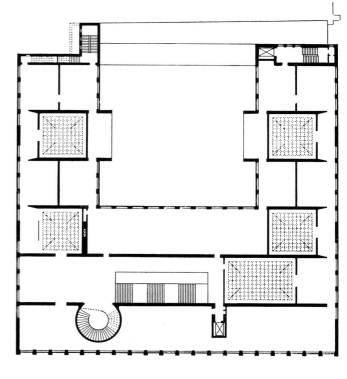

Ground floor plan

Ground plan of the first floor

0 2   10 m

historical structural fabric, but justified primarily functionally by the architect. The rhythm of the windowed and closed façade sections and their alternating crowning by blind gables and gables of glass resulted mainly from the intention to illuminate the exhibition rooms alternately with side light and top lighting; even the glazing of the gables prevents shadows on the illuminated ceilings. The stacked up supporting pillars on the largely closed northern façade are probably an allusion to the buttresses of the mediaeval ecclesiastical buildings. Apart from their articulating function, the pillars also fulfil a real structural function, as the supporting brick walls are not stabilized by any reinforced concrete constructions.

The interior, which one accesses through a discreetly-placed entrance on the north side, opens into a grand hall, itself opening onto the courtyard dominated by a flight of steps articulated by a number of half-landings and leading up to the main floors of the museum. Rooms of varying sizes, with ceilings of different heights and with varied lighting arrangements surround and interpenetrate each other – although they are arranged essentially in straight lines – whereby Schwarz, as the "most natural" lighting favoured the side light falling in from windows and expressly distanced himself from any "effect lighting." It was above all the explosive growth of twentieth century artworks from the Stiftung Ludwig that led in 1986 to the transfer of

the picture gallery to a new building. After a sensitively carried out restoration, the building, in the meantime extolled as a classic of museum architecture, has proven to be a surprisingly suitable domicile for Cologne's Museum of Applied Arts.

Bauen + Wohnen 1954, pp. 6-8 • *Glas Forum* 5/1957, pp. 8-15 (Otto Völckers) • *Baukunst und Werkform* 11/1958, pp. 5-12 (Hannelore Schubert) • *Die Bauzeitung* 64/1959, pp. 134-139 (Harbers) • Mathias Schreiber (ed.), 40 Jahre Moderne in der Bundesrepublik, Stuttgart, 1986, pp. 35-37 • *Kunstchronik* 43/1990, pp. 111-123 (Barbara Mundt) • Wolfgang Pehnt/ Hilde Strohl, Rudolf Schwarz, Stuttgart, 1997, pp. 169-175, pp. 270-272

Schubert, pp. 38-40

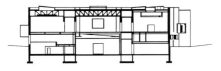

Cross sections

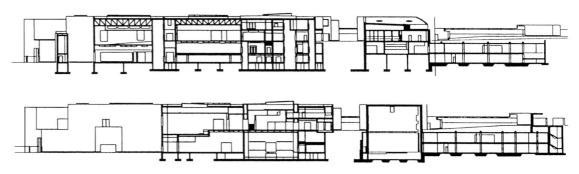

Longitudinal sections

from left to right
Like a leitmotif, the roofed-over entrance shows the characteristic qualities of this architecture: paths, light, lines | Initially, only the smooth, slightly curving wall of the auditorium is seen while the rest of the complex extending between two walls is hidden from view | View from the park of the two museum hills | The first courtyard with the diagonally projecting oriels

Museu de Serralves

Porto, Portugal

Client	Fundação de Serralves, Porto
Architect	Álvaro Siza Vieira, Porto
Enclosed space	88,000 m³
Net floor area	15,000 m²
Exhibition area	4,500 m²
Construction time	1996-1999

Portugal's first public museum of contemporary art lies on the outskirts of a large park. The 160-metre long building, for the most part four storeys, is fitted into the sloping landscape so that its enormous volume can hardly be guessed at from the entrance area – at best, its size could be gauged by walking round the outside. Between two slices of wall that are penetrated only by window openings and a bridge into the park are situated (apart from a two-storey underground garage with a grass roof) the auditorium that belongs to the complex and, separated from it by a courtyard, the U-shaped museum itself, with two asymmetric wings around another courtyard opening to the park.

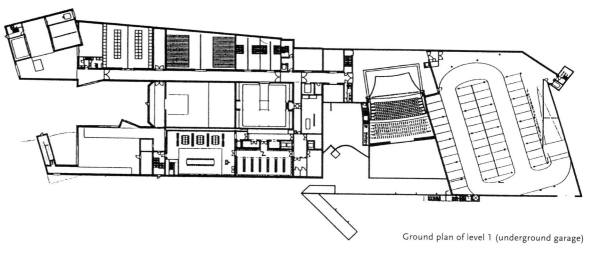

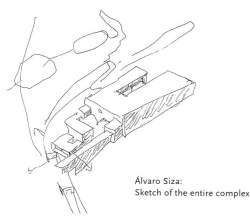

Álvaro Siza:
Sketch of the entire complex

The quality of this architecture consists in the tension between regularity and carefully calculated discomfiture, in the interplay between inside and outside, in the visitor routing, and not least in the treatment of light. The long trajectory that leads from the exterior portal to the actual museum entrance already brings into focus significant elements almost as leitmotifs: it begins with a bend which is transferred to the third dimension in the fracturing of the roofing at the portal into multiple obtuse angles, making it immediately clear to those entering that spatial laws are being demonstrated here and at the same time, relativized by their reduction to a play of sharply-drawn lines. The trajectory staged in this way, carefully set off from the green lawn by stone slabs and

roofed over, its further course narrowed and rhythmicized by the gatehouse placed at an angle, leads – first on the one side hermetically closed by a wall, but on the other side entirely open – past a large inner courtyard bounded on its south side by the immaculate white wall of the auditorium. While this windowless wall, the effect of which is inhospitable despite the elegance of its curving roofline, suggests that the visitor is still outside the building, the windowed walls, some of them angled, lend the neighbouring courtyard placed between the auditorium and the actual museum a significantly more intimate character that appears to blur the boundary between external and internal space. At many places in the building the interplay between inside and out-

side becomes a dialogue between architecture and nature carefully staged by means of refined wall cut-outs, room-high window openings or oriels that are occasionally twisted out of the walls in sharp, balcony-like angles.

The interior of the museum – accessed by the route taking visitors from the two-storey high atrium on a labyrinthine excursion leading occasionally via stairways and ramps and interrupted repeatedly by views of the complex – consists of seven large and a series of smaller rooms, each of which has a specific character created by variations in their dimensions and proportions as well as the form and size of the wall and ceiling openings. However, light plays the most

91

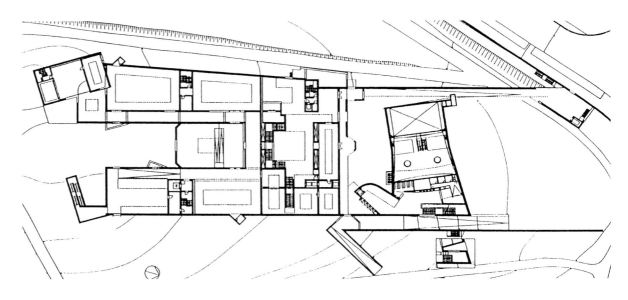

Ground plan level 3 (entrance level)

Álvaro Siza: Sketch of the interior

from left to right
In the entrance area | The unconventionally linked exhibition rooms are characterized by graduated ceilings and light directed in a variety of ways

important role: its incidence is subtly directed and its targeted nuancing by means of a multiplicity of reflections and refractions of the spatial boundaries, always white, allow this architecture sometimes to appear weightless. The fragmentation of the prismatic stereometry – never obtrusively staged, yet unmistakable – contributes decisively to the impression of this lightness that allows one to almost forget the structural necessities, which are nowhere put on display. However, on no account does this fragmentation of the prismatic stereometry take on deconstructionist traits. The rooms are often bounded not by wall and ceiling surfaces in the traditional sense, but instead seem to develop a life of their own that now and then shifts right angles, inter-

rupts walls by means of oriel-like protrusions or sometimes makes them appear to be tilted, and again and again alienates the ceilings – at times in counterpoint to varying floor levels – by means of multiple layerings, to the extent that the light effects thereby created seem to overrule spatial laws. In addition to several rooms in which the ceilings are virtually 'turned upside down' by 'hanging tables,' out of which indirect light falls on the walls, there are also conventional rooms lit from above, whose glass ceilings are not flat, however, but slightly swollen like sails. Herein too, we see Siza's unmistakeable style – as we do in the organically curved contour of the auditorium wall – that is probably to be explained not only by the admired model provid-

ed by Alvar Aalto, but is also perhaps to be interpreted as an expression of that mentality that has its linguistic equivalent in the soft ductus of Portuguese. The fact that these thoroughly manneristic characteristics of Alvaro Siza's language of form do not detract from the functional capabilities of his buildings, but instead are able to intensify them, is proven here, for example, by the largely asymmetric arrangement of the doors of the museum's rooms, whose spatial sequence, almost always regular and therefore conventionally appropriate for museums, is thereby eventfully alienated and often found surprising. The routing, already intentionally emphasized in the entrance area thus proves to be not only an important architectural motif, but also at

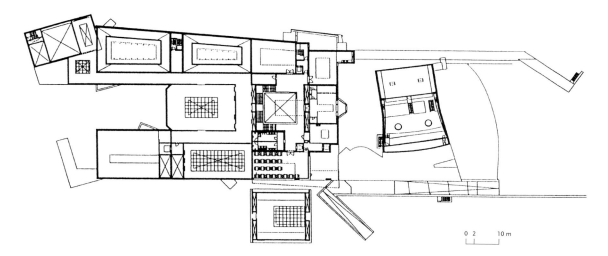

Ground plan level 4 (cafeteria)

Álvaro Siza: Sketch of the interior

the same time an effective solution to a central
problem of museum architecture as such.

Baumeister 7/1999, pp. 6-7 (Gerd Hammer) • *Bauwelt* 32/
1999, pp. 1739-1747 (Christian Gänshirt) • *Deutsche Bauzeitung* 9/1999, pp. 96-103 (David Cohn) • *The Architectural
Review* 1230/1999, pp. 32-33 (Guy Marc) • Philip Jodidio,
Álvaro Siza, Cologne, 1999, pp. 164-167 • *architektur aktuell*
237-238/2000, pp. 144-156 (Paul von Naredi-Rainer) • Álvaro
Siza. Museu de Serralves/Serralves Museum (Paulo Martins
Barata, Raquel Henriques de Silva, Bernardo Pinto de Almei-
da), Lisbon, 2001

Maier-Solgk, pp. 200-205 • Trulove, pp. 70-79

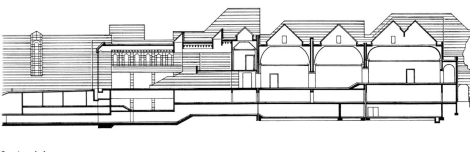

Section A-A

Section B-B

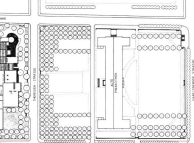

Site plan

from left to right
The museum part from the southeast | View of the museum part from the southwest | Entrance hall | One of the roofed-over ramps between the interior courtyard and the exhibition rooms | Marées Room | Exhibition room with stairway to the elevated level beyond

Neue Pinakothek

Munich, Germany

Client	Bavarian Ministry of Education and Culture
Architect	Alexander Freiherr von Branca, Munich
Enclosed space	147,000 m³
Net floor area	11,500 m²
Exhibition area	7,250 m² (including depots)
Construction time	1974-1981 (Award 1967)

The nineteenth century stocks that were rescued, along with those of modern art and the graphic collection of the Bayerische Staatsgemäldesammlungen were to be united in a Neue Pinakothek that was to replace the destroyed counterpart to Klenze's Alte Pinakothek. The design of Alexander von Branca from Munich was the one that was selected, among other reasons, because of his "balanced height development and [the way he] positioned [his building] on the complex and in relation to the Alte Pinakothek." A programmatic change with far-reaching consequences – instead of twentieth century art and graphics, extensive administrative and institutional facilities were to be accommodated – resulted in the building´s current appearance.

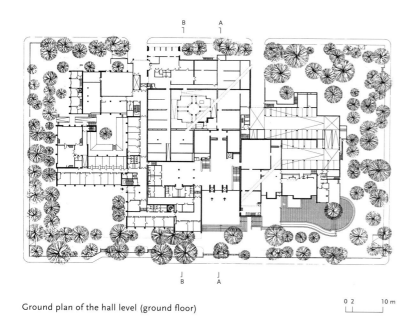

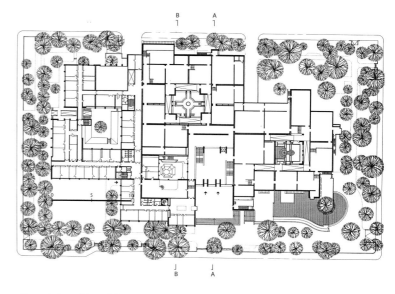

Ground plan of the hall level (ground floor)

0 2   10 m

Ground plan of the exhibition level (upper storey)

The administrative wing laid out to the west is distinguished by rows of round-arched windows between wall projections with rounded off front ends. In the eastern half, in the museum part identifiable through its sawtooth roofs, this uniform, small-scale articulation is contrasted with large wall surfaces and cubic blocks. Because of the natural stone cladding, the impression that is initially generated is one of pathos-evoking detachment, which, however, is alienated by the occasionally entirely unmotivated details like copper oriels or functionless gargoyles; it hardly allows any conclusions to be drawn as to the function and importance of this building.

The interior of the museum, which is accessed via an entrance hall of gloomy solemnity, the interface between the administration part and the exhibition area, is laid out approximately on the ground plan of a figure eight on its side, around two richly styled interior courtyards. Around these courtyards surrounded by wheelchair-accessible but bunker-like ramps are 35 exhibition rooms of different sizes, each with additional cabinets, arranged so that they rise step by step; the first half of a circular tour (from which visitors can deviate at will) thus ends on the gallery of the entrance hall and subsequently leads back to the entrance level. Through historicizing mouldings on frames, doors and ceiling vaults and fabric-covered walls in discreet colours, the

comfortably proportioned exhibition rooms, perfectly illuminated by complicatedly filtered top lighting, are, in a way, transported back to the time when the pictures shown here came into being.

Der Architekt 9/1980, pp. 420-426 (Dieter Osterlen) • *Baumeister* 10/1981, pp. 1001-1009 • *The Architectural Review* 169/1981, pp. 334-340 • Festgabe zur Eröffnung der Neuen Pinakothek in München am 28. März 1981, Munich, 1981 • *Bauwelt* 19-20 /1981, pp. 783-794 • Pantheon 39/1981, pp. 104-110 • *deutsche bauzeitung* 1/1982, pp. 30-32 (Gerhard Ullmann) • *Museumskunde* 47/1982, pp. 26-39 (Norbert Knopp) • Ingeborg Flagge (ed.), Museumsarchitektur, 1985, pp. 20-22 • Michael Künne, Die Neue Pinakothek. Photographisch erlebte Architektur, Munich, 1985

Klotz/Krase, pp. 24-26 and pp. 44-48 • Schilgen, pp. 8-25 • Schubert, pp. 130-133

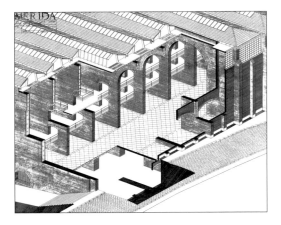

Axonometric projection of the room plan

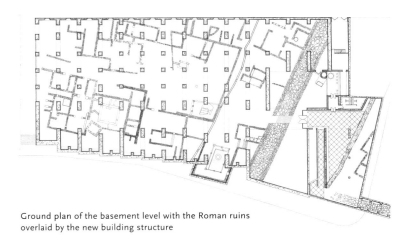

Ground plan of the basement level with the Roman ruins overlaid by the new building structure

from left to right
Façade on Calle José Ramón Mélida (from the southeast) | General view of the administration buildings and the museum (from the southeast) | Great hall | View into one of the transepts

Museo Nacional de Arte Romano

Mérida, Spain

Client	Spanish Ministry of Culture
Architect	José Rafael Moneo Vallés, Madrid
Total area	10,380 m²
Net floor area	9,650 m²
Exhibition area	7,525 m²
Construction time	1981-1985

Colonia Augusta Emerita, now Mérida, is one of the most important cities of the Roman empire on the Iberian peninsula; its remains – among them a theatre and an amphitheatre – are currently being excavated. The museum, erected on a part of the excavation site with the remains of a Roman settlement, seeks not only to be a neutral container for the archaeological finds, but as a part of the ancient site, also seeks to elucidate the fundamental principles of the architectural culture that belongs to the objects kept there. Thus Rafael Moneo makes the characteristics of Roman architecture, the feeling for the monumental space and structural solidity into the determining factors for his museum building which, moreover, because of its situation,

0   5   20 m

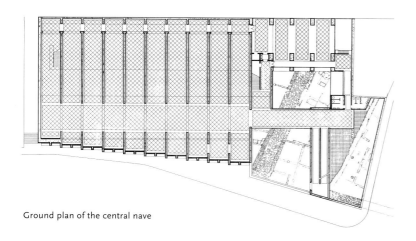

Ground plan of the central nave

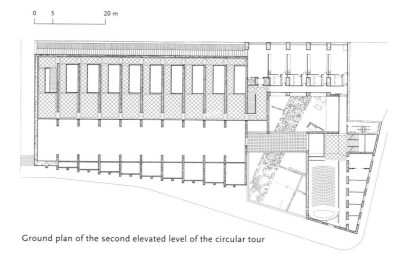

Ground plan of the second elevated level of the circular tour

represents the connecting link between the field of classical ruins and the fringes of today's city.

His building is laid out in two clearly distinguishable parts, the administrative wing that adopts the dimensions of the neighbouring residential development, and the actual museum block itself, much bigger, that stands on top of an excavation site accessible from the museum and separated from it by a ceiling. On the entrance side, the strictly rectangular ground plan of the museum overlaying the structure of the Roman development follows in the form of a stairway the course of the street, whereby a graduated series of buttressed walls is created, which are to point programmatically to Roman con-

struction principles. The brickwork of the entire museum is executed using the technique favoured by the Romans, opus caementitium, a brick shell filled with concrete. It is the arches, however, that really are the epitome of the Roman incantatory formula – they lend the interior a monumental simplicity. Room-height archway openings cut enfilade-like into brick walls parallel with each other and six metres apart create the spatial effect of looking down the length of a nave in which the most valuable objects are displayed. Naturally lit by glass gable roofs and windows placed high on the walls, the corridors running across the main nave between these walls are laid out by means of corridors and galleries on several levels, which enable

one to experience the spatial structure of intercrossed wall and arch systems again and again.

Arquitectura 5-6/1984, pp. 23-45 (Javier Frechilla) • *Casabella* 4/1984, pp. 52-63 (Giacomo Polin) • *Werk, Bauen + Wohnen* 12/1984, pp. 18-23 (Paolo Fumigalli) • *The Architectural Review* 1065/1985, pp. 38-47 (Peter Buchanan) • *Lotus International* 46/1985, pp. 22-35 (Francesco Dal Co) • *Baumeister* 2/1987, pp. 13-21 • Rafael Moneo. Bauen für die Stadt, Vienna Exhibition Catalogue, Stuttgart, 1993, pp. 46-53

Allégret, pp. 94-105 • López Moreno/López Rodríguez/ Mendoza Castells, pp. 320-329 (Enrique de Teresa) • Montaner/Oliveras, pp. 80-83 • Stephens, pp. 66-69

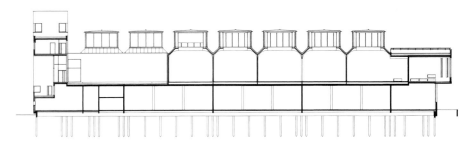

Longitudinal section through the gallery wing with the toplighted rooms

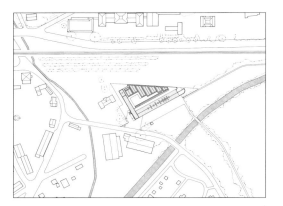

Site plan

Longitudinal section through the exhibition wing (with the great hall)

from left to right
View from the northwest | Inner courtyard on the first floor
(on the left, the gallery wing, on the right, the exhibition wing) |
Toplighted rooms in the gallery wing (first floor) | Rotunda
(on the first floor) and great hall (on the second floor) of the
exhibition wing

Essl Collection

Klosterneuburg, Austria

Client	Agnes and Karlheinz Essl, Klosterneuburg
Architect	Heinz Tesar, Vienna
Enclosed space	38,603 m³
Net floor area	7,620 m²
Exhibition area	3,200 m²
Construction time	1998-99

Not far from Vienna, a museum for the most extensive collection of Austrian post-war paintings, recently supplemented by foreign works, came into being within a very short time and without any public support. A knowledgeable critic of architecture has interpreted its puzzling design as the embodiment of the genuinely Austrian ambivalence between baroque sensuality and Enlightenment sobriety manifested here in particular in the personalities of the client and the architect.

The white-plastered volume rises above a high plinth of rough concrete on the ground plan of a right-angled triangle broken open into a trapezium that follows the form of the site – situated between

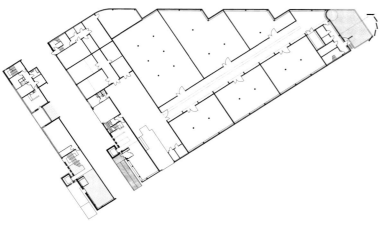

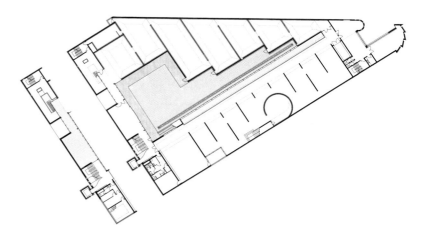

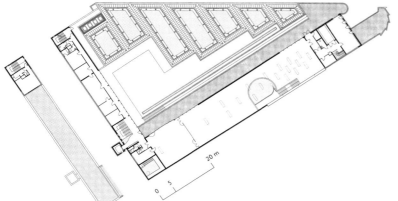

from bottom left, clockwise to top right
Ground floor plan | Ground plan of the first floor |
Ground plan of the second floor.

20 m

0   5

the railway line and a tributary of the Danube – and points to the baroque convent Klosterneuburg to the northwest, with the tip of the triangle capriciously dissolved in a fan of concrete slabs. Visitors enter the building at the opposite end, the narrow access wing to the southeast, and are led directly from the foyer to the next level where a real architectural landscape unfolds. On the right, the long exhibition wing – organized by walls positioned crosswise and an inserted rotunda – opens onto a garden in an inner courtyard. The wing's wall of windows also lights at least partially the enormous storage area underneath it, into which we can see by means of a shaft that the architect calls a "room cut-out." A narrow ramp leads along the outside of this wall of

windows to the great hall for temporary exhibitions above it (which is also accessible from inside). Its curving roof, shot through with narrow bands of light, presents an exciting contrast to the glass lanterns on the opposite side that mark the silhouette of the longest building wing in a meaningful way. Through these lanterns falls conventional light from above into seven variously-sized gallery rooms – all trapezoid because of their orthogonal grid. In an eventful rhythm – which, however, eventually submits to a straight sequence of rooms – the rooms are linked to each other and open gradually toward the courtyard, from which lateral light also comes in through high, narrow openings.

Sammlung Essl. The first view, Cologne 1999, pp. 352-369 •
architektur aktuell 237-238/2000, pp. 130-143 (Matthias
Boeckl) • *Bauwelt* 2/2000, pp. 30-35 (Friedrich Achleitner) •
Gottfried Knapp, Heinz Tesar. Sammlung Essl, Klosterneuburg, Stuttgart/London, 2000

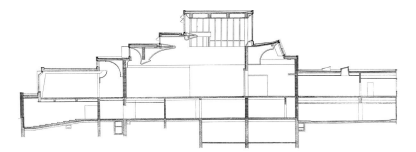

Section through the central hall

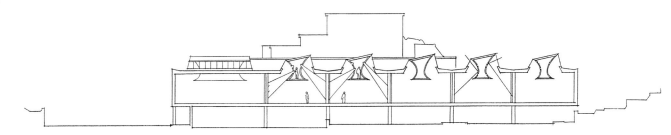

Section through the large exhibition hall (with schematic representation of the incidence of light)

from left to right
General view from the street (from the north) | View from the northwest | Central hall | The large, flexibly divisible exhibition room structured by the dominant lighting architecture

Nordjyllands Kunstmuseum

Ålborg, Denmark

Client	Nordjyllands Kunstmuseum
Architects	Elissa & Alvar Aalto, Jean-Jacques Baruël
Construction time	1968-1972 (Competition 1958)

The external appearance of North Jutland's sculpturally-designed art museum, marked by a stepped roof and clad with white marble, glass, and copper sheets is to be understood as a reaction as well to the topographic situation, a valley surrounded on three sides by tree-covered slopes, the bottom of which is somewhat lower than the access road. It is above all, however, as it almost always is with Aalto, the consequence of his spatial arrangement of the interior.

The main floor on the street level is arranged around a high central hall that can be used both as an auditorium and an exhibition room. It is surrounded on two sides by the angled entrance foyer accessed via

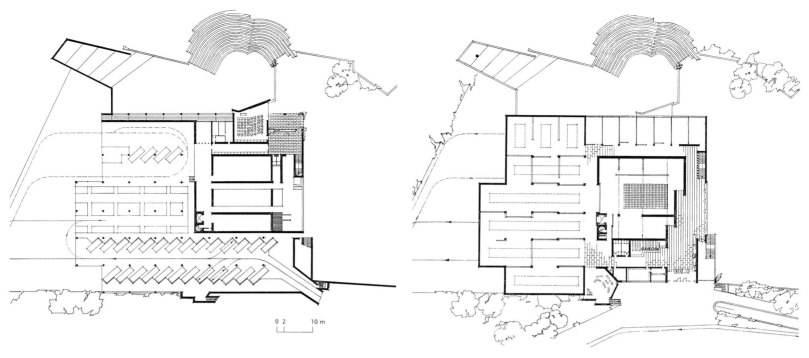

Ground plan of the lower floor   Ground plan of the main floor

the northern corner of the building. With its glass walls the height of the room, the foyer opens to the exterior and leads on one hand via a stairway to the reading rooms situated underneath, the restaurant, the underground garage partly slid into the mountain, and into the sculpture garden closed off by a theatre of an unusual shape, and on the other hand, leads in both directions into the exhibition area. The exhibition rooms are connected to the circulation around the central hall in such a way that they themselves never function as thoroughfares so that visitors are able to contemplate the artworks undisturbed. On the side facing the sculpture garden are situated seven small rooms lit from the side. Right-angled to this, oriented toward the southeast, an enormous exhibition room takes in approximately half of the entire floor area; although structured by columns arranged in a grid and the very dominant lighting architecture, it is basically open and can be subdivided at will by moveable walls.

While the high-ceilinged hall is lighted through the glass walls of the vaulted-over roof terraces, the large exhibition room receives its light through slanting, asymmetric roof crowns. From here, the light falls at an angle of 90 degrees on the north side and 56 degrees on the south side onto enormous parabolic reflectors hanging in the depths of the room; the reflectors cast shadowless light onto the whitewashed walls – a construction that Aalto first used in 1955 in the Finnish Pavilion of the Biennale in Venice.

Arkitektur 16/1972, pp. 182-199 • Karl Fleig, Alvar Aalto, Vol. I 1922-1962, 3rd ed. Zurich, 1970 • Karl Fleig, Alvar Aalto, 2nd ed. Zurich, 1979, pp. 81-83 • *Architecture and Urbanism*, extra edition 5/1983, pp. 144-147 • Else Bülow, Art and Alvar Aalto, Nordjyllands Kunstmuseum, 1991 • Göran Schildt, Alvar Aalto. A Life's Work – Architecture, Design and Art, Keurun, 1994, pp. 120-122 • Aase Bak/Christoffer Harlang, Nordjyllands Kunstmuseum. Elissa & Alvar Aalto, Jean-Jacques Baruël, Copenhagen, 1999

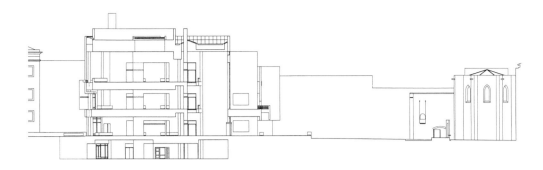

Cross section

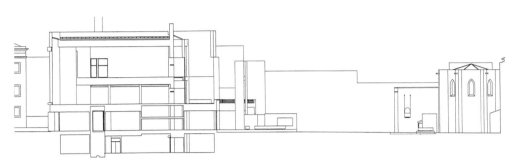

Cross section

Site plan

from left to right
Main façade on the south side | Detail of the main façade
(including the main entrance) | Hall on the ground floor|
Ramp | Exhibition room on the second floor.

Museu
d'Art Contemporani

Barcelona, Spain

Client	Museu d'Art Contemporani Foundation, Barcelona
Architects	Richard Meier & Partners, New York
Built area	14,647 m²
Net floor area	13,800 m²
Exhibition area	5,087 m²
Construction time	1991-1995 (commissioned in 1987)

It was not an existing collection of modern art, but primarily the desire to see a work of Richard Meier's in Barcelona that led to that prominent architect being awarded the brief and given the opportunity to influence the choice of location. Although the rectangular ground plan of the building, 120 metres long and 35 metres wide – necessitating the demolition of several blocks in the densely populated port quarter of Raval – follows the block development of the quarter, in its radiant brightness and artificial immaculateness, it forms a sharp contrast on the whole to the dilapidated gloominess of its surroundings.

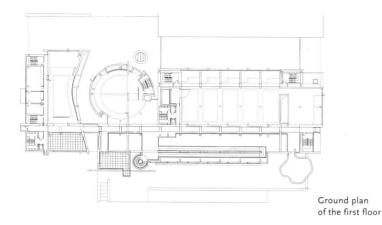

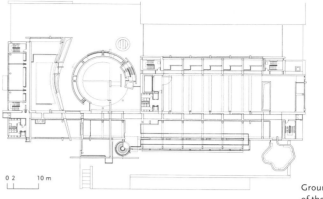

Ground plan
of the first floor

0 2   10 m

Ground plan
of the second floor

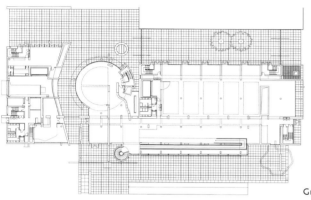

Ground floor plan

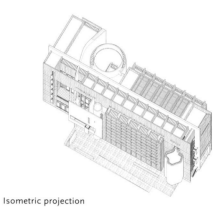

Isometric projection

The museum consists of three different parts that are very evident from the north, while on the south side, the independently-structured show façade integrates them: a long, three-storey main block for the exhibition rooms, a rotunda serving as an atrium and reading room, and finally, separated from that block by a passageway running across the building, a narrow, seven-storey wing for the administration, the library, and other facilities.

The effectively staged access leads visitors from a dark entrance area, through the rotunda, partially lit by bands of glass, into an enormous triple nave flooded with light. Beyond the glass entrance wall, a ramp leads upwards in a series of counterpoised diagonals and opens views to the exterior and, over a ravine lit from above by a glazed band in the roof, onto the gallery wing. Two bridges lead into the axially-arranged exhibition rooms that are lit from above on the topmost floor, and on the floors below are lit laterally by light slits and wall openings.

As the space-creating element, light is the dominant theme of this architecture that seeks not only to be a neutral container, but also to represent its own possibilities in the dissolution of very complex volumes and the combination of different forms.

Architectural Design 3-4/1991, pp. 46-53 • *architektur aktuell* 190/1996, pp. 42-53 (Juli Capella and Quim Larrea) • *Bauwelt* 17/1996, pp. 1013-1017 (Lluis Permanyer) • Silvio Cassarà, Richard Meier, Basel/Boston/Berlin, 1996, pp. 156-157

Maier-Solgk, pp. 26-33 • Museo d'arte e architettura, pp. 134-141 • Newhouse, pp. 66-72 • Steele, pp. 130-131

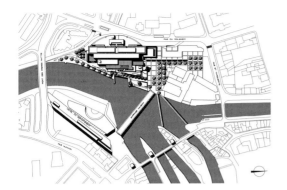

Site plan

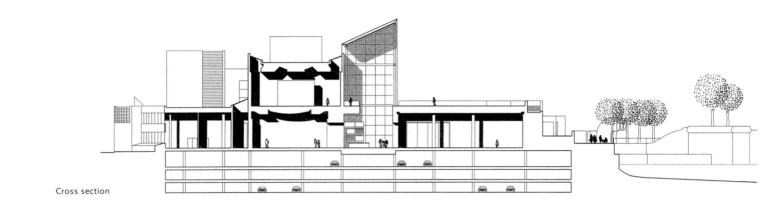

Cross section

from left to right
Entrance side (from the north) | General view from the southeast across the Ill | Glazed hall | View of the minster from one of the exhibition rooms | Exhibition room on the upper floor

Musée
d'Art Moderne
et Contemporain

Strasbourg, France

Client	City of Strasbourg
Architect	Adrien Fainsilber, Paris
Net floor area	12,980 m²
Exhibition area	4,633 m²
Construction time	1994-1997 (competition 1988)

Diagonally across from the picturesque Petite France quarter and in sight of Strasbourg's old city with the cathedral towering above it, the location of the museum (whose collection represents a cross-section of the art of the last 150 years) was decisive for its design. The imposing volume results not least out of the intention to create a counterpart for the headquarters of the European Parliament and the European Court of Human Rights.

The museum consists essentially of two prisms on their sides that are linked to each other by means of a glass hall 104 metres long and 25 metres high that towers over the entire complex. While the convex part of the building with its white Eternit cladding

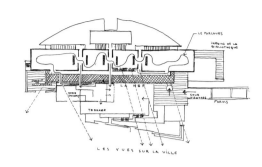

Plan of the circular tour
with views to the outside

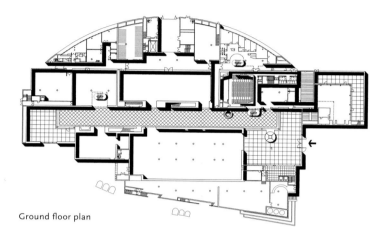

Ground floor plan

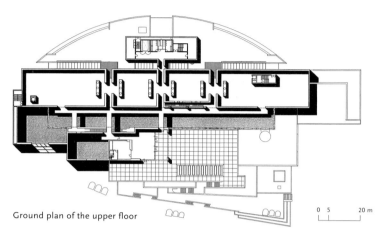

Ground plan of the upper floor

0 5   20 m

picks up the sober formal language of the new town behind it, the red granite of the monumentally structured show side facing the river is a reference to the city's historic buildings of red sandstone from the Vosges. The museum thus fulfils the function of an urban hinge. But as a secular and modern counterpart to the cathedral (to which Adrien Fainsilber refers by means of numerous artistically staged views), it seeks above all to be a public space and a place of community. It is not by chance that the dominant form of the glass hall – originally supposed to be open to the public – is reminiscent of the halved nave of a cathedral.

Spanned by bridges, the hall is accessed from the north. On both sides of it on the ground floor are the relatively low-ceilinged exhibition rooms of varying sizes; their artificial lighting is based on aircraft lighting systems, according to the architect. Only the western part of the upper storey contains museum rooms of varying sizes lit by a combination of artificial and natural light from above. Their arrangement in enfilade is interrupted by wall pieces placed transversally. On the side facing the river, an enormous panorama terrace (including a restaurant) provides a marvellous view of the city and thereby emphasizes the urban aspect as the primary design-determining factor of this architecture.

Bauwelt 44/1998, p. 2454 (Amber Sayah) • France musées récents (le moniteur architecture amc), Paris, 1999, pp. 84-89

Maier-Solgk, pp. 212-219

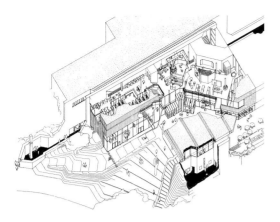

Isometric projection of the first building phase

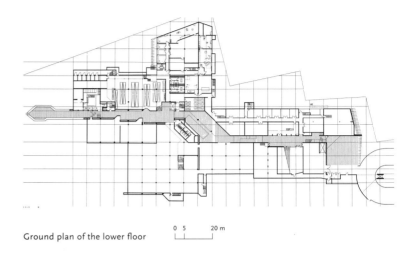

Ground plan of the lower floor

0 5   20 m

Sprengel Museum

Hanover, Germany

Client	Hanover State Capital
Architects	Peter and Ursula Trint, Cologne / Dieter Quast, Heidelberg
Enclosed space	92,665 m³
Net floor area	15,485 m²
Exhibition area	5,373 m²
Construction time	1975-79 (1ˢᵗ building phase) 1989-92 (2ⁿᵈ building phase) (Competition 1972/73)

Created for a substantial collection of twentieth-century artworks, the building (voluminous, but without giving the appearance of being monumental) on the bank of Lake Masch near Hanover's city centre turns its inside outwards in places. In correspondence with the spirit of the nineteen-seventies, it goes to some trouble to avoid provoking a fear of the unknown and instead, awake visitors' curiosity. At the same time, the hint of a city wall around the building illuminates the function of conservation in an enclosed safe retreat into which public space is supposed to enter dialogically.

The entrance positioned asymmetrically between two building wings is therefore welcoming. It is roofed

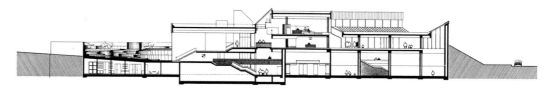

Section

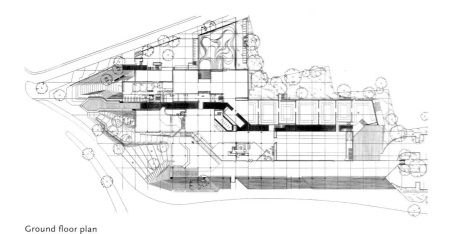

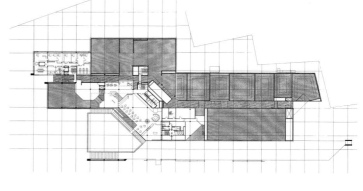

Ground floor plan

Ground plan of the first floor ("educational level")

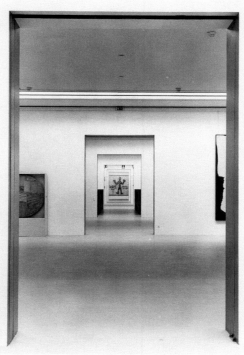

from left to right
Main entrance | View from the north of the museum street extending beyond the building | Museum street | Top lighted rooms on the ground floor (second building phase) | Collection rooms on the lower floor (first building phase)

over by a paraphrase of the classical columned portico and situated on the ridge of a hill accessed by stairs. The hill's surface structure continues over the building's boundary into the interior. Through a spacious entrance, one reaches the 'museum street,' 17 metres high and 120 metres long, bent at the interface between the parts of the building and receiving natural light from above through the glass roof. Like a ravine bridged over many times, this 'street' is the axis that forms the museum's backbone, offering a variety of views over all the floors, and continuing beyond its external boundaries. From this one accesses the collection rooms which are arranged on one hand in enfilade as a sequence of six light, high-ceilinged rooms of varying dimensions,

and on the other hand, are variable and interlinked in a complex fashion. The enormous 17-metre-wide, 41-metre-long temporary exhibition room on the ground floor can be flexibly partitioned by moveable walls. Although the building's shape, sometimes irregular, and the variety of connections – primarily between the collection rooms in the basement – make orientation more difficult, in exchange ever-changing perspectives are offered. Various different tours thematically organized and each containing a 'didactic room' always lead back to the museum street. While the exhibition rooms in the basement are lit by artificial light, the atmosphere of the rooms on the main floor lit from above is determined by daylight supplemented ingeniously by artificial light.

Bauwelt 37/1979, pp. 1585-1596 (Peter and Ursula Trint/ Dieter Quast; Joachim Büchner) • *Techniques et Architecture* 326/1979, pp. 62-63 • *Detail* 3/1980, pp. 377-381 • *Baumeister* 8/1980, pp. 785-789 • Klaus Kowalski, "Das Kunstmuseum Hannover mit Sammlung Sprengel," in: *Museumskunde* 46/1981, pp. 155-164 • *Bauwelt* 28-29/1992, pp. 1600-1601 (Christoph Gunßer)

Schubert, pp. 124-126

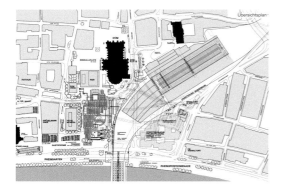

Site plan

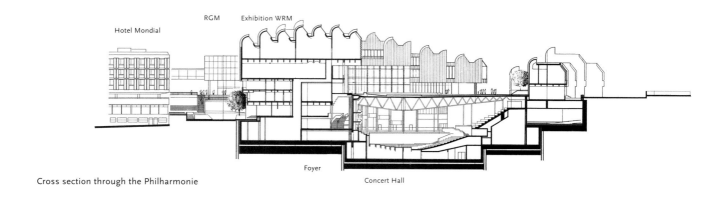

Hotel Mondial   RGM   Exhibition WRM

Foyer   Concert Hall

Cross section through the Philharmonie

from left to right
Some exhibition rooms open to the hill on which the cathedral
was erected | The volume of the museum, articulated by shed
roofs and descending to the Rhine | The "Museumsstraße"
(here still with paintings from the collection of the Wallraf-Ri-
chartz-Museum, moved into a new building in 2001) | The wide
stairway runs transversally to the main direction of the museum

Museum Ludwig

Cologne, Germany
formerly
Wallraf-Richartz-Museum / Museum Ludwig
(and Cologne Philharmonic)

Client	City of Cologne
Architects	Peter Busmann and Godfrid Haberer, Cologne
Enclosed space	260,000 m³
Net floor area	24,500 m²
Exhibition area	9,445 m²
Construction time	1981-1986 (competition won in 1976)

The real challenge for this project consisted in inte-
grating a volume equal to that of Cologne Cathedral
(and containing in addition to two museums, a
concert hall as well) into the urban situation on the
banks of the Rhine in Cologne – sadly neglected since
the end of the war – at the foot of the Gothic cathedral. Chosen primarily for its virtues in relation to
urban planning, the design recreates the old cathedral hill, sinking the concert hall into its interior (the
technical difficulties that had to be overcome were
enormous) and distributes the remaining spatial program over two volumes of different sizes which extend in an east-west direction, diminishing in height
and breadth the closer they come to the Rhine, the
larger of them containing the actual museum rooms.

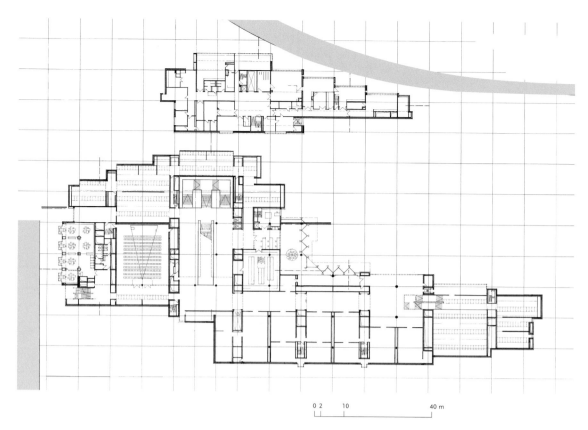

Ground plan of the first floor

0 2   10   40 m

Between them there is a plaza that contracts toward the cathedral into a narrow passageway effectively staged as a view axis, while toward the Rhine, it broadens out into a wide stairway. The distinguishing characteristic of this architecture clad with red brick and titanium-zincked sheet metal is its sawtooth roof structure, consistent throughout, which on one hand organizes the building mass into small-scale units and probably also seeks to set it in relation to the filigree structure of the Gothic cathedral, while on the other hand resolving the problem so thorny for museums, the lighting, at the same time bringing it into view.

These sawteeth light the pictures and objects on the upper floor with a comfortable northern light, but

their imposing form 'overwhelmes' the exhibits, particularly in the smaller and lower-ceilinged exhibition rooms where the uniform dimensioning of the sawteeth appears to be quite out of proportion. On the two upper exhibition storeys, the 'museum street' runs along these sawteeth as a central access way from which the exhibition rooms, clearly organized and mostly axially interlinked, can be accessed. The access to this circulatory axis is via an enormous stairway leading right-angled to it, its almost baroque gesture in unexpected contrast to the discreet modesty of the entrance at the western end of the building facing toward the cathedral. It is true that the drama of this cascade of steps effectively opens perspectives, but in the final analysis, it leads to nothing

because it ends in a room that feels far too low-ceilinged under the omnipresent sawtooth roof.

wettbewerbe aktuell 4/1976, pp. 235-254 • Bulletin der Museen der Stadt Köln, special issue 2/1986 • Zwischen Dom und Strom. Neubau Wallraf-Richartz-Museum, Museum Ludwig und Kölner Philharmonie, ed. Hochbaudezernat der Stadt Köln, Cologne, (1986) • *Bauwelt* 37/1986, pp. 1408-1419 (Peter Rumpf) • *Techniques et Architecture* 368/1986, pp. 84-89 • *The Architectural Review* 1088/1987, pp. 38-45 (Colin Davies) • *Architecture and Urbanism* 199/1987, pp. 21-84 • *Deutsches Architektenblatt* 19/1987, pp. 267-272 (Christian Marquart, Replique der Architekten; Hugo Borger) • "Stimmen zum Kölner Museumsbau," in: *Kunstchronik* 40/1987, pp. 293-329 (Judith Breuer, Christoph Bellot, Wolfgang Augustyn) and pp. 497-503 (Hugo Borger) • *Werk, Bauen und Wohnen* 4/1988, pp. 11-13 (Klaus-Dieter Weiss)

Allégret, vol. 2, pp. 82-89 • Montaner, pp. 50-57 • Schilgen, pp. 136-157 • Schubert, pp. 173-177

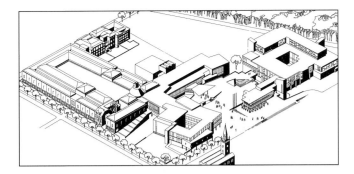

Bird's eye view of the entire Kulturforum complex

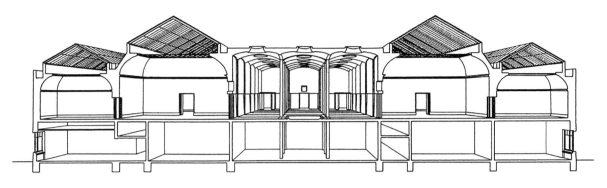

Cross section

from left to right
View of the exterior | The large octogonal exhibition room |
Central columned hall | Glazed dome of the entrance rotunda |
Corner pavilion 'slid into' an exhibition room

Gemäldegalerie

Berlin-Tiergarten, Germany

Client	Staatliche Museen zu Berlin – Preußischer Kulturbesitz
Architects	Heinz Hilmer and Christoph Sattler, Munich
Enclosed space	152,000 m³
Total area	24,000 m²
Exhibition area	7,000 m²
Picture-hanging walls	2,200 running meters
Construction time	1991-1997 (restricted, two-stage competition 1986/87)

When Hilmer & Sattler took over building the Kulturforum that was originally planned in the sixties and in the intervening time had become the object of virulent criticism, they replaced the originally planned idea of a "Stadtlandschaft" with a design for a closed urban space. Its cornice height and alignment matching those of two old buildings that had been conserved, the block-like volume of the Gemäldegalerie forms the conclusion of the Kulturforum on two westwardly directed streets. Its upper storey clad with terracotta slabs and, bay by bay, enclosed by yoke-like steel frames above an allusively rusticated granite plinth, the modest building cites the instruments of classical palace architecture, but is also reminiscent of Schinkel and Stüler, as well as Mies van der Rohe,

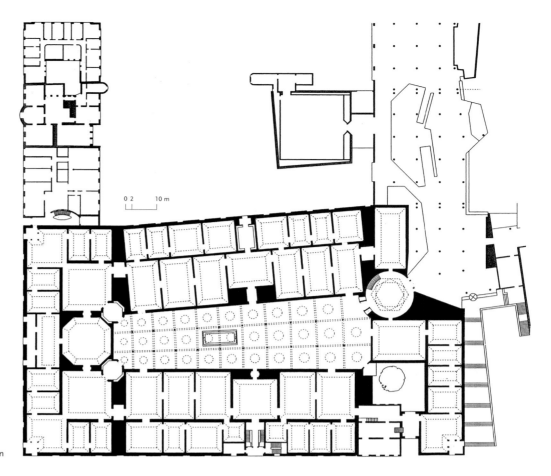

Ground plan

but it does not compete at all with the latter's Nationalgalerie next to it. Berlin's Gemäldegalerie combines the atrium building type with the ground plan structure of Leo von Klenze's Alte Pinakothek in Munich, a sequence of interconnected, toplit rooms, each also directly accessible from a loggia, and each with additional cabinets. Repeating this scheme, a double ring of exhibition rooms of different sizes is laid out around an enormous hall of columns effectively lit by round skylights in the Welsh vaults. Instead of a courtyard, it is this that does duty as an orientation and communication centre. With three naves and conically narrowing, this circulation hall is accessed by a rotunda that sets accents as leitmotifs. In accordance with its function – the articulation between the entrance area

and the exhibition rooms – the cupola construction of glass hexagons stacked inside and on top of each other formulates light as the theme and mission of the building. Housing one of the most important collections of European painting (13th – 18th century), the exhibition rooms – numbering more than fifty – are all on a single level and either six or nine meters in height. They are designed more to be walked around rather than to be paced out, and they are laid out in such a way that there is never more than an enfilade of four rooms. They are lighted exclusively by daylight from every direction, filtered many times over by enormous slightly inclined glass roofs and evenly disseminated in the exhibition rooms by deep coving. With dark oak floors, walls divided in three with textile-

covered coloured hanging surfaces, the design of the rooms evokes the atmosphere of a classical nineteenth-century picture gallery, but above all provides for optimum presentation of the pictures, for it is on them that the whole abundance of light is concentrated.

Lotus international 55/1988, pp. 69-83 (Hilde Leon) • Michael Zimmermann, "Der Neubau von Hilmer & Sattler für die Gemäldegalerie", in: Berlins Museen. Geschichte und Zukunft, ed. Zentralinstitut für Kunstgeschichte München, Munich/Berlin, 1994, pp. 307-309 • Bauwelt 25/1998, pp. 1464-1467 (Peter Rumpf) • Staatliche Museen zu Berlin – Preußischer Kulturbesitz (ed.), Gemäldegalerie Berlin. Der Neubau am Kulturforum, Berlin, 1998 • Hilmer & Sattler. Bauten und Projekte, Stuttgart/ London, 2000, pp. 162-171 • Falk Jaeger, Architektur für das neue Jahrtausend. Baukunst der neunziger Jahre in Berlin, Stuttgart/ Munich, 2001, pp. 95-97

Maier-Solgk, pp. 49-54 • Peressut, pp. 184-189

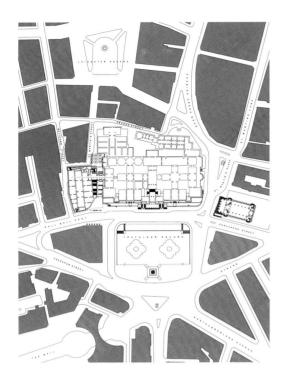

Site plan

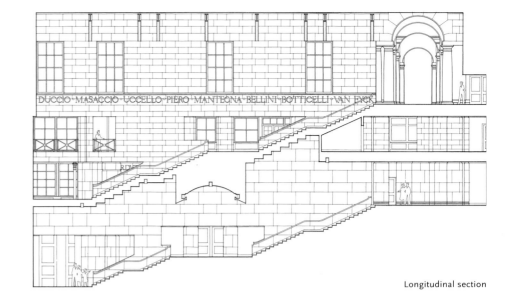

Longitudinal section

from left to right
Jubilee Walk between the old building and the Sainsbury Wing |
Façade facing Trafalgar Square | The great stairway | Galleries,
first axis, view from the topmost stair landing perpendicular to
the main direction | Galleries, central axis

National Gallery Sainsbury Wing

London, UK

Client	National Gallery Services Ltd.
Architects	Robert Venturi, Denise Scott Brown and Associates, Philadelphia
Total area	15,810 m³
Exhibition area	4,180 m²
Construction time	1988-1991 (invited competition 1985)

It was above all the external appearance of the Sainsbury wing (named after the donors) of the National Gallery in the centre of London that triggered off the most vehement controversies. The building – in which the new main entrance to the entire museum is located in addition to the galleries for one of the most important collections of early Renaissance paintings – is endowed with four different façades; in a continuing formal transformation, each one is a variation on its neighbour. Thus the façade facing Trafalgar Square takes up the neoclassical language of the old building designed by William Wilkins in 1838, but forms the Corinthian pilasters into a new, irregular rhythm, increasingly losing plasticity (legible in the blind windows and

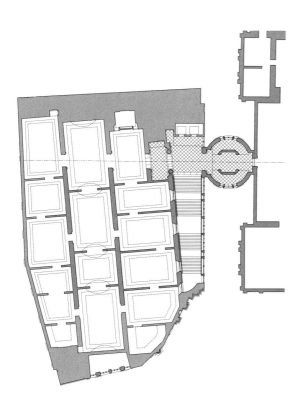

Cross section

0 1   5m

Ground plan of the gallery level (second floor)

the moulding breaking off) and, moreover, torn open by large, frameless entrance hollows. Like the glass wall facing the old building and attached directly to the pilaster façade – whose lack of structural relationship to the interior it thus reveals – the hollows thematize the idea – developed by Venturi in his influential 1966 book *Complexity and Contradiction in Architecture* – that contrary to the dogma of modernism, exterior and interior do not have to correspond to each other at all, because architecture is the object of a complex and contradictory reality and perception.

Behind the glass wall and thus half outside space, half inside space, a stairway widening conically (and

thus citing in reverse Bernini's Scala Regia in the Vatican) leads to the gallery rooms on the second floor. Here, in the connecting axis to the old building, visitors are treated to a magnificent enfilade, which is continued in the dominant central axis of the exhibition rooms. This axis running almost perpendicular to the connecting axis is laid out clearly but not monotonously in three rows. Classical but nevertheless recognizably alienated elements in pietra serena suggest the illusion of Italian Renaissance rooms. However, a glance into the lantern lights filtering the daylight through matt glass panes reveals them to be deliberate quotations of Sir John Soane's Dulwich Picture Gallery: a solution which is anything but simple for the ambivalent task of the museum, which is

to create an aesthetic ambience adequate to the work of art without cancelling out the historical distance.

The National Gallery (Architectural Design Profile 63), London, 1986 • *Domus* 684/1987, pp. 25-31 (Stanislaus von Moos) • *Archithese* 17.6/1987, pp. 49-62 (Peter Blundell Jones) • *Lotus International* 55/1987, pp. 84-117 (Janet Y. Abrams) and 72/1992, pp. 71-89 (Robert Venturi) • *Bauwelt* 37/1991, 1988-1997 (Peter Buchanan) • *Architectural Design* 11-12/1991, pp. 16-19 (Geoffrey Baker) • *The Architectural Review* 1133/1991, pp. 30-36 (Rowan Moore) • *Zodiac* 6/1991, pp. 116-135 (Robert Venturi) • Colin Amery, A Celebration of Art and Architecture. The National Gallery Sainsbury Wing, London, 1991 • *Architecture and Urbanism* 260/1992, pp. 10-49 (Marc Linder) • Carolina Vaccaro/Frederic Schwartz, Venturi, Scott Brown und Partner, Zürich/Munich/London, 1992, pp. 164-169

Muso d'arte e architettura, pp. 110-117 • Newhouse, pp. 182-185 • Peressut, pp. 54-63 • Steele, pp. 246-249 • Tzonis/Lefaivre, pp. 272-275

Matrix-like Arrangement of Rooms

The term "matrix" used in biology to designate topsoil, and in connection with physics, referring to the simultaneous control of different parameters and finally, in mathematics, designating a particular scheme of figures and other quantities, here stands for the overlapping and ambiguity of spatial structures. Exhibition rooms are linked to each other in such a way that visitors are no longer conducted by a single route associated with auxiliary routes, but instead they are always offered a number of equal alternatives for continuing on their way. Beginning with the relatively simple spatial structure of the Kunstsammlung Nordrhein-Westfalen in Düsseldorf, which in many respects still exhibit the traits of a "directed sequence of rooms," the complexity of the spatial connections increases in the subsequent examples and in the end, does not remain limited in each case to one level (particularly in Hans Hollein's museums) but extends to the vertical interlinking of levels staggered in counterpoint to each other by means of an almost extravagant use of ramps and stairways.

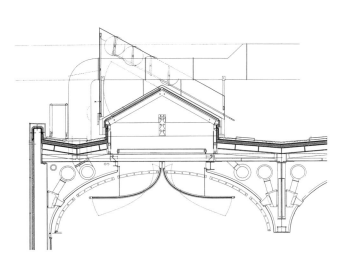

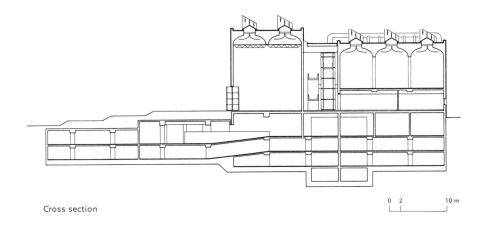

Cross section

0 2   10 m

Lighting technology construction

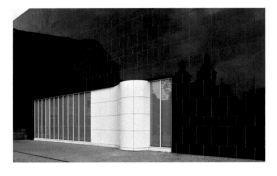

from left to right
The sculptural, curving form of the main façade, repeated
in miniature, gives no hint that it conceals an orthogonal
spatial structure behind it | Stairway| Triple-axis exhibition
room on the first floor | Exhibition room on the second floor;
as a module, the band of lighting determines its width

Kunstsammlung Nordrhein-Westfalen

Düsseldorf, Germany

Client	State of North-Rhine/Westphalia
Architects	Hans Dissing and Otto Weitling, Copenhagen
Enclosed space	125,000 m³ (incl. underground garage)
Net floor area	6,259 m²
Exhibition area	3,200 m²
Construction time	1979-1985 (competition 1975)

This collection of modern painting, extant since 1960
and one of the most exquisite of its kind, acquired a
fitting domicile in this new building. The building by
the Danes Hans Dissing and Otto Weitling, who were
students of Arne Jacobsen, is characterized by solid
nobility and a high degree of functionality. The extended layout and elegant, laterally curving façade of
weatherproof black granite from Bornholm, polished
mirror-smooth, not only gives the rather heterogeneous Grabbeplatz – whose disparate buildings cast
multi-faceted reflections on it – a properly urban setting, but also intimates the treasures hidden within
its hermetic secrecy. The interior, fully air-conditioned
in the collection area, is accessed by a rather too
casual entrance area and a narrow, but cleverly laid

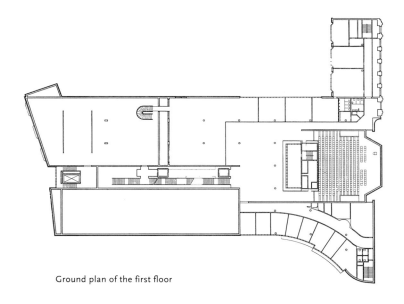

Ground plan of the first floor

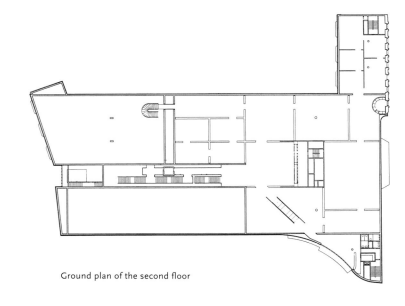

Ground plan of the second floor

out and very detailed, carefully worked out cream-coloured staircase with two glass lift shafts and three stairways staggered in parallel. The collection rooms of varying sizes, organized by an orthogonal structure, are interlinked by openings arranged in enfilade but without any kind of framing to emphasize them. Sometimes they offer only one way of circulating, sometimes two. These rooms are lighted by daylight from above, with the exception of several rooms in the annexe for the collection of small pictures by Paul Klee. This very significant requirement induced the architects to plan the building from top to bottom so to speak, and to extend the exhibition rooms of varying heights to the roof. Thus the circular tour of the museum (which does not in fact prescribe a

necessary sequence of rooms) descends from the smaller gallery rooms on the third floor via a sculptural stairway to the larger room for post-war art two storeys high, down to the enormous 12-metre-high room for temporary exhibitions. The rooms are lit by transparent reflecting screens of matt acrylic glass which, as bands of skylights all running in the same direction together with their concave longitudinal beams, form an elegant double curve coming to a pointed end in the ridge line. These bands of light – a refined structure first tried out in principle by Louis Kahn in the Kimbell Art Museum – also form the module whose multiplication results in the different dimensions of the museum rooms. Even though they are somewhat overemphasized from a decora-

tive perspective, these bands of light nonetheless generate an almost ideal illumination; the fact that the skylights are sheltered by shade constructions means that they let in not only northern light, but also a little southern light.

wettbewerbe aktuell 2/1976, pp. 83-100 • *Bauwelt* 19-20/1976, pp. 582-586 (competition) and 17/1986, pp. 620-626 (Peter Rumpf) • Ingeborg Flagge, Kunstsammlung NRW (Architektur in der Demokratie 2), Düsseldorf, 1986 • Manfred Sack/Dieter Leistner, Kunstsammlung Nordrhein-Westfalen Düsseldorf, Stuttgart, 1986 • *Techniques et Architecture* 386/1986, pp. 78-83 • *Architecture and Urbanism* 2/1987, pp. 19-40 • *Baumeister* 1/1987, pp. 44-51 • *Deutsche Bauzeitung* 1/1987, pp. 22-27 (Ingeborg Flagge)

Montaner, pp. 58-63 • Schilgen, pp. 106-121 • Schubert, pp. 169-171

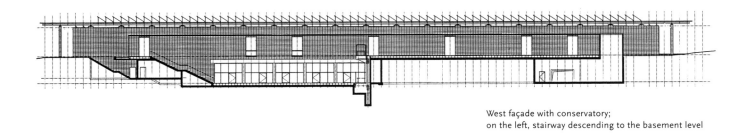

West façade with conservatory;
on the left, stairway descending to the basement level

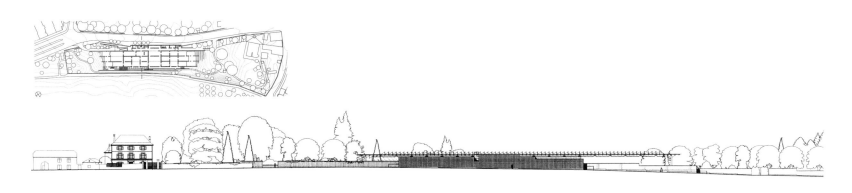

Site plan and general view of the complex from the east

from left to right
West façade, detail | General view from the west |
Entrance side on the south | Entrance side on the south:
temple-like façade and water-lily pool

Fondation Beyeler

Basel, Switzerland

Client	Beyeler Foundation, Riehen
Architect	Renzo Piano Building Workshop, Paris/Genoa
Enclosed space	42,800 m³
Total area	5,490 m²
Exhibition area	2,710 m²
Construction time	1994-1997; extension 2001 (planning commission 1991)

The museum that the Basel gallery owner Ernst Beyeler commissioned from Renzo Piano for his exquisite collection of modern art was to convey "luxe, calme et volupté." Beyeler had found Piano's building for the Menil Foundation in Houston particularly pleasing. Tranquillity as the opposite of the excited staging of architecture, luxury as high standards in materials and (invisible) technology, and finally, absolute delight as the harmony between the collection, the building, and the surroundings correspond to Piano's expectation of a museum building that seeks "to suggest the quality of the collection and its relation to the world outside."

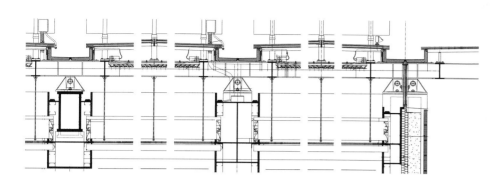

Cross section through the roof

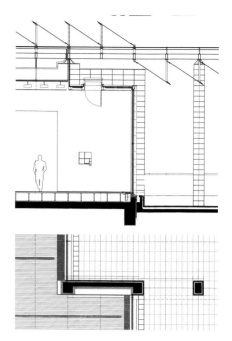

Detail of longitudinal section and ground plan
(temple-like façade in the water-lily pool)

The site in Riehen, a suburb of Basel, a long, narrow park with a baroque mansion, is enclosed by walls on its long sides separating it on the east from a heavily travelled road and on the west from open farmland. Piano takes these enclosure walls running north-south as the starting point of his planning. Four walls running parallel to them, each 130 meters in length, determine the five-naved basic structure based on a grid of 7.8 x 6 metres as well as the spatial concept of the museum. Only the outer walls are solid, while the inner walls are reinforced concrete supports clad with plasterboard, their hollow spaces containing the services. The walls clad with reddish Argentine porphyry – in homage to the red sandstone characteristic of the

buildings of the region but not very durable – are one of the two basic motifs that determine the appearance of the long, low building.

In calculated contrast to these walls that run out in the park – they have something ruinous about them and thus appear to be almost at one with the earth – the light roof of white-painted steel and glass, more than 5,000 square metres in size and projecting far out beyond the walls, seemingly hovering over the building – in the architect's words, like a "flying carpet" – forms the second basic motif of this architecture. This roof slab was developed in a long design process as an autonomous element supported by columns. It consists of four layers

lying one on top of the other; it also contains an air space functioning as heat buffer. Adjustable lamella as the lowest level filter the light, while the topmost level, a shed construction of tilted glass plates that only let in light to a certain extent serves for solar protection and distinctively defines the silhouette of the museum.

Access to the museum is on its narrow sides. While delivery and technical supply takes place on the north, the visitor entrance is located on the main façade to the south. The museum presents itself to the visitors who enter the site between the old villa (in which the administrative functions and the museum café are accommodated) and the new

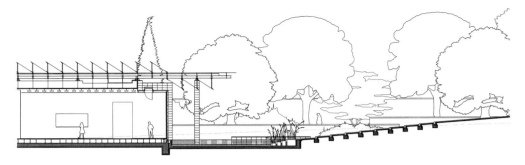

Longitudinal section (detail of the southern part)

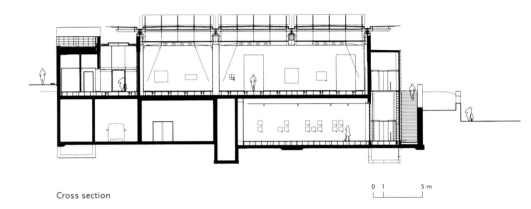

Cross section

0 1 5 m

from left to right
Giacometti room with view of the water-lily pool | Entrance
(in the eastern "aisle") | Exhibition room in the southern part
of the building | "American room" in the northern part of the
building | Exhibition rooms in the southern part of the building

museum as pavilion-like architecture, in front of
whose glass wall four slender porphyry pillars rise
out of a pond of water lilies to support the projecting glass roof that appears almost weightless. In
spite of the serene effortlessness of this staging, in
which Japanese architectural influences are just as
noticeable as that of Carlo Scarpa, the allusion to
the form of an ancient amphiprostyle nonetheless
remains recognizable, that form of classical temple
whose outer walls only have pillars on the narrow
sides: on the northern side too of the museum,
four free-standing columns support the projecting
roof. Thus Renzo Piano places his museum in an
architectural history context that includes both the
building type of the pavilion-like exhibition hall and

the temple motif signifying dignity that has been
established as an iconological constant in museum
architecture since Schinkel.

Visitors are led past one side of the water lily pond
and the temple front through a glass door into the
easternmost of the five naves that distinguish the
largely symmetrically laid out ground plan. This
narrow corridor – which allows a view through the
entire length of the building and thereby allows its
size to become perceptible – leads past cloakrooms
and counters to a forum that opens in the middle
of the museum. From here both the exhibition
rooms and a conservatory are accessed, the latter
located in the westernmost nave along with an

impressively staged stairway to the large underground media room. The three wider middle naves,
each open to the park by means of glass walls at
their ends, cannot be spatially experienced as such
because of the walls running crosswise. These are
laid out more or less symmetrically around the central forum to generate a matrix-like spatial structure; in it, never more than three exhibition rooms
are linked with each other in enfilade. The unobtru-
sive sequence of richly varied spatial relations thus
created, never appearing rigid, but never aleatory
either, corresponds to the unpretentious form of
the light, well-proportioned exhibition rooms bathed
in natural daylight by a glazed roof; their clarity is
not diminished at all by any disruptive details.

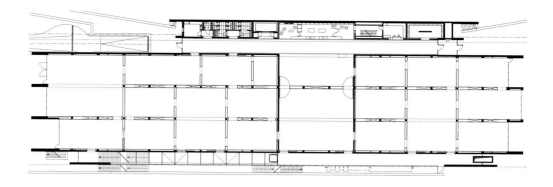

Ground floor plan

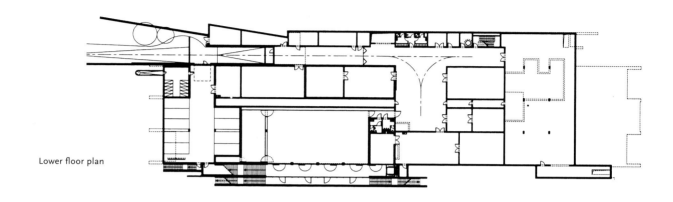

Lower floor plan

Peter Buchanan, Renzo Piano Building Workshop. Opere complete, vol. 2, Turin, 1996, pp. 170-179 • *The Architectural Review* 1210/1997, pp. 59-63 (Raymund Ryan) • *Bauwelt* 40/1997, pp. 2272-2279 (Reinhardt Stumm; Andrea Compagno) • *Deutsche Bauzeitung* 12/1997, pp. 18-20 (Holger Fischer) • *Domus* 798/1997, pp. 54-60 (Markus Brüderlin) • Renzo Piano, Mein Architektur-Logbuch, Ostfildern-Ruit, 1997, pp. 220-223 • *architektur aktuell* 213/1998, pp. 78-89 (Cornelia Fröschl) • *Baumeister* 2/1998, pp. 48-55 (S. Schneider) • Detail 3/1998, pp. 381-386 • *El Croquis* 92/1998, pp. 48-59 • *Werk, Bauen und Wohnen* 1-2/1998, pp. 24-29 (Ernst Hubeli) • Fondation Beyeler (ed.), Renzo Piano – Fondation Beyeler. A Home for Art, Basel/Boston/Berlin, 1998 (Werner Blaser/Lutz Windhöfer/Andrea Compagno/Roman Hollenstein/Jochen Wiede/Markus Brüderlin)

Lampugnani/Sachs, pp. 154-161 (Benedikt Loderer) • Mack, pp. 86-97 • Maier-Solgk, pp. 34-41 • Newhouse, pp. 23-26 • Peressut, pp. 222-229

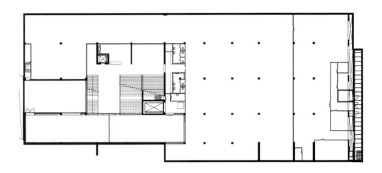

from left to right Ground plan of the lower floor | Ground floor | Upper floor

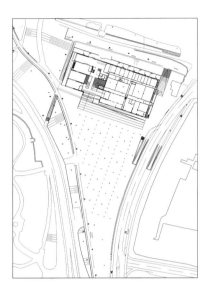

Site plan

Circular exhibition tour variants

from left to right
General view from the marketplace | Part of the main façade | Exhibition level | Stairway | Gallery facing the park on the exhibition level

Museum Het Valkhof

Nijmegen, Netherlands

Client	Museum Het Valkhof Foundation, Nijmegen
Architect	Ben van Berkel (UN studio van berkel & bos), Amsterdam
Enclosed space	39,382 m³
Net floor area	ca. 8,800 m²
Exhibition area	ca. 2,700 m²
Construction time	1996-1999 (competition 1995)

The Het Valkhof Museum, erected at the northern end of the triangular marketplace and parallel to the historic town wall, brings together different collections ranging from archaeology to the modern era. It is shaped in the form of a prism laid transversely over a lightly trapezoid ground plan. The 80-metre wide façade of pale green opaque glass leads visitors by means of a three-stage arrangement gradually developing from right to left and opening into transparent corners almost unnoticeably to the asymmetrically positioned entrance. In this way, the building reacts discreetly to the topographic situation, but as for the rest, avoids any historical references or symbolic gestures.

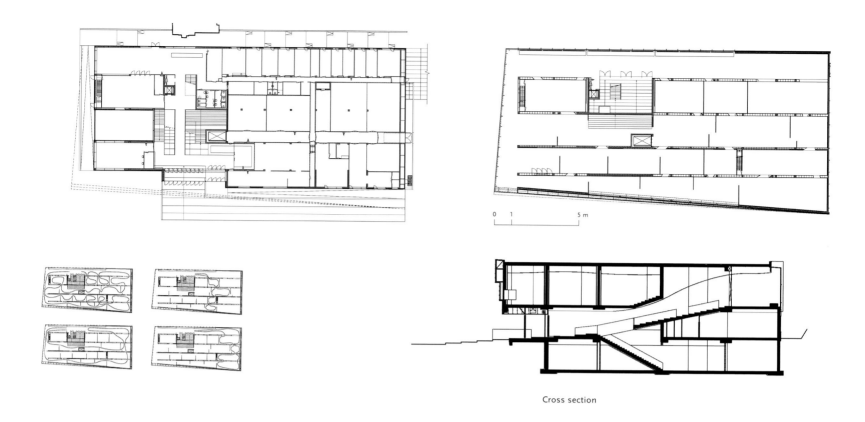

Cross section

The architect declares that his program is "to create all-inclusive spatial structures that unite construction, function, and visitor circulation into a whole." Correspondingly, the access, the building's structure, the organisation, the HVAC, and the lighting technology all determine the form of the museum to the same extent: from the entrance, one already has an overview of the functional structure of the important areas of the museum, accessible directly via the dominant stairway formation that serves statically as the stiffening core. In combination with the second principal element, which immediately catches the eye – an undulating ceiling extended across the whole building – visitors are almost literally drawn in a flowing movement upwards into the real exhibi-

tion level. Accessed via a gallery opening toward the city wall and taking in the entire length of the building, it is divided into five parallel 'streets' of varying widths. Numerous irregularly placed, diagonally cut wall openings repeatedly generating diagonal views prevent visitors becoming habituated in any way; they allow no less than 88 theoretically possible tours. The moment of movement implicit in the tours is brought into sensory focus in the undulating ceiling that optically summarizes the exhibition area, undulating more intensely at the points where the circulation flow is stronger than it does in quieter places. This moment of movement is what Ben van Berkel considers to be the central motif of his architecture. Discreetly shielded, but still quite visible

behind the suspended aluminium strips of this ceiling – which fulfils more than just an aesthetic function – is the entire technology, from the lighting to the HVAC system.

Caroline Bos (ed.), museum het valkhof, Amsterdam, 1999 • Architectural Review 3/2000, pp. 54-57 (Connie van Cleef) • architektur April 2000, pp. 44-49 • Bauwelt 2/2000, pp. 12-17 (Ludger Fischer) • Werk, Bauen und Wohnen 3/2000, pp. 30-37 (Hans Ibelings)

Trulove, pp. 86-91

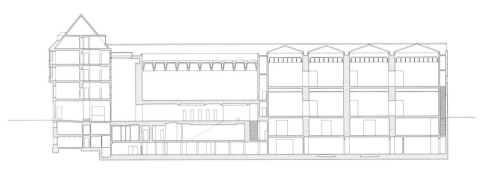

Longitudinal section

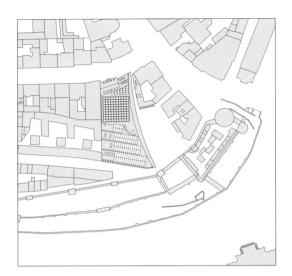

Site plan

from left to right
Library and administration building on the Luitpoldstraße |
Auxiliary building and main façade | The exhibition rooms on
the upper floor open balcony-like toward the glass wall | The
foyer with the spiral stairway to the exhibition levels

Neues Museum

Nuremberg, Germany

Client	Freistaat Bayern/Staatliches Hochbauamt Nürnberg I
Architect	Volker Staab, Berlin
Enclosed space	82,332 m³
Net floor area	7,097 m²
Exhibition area	2,897 m²
Construction time	1996-1999 (competition 1991)

A collection of art and design from post-war times to the present, and in addition, an institute for modern art and the Designforum Nürnberg were to be accommodated in a new building right next to the mediaeval city wall. On the narrow side where the main access is located, Volker Staab integrated a historicist residence building into an extension that takes up the material and arrangement of its surroundings without excessive deference. Behind these two buildings facing the street (for the library and the museum administration) the rest of the building volume is shifted to the western edge of the site, so that on the other side a new square is created between the city wall, the residences of well-to-do citizens, and the expansive museum façade.

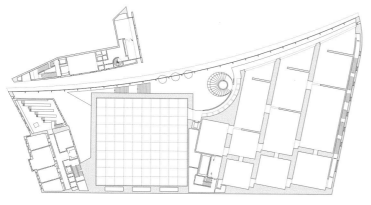

Mezzanine floor

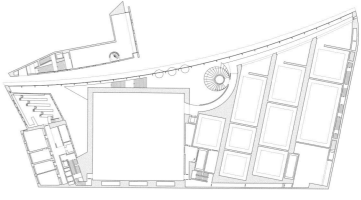

Upper floor

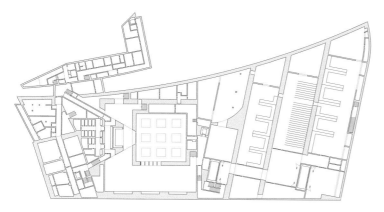

Ground plan of the lower floor

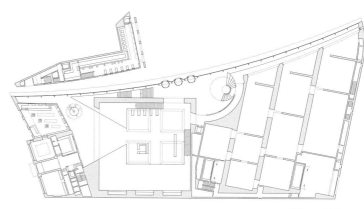

Ground floor

0 2   10 m

Placed in front of a backyard and separate from the rest of the museum, a strictly organized, angled wing for the Designforum and the museum café allows a narrow alley to come into being. Visitors are virtually sucked through it, along the curving concave glass wall terminating above in the sharp, protruding edge of a flat roof. At the point where the narrow passageway widens out to the square, three revolving doors lead into the museum.

In the interior, each building element corresponds to a different function which, according to the architect, becomes clear as by a "surgical incision": an inserted concrete cube surrounds the auditorium in the basement, the foyer on the lower ground floor,

and on the higher upper floor, a room lit from above, without columns, for temporary exhibitions. To the north, this cube opens via a conical footbridge into an atrium adjoining the library and administration buildings and thus becomes the exterior space in the interior of the museum. South of the cube, the foyer broadens out into a light and airy hall in which an elegantly formed spiral stairway accesses both exhibition levels that open like balconies into the glass wall. Rooms of varying sizes arranged in three parallel room sequences are interconnected with each other in a matrix – not only by means of passageways positioned in enfilade in the corners, but also via two diagonal passageways and view axes. On the upper floor, these rooms – whose white walls

ascend from the grey sandstone floor without baseboards – are naturally lit from above through a filigree ceiling grid, while below, spotlights illuminate the design objects.

wettbewerbe aktuell 1/1992, pp. 49-60 and 1/2000, pp. 91-96 • Ansichten zur Architektur – Neues Museum in Nürnberg, Ostfildern-Ruit, 2000 • *Bauwelt* 2/2000, pp. 18-23 (Nils Ballhausen) • *Detail* 1/2000, p. 35 and 2/2000, pp. 230-233

Jahrbuch 2000, pp. 128-133 (Karin Leydecker) • Herwig, p. 28-57 • Maier-Solgk, pp. 188-194

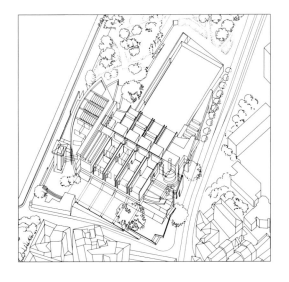

Axonometric projection of the site plan

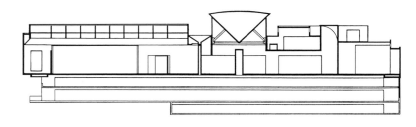

Cross section

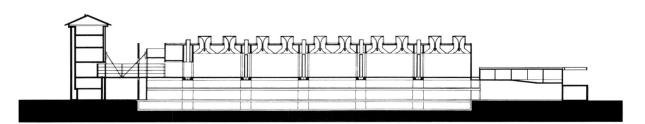

Longitudinal section through the main gallery

from left to right
Entrance side | Museum street | View from the atrium onto the museum street | Sculpture room in the northern part of the main gallery | Painting room in the main gallery | Museum street

Musée de Grenoble

Grenoble, France

Client	City of Grenoble
Architects	Groupe 6, Grenoble (Olivier Félix-Faure, Antoine Félix-Faure, Philippe Macary)
Net floor area	10,641 m²
Exhibition area	6,500 m²
Construction time	1990-1993 (two-stage invited competition 1985/87)

In addition to the requirements that the important collection of paintings and sculptures of the fifteenth to the twentieth century be presented chronologically and that a department of antiques be accommodated, the architects also had to take into account the tower of a mediaeval fortress and on top of that, had to include a sports facility and an underground garage. They made use of this last requirement to raise the building, clad in white stone on the main show side above the street level, by means of an embankment covered with vegetation. A wide, gently rising stairway leads at that corner of the building that faces the city centre to the level of the museum, whose 65 gallery rooms are for the most part on one level.

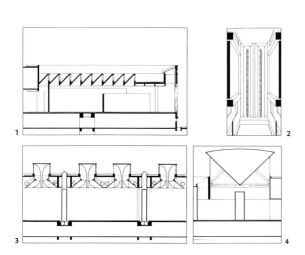

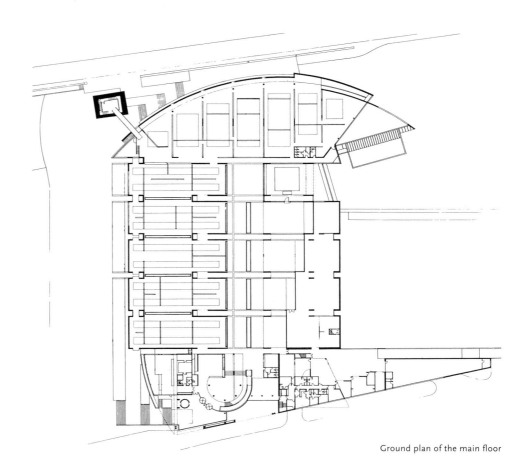

Lighting systems: **1** north light shed roofs in the Modern Department | **2+3** Lantern system in the main gallery | **4** Lighting of the museum street

Ground plan of the main floor

From the exterior, the museum – whose ground plan is composed of one square and two circular segments – appears as a flat, largely closed volume that is gently rounded on the northern side facing the River Isère and on the entrance side, is arranged as five blocks separated from each other by narrow light slits. These vertical wall openings that continue over glazed saddleback roofs into the interior of the building as space-forming tracks of light, not only contrast with the horizontals of the rhythmically drawn masonry, but also allow views into the interior of the building, thus recognisable as a museum.

It is accessed from the round atrium derived from classical modernism. To the right of it, one can gain

access to the antique department housed in the basement, while to the left, one can get to the cafeteria. Above all, though, one will be lead into the museum 'street' brightly lit from above. As the central orientation axis, it connects the museum's three main departments: to the left, the rooms for the permanent collection, lit by means of rooflights through double metal reflectors with subdued light from above but on the perimeters also lit from the side; to the right of this passage, the rooms for temporary exhibitions, and, at its end, the rooms for modern art lit with northern light via sawtooth roofs. This way a double circular tour through the museum is achieved allowing visitors to be as leisurely as they wish or to reach every room without going a step out of their way.

Techniques et Architecture 387/1990, pp. 98-101 • *Techniques et Architecture* 408/1993, pp. 24-32 • France musées récents (le moniteur architecture amc), Paris, 1999, pp. 90-95

Maier-Solgk, pp. 118-123 • Räume für Kunst, pp. 30-31

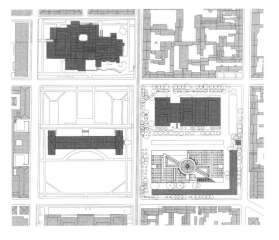

Site plan that shows the containment of the Pinakothek by a slender, L-shaped volume planned as the second building phase

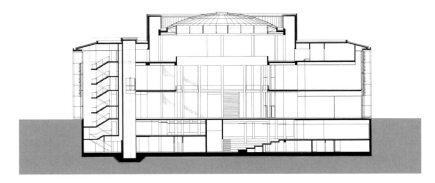

Cross section north-south

Longitudinal section, east-west

from left to right
General view from the north | View of the Alte Pinakothek through the entrance loggia | The diagonal stairway leads in the form of a wedge from two sides to the central rotunda linking three levels | The central rotunda, embraced by a spatial shell is the starting and ending point of all circuits | The exhibition rooms on the upper floor are interconnected by room-height openings alternately diagonally and in enfilade

Pinakothek der Moderne

Munich, Germany

Client	Freistaat Bayern
Architect	Stephan Braunfels, Munich
Enclosed space	258.527 m³
Total floor area	33.284 m²
Exhibition area	12.000 m²
Construction time	1996-2002 (competition 1992)

Two incunabula of museum architecture – the concrete presence of Klenze's Alte Pinakothek and the central rotunda motif historically determined by Schinkel's Altes Museum – characterize the basic structure of Munich's third Pinakothek in different ways. Braunfels shifts his own building – which houses four heterogenous collections – so close to the edge of the site between the city centre and the two older Pinakotheks that a perspectival axis to Klenze's museum comes into being. Its height is deliberately constrained, moreover, by partially sinking the enormous volume of the new building so that it does not rise above Klenzes's building. The second essential motif, the diagonal running through the building, results from the anchoring of the new museum in its

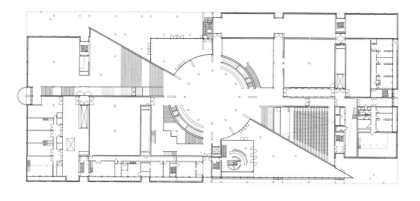

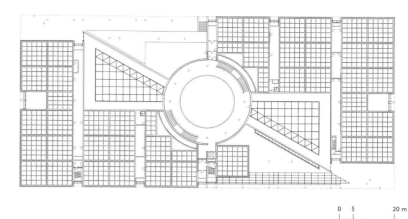

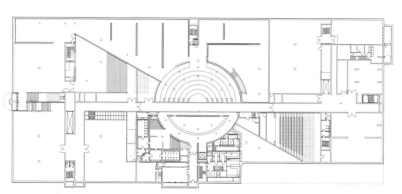

0   5   20 m

from bottom left, clockwise to above right
Lower floor (first level) | Ground floor| Gallery rotunda

urban context and the opening on both sides that this requires. Lending the building, the unpretentious exterior of which has been executed in exposed concrete, its inner tension, this motif, in combination with the central rotunda, also determines the circulation and in so doing, the organisation of the various museum areas.

It is not least the structure of the building, on the whole developed on a foundational square grid – undogmatically developed at all levels, yet recognizably square – that determines the imposing funnel-form of the diagonally placed stairway, 100 metres long, rising over a height of 12 metres and linking the three main levels of the museum uninterruptedly. Below a huge domed roof light, the stairway's two wedges meet in the rotunda (34 metres in diameter) which is also the starting point and finishing point of all other routes. The stairs integrated into the rotunda's double skin not only reveal exciting, continuously changing perspectives, but above all, enable the spatial matrix of a variety of short cuts and combinations of tours through the almost innumerable exhibition rooms, which as large squares or double squares of different sizes are variously accessed by means of median or diagonal axes. In the rooms rigorously devoid of all technical apparatus (although they nevertheless contain concealed high calibre HVAC, security and lighting technology), whose dazzlingly white walls rise plinthless from behind sunken ventilation grilles out of the grey terrazzo floor, ingen-

iously combined light coming through deep, square ceiling coffers creates objectively ideal presentation conditions – a situation to which not all works of art – nor indeed all visitors – will be equal.

wettbewerbe aktuell 7/1992, pp. 27-44 • *Bauwelt* 22/1992, pp. 1198-1199 (Gerhard Matzig) and 22/2002, pp. 26-33 (Martina Düttmann) • *Architectural Record* 10/1997, p. 37 (Claudine Weber-Hof) • *architektur aktuell* 9/2002, pp. 80-93 (Jean Stock) • *Deutsche Bauzeitschrift* 7/2002, pp. 18-19 • *Domus* 853/2002, pp. 14-17 (Deyan Sudjic) • *Museumsjournal* 11/2002, pp. 26-29 (Corinna Lotz) • Stephan Braunfels – Pinakothek der Moderne. Art, Architecture, Design (Stephan Braunfels, Michael Mönninger, Winfried Nerdinger), Basel/Berlin/Boston, 2002 • Gottfried Knapp, Stephan Braunfels. Pinakothek der Moderne München, Munich/Berlin/London/New York, 2002 • Oliver Herwig, Pinakothek der Moderne München (*Die Neuen Architekturführer* No. 40), Berlin 2002

Site plan

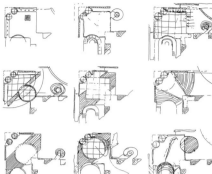

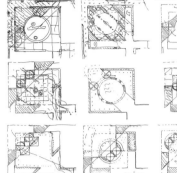

Sketches:
Variations on the design of the exhibition rooms | Entrance situation | Circulation at the main entrance

from left to right
External view from the south (from the Bundeskunsthalle) | External view from the northeast (from the street) | Inner courtyard to the north; on the right, the administration wing | South side; on the left, the glass walls of the exhibition rooms

Kunstmuseum

Bonn, Germany

Client	City of Bonn
Architect	Axel Schultes, Berlin
Enclosed space	110,000 m³
Total floor area	12,000 m²
Exhibition area	4,700 m²
Construction time	1988-1992 (competition 1985 and 1986)

"Inventing 'city' – in this case, 'art city' – in the no-man's-land somewhere between Bonn and Bad Godesberg," was the way Axel Schultes described the problem of designing his museum building. The architect reacted to the position of the site on a four-lane road in a boring and faceless development at the edge of Bonn's government quarter (which had never been properly developed) by rigorously cutting it off. On three sides, his volume executed in exposed concrete (and subsequently brightened up by glazing) is stereometrically and austerely closed. It is only on the fourth side that it demonstratively opens up to the Bundeskunsthalle that Schultes had conceived with the Kunstmuseum as a closed museum area. However, after an additional competition,

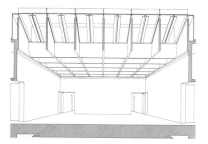

Exhibition room on the upper floor:
Section through the "troughs"

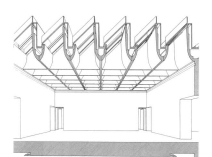

Exhibition room on the upper floor:
Section through the "crosspieces"

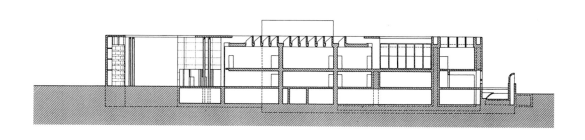

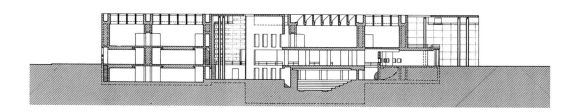

Sections

it was Gustav Peichl's design that was chosen for the Bundeskunsthalle, (see page 192-193), and it only took up Schultes' idea of the "city within a city" to a very limited extent.

A smooth wall, broken through only in sections by severely drawn window openings, concludes the museum to the north and toward the road to the east. It is only at a second glance that it becomes clear that not all of the 13-metre high wall is part of the museum building, but instead, it goes beyond this to become a kind of city wall – partially cut open at its full height – behind which there is a courtyard bounded on the other side by the real museum façade, now no longer hermetically closed

but instead at least in part invitingly opened. One does not realize until one passes through the outer wall that on its inner side there is a narrow building wing (destined for the administration) whose roof is carried beyond the wall opening, so that the 'city wall' eventually turns into an integral part of a stereometric whole again. As a bounded area, this formal dialectic – from the perspective of content an apt and easily comprehensible metaphor for a museum – not only continues at the southern façade facing the Bundeskunsthalle, but instead becomes a virtuoso interplay of geometric volumes and elementary tectonic motives, in which architecture thematizes itself. Slender columns that only seem to be placed without any rhyme or rhythm and the elegantly curv-

ing roof show that architectural design includes not only tectonic weight and static austerity but also graceful lightness and dynamic movement.

The basic structure of this museum building is developed out of the elementary geometric figures of the square and the circle that interpenetrate each other several times and in so doing, generate a complex figuration. The starting point is the basic square of 93 metres per side that is divided by a diagonal into two triangles. While one of these two triangles contains only the entrance area and the administration wing, the rest of it remaining open to a large extent, in the second are located the square or rectangular exhibition rooms, whose

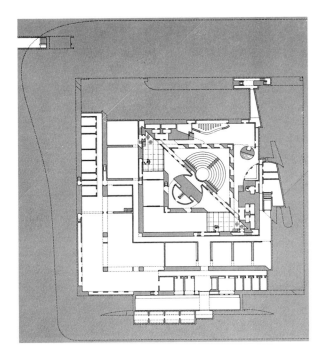

Ground plan of the lower floor

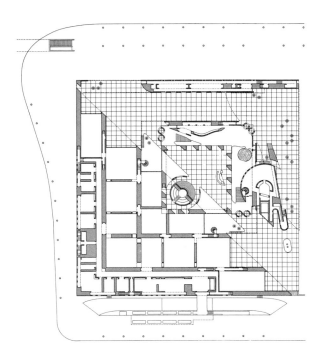

Ground floor plan

positioning and varying sizes are generated by a concentric reduction of the original square at varying intervals.

Situating the access between the individual rooms in their corners not only produces the largest possible expanses of hanging areas, but above all, results in exciting diagonal view axes that often open onto the room-height glass walls, which in turn open the outermost rooms of the three directed sequences of exhibition rooms arranged at angles to each other to the courtyard. Apart from these rooms with lateral light, the remaining rooms on the lower floor are illuminated by artificial light while on the upper floor, evenly distributed, shadow-free daylight

comes in through square cassettes formed of cross-pieces and troughs.

However, the architectural core in all the senses of the word is the stairway laid out in the form of a double cone in the centre of the building. Accompanied by a correspondingly dramatic staging of light, visitors are almost literally drawn up its steps, at first convex and then concave. This central rotunda – a motif repeatedly taken up and varied in museum architecture – is accommodated in the corner of a cubic volume whose ground plan outline is precisely developed from the total structure, appearing to shift itself out of the museum forecourt and into the collection wing, thereby endowing the building with

additional complexity and tension. On the lower floor it contains a lecture hall laid out like an arena, on the ground floor, the spacious foyer and on the upper floor, exhibition rooms, whose position shifts the rotunda to the centre visually as well. From here, a multitude of views both inward and outward are opened; as a constant puzzle play between inside and outside, once again it makes architecture itself into an exhibition object before it discreetly withdraws itself in the exhibition rooms and enables a presentation of the collections – pictures and drawings of the Rheinischer Expressionism around August Macke as well as contemporary works by German artists – as unpretentious as it is generous.

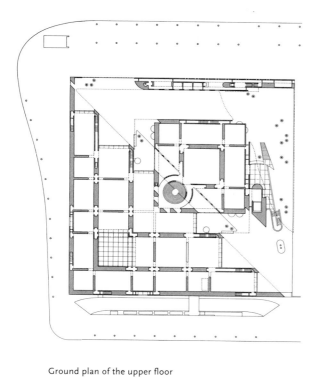

Ground plan of the upper floor

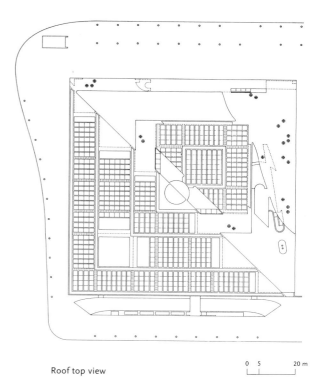

Roof top view

0　5　20 m

from left to right
Central stairway (with a sculpture by Markus Lüpertz) |
Exhibition rooms on the upper floor | Auditorium

wettbewerbe aktuell, 5/1985, pp. 251-270 and 7/1992, pp. 89-
100 • *Baumeister* 8/1985, pp. 17-21 • *Baumeister* 9/1992, pp.
16-21 (Wolfgang Bachmann) • *Bauwelt* 26/1992, pp. 1518-
1527 • Ingeborg Flagge, Kunstmuseum Bonn, Bonn, 1992 •
Deutsche Bauzeitung 4/1993, pp. 40-49 (Ingeborg Flagge) •
Techniques et Architecture 408/1993, pp. 60-65 • Charlotte
Frank (ed.), Axel Schultes. Kunstmuseum Bonn, Berlin, 1994
• Friedbert Kind-Barkauskas/Bruno Kauhsen/Stefan Polónyi/
Jörg Brandt, Concrete Construction Manual, 2nd ed. Basel/
Boston/Berlin, 2002, pp. 206-209

Maier-Solgk, pp. 80-89

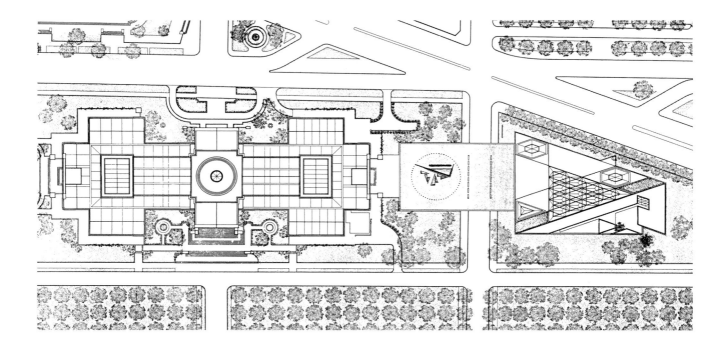

Site plan

National Gallery of Art, East Wing

Washington D.C., USA

Client	Trustees of the National Gallery of Art, Washington DC
Architect	Ieoh Ming Pei & Partners, New York
Total area	56,200 m²
Construction time	1971-1978 (commissioned in 1968)

The extension of the neo-classicist building designed by John Russell Pope and opened in 1941 as the National Gallery was significantly determined by the trapezoid form of the site provided for it (an extension had been intended from the outset) separated from the main building by a street running along its narrow eastern side. I.M. Pei developed a modular triangular structure out of the asymmetric trapezium and the plan of taking up and continuing the longitudinal axis of the old building's double axis. This modular structure determines the building in terms of leitmotif and detail. Thus the entire complex is organized as a large isosceles triangle and a somewhat smaller right-angled triangle whose longer side is aligned with the main building. This division

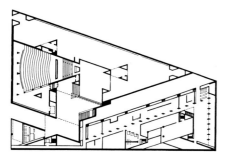
Level 1 (atrium)

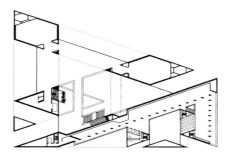
Level 4 (main gallery)

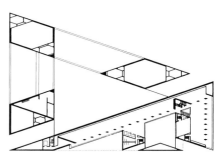
Level 6

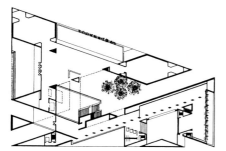
Level 0

Level 2 (mezzanine)

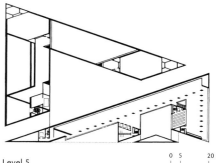
Level 5

0   5   20 m

Ground plan of 6 levels of the East Wing

from left to right
The aerial view with the Capitol in the background shows how the structure of the building is integrated into the geometry of the city's layout | The entrance side of the east wing facing the old building | The light-flooded atrium in whose form the modular structure of the building is legible | One of the hexagonal exhibition rooms on the top floor

of the plot of land into two complementary triangles reflects the different uses to which they are put. While the smaller, eight-storey building segment accommodates the administrative functions and a study centre for visual arts, the larger one serves as an exhibition wing. A 16,000 square metre atrium, also triangular, roofed over with a glazed lattice of tetrahedrons, not only links the two parts, but also serves as access and orientation space for the entire museum. Because its alignment cuts the ground plan of the striking corner towers out of the complex as a whole, the dimensions of this inner courtyard also determine the vertical structure and in so doing, the sharp-edged external form of this pink marble-clad architecture, which presents a self-

assured counterpoint to the old building, with which it is connected by an underground passageway.

The towers in the corners of the large triangle house the majority of the exhibition rooms. Those on the uppermost floors and the galleries in the wing between are lit by natural light from above. The implementation of a largely six-cornered ground plan for the exhibition rooms – developed through the consistent use of the modular structure – means that not only are sharp angles unsuitable for exhibition purposes avoided, but also that surprising spatial experiences and a variety of spatial connections are created. Again and again these lead back to the light-flooded 18-metre high atrium spanned by cat-

walks and footbridges. It is not least this atrium's communicative qualities that bring to expression a significant aspect of today's museum design.

Baumeister 4/1976, pp. 306-307 • *Architectural Record* 8/1978, pp. 79-92 (William Marlin) • *werk.archithese* 25-26/1979, pp. 33-36 (Werner Oechslin) • *Progressive Architecture* 10/1978, pp. 49-59 and 8/1983, pp. 76-79 • *The Architectural Review* 983/1979, pp. 22-31 (Colin Amery) • *Casabella* 43/1979, pp. 34-37 (Nico Calavita) • *Techniques et Architecture* 326/1979, pp. 56-57 • Bruno Suner, Ieoh Ming Pei, Basel/Boston/Berlin, 1989, pp. 92-103 • Carter Wiseman, I.M.Pei. A Profile in American Architecture, 2nd ed. New York, 2001, pp. 155-183

Montaner/Oliveras, pp. 54-57 • Tzonis/Lefaivre/Diamond, pp. 174-175

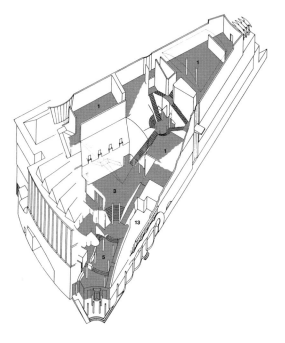

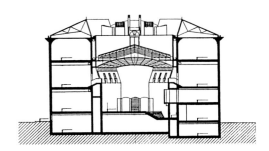

Cross section

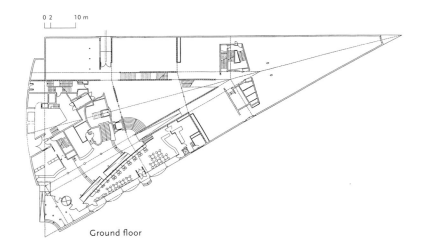

Ground floor

Isometric projection of exhibition rooms:
access system

from left to right
View of the eastern corner from the north | View from the
southwest (with the main entrance) | Central hall | Stairway:
view down from the second floor to the west | View through
the central stairway area to the north (first floor)

Museum für
Moderne Kunst

Frankfurt on Main, Germany

Client	City of Frankfurt on Main
Architect	Hans Hollein, Vienna
Enclosed space	50,530 m³
Net floor area	9,100 m²
Exhibition area	4,150 m²
Construction time	1987-1991 (competition 1982)

Hans Hollein's museum building fills its site, a plot
of land in the form of an extended right-angled triangle at the edge of Frankfurt's old city, right up to
the very edge of the road. The form that thus came
into being, referred to as the 'slice of pie,' allows
the volume to appear as a solitaire, although it does
refer to its surroundings through its use of light
coloured plaster and red sandstone. The monolithic-
seeming block, whose façades consist of an interplay between large, closed areas and decorative,
convex and concave fanned out window openings,
concludes at its sharp angle as a stepped sculpture.
In combination with the carefully arranged structures on the roof, it evokes associations with the
steamship motif (important in recent architectural

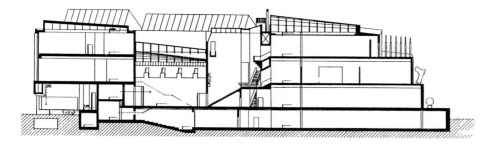

Longitudinal section

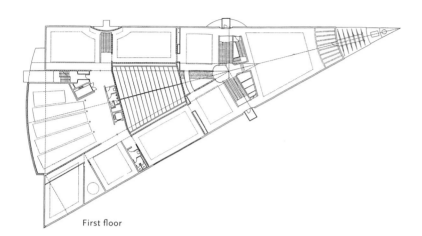

First floor

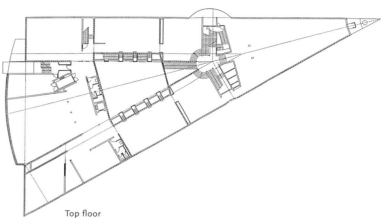

Top floor

history) that is used as an ambiguous symbol. The main entrance is not located in the middle of the largely symmetrically designed narrow side as the large flattened arch under the projecting window front seems to suggest, but instead, to the right of it, at the corner of the building, thus creating a connection – sensible from an urban planning perspective – to the historical city centre and to the cathedral. Above all, though, this way, the diagonal for accessing the building is introduced, from which the entire tension of the internal spatial structure derives.

By inscribing another triangle for the three-storey building onto the triangular ground plan, a symmetric structure was created, whose apparent clarity is overlaid and deliberately disrupted by a masterly system of stairways, ramps, bridges, and galleries that render each of the museum's rooms accessible in at least two ways. According to his maxim that there is "no neutral space, but only characteristic spaces of different sizes," Hollein grouped the exhibition rooms in a refined interplay of toplight, lateral light and artificial light around the central trapezoid-shaped hall with a glass roof, its walls studded with balconies slanting outwards in the upper third of the room, and the adjoining staircase. It is not only both the goal and starting point of the complex, three-dimensionally laid out circulation, but also celebrates architecture itself as a veritable spatial work of art.

wettbewerbe aktuell 8/1983, pp. 459-474 • *Baumeister* 8/1991, pp. 12-23 • *Bauwelt* 28/1991, pp. 1474-1483 (Peter Rumpf) • Connaissance des arts 473-474/1991, pp. 58-63 • *Domus* 731/1991, pp. 29-41 (Jean-Christophe Ammann/Joseph Rykwert) • *GA document* 31/1991, pp. 22-43 • Museum für Moderne Kunst Frankfurt am Main, ed. Magistrat der Stadt Frankfurt am Main, Frankfurt, 1991

Lampugnani, pp. 74-87 (Michael Mönninger) • Maier-Solgk, pp. 112-117 • Montaner/Oliveras, pp. 96-97 • Räume für Kunst, pp. 36-37

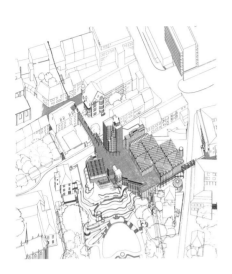

Isometric projection

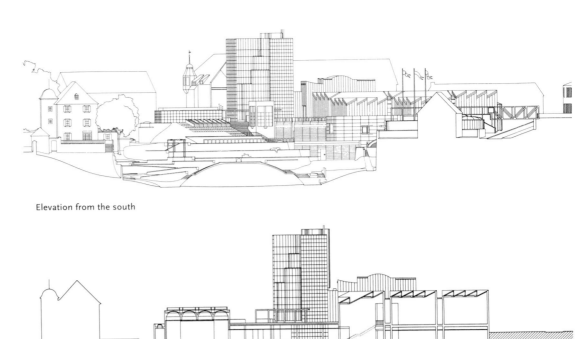

Elevation from the south

Section (west-east)

from left to right
View from the garden, in the foreground the little entrance temple | "Rice terraces" | Mirrored wall of the administration tower | Upper main floor with the overhanging cafe, whose panorama windows face the Propsteikirche | Square museum rooms clad with sheet zinc on the upper floor, seen from the terrace

Museum Abteiberg

Mönchengladbach, Germany

Client	City of Mönchengladbach
Architect	Hans Hollein, Vienna
Enclosed space	40,754 m³
Net floor area	6,000 m²
Exhibition area	3,500 m²
Construction time	1976-1982

There is probably no other museum building from the last decades that has been so unanimously praised by architecture critics as the Städtische Museum Abteiberg in Mönchengladbach, opened after ten years of planning and construction time on 23rd June 1982, the first large project realized by the Viennese architect Hans Hollein. It marks the beginning of the real boom in museum-building in Germany in the last quarter of the twentieth century and it has definitively established the museum as the preferred type of building commission there.

From a number of design variants developed by the architect commissioned by the museum director, Johannes Cladders – who did not invite competition

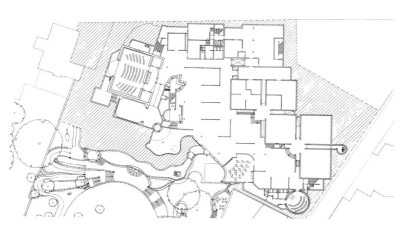

Ground plan of the lower main floor (Garden level)

Ground plan of the upper main floor (Abteistraße level)

0 5   20 m

submissions – was chosen the concept described as "rice terraces;" it reacts in a very original and at the same time very sensitive fashion to the topographical situation. Hollein used the hillside location of the building site on the southern outskirts of the city centre, next to the Romanesque-Gothic minster and the Baroque provost´s residence to stage a real architectural landscape that presents itself from the foot of the Abteiberg as a collage-like ensemble of heterogeneous components that looks like the silhouette of a town.

Above curving brick walls climbing in terraced forms that are as much part of the landscape as they are part of the architecture, on a roof plateau

accessible from the city via a footbridge, rises an exciting group of buildings executed in a great variety of materials. The highest one is the administration tower clad in sandstone from the Rhineland, broken open on the side facing the garden by a folded, crystalline mirrored glass wall; next to it is a low hall, also clad in sandstone, for temporary exhibitions. This presents a counterpoint to a group of square exhibition rooms with diagonal, sawtoothed shed roofs, whose lead-coloured zinc cladding provides an effective contrast to the costliness of the little entrance temple of dazzling white marble and shining stainless steel columns. This apparently unintentional ensemble – in fact artfully related by means of different alignments and perspectival axes

to the existing development – and not unjustifiably interpreted as the abbreviation of a city and its building types (occasionally ironically distanced) can be considered a virtual demonstration of that multifariousness aiming at manifold associations that has become a central idea in architecture as a protest against the monotony of our towns.

Largely hidden in the Abteiberg, the interior of the museum, into which one descends from the entrance temple as if into a secret cave, is not laid out as a consistent linear course, but instead as a three-dimensional matrix of varied spatial overlappings, entrances and views. Following two principal distribution zones opening toward the mountainside are

139

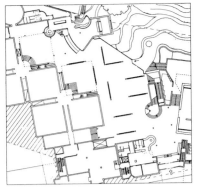
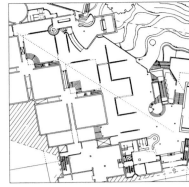

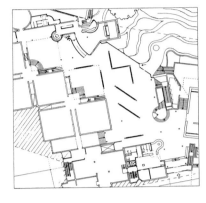
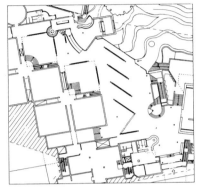
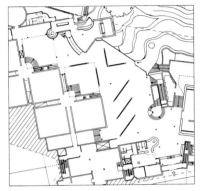
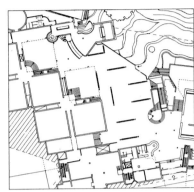

Possible arrangements for the moveable partition walls in the main museum levels

three floors, set counter to these zones at half-storey intervals and playfully connected with them by stairways, every one of them different. On these three levels are square exhibition rooms diagonally joined together on the cloverleaf principle and separated from each other by narrow inter-mediate zones where the supply systems and fire escapes are located. Corner access to these rooms presents an alternative to the principle of the enfilade usual in museum architecture since the nineteenth century – deriving from Baroque palace architecture – and repeatedly adopted since then. It also offers the enormous advantage of providing uninterrupted areas to hang pictures. This rational, geometric spatial organization is broken up by unexpectedly opening, freely

expanding organic spatial forms, so that in the interplay of spaciousness and intimacy, clarity and moments of disorientation, comes into being the flexibility that Hollein understands as "not mobility of walls and ceilings, but the provision of multi-layered situations." However, some spatial situations prove to be so specifically coordinated to certain objects – some of them unfortunately only temporary exhibits – that they could hardly be used adequately once the objects were removed.

The almost unsurpassable variety of lighting not only satisfies viewers' need for change very conveniently, but is also carefully based on the sophisticated spatial organisation. Natural lighting from the

side, light coming in through shed roofs or domed roof lights, artificial light from luminous ceilings, decorative spotlights, and fluorescent tubes arranged in geometric figures create a continually changing illumination that is sensitively based as much as the complex spatial organisation on Mönchengladbach's collection of contemporary art, and at the same time, avoids any monotony. The self-assured architect programmatically describes his museum designed with a virtually inexhaustible abundance – occasionally found too rich – as an "autonomous work of art for artworks and people."

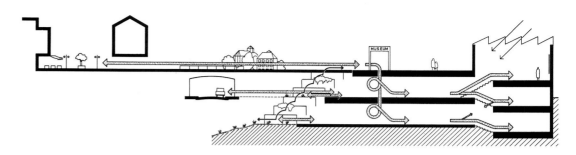

Circulation (schematic longitudinal section)

Exhibition room access

from left to right
View from the exhibition level on the upper main floor into the square exhibition rooms set at half-storey intervals | Square exhibition rooms, diagonally interlinked, on the top and bottom levels | Stairways as a multifarious, ever-recurring design element | The spatial layerings between the exhibition rooms serve alternately for the provision of light, for supply, or as connecting elements or fire escapes | Flowing exhibition space on the lower main floor

Baumeister 10/1982, pp. 965-975 • *Bauwelt* 30/1982, pp. 1192-1213 (Peter Rumpf) • *Deutsche Bauzeitung* 12/1982, pp. 40-50 (Gerhard Ullmann) • *Domus* 632/1982, pp. 2-17 (Joseph Rykwert) • Ekkehard Mai, "Städtisches Museum Abteiberg Mönchengladbach – Vom Luxus der Avantgarde: Architektur als Muse des Museums," in: *Museumskunde* 47/1982, pp. 150-159 • *The Architectural Review* 1030/1982, pp. 55-71 (Jonathan Glancey) • *Architectural Design* 7-8/ 1983, pp. 110-120 • *Baukultur* 5/1983, pp. 18-22 (Dagmar von Naredi-Rainer) • *L'architecture d'aujourd'hui* 225/1983, pp. 84-103 (P. Goulet) • *GA critique* 6/1983, pp. 34-53 (Riichi Miyake) • Heinrich Klotz, Die Revision der Moderne, Munich, 1984, pp. 104-109 • Hans Hollein (Architecture and Urbanism), Tokyo, 1985, pp. 66-91 and pp. 137-144 • Wolf-gang Pehnt, Hans Hollein. Museum in Mönchengladbach. Architektur als Collage, Frankfurt, 1986 • Johannes Cladders, "Eine gebaute Museumstheorie: das Museum Abteiberg Mönchengladbach," in: Luisa Lopez Mòreno/José Ramón

Lopez Rodríguez/Fernando Mendoza Castells (eds.), El Architecto y el Museo, Jerez, 1990, pp. 38-51 and pp. 367-371 • Steffen Krämer, Die postmoderne Architekturland-schaft. Museumsprojekte von James Stirling und Hans Hollein, Hildesheim/Zürich/New York, 1998

Allégret, Vol. 2, pp. 100-107 • Klotz/Krase, pp. 17-20 and pp. 91-103 • Montaner/Oliveras, pp. 90-95 • Schilgen, pp. 26-45 • Schubert, pp. 137-139

Spatial Interpenetration and Spatial Isolation

While the relationship of the rooms to each other and their spatial interconnection were the selection criteria in the first two parts of the project section, in the three following, the criterion is the quality of the spaces themselves. That pair of opposites, spatial interpenetration and spatial isolation, attempts to name a phenomenon that is associated with two important design principles of classical modernism: the concept of flowing space and the preference for pavilion-like structures. These two architectural phenomena are often combined, but they can also be mutually exclusive. Therefore we find very different buildings here, from the monumental solidity of Bielefeld's Kunsthalle, whose open exhibition levels can, however, also be regarded as classic examples of flowing spaces, to the staggered ensemble of Davos' Kirchner Museum, which consists of largely isolated pavilions. In the refined spatial structure of the Kunsthal in Rotterdam, the principle of flowing spaces is elevated to a complex interpenetration of spaces with spiral-form access, and in the layout of the Louisiana Museum – which has been repeatedly extended – we find individual pavilions connected by long passageways linked together into a unified whole composed of a number of rooms enclosing and interpenetrating each other.

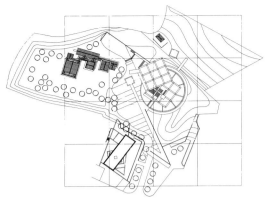

Site plan

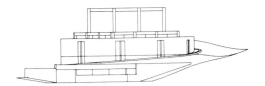

Elevation of Himeji I

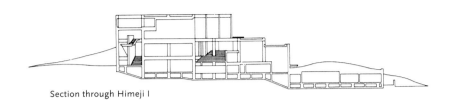

Section through Himeji I

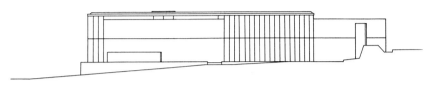

Elevation of Himeji II

from left to right
Entrance area of Himeji I | Himeji I | The ramp between the cube and the cylinder, also used as an exhibition room (Himeji I) | The glazed prism of Himeji II, interpenetrated by a concrete cube

Literature Museum

Himeji, Japan

Client	City of Himeji
Architect	Tadao Ando & Associates, Osaka
Built area	1,324 m² / 1,360 m²
Total area	3,815 m² / 2,532 m²
Construction time	1989-1990 / 1994-1996

The location on a hill in sight of one of Japan's most famous fortifications was decisive in determining the design for the museum dedicated to the philosopher Tetsuro Watsuji (1889-1960). Built in two phases, it contains a collection of documents about the region's literary figures. While the main building serves primarily for exhibition purposes, the extension contains a library and an archive for the work of the writer Ryotaro Shiba (1923-1996).

The museum itself (Himeji I) consists of two volumes of different heights above a square ground plan; they intersect with each other at an angle of 30 degrees. The tripartite division of the 22.5-metre sides of this square results in a nine-part grid struc-

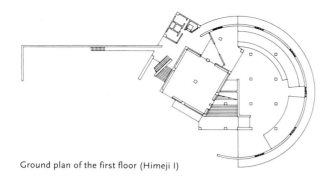

Ground plan of the first floor (Himeji I)

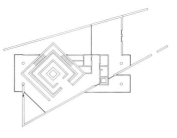

Ground plan of the first floor (Himeji II)

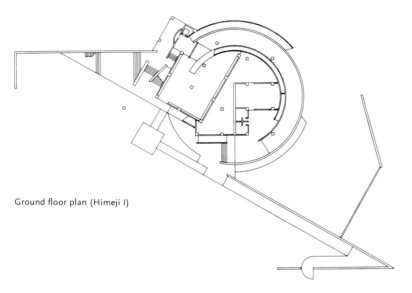

Ground floor plan (Himeji I)

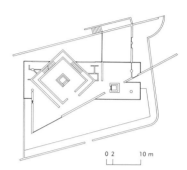

0 2   10 m

Ground floor plan (Himeji II)

ture. Projected into the third dimension, this becomes a spatial grid that allows the two prisms to appear as more or less deeply sunken cubes that are variously subdivided into open and closed volumes. Around the lower of these two volumes is positioned a cylinder penetrated only by a few narrow window openings. Like the other parts of this ensemble, the cylinder is exposed concrete. Partially girdled by water falling in low cascades, over which a carefully circled ramp leads into the building, the reticence of this architecture reduced to the bare essentials conveys the meditative peace and quiet that is one of the most significant ideals of Zen Buddhism. Serving almost entirely for the presentation of the documents and pictures, the interior intentionally offers

continually changing spatial experiences generated by the intersection of the two cubes and a ramp leading along the cylinder wall. Nonetheless, visitors will still be able to find the concentration necessary for the study of the small-scale objects on display.

The extension (Himeji II), laid out on the axis of the existing museum and also partially ringed by water, obeys the same design principles although it is quite different in appearance. An extended glazed cube is also cut through – this time at an angle of 45 degrees – by a cube of concrete, for its part concentrically subdivided.

GA Document 30/1991, pp. 80-91 • The Japan Architect 1/1991, pp. 72-75 • Architectural Design 99/1992, pp. 52-55 • Casabella 599/1993, pp. 52-55, p. 70 and 645/1997, pp. 16-25 • GA Architect 12/1993, Tadao Ando 2, pp. 103-112 • Masao Furuyama, Tadao Ando, Zürich/Munich/London, 1993, pp. 164-165 • Philip Jodidio, Tadao Ando, Cologne 1997, pp. 100-105 • "Tadao Ando 1983-2000." El Croquis 44+58, Madrid, 2000, pp. 230-245

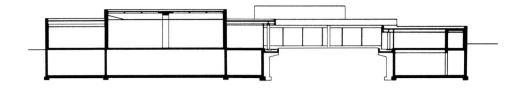

Cross section

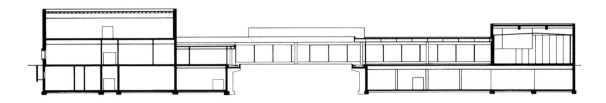

Longitudinal section (parallel to the bank of the Aachener Weiher)

from left to right
The Japanese rock garden | The terrace overlooking the
Aachener Weiher | Exhibition rooms

Museum of
Eastern Asian Art

Cologne, Germany

Client	City of Cologne
Architects	Kunio Mayekawa, Tokyo Masayuki Nagare (rock garden) Jochen Jacobs, Cologne (extension)
Enclosed space	29,000 m³
Exhibition area	910 m² (+ 480 m² extension)
Construction time	1973-1977; 1992-1995 extension (Planning commission 1966)

For Cologne's renowned Museum of Eastern Asian Art – whose original domicile was destroyed in the Second World War – the Japanese architect Kunio Mayekawa (1905-1986) who, himself a student of Le Corbusier, significantly influenced a whole generation of Japanese architects, planned a new building in Cologne's green belt, right next to the Japanese cultural institute on the banks of the Aachener Weiher, which is conveniently located for public transport purposes. Opened in 1977, the museum was endowed with additional exhibition areas in 1992-1995 by Jochen Jacobs, who stuck to the original design to a very large extent. The low building, multiply articulated, a balanced composition of interlocking blocks, fits discreetly into its surroundings, which

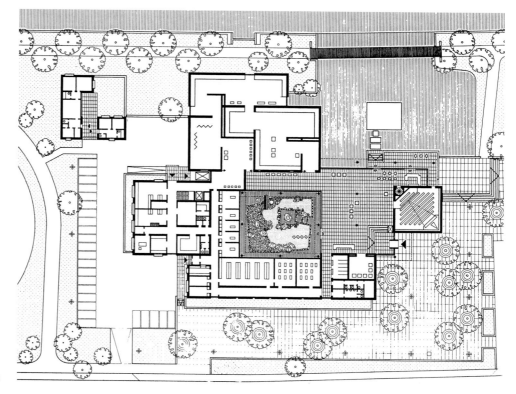

Ground plan

0   5   20 m

for their part are incorporated into the architecture. Japanese ideas inform the rock garden at the centre of the complex and the bringing of the water of the Aachener Weiher – which was originally intended to have a curving bank – right up to the museum. The iridescent golden brown tiles fired in Japan with which most of the architecture is clad form a harmonious contrast to the sparely used grey stone cladding of a few remaining parts.

One enters the spacious foyer via an esplanade tiled with ceramic slabs. Descending in shallow steps, the foyer gives visitors a view inside, toward the rock garden, and toward the outside, of the Aachener Weiher, which extends up to the publicly-accessi-

ble roofed-over terrace of the café. The room-height glazing of the foyer presents an intentional contrast to the closed, ceramic-clad walls of the somewhat higher volume that contains the exhibition rooms and only reveals a view to the outside at the interfaces between the individual room groupings. As for the rest, the exhibition rooms of varying sizes and different heights flowing into each other are lighted exclusively with artificial light. Partly surrounding plinths as well as built-in, fully air-conditioned display cases of light-coloured Japanese ashwood allow optimum presentation of the objects, some of them as fragile as they are valuable, which means that the displays have to be changed at frequent intervals for curatorial reasons.

Baumeister 5/1978, pp. 444-445 • *Museen in Köln. Bulletin* 16/1977, Heft 8, pp. 1545-1547 (Roger Goepper) • *Kölner Museums-Bulletin* 3/1995, pp. 4-29 (Adele Schlombs, Eva Ströber)

Schubert, pp. 112-113

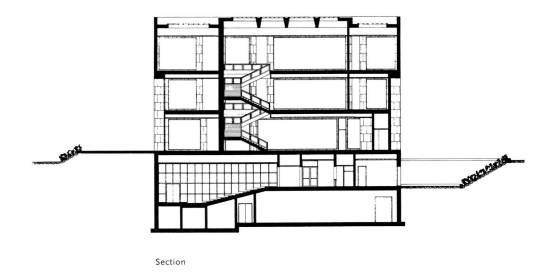

Section

Site plan

from left to right
Entrance side from the street (northwestern side) | View from the park (from the east) | Central hall on the ground floor | Exhibition area on the first floor

Kunsthalle

Bielefeld, Germany

Client	City of Bielefeld
Architect	Philip C. Johnson, New York
Enclosed space	28,700 m³
Net floor area	2,422 m²
Exhibition area	1,099 m²
Construction time	1966-1968 (Commissioned in 1963)

At the instigation of Rudolf August Oetker, an industrialist and patron of the arts from Bielefeld, this commission was awarded to Philip Johnson, who had already built six museums in the United States.

Located on a large traffic axis, the building – which appears massive at first glance – opens with two expansive glazed fronts toward a park. It consists of five floors on a square ground plan of 30 x 30 metres (originally it was supposed to be 40 x 40 metres), of which only the three uppermost ones with the exhibition rooms are visible above the level of the street. Two underground floors contain offices, a conference hall, a library, depots, and workshops. The structure of the cube develops out of the tension between the

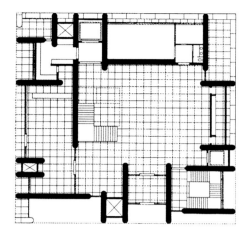

Ground floor plan

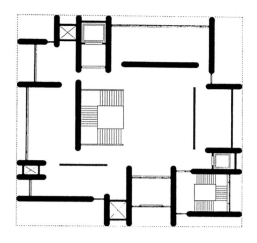

Ground plan of the first floor

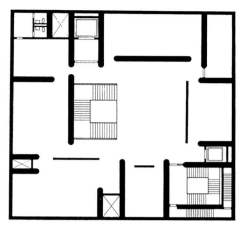

Ground plan of the second floor

0 2   10 m

heavy, closed volume of the top floor and the asymmetrically organized verticals of the rounded-off walls that protrude from the recessed parts of the remaining volume, which are partially glazed, up to the alignment of the top storey. It thus suggests an interpenetration between interior and exterior. In addition to the solidity of the materials used – a reddish sandstone for the cladding of the reinforced concrete – the most simple proportions based on whole-number units (which probably were inspired by the studies of Johnson's friend, the art historian Rudolf Wittkower, on the aesthetic proportions of Renaissance architecture) emphasize the significance of this building task.

On the top floor the interior is lit from above through a gridwork ceiling, while the remaining floors are illuminated by a combination of lateral and artificial light. By means of walls of varying lengths arranged perpendicularly to each other, visible from the outside, it is divided the same way on all the floors into rooms of different sizes that flow into each other. From the spacious entrance hall, a stairway placed in the centre of the building leads to the exhibition levels, which are also accessible via a second stairway next to the entrance.

In spite of the evident sophistication of the architecture, the spatial organisation oriented toward the centre, varied but never confusing, enables an entirely appropriate presentation of the twentieth-century artworks.

J.W. von Moltke, "Das Richard Kaselowsky-Haus, Kunsthalle der Stadt Bielefeld", in: *Museumskunde* 32/1967, pp. 76-85 • *Bauwelt* 42/1968, pp. 1300-1301 • *Deutsche Bauzeitschrift* 1/1969, pp. 37-40 • Georg Syamken, "Die Kunsthalle der Stadt Bielefeld", in: Museum und Kunst. Beiträge für Adolf Hentzen, Hamburg, 1970, pp. 266-276 • Henry-Russel Hitchcock, Die Bielefelder Kunsthalle, Bielefeld, 1974 • Peter Blake, Philip Johnson, Basel/Berlin/Boston, 1996, pp. 114-115

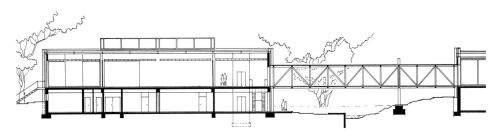

Josef Albers Museum, section D-D

Josef Albers Museum, section C-C

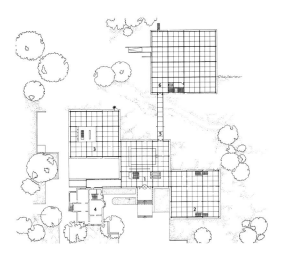

Plan of the entire complex
1 Media room | **2** Modern gallery | **3** Museum of Prehistory |
4 Old building, Local History Museum | **5** Bridge | **6** Josef Albers
Museum

from left to right
Josef Albers Museum | Forecourt with main entrance | Josef
Albers Museum, view from the external circulation way into
the large exhibition hall | Modern gallery: sculpture hall

Museum Quadrat and Josef Albers Museum

Bottrop, Germany

Client	City of Bottrop
Architect	Bernhard Küppers, Bottrop
Enclosed space	14,500 and 7,500 m³
Net floor area	2,670 and 1,350 m²
Exhibition area (i.e. length of walls for pictures)	1,170 m² (resp. circa 200 m)
Construction time	1975-1976 and 1981-1983

Ice age artifacts and a stock of paintings and drawings by the Bauhaus artist Josef Albers (1888-1976), who emigrated in 1933 and since 1970 has been an honorary citizen of the city of his birth occasioned the building of a new museum in the Stadtpark. It was to be linked to a villa serving as a local museum, and Bernhard Küppers, at the time director of the municipal building department of the city of Bottrop, designed a new building of steel, aluminium, and glass, strictly geometrically organized and stylistically inspired by Mies van der Rohe. It gains its significance from the contrast with the old building and above all, the mature growth of the lovingly maintained park landscape. Three diagonally linked volumes of different heights, each on a square ground plan of 21.15 x

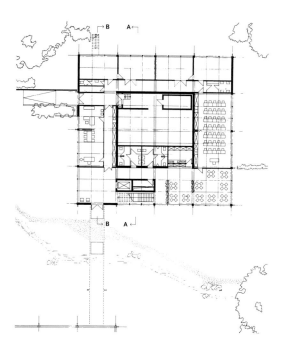

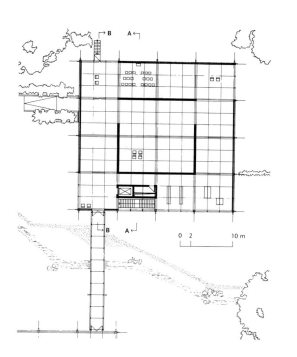

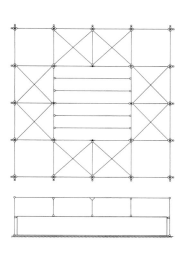

Josef Albers-Museum, structural system

Josef Albers Museum, ground floor plan

Josef Albers Museum, ground plan of the upper floor

21.15 metres, are accessed from the central pavilion. They house very different facilities, a media centre (in the middle), a museum for prehistory, and a modern gallery. The daylight illumination by means of asymmetrically arranged storey-height glazing, its dimensions derived from the modular grid structure, can be supplemented at any point by additional spotlights that are concealed in the gridwork of the ceiling.

A large donation from the estate of Josef Albers led in 1977 to the extension (planned from the inception) of the first building phase, called the "Quadrat." The ground plan – again square – and its interior layout are definitely to be understood here as a homage to Josef Albers, whose geometrically abstract picture

forms found their final simplification in the famous Square pictures. Larger dimensions (28.2 x 28.2 metres ground plan) and a clear distinction from the existing building volume emphasize the specific significance of the two-storey Albers Museum. On the other hand, the integration and linking of the building into the complex as whole takes place structurally by retaining the basic module of 7.05 metres – now quadrupled – and spatially by means of a transparent bridge from the central media space. While the rooms of the first building phase were easily perceptible, the new building, strictly governed by the modular grid and opened to exciting perspectives by means of asymmetric wall openings, develops its height in a graduated fashion. A relatively low surrounding corridor economically lit

from the side circumscribes a higher, square central room provided with overhead light by sawtooth roofs. In this room, Albers' meditative Square pictures, the heart of the collection, invite visitors to linger.

Baukultur 5/1983, pp. 4-6 (Bernhard Küppers) • Bauwelt 20-21/1985, pp. 792-95 (Jörg Johnen) • Ulrich Schumacher/Bernhard Küppers, Architektur – Kunst – Natur. Das Museum in Bottrop, Bottrop, 1988

Allegret, pp. 48-53

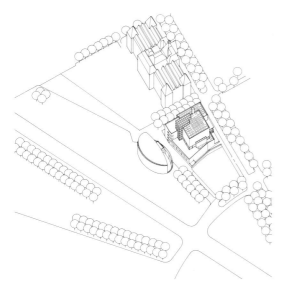

Axonometric projection

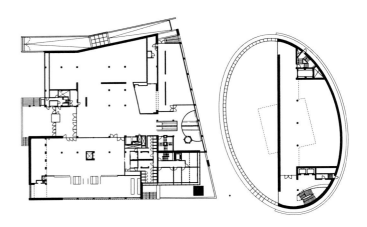

Ground plan of the lower floor

above and right
The first building of the Van Gogh Museum (without the additions by Martien van Goor) | The flowing space of the exhibition rooms in the first building opens onto the central void

Van Gogh Museum

Amsterdam, Netherlands

Client	Rijksgebouwdienst, The Hague and Van Gogh Museum Foundation, Amsterdam
Architects	Gerrit Rietveld, J. van Dillen, J. van Tricht (first building) Kisho Kurokawa, Tokio (extension)
Total area	6,575 m² (first building) 5,083 m² (extension)
Construction time	1969-1973 (first building; design 1963) 1996-1998 (extension; commissioned in 1990)

One of Gerrit Rietveld's last works, this peaceful museum building composed of rigid prisms was executed after his death by Van Dillen and Van Tricht. The fundamental idea was to group the exhibition spaces flowing into each other (and lit for the most part by pyramidal glass skylights shaded by sun shields) around an empty central space lit from above, its open stairway inspired by the de Stijl aesthetic. By opening the exhibition rooms toward the centre, the aspect of the communicative that has since then played an increasingly important role in museum architecture is emphasized here relatively early.

In the end, the unexpectedly large numbers of visitors necessitated not only extensive renovations,

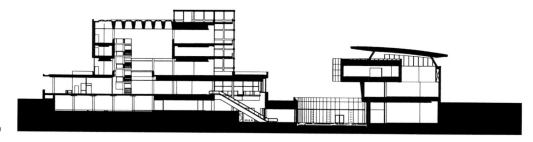

Cross section through the first building and the addition

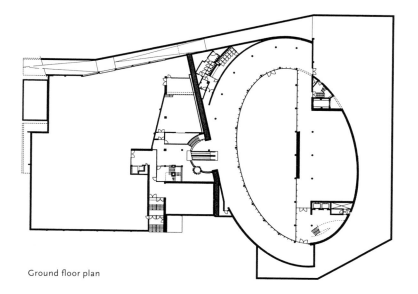

Ground floor plan

0 2   10 m

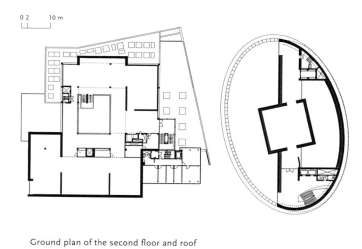

Ground plan of the second floor and roof

above and right
The addition and the first building, supplemented by a glazed entrance area, are opposite to each other | The exhibition room on the ground floor of the addition, into which the cube for the prints projects, is lit by a band of windows below the titanium roof

but also the enlargement of the existing museum. While Martien van Goor adopts the language of the existing architecture in his extensions, above all in a glazed volume for the access area, the curved lines of the new building designed by Kisho Kurokawa present a crass contrast to Rietveld's prismatic forms with their rough concrete surfaces. The new building is covered instead with polished granite and shimmering titanium. Under a shell-like roof, it rises over the ground plan of a half ellipse asymmetrically divided lengthways (the original circular ground plan was rejected for reasons related to town planning) whose second half as a sunken pool of water effectively stages not only the relation between the old and the new building, but also brings into focus the

tension between volumes and voids as an elementary principle.

Because more than half its spatial volume is underground, the new building, whose large, oddly blurred rooms almost double the exhibition area, is kept significantly lower than the old building to which it is linked underground. The positioning of the square placed in the upper exhibition room serving for the display of prints, jutting out at an angle over the water from the forward-leaning front and thus disturbing the symmetry of the new building – while at the same time forming an exact parallel to the alignment of the old building – is characteristic of the ambivalence of this architecture that not only oscil-

lates between deliberate autonomy and subtle reference to that which already exists, but also seeks to unite ancient Japanese tradition with uncompromising modernity.

The Architectural Review 922/1973, pp. 376-385 (Richard Padovan) • *Bauen und Wohnen* 1973, pp. 434 • *International Lighting Review* 41/1990, pp. 50-61 • Marijke Küper/Ida van Zijl, Gerrit T. Rietveld. The complete works 1888-1964, Utrecht, 1992, pp. 352-353 • Andreas Blühm (ed.), Van Gogh Museum Architecture. Rietveld to Kurokawa, Rotterdam, 1999 (Hans Ibelings) • *architektur aktuell* 227/1999, p. 8 • *Bauwelt* 16/1999, pp. 844-845 (Peter van Asche)

Trulove, pp. 112-119

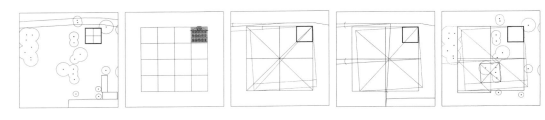

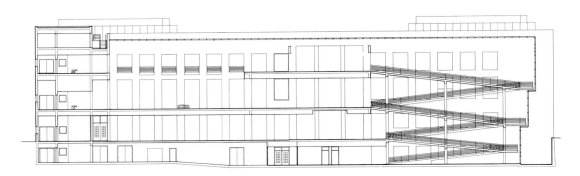

Development of the basic structure derived from the cube of the Villa Metzler

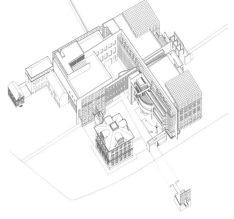

Isometric projection

Section

from left to right
The west side facing the museum park is dominated by the corner cubes clad with white steel plates, whose dimensions correspond to those of the Villa Metzler | West façade | The inner courtyard accentuated by a fountain and also derived from the square grid, through which the required public foot-path leads | The ramps – a motif quoting Le Corbusier | Exhibition rooms on the first floor with the display-cases also designed by Richard Meier

Museum für Kunsthandwerk

Frankfurt on Main, Germany

Client	City of Frankfurt on Main
Architect	Richard Meier & Partners, New York
Enclosed space	61,141 m³
Total area	9,925 m²
Exhibition area	4,810 m²
Construction time	1982-1985 (restricted competition 1980)

The neoclassicist Villa Metzler on the southern bank of the River Main, which had provisionally housed the renowned Frankfurt Museum für Kunsthandwerk since 1965, formed the starting point for the museum building which carries on the tradition of the modernism of the 1920s. The cube of the old building becomes the module for the angled new building laid out around it, kept in brilliant white and linked to it only by a glass bridge. In their ground plan and their elevation, both the three corner cubes with their regular window openings and the playfully emphasized, asymmetrically arranged passages, galleries, arcades, and freestanding walls around them obey down to the last detail the strict stereometry governed by a square grid whose sides each

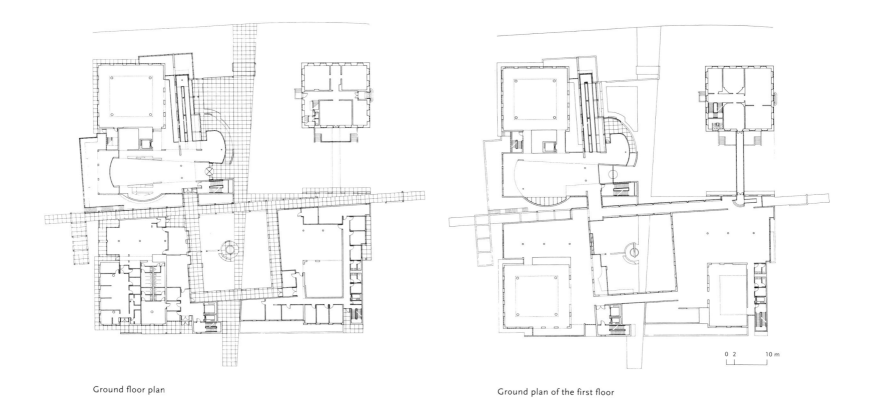

Ground floor plan

Ground plan of the first floor

measure 1.10 metres in length. Over the grid oriented on that of the Villa Metzler is laid a second grid network aligned with the river bank and therefore deviating noticeably from the first one, so that between the four quadrants of the building site, an axial intersection of routes widening out conically comes into being. It not only emphasizes the caesurae between the volumes and allows selective views, but also contributes significantly to the tension of this architecture through its form gained by slightly turning the basic square.

The interior of the museum is accessed by means of a light-flooded ramp positioned transversally to the entrance axis. In changing perspectives and varied

overlappings, the ramp allows the interpenetration of interior and exterior space to become an intellectual game. The circulation system leads visitors counterclockwise through a succession of exhibition rooms whose sequence mirrors the basic structure of this architecture. Sophisticated display-case architecture, which is staged using the same means and as effectively as the whole building, renders the exhibition rooms – most of them illuminated naturally from the side – a logical continuation of the external architecture and only rarely allows the primacy of the architecture over the works of art on display to be forgotten.

Baumeister 8/1980, pp. 767-775 (Competition) • *Bauwelt* 71/ 1980, pp. 1132-1141 (Competition) and 20-21/1985, pp. 766- 777 (Peter Rumpf) • *Architectural Record* 4/1981, pp. 87-95 • *The Architectural Review* 1012/1981, pp. 34-38 (Lance Knobel) • *Lotus international* 28/1981, pp. 95-110 (Competition) • Norbert Huse, Richard Meier. Museum für Kunsthandwerk Frankfurt am Main, Berlin, 1985 • Museum für Kunsthandwerk, ed. Hochbau- amt der Stadt Frankfurt am Main, 1985 • *Casabella* 515/1985, pp. 4-17 (Mirko Zardini, Kenneth Frampton) • *Detail* 5/1985, pp. 457-465 • *Deutsche Bauzeitung* 8/1985, pp. 22-27 (Falk Jaeger) • *Domus* 662/1985, pp. 3-11 (Fulvio Irace) • *Techniques et Archi- tecture* 359/1985, pp. 103-108 • Werner Blaser (ed.), Richard Meier. Building for Art/Bauen für die Kunst, Basel/Boston/Berlin, 1990, pp. 53-89 • Silvio Cassarà, Richard Meier, Basel/Boston/ Berlin, 1996, pp. 92-95

Allegret, Vol. 2, pp. 18-23 • Klotz/Krase, pp. 22-24 and pp. 121- 132 • Lampugnani, pp. 113-115 (Kenneth Frampton) • Monta- ner/Oliveras, pp. 102-105 • Schilgen, pp. 82-105 • Schubert, pp. 162-164 • Twentieth-Century Museum I (Michael Brawne)

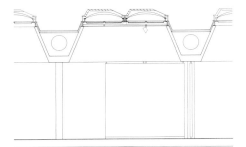

Section through the gallery rooms on the third floor

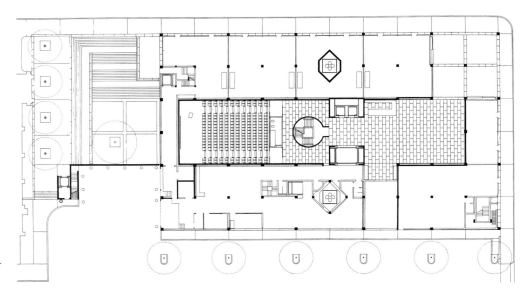

Ground plan of the lower floor

from left to right
The general view clearly reveals the modular organization |
The roofed-over library courtyard | Exhibition rooms on the
third floor | Exhibition rooms on the third floor with view over
the library courtyard

Yale Center
for British Art

New Haven / Connecticut, USA

Client	Yale University
Architects	Louis Isidore Kahn, Philadelphia (completed by Anthony Pellecchia and Marshall D. Meyers)
Total area	34,816 m²
Net floor area	18,000 m²
Construction time	1969-1977

Kahn's last work, almost entirely designed by him but completed by his pupils, still gets a mixed reception. The purpose of the building is to accommodate a collection of British art donated to Yale University as well as an important library. The requirement was that the building's scale should correspond to the collection that contains many small-scale pictures, watercolours and drawings. A strict quadratic grid of 20 feet per side is the basis of the four-storey building, its ground plan measuring 10 x 6 modular units. This austere structure becomes clearly recognizable through the minimalist exterior – a subtly chosen texture of cast concrete framework and fillings of stainless steel plates, rhythmically punctuated by window openings. The articulation in the interior takes place by means of two

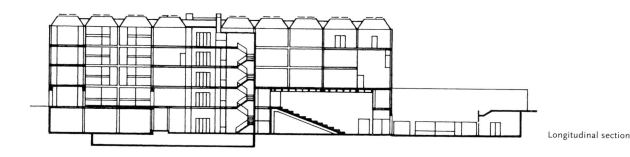

Longitudinal section

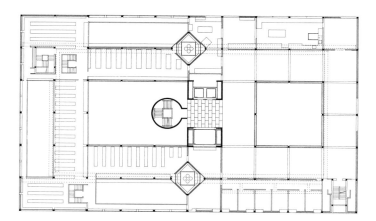

Ground plan of the second floor

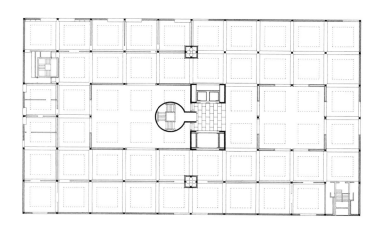

Ground plan of the third floor

0 2   10 m

glass-roofed courtyards of differing sizes, of which the larger, called the "library courtyard," occupies only the three upper floors and conceals the main stairway in a cylindrical concrete casing. The sculptural dominance of this element not only breaks with the proportions of the building structure readable everywhere else, including inside, but also raises the question as to the relation between "serving" and "served" rooms, on whose suitability Kahn otherwise used to lay great value.

The exhibition rooms – on the first and second floors for temporary exhibitions, on the third floor intended for the permanent presentation of the picture collection – are laid out around the square courtyard in the two mezzanine storeys. (The library is laid out around

the larger, rectangular court.) On the top floor, the exhibition rooms surround both the interior courtyards. Although the modular structure remains recognizable here too, not only in the column system and the removable partitions, but also in the wall articulation (the fillings between the concrete framework consist of light oak or unbleached linen), the impression of a flowing spatial continuum prevails nonetheless. The lighting of the exhibition rooms – apart from the lateral light distributed by sporadically distributed windows that open both to the inner courtyards and the outside – is accomplished in the mezzanine storeys by means of spotlights, on the top floor through filtered daylight which falls through almost room-height superstructures corresponding to the module grid. Whether

these rooms also radiate the sought-after atmosphere of the English mansions in which such art works were once to be found is a question that remains open.

Architectural Record 7/1977, pp. 95-104 (Vincent Scully) • *The Architectural Review* 965/1977, pp. 37-44 (W.H. Jordy) • *L'architecture d'aujourd'hui* 193/1977, pp. 70-74 • Jules David Prown, The Architecture of the Yale Center for British Art, New Haven, 1977 • *Domus* 579/1978, pp. 1-5 (Agnoldomenico Pica) • *Progressive Architecture* 5/1978, pp. 76-82 (Martin Filler) • *Architecture: the AIA journal* 6/ 1978, pp. 80-89 (A.O. Dean) and 1/1986, pp. 64-67 (M.J.Crosbie) • *Baumeister* 3/1979, pp. 239-242 • *Casabella* 43/ 1979, pp. 38-39 • *A+U: extra edition* 11/1983, pp. 172-184 • *The Architect's Journal* 9/ 1992, pp. 50-53 (D. Hawkes) • Romaldo Giurgola/Jamini Mehta, Louis I. Kahn, 4th edition, Zürich/ Munich/ London, 1992, pp. 87-90 • Bruno Jean Hubert, Louis I. Kahn: Le Yale Center for British Art, Marseilles, 1992 • Duncan Robinson, The Yale Center for British Art: A Tribute to the Genius of Louis I. Kahn, New Haven, 1997 • Klaus-Peter Gast, Louis I. Kahn, Basel/ Berlin/Boston, 1999, pp. 24-27

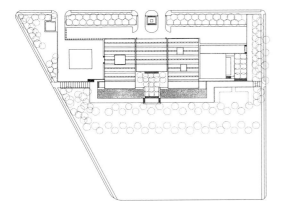

Site plan

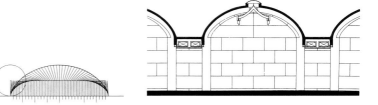

Diagrammatic representation of the cycloid arch and section through the vault

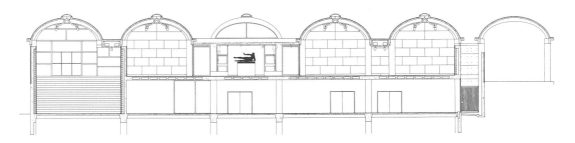

Cross section

from left to right
General view from the south | Exhibition rooms on the upper
floor | Stairway to the lower floor

Kimbell
Art Museum

Fort Worth / Texas, USA

Client	Kimbell Art Foundation, Fort Worth
Architect	Louis Isidore Kahn, Philadelphia
Total area	11,148 m²
Exhibition area	4,831 m²
Construction time	1969-1972 (commission 1966)

Kahn's maxim that architecture is the art of creating spaces with light is evident in the Kimbell Art Museum building, which is considered a milestone in modern museum architecture, in a special way. In order to be able to present an exquisite private art collection under the southern sun of Texas in evenly lit rooms yet all the same in natural daylight (with the latter to have a mystic character, moreover), the architect developed a concrete shell structure of circular segments, with a skylight running down its entire length. In addition, the apex of the vaults is shielded by perforated, curved aluminium reflectors that transform the roof into a "natural source of light." Logically, Kahn also makes the barrel vault turned thus into an ingeniously refined zenith light into the modulus for the complex, for the

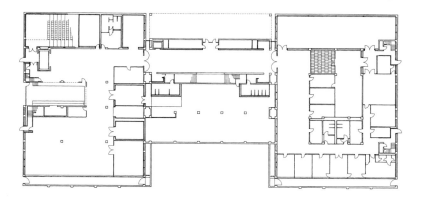

Ground plan of the lower floor

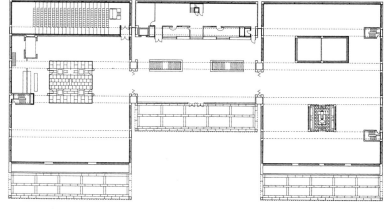

Ground floor plan

0 2   10 m

ground plan organisation of which he designed four versions. The building that was eventually built – which because of external conditions was to be only one storey high from the outside – consists of sixteen rectangular elements, each spanned with a barrel vault, each with a clear width of circa 30 x 7 meters. They are arranged in such a way that two blocks of six on the sides and a block of four between them cut out a central courtyard. The two outermost units on the garden side are developed as open loggias and thereby dovetail the building not only into its surroundings, but also create an almost Arcadian atmosphere through the harmonious effect of the carefully worked, lead-roofed concrete skeleton and the walls of yellowish travertine, with the fountains in the park. In the middle

of the three-part symmetrical basic structure consisting of layers stacked up behind each other are the foyer, a symmetric stairway connecting to the lower floor that houses the service rooms, and an administrative zone. On the left, a room for temporary exhibitions, an auditorium, and a café are linked to these, and on the right is the actual exhibition area, whose columnless spatial continuum is articulated not only by partition walls whose positions can be varied, but above all by the dominant modular vault structure. Three atria of different sizes and containing gardens punctuate the spatial flow and supplement the silvery light from above with a greenish lateral light. Plans for an extension were dismissed in 1990, because although they used the same design elements, they would have

destroyed the subtle structural proportions of the building.

Nell E. Johnson, Light is The Theme. Fort Worth, 1975 • David M. Robb, Louis I. Kahn: Sketches for the Kimbell Art Museum, Fort Worth, 1978 A+U extra edition 11/1983, pp. 128-157 • Via 7/ 1984, pp. 76-85 (A. T. Seymour) • In Pursuit of Quality: The Kimbell Art Museum Fort Worth, New York 1989 • Patricia Cummings Loud, The Art Museums of Louis I. Kahn, Exhibition Catalogue, Durham/ London, 1989, pp. 100-171 • Gioia Gattamorta, Louis I. Kahn: Kimbell Art Museum, Florence, 1991 • Michael Brawne, Kimbell Art Museum. Louis I Kahn, London, 1992 • Louis I. Kahn. The Construction of the Kimbell Art Museum, Exhibition Catalogue, Mendrisio, 1997 • Klaus-Peter Gast, Louis I. Kahn. The Idea of Order, Basel/Berlin/Boston, 1998, pp. 88-97 • Klaus Peter Gast, Louis I. Kahn, Basel/Berlin/ Boston, 1999, pp. 144-149 • Twentieth-Century Museums I, London 1999 (Michael Brawne)

Tzonis/Lefaivre/Diamond, pp. 148-151

Bird's eye view from the northeast

Site plan

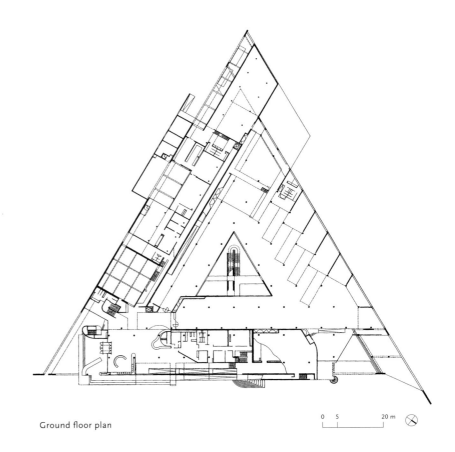

Ground floor plan

0   5   20 m

from left to right
View from the north | View from the entrance hall of the "sarcophagus" gallery | Exhibition rooms | Main entrance at the eastern corner, facing the city

Musée de l'Arles antique

Arles, France

Client	City of Arles
Architect	Henri Ciriani, Paris
Net floor area	7,400 m²
Exhibition area	3,000 m²
Construction time	1989-1995 (Two-stage competition 1983/84)

The form of the tongue of land available as a building site, between a lock on the Canal du Midi and the Rhône to the south of the Provencal city of Arles (which has a plethora of monuments from Roman antiquity) made Henri Ciriani choose a triangular ground plan for the building. In addition to an archaeological museum, it also houses a research institute for classical antiquity and the central administration for the museums in Arles. These three functional areas are grouped around the interior courtyard, which not only repeats the ground plan form of the equilateral triangle – determined at the outset by urban planning reasons – but, in contrast, also becomes the starting point of a spiral-form movement which becomes visible on the outside as

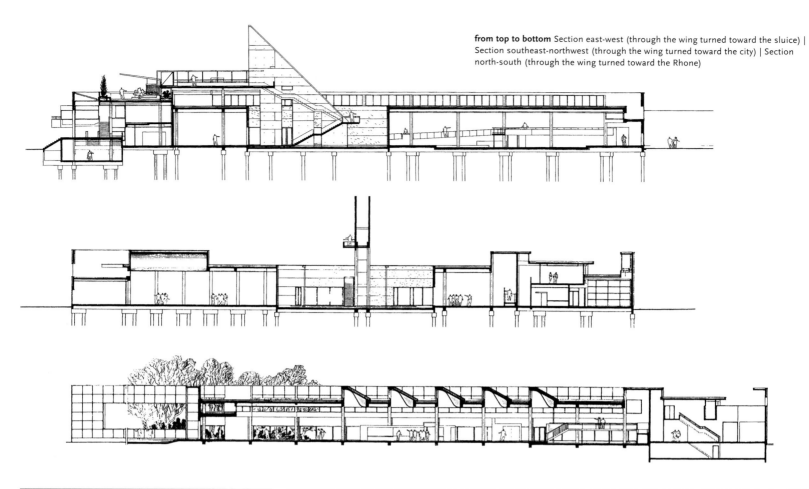

from top to bottom Section east-west (through the wing turned toward the sluice) | Section southeast-northwest (through the wing turned toward the city) | Section north-south (through the wing turned toward the Rhone)

a dynamic effect in the "open façades" jutting out above the geometric corner points. These three different façades of the transversally positioned building are partly closed and partly cut-out, structurally independent walls. Repeatedly, three-dimensional volumes break through these walls, which occasionally permit views deep inside the building as well. In this way, the façades are both a spatial skin and a space-forming element at the same time. The vivid colour of its blue enamelling, which is undoubtedly also to be understood as a homage to the sky of southern France, contrasts with the matte white and grey tones of the other architectural elements and thus emphasizes an architectural understanding of plastic-geometric three-dimensionality following the

tradition of classical modernism. A vast hall at the eastern corner gives access to the building, the museum part of which is homogeneously lit by means of sawtooth roofs opening northwards and also by bands of windows placed high in the walls. The use of slender columns permits this exhibition area to function as a flowing continuum without subdivisions around the interior courtyard, allowing circular tours of varying length. Slight differences in level not only enable the objects to be presented effectively, but also generate the moment of movement that eventually leads over a narrow stairway in the inner courtyard to the roof of the museum, from which a wonderful 360 degree view is to be had. Two triangular wall segments framing this stairway

and towering above the museum to good effect illustrate its ground plan structure once again in the third dimension, as it were.

Architectural Design 11-12/1984, pp. 44-47 • *Casabella* 523/1986, pp. 4-13 (Jean-Paul Robert) • *L'architecture d'aujourd'hui* 282/1992, pp. 102-111 • *Deutsche Bauzeitschrift* 8/1995, pp. 84-85 • *Bauwelt* 10/1996, pp. 507-509 (Kaye Geipel) • Luciana Miotto, Henri E. Ciriani. Contextual architecture and the pièce urbaine, Turin, 1996, pp. 74-82 • Mauro Galantino, Henri Ciriani. Architecture 1960-2000, Milan, 2000, pp. 60-61, pp. 72-85

Allégret, pp. 106-109 • Cerver, pp. 108-119 • Kind-Barkauskas/Kauhsen/Polónyi/Brandt, Concrete Construction Manual, pp. 212-215 • Mostaedi, pp. 32-41

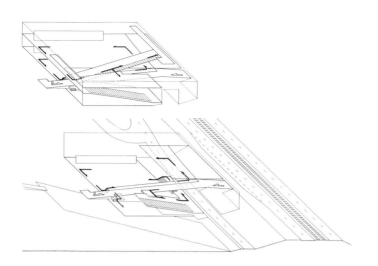

Isometric projection of the spiral circulation

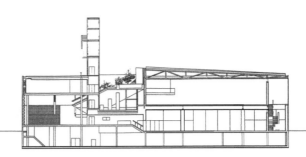

Longitudinal section

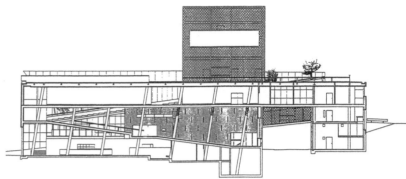

Cross section

from left to right
View of the exterior | The view from the west shows how the building bridges the difference between the embankment and the lower-lying park level and reveals the slanted levels inside when lit up at at night | The sloping hall that also serves as an auditorium and the inside part of the ramp that runs through the building | The ceiling of the dark exhibition rooms for displaying light-sensitive objects is supported by five asymmetrically-placed tree-trunks

Kunsthal

Rotterdam, Netherlands

Client	Dienst Gemeentelijke Musea, Rotterdam
Architect	Rem Koolhaas, Office for Metropolitan Architecture, Rotterdam
Enclosed space	ca. 40,000 m³
Exhibition area	ca. 3,000 m²
Construction time	1987-1992

From the requirement to unite three large exhibition rooms usable together or separately, an auditorium, and a restaurant with its own entrance all into a single building that would be bounded on one side by a dual carriageway on the crest of a dyke and on the other by a lower-lying park, Rem Koolhaas developed an architectural creation that attempts to do justice to the "principles of metropolitan architecture" that he propagates. The essential design idea that grew out of the functional program consists in a continuously developed circular tour in accordance with the basic concept of a continuous loop, its linear sequence – repeatedly broken open by unexpected views backwards – imparting a succession of contrasting spatial experiences. This spindle-form movement

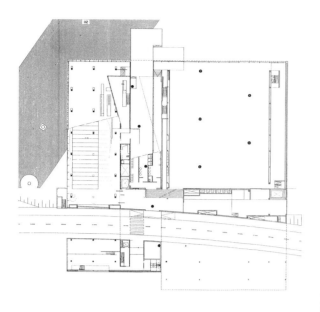
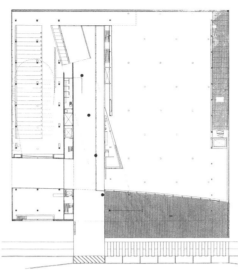
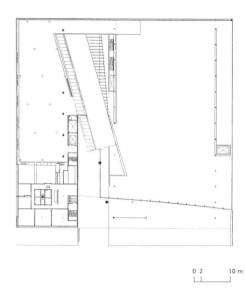

0 2 10 m

from left to right Ground plan of the lower floor (park level) |
Ground floor plan (embankment level) | Ground plan of the upper floor

has its starting point at the ramp that cuts right through the building. This ramp is divided by a glass wall into a public external area and an internal area belonging to the museum tour, whose spatial program is basically distributed across two levels tilted counter to each other. The constant interchange of materials and colours, varying from coloured raw concrete and metal screens to different forms of more or less transparent glass to plastic, creates a continuously changing, sometimes surreal atmosphere in which the machine-like, often gruff character of this architecture is never hidden.

At best, the complexity of the spatial organization can only be guessed at from the deliberately sober

external form when nocturnal lighting allows the tension between the slanting levels and the prismatic form of the external shell to become visible. Apart from that, the design and materiality of the low volume – different on each of the four sides – only indicates that here, neither a balanced composition nor a typological representation of any kind, and certainly not an exorbitant intensification of the museum idea is intended. Rather, this building – whose tall service tower functions on purpose as a billboard – appears to be an unambiguously realistic example of urban architecture in the fragmented and contradictory urban environment.

Baumeister 11/1992, pp. 40-44 (Sabine Schneider) • *AIT* 7-8/1993, pp. 48-51 • *ARCH+* 117/1993, pp. 50-53 • *Architectural Record* 3/1993, pp. 66-73 (Tracy Metz) • *L'architecture d'aujourd'hui* 285/1993, pp. 6-14 (Emmanuel Doutriaux) • *Bauwelt* 46/1993, pp. 2490-2497 (Hans van Dijk) • *Domus* 747/1993, pp. 38-47 (Kenneth Frampton) • *Techniques et Architecture* 408/1993, pp. 81-88 • *Architecture and Urbanism* 287/1994, pp. 108-143 (Andrew MacNair) • *El Croquis* 79/1996, pp. 74-105

Cerver, pp. 120-127 • Newhouse, pp. 232-234 • Peressut, pp. 64-93 • Räume für Kunst, pp. 48-49 • Wang, pp. 234-237

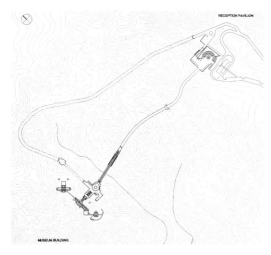

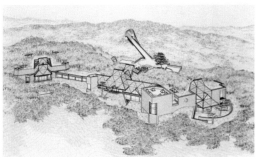

Ground plan of the lowest level

0 5   20 m

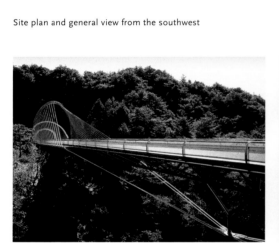

Site plan and general view from the southwest

from left to right
Access to the museum – tunnel exit and bridge | Entrance |
Entrance hall | North wing with rock garden | Room in the
south wing

Miho Museum

Shigaraki, Japan

Client	Shumei Culture Foundation
Architect	Ieoh Ming Pei & Partners, New York
Building site area	1,002,000 m²
Net floor area	20,780 m²
Exhibition area	17,429 m²
Construction time	1994-1997

Commissioned by Shinji Shumeikai, a religious community founded in 1970 by a group of exceptionally wealthy Japanese, the Chinese-American architect Ieoh Ming Pei designed a museum for antique art objects of both Eastern and Western provenance that lies in the midst of the Shigaraki nature reserve near Kyoto.

As leitmotif for his design, Pei cites the ancient Chinese tale "Peach Blossom Spring," according to which a fisherman is lured into a cave by the scent of flowers and discovers the valley of a lost paradise through a crack in the rock wall. Pei really has created an imposing design in the apparently untouched mountain landscape. From the isolated reception

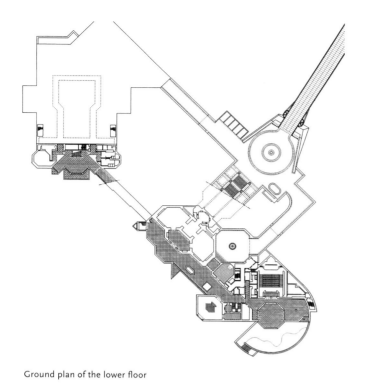

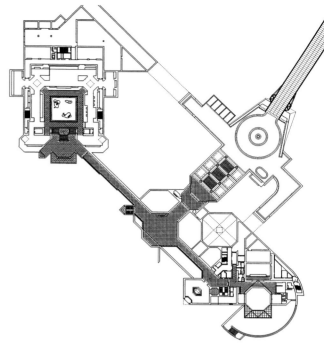

Ground plan of the lower floor

Ground plan of the entrance level

building leads a path – to be understood as inner preparation for the artistic experience – initially into a tunnel through the mountain and then across a filigree bridge suspended by steel cables over a deep ravine and onto the round forecourt, from which a terrace-form ramp climbs to the museum that receives visitors first of all with a light-flooded entrance hall. Using modern means, its form and construction paraphrase the structures of traditional Japanese temple architecture and refer – this is a significant element – in varied and subtle ways to the surrounding landscape. The consideration for nature expressed in strict building regulations that only allow a very limited building height and roof area resulted in almost 80 percent of the entire

building volume, of which only a few parts and glass roof pyramids are to be seen from outside, having to be sunk at great cost into the mountain.

The actual exhibition rooms, some of them tailored to specific objects, are situated in two differently formed wings that are accessible from the entrance hall, each via a narrow gallery. Their window walls stage the features in the landscape panorama – with exactly placed trees carefully planted in the earth on top of the concrete roof – to appear as if they were on show, like precious objects specially presented. In contrast to this, the exhibition rooms, lit by lamella-directed light from above, are of varying sizes and shapes, each of a geometric clarity, their severity

mitigated by the warm tones of the honey-coloured limestone. Three garden courtyards complete the ensemble, transforming it into a modern temple for the meditative contemplation of art.

The Japan Architect 4/1996, pp. 24-25 • Miho Museum. Connaissance des arts, Paris, 1997 • *Casabella* 658/1998, p. 26-33 • *Bauwelt* 33/1999, pp. 1776-1777 (Ulf Meyer) • Carter Wiseman, I.M. Pei. A Profile in American Architecture, 2nd ed. New York, 2001, p. 317 ff.

Trulove, pp. 58-63

Axonometric view (1982)

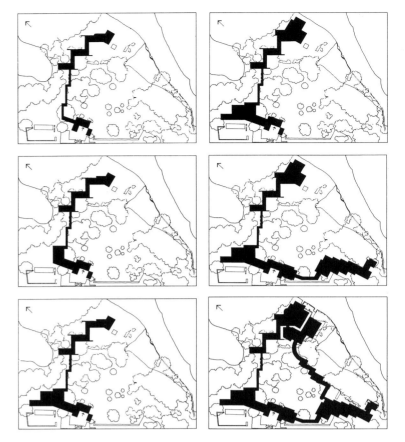

Stage by stage development
of the museum:
1958, 1966, 1971, 1976, 1982, 1991

from left to right
View of the one and two-storey exhibition room in the north
wing from the pond (1958) | View of the Øresund from the
entrance; on the right, the print wing (1991) | Connecting pas-
sage between the entrance and the south wing (1982) | Exhibi-
tion room in the south wing (1982)

Louisiana Museum
for moderne Kunst

Humlebæk near Copenhagen, Denmark

Client	Louisiana Foundation
Architects	Jørgen Bo and Vilhelm Wohlert
Net floor area	ca. 11,000 m²
Exhibition area	6,000 m²
Construction time	1956-1998

The architects commissioned by Knud W. Jensen
had to take into account two significant factors.
The new building had to harmonize well with the
nineteenth-century country house to which it was
to be attached. He had acquired it, together with a
park high above the Øresund with a small lake and
old trees, in order to erect a museum there for his
private art collection. Above all, however, the museum was to be designed in such a manner that it
exploited to the full the beauty of the park without
destroying it. During no less than eight building
phases over the course of more than forty years,
Jørgen Bo and Vilhelm Wohlert have remained true
to the basic principle of keeping nature, architecture
and art in balance.

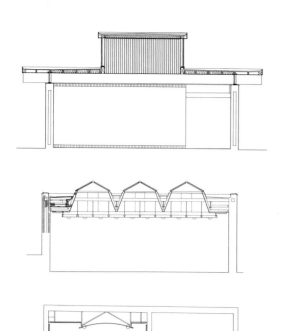

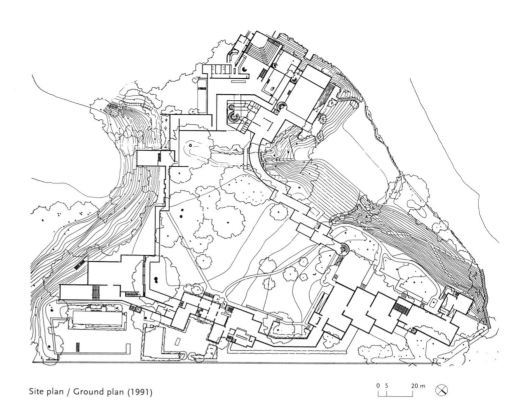

Cross sections from top to bottom
Exhibition rooms in the north wing (1958) |
Exhibition rooms in the south wing (1982) |
Subterranean print wing (1991)

Site plan / Ground plan (1991)

0 5   20 m   ⊗

The concept was to make art experienceable in an unceremonious way in a more or less everyday environment. For that reason, the new museum was to be like a large country house, friendly, rustic, with whitewashed walls, wood and clinker brick, and open to the park. Erected in the first phase, the three pavilions of the southern wing, inspired by the traditional Danish architecture, but also by Japanese and American architecture, were sensitively integrated into the landscape and linked via glass passageways with frequent bends to the old building, which functioned as the entrance. The variation between views and concentrated interior spaces, the avoidance of longer view axes, and the natural lighting by means of overhead and lateral light only supplemented

occasionally with spotlights assured the museum exceptional acceptance.

In 1966 and 1971 extensions for temporary exhibitions were added to the northern wing, and in 1976 a concert hall and event venue was added to its end. A new exhibition wing in the southern wing was opened in 1982, this time as a row of diagonally placed rooms set next to each other, closed off to the outside and illuminated by somewhat more sophisticated overhead lighting structures. In 1991, Vilhelm Wohlert's son Claus designed the subterranean wing for prints, which is accessible via a conservatory. It links the two wings with each other and thus enables a complete circular tour of the

museum. In addition to a café and a children's museum, a new museum shop was built in 1998; it shall soon be followed by an extension for a "House of Twentieth-Century Architecture" planned by Jørn Utzon.

Arkitektur DK 5/1958, pp. 145-165 (Kay Fisker); 7/1982, pp. 253-273; 4/1989, pp. 184-187 (Lisbet Balslev Jørgensen); and 7/1991, pp. 309-321 (Thomas Kappel) • Michael Brawne, *The New Museum*, New York/Washington, 1965, pp. 80-83 • *Baumeister* 3/1979, pp. 258-259 • *Progressive Architecture* 8/1983, pp. 82-87 (John Morris Dixon) • Knud W. Jensen, Mein Louisiana-Leben. Werdegang eines Museums, Klagenfurt, 1991 • Michael Brawne, Jørgen Bo, Vilhelm Wohlert. Lousiana Museum, Humlebæk, Tübingen/Berlin, 1993 • *Detail* 8/2000, pp. 1450-1454 (Heide Wessely)

Allegret, pp. 54-61 • Aloi, pp. 92-100

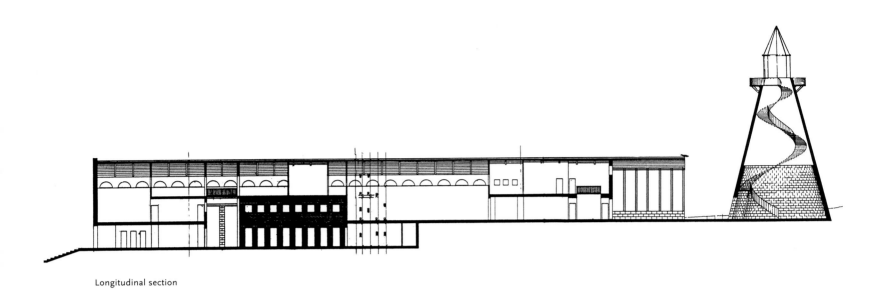

Longitudinal section

from left to right
Exhibition building, details: classical motifs | General view |
View of the lighthouse from the entrance portico | Central
exhibition hall | Exhibition room above the café

Centre d'art contemporain

Vassivière-en-Limousin, France

Client	Région du Limousin
Architect	Aldo Rossi, Milan
Enclosed space	7,600 m³
Net floor area	1,373 m²
Exhibition area	1,024 m²
Construction time	1988-1991

Integrated into in a wide-ranging network of paths, a large sculpture park on an island in the Lac du Vassivière, which is accessible only by a footbridge, has at its centre an unusual building that visitors are surprised to see when they come out of the forest. On the highest point of a sloping meadow is a 27-metre high lighthouse crowned by a glassed-in viewing platform. Aldo Rossi, the architect who was deliberately entrusted with this building task, says that the tower "has always been one of my obsessions," and here it not only makes the island into the central point of the lake, but functions as a beacon or signal in archetypal symbolism. Thus it indicates the long building lying at the foot of it, an art centre that contains a succession of rooms that can

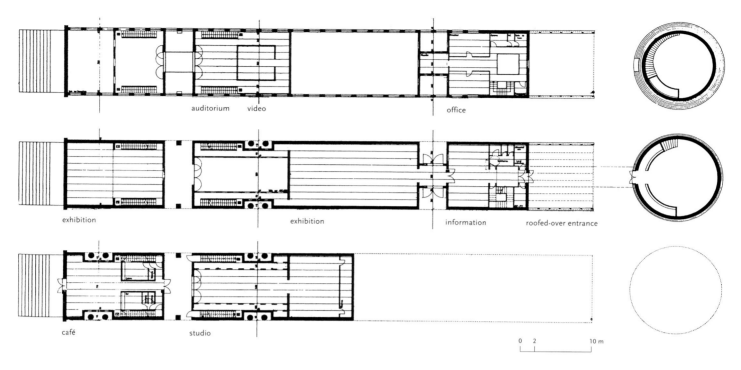

auditorium   video   office

exhibition   exhibition   information   roofed-over entrance

café   studio

0 2   10 m

Ground plans

serve equally well as artists' ateliers, exhibition halls or seminar rooms. Like the conical tower, its exterior is characterized by grey granite and red brickwork. Sparingly used motifs from the repertory of classical architecture awaken associations to an Arcadia that admittedly evades any concrete determination.

The way through the 80-metre long building laid out in five areas one behind the other, its interior sophisticatedly stacked in several levels, begins at the foot of the tower, at an open portico whose metal structure appears to be a modern abbreviation of a classical columned hall. The small-format, two-storey entrance area is followed by the long exhibition hall as the central space, spanned by a

segmented wooden roof and lit by arched windows placed high in the walls that again evoke the classical without it really being possible to consider them quotes. Under one part of this exhibition hall is an artist's atelier. On the main level, the last building section – separated from the rest of the building by an open, transversal passage – contains another exhibition room, and there is a café on the lower floor from which visitors can go outside.

L'architecture d'aujourd'hui 258/1988, pp. 72-73 (Didier Laroque) • Techniques et Architecture 387/1990, pp. 102-105 • Techniques et Architecture 399/1991, pp. 103-108 • Architectural Digest 3/1992, pp. 58-64 (M. Peppiatt) • Baumeister 9/1992, pp. 42-45 (Richard Maillinger) • Bauwelt 10/1992, p. 469 • Gianni Braghieri, Aldo Rossi, 4th ed. Zürich/Munich/London, 1993, pp. 248-249 • Alberto Farlenga, Aldo Rossi. Das Gesamtwerk, Cologne, 2001, pp. 192-195

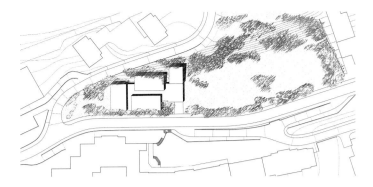

Site plan

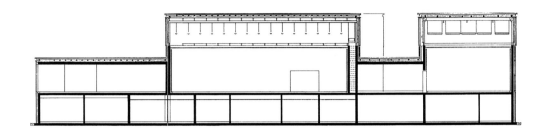

Cross section   Longitudinal section

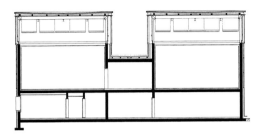

from left to right
General view from the terrace of a hotel up the hill | View of
the entrance area from the southeast | Collection room | Ent-
rance area (corridor), used as an exhibition room | Collection
room with view of the corridor

Kirchner Museum

Davos, Switzerland

Client	Kirchner Foundation Davos
Architects	Annette Gigon + Mike Guyer, Zurich
Enclosed space	12,830 m³
Net floor area	1,960 m²
Exhibition area	1,070 m²
Construction time	1991-1992 (invited competition 1989)

The occasion for the erection of this museum in
Davos in Switzerland was supplied by a donation of
circa 400 works by the German Expressionist Ernst
Ludwig Kirchner (1880-1938), who spent the last 21
years of his life there. The first large project by the
Zurich architects Annette Gigon and Mike Guyer
started from the basic idea of counterbalancing
Kirchner's expressive, colour-intensive pictorial
vocabulary with a purist architectural language of
reserved rigour. Four exhibition rooms (three of
them the same size, 18 x 9 x 4.75 metres, and a
smaller one of 11 x 9 x 4.75 metres) as cubic blocks
linked to each other by the lower entrance and
access hall determine the museum's appearance,
which functions like a paraphrase of the loosely

Structural details of the exhibition rooms

Ground floor plan

0　2　　　　　　　　10 m

jumbled flat roofs of Davos. However, this well-thought-out ensemble is marked above all by its glass cladding articulated by chromed steel bands. In part opaque and shimmering matte, in part transparent and reflecting, it covers the entire building like an external skin (even the flat roofs are covered with shards of glass instead of the usual gravel).

The interior lighting significantly determines the design of the building structure as a whole. In order to illuminate the collection rooms even in the winter months by means of a squared skylight extending from wall to wall, a well-proportioned glass housing was set over their volumes. This enables natural overhead lighting for the most part even when the snow is deep, by means of the lateral light regulated with the aid of lamellas (which can be infinitely variably supplemented by artificial light whenever necessary). The insulation necessary as a prerequisite for the exhibition rooms – their layout also had to take into account the existing trees – determines both the ground plan and the lower height of the corridor-like access hall to which visitors return again and again, and from which they can see outside. Exposed concrete and reduced lighting demonstratively differentiate this circulation area (which is not at all suitable for hanging pictures) from the white collection rooms with parquet floors, each accessed individually via doorless openings.

Faces. Journal d'architectures 26/1992-93, pp. 15-19 (Dorothee Huber) • *Werk, Bauen und Wohnen* 12/1992, pp. 24-29 (Walter Zschokke) • Annette Gigon/Mike Guyer, Werkstoff. Exhibition Catalogue, Lucerne, 1993 • *Domus* 748/1993, pp. 40-47 • *Techniques et Architecture* 408/1993, pp. 50-53 • *Deutsche Bauzeitung* 8/1994, pp. 64-69 (Hans Binder) • Christoph Mayr Fingerle (ed.), *Neues Bauen in den Alpen. Architekturpreis* 1995, Basel, 1996, pp. 8-17 • J. Christoph Bürkle (ed.), Gigon Guyer. Arbeiten 1989 bis 2000, Zürich, 2000, pp. 6-27

kunst im bau, pp. 100-105 • Maier-Solgk, pp. 96-103 • Meseure/Tschanz/Wang, pp. 280-281 (Anna Meseure) • Newhouse, pp. 87-89

Open Plans

Especially in the sixties and seventies, the open plan was not only considered a model of democratic transparency, but also, as a supposedly neutral pattern, provided the prerequisite for a multitude of transformation possibilities achievable by technical means. The most spectacular example of this is the Centre Pompidou, whose original conception has to a large extent been lost, however, by the subsequent addition of fittings. Nonetheless, this architecture conceived as a "flexible container" is programmatically placed at the beginning of our selection of museum buildings whose open structure is appropriate not least for didactically arranged science museums like the newMetropolis or Domus. This section ends intentionally with two museums, the Kunsthaus in Bregenz and the Neue Nationalgalerie in Berlin, whose very different rooms – that are in any case to be classified as "open" – are no longer intended to be understood as neutral envelopes, but instead as manifestations of the epitome of architectural space.

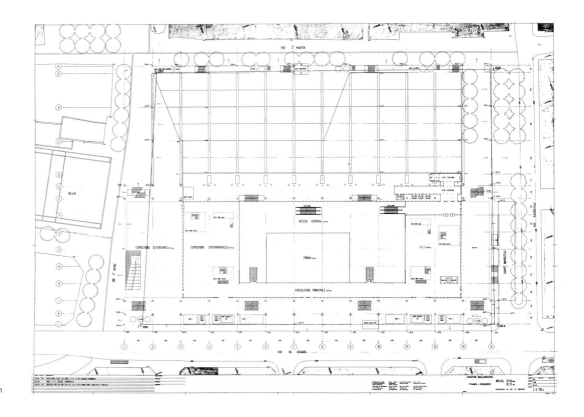

Ground floor plan

Aerial view | View from the tower of Notre Dame cathedral: painted white like the entire supporting structure, the side façades are determinated by the wind guys | East façade with the characteristic white ventilation shafts | The west side facing the square, is the main show side with the distinctive escalator

Centre National d'Art et de Culture Georges Pompidou

Paris, France

Client	Ministries of Culture and Education, Paris
Architects	Renzo Piano and Richard Rogers, Milan/London
Enclosed space	430,000 m³
Total area	92,900 m²
Exhibition area	17,000 m²
Construction time	1972-1977 (competition won 1971); Alterations 1985 and 1997-2000

To erect "an architectural and urban complex that will mark our century" – as the task was formulated in the invitation to the competition for the first of the "grands projets Parisiens," whose initiation has since then come to belong to the image of the historically-conscious French presidents – was a challenge that 681 architects' offices in 49 countries rose to meet. Posthumously named after its initiator, the project was to house in addition to the exhibition rooms for contemporary works of art, a library, a design centre, and music studios as well. It does credit to the project's initiator that he accepted the competition judges' courageous decision in favour of the design that, as the embodiment of the anti-museum spirit rooted in the utopias of the late six-

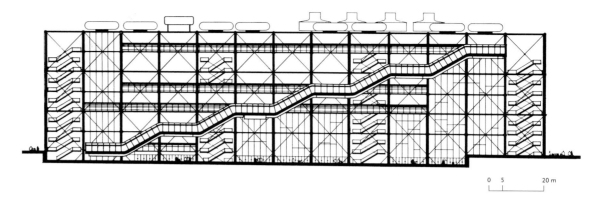

Elevation of the east façade on Rue Renard

0 5   20 m

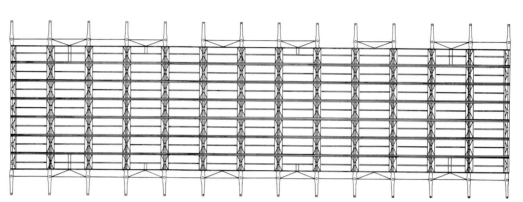

Plan of the construction system

ties, was virtually the antithesis to the existing cultural monuments. Piano and Rogers, who wanted the desired cultural centre to be understood as a "theme park with information and entertainment," determined that half of the available building site was to be a public square. Facing it was to be the façade – equipped with neon lights and enormous video screens – of a "cheerful city machine," which as a "flexible container and dynamic communication machine made of prefabricated parts" represented a technically and functionally provocative architecture. Their basic idea was to erect the building as a huge scaffolding that allowed all manner of changes inside. The interior space was to be totally flexible and even variable in the third dimension by means of

pneumatic ceilings. Financial considerations led to the moveable ceilings being abandoned, while fire safety regulations dictated the storeys be subdivided by partition walls, and ideologically motivated concerns led to the rejection of the media façade. In the end, for security reasons, the numerous entrances that had originally been planned were also reduced to a minimum. In spite of the restrictions imposed and the numerous alterations required in the course of many changes of plan, the conceptual focuses of movement, variability, and flexibility were realized here in an exemplary fashion.

The building, 166.4 metres long, in front of the transparent glass skin is dominated by a huge sup-

porting structure of cast steel, its elements developed, shaped, and manufactured specially for this project. Suspended from hollow steel supports eighty centimetres in diameter, 8.9-metre long "gerberettes" (cantilevers named after their inventor, Heinrich Gerber, a nineteenth-century German engineer) carry fourteen oversized trussed beams per storey. Spaced at intervals of 12.8 metres, these each span 48 metres without supports and thereby enable flexible interior spaces. Six metres in front of the main supports are positioned strengthening cross struts that are linked to the gerberettes by means of tension rods. This way, two parallel vertical zones, both 7 metres deep, are created on the two long sides of the building. These provide access

175

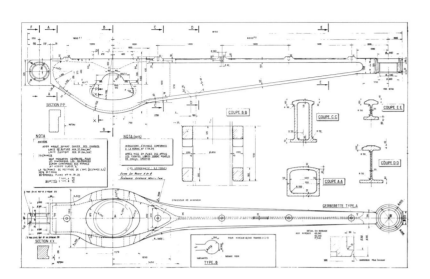

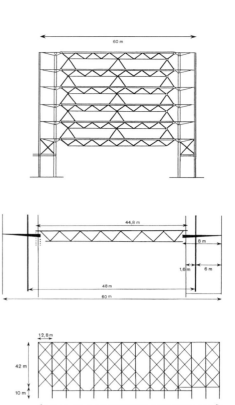

The specially developed gerberette, cast by Krupp

Plan of the wind guys on the side facing
the square and the transverse sides

from left to right
As the main connecting element, the escalator demonstratively
puts on display the high-tech character of this architecture |
External access | Entrance area, with the newly designed signa-
ge by Rudi Baur | The 'boulevard' running through the whole
building as the access to the exhibition rooms

and supply functions. Caterpillar chain-like tube
escalators climb diagonally across the building's
western façade facing the open space; as the primary access route for all the floors, they not only
mark the appearance of the building decisively, but
also illustrate directly the myth of movement and
mobility that has become a leitmotif of the modern
age. On the back of the building too, all the supply
lines are shifted to the exterior, thus determining its
appearance. The fact that they are painted in bright
colours – ventilation shafts in blue, water pipes in
green, electrical installations in yellow – is to be
understood neither as decoration nor as provoca-
tion, but is instead to render elementary architectural functions visible in pithy symbolism.

The building's spatial system is simple; in addition
to an extensive entrance area in which the usual
service facilities are accommodated, it includes five
more or less open levels in which are housed the
library, the museum for modern art, and temporary
exhibition spaces. (The IRCAM music institute and
its sophisticated sound studios were transferred in
their entirety to a subterranean level and then subsequently extended below the square next to the main
building.) The floors of the museum at first were
only subdivided by suspended walls, a solution
which was problematic especially for the presentation of more traditionally-sized pictures. They were
then subdivided for the first time into smaller museum rooms organised as a rhythmic sequence by

Gae Aulenti in 1985. During the general refurbishment of the building, undertaken under the direction of Renzo Piano between 1997 and 2000 (made
necessary not least by the extraordinary success
of the Centre Pompidou, which was expected to
attract 5,000 visitors daily, and in fact is inundated
by five times that quantity per day) Jean-François
Bodin organized the storeys into a large boulevard
running the entire length of the building and giving
access to the small-scale exhibition areas on both
sides. The basic principle of the supporting structure – which has remained visible – conveys an
impression of the original architectural conception,
but not without diverting attention away from the
objects on exhibition as it always has done.

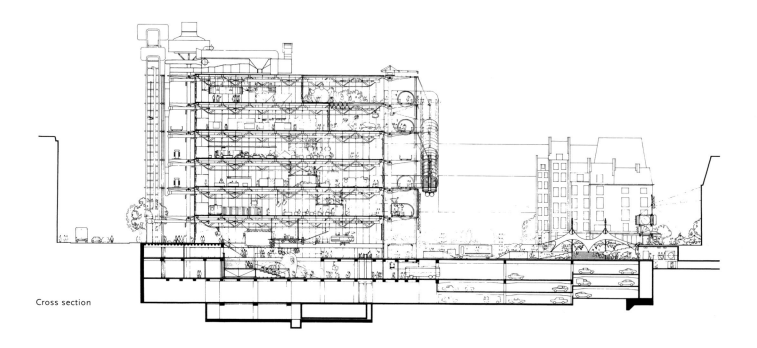

Cross section

The Centre Pompidou, which as the first actually erected building in a long tradition of construction ideas that had never before been consistently implemented (among others, the Russian Constructivists, Buckminster Fuller, Yona Friedman, Serge Chermayeff and the British group Archigram) has become the showpiece of a new building type in which the boundaries between technology and architectural form are dissolved, and has at the same time become the epitome of a provocative, boundary-blurring conception of culture that represents a counterweight to the design of the museum as temple.

Domus 503/1971, pp. 1-7; 511/1972, pp. 9-13; 558/1976, pp. 48-55; 566/1977, pp. 1-37 (Cesare Casati); 570/1977, pp. 17-24 and 575/1977, pp. 1-11 • *Architectural Design* 42/1972, pp. 407-410 (Peter Rawstorne) • *Deutsche Bauzeitung* 9/ 1972, pp. 974-976 and 4/1977, pp. 25-31 (Gerhard Ullmann) • *Techniques et Architecture* 298/1974, pp. 62-69; 317/1977, pp. 62-66 and 326/1979, pp. 33-38 • Alan Colquhoun/Andrew Rabeneck and others, Centre Pompidou (*Architectural Design* Profiles no. 2), London, 1977 • *The Architectural Review* 963/1977, pp. 270-294 (Reyner Banham) • *L'architecture d'aujourd'hui* 189/1977, pp. 40-81 (Hélène Demoraine/J. Prouvé/François Barré) • *Baumeister* 4/1977, pp. 329 (Adam W. Löffler) and 8/1984, pp. 78-79 • *Bauwelt* 11/1977, pp. 316-334 (Jochen Bub/Wim Messing); 7/1978, pp. 254-260 (Jochen Bub) and 4/2000, pp. 26-31 (François Chaslin; Helga Fassbinder) • *Werk. archithese* 9/1977, pp. 13-28 (Maurice Besset, Franz Meyer, Leonardo Bezzola, Cathérine Mitsion/Magda Zakarian, Corinne Jacopin) • Yukio Futagawa, Piano + Rogers Centre Beaubourg, GA no. 44, 1977 • *Museumskunde* 43/ 1978, pp. 2-10 (Manfred Eisenbeis) • Jean Baudrillard, "Der Beaubourg-Effekt," in: Jean Baudrillard, Kool Killer or: Der Aufstand der Zeichen, Berlin, 1978, pp. 59-82 • Alexander Fils, Das Centre Pompidou in Paris, Munich, 1980 • Centre national d'art et de culture Georges Pompidou, (Stahl und Form 1980) • *Casabella* 515/1985, pp. 54-59 (Pierre-Alain Croset /Silvia Milesi) • Peter Buchanan, Renzo Piano Building Workshop. Complete Works, vol. 1, London, 1994, pp. 52-63; vol. 3, London, 1997, pp. 1 ff. • Kenneth Powell, Richard Rogers, Zürich/Munich/London, 1994, pp. 44-51 • Deyan Sudjic, Richard Rogers. Buildings and Projects, London, 1994, pp. 52-65 • Nathan Silver, The Making of Beaubourg. A Building Biography of the Centre Pompidou Paris, Cambridge, Mass., 1994 • *GA Architect* 14/1997, "Renzo Piano Building Workshop," pp. 30-45 • Winfried Nerdinger (ed.), Konstruktion und Raum in der Architektur des 20. Jahrhunderts, Munich/Berlin/London/ New York, 2002, pp. 78-81

López Moreno/López Rodríguez/ Castells, pp. 18-25 • Montaner/Oliveras, pp. 32-35 • Newhouse, pp. 193-198 • Tzonis/ Lefaivre 1992, pp. 84-89

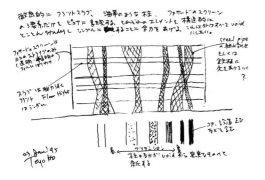

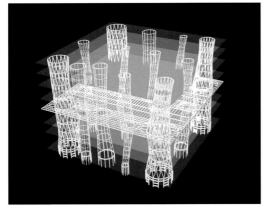

Toyo Ito: Design sketch "seaweed dancing in the water" | Schematic representation of the structural system of tubes and plates

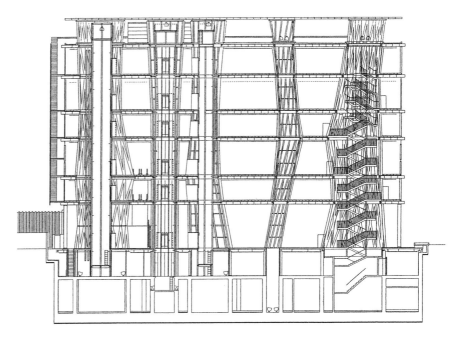

Section

From left to right
The storeys of varying heights differ in their lighting and the structure of the glass walls | The nocturnal appearance reveals the combination of geometric and organic elements | As a sort of 'second nature,' tree-like supports dominate the appearance of the flowing spaces

Mediatheque

Sendai, Japan

Client	City of Sendai
Architect	Toyo Ito & Associates, Tokyo
Total area	21,600 m²
Construction time	1995-2001 (Competition 1995)

For the task of bringing together in a single building a library, media ateliers open to the public, audio-visual facilities, and not least, an exhibition centre (which was expressly intended to be a prototype for a public building in the twenty-first century), the architect developed a design that is aptly described as a synthesis of minimalism and formal abundance. On an almost square ground plan, each of its sides 50 meters long, and surrounded on three sides by a transparent glass skin, the building – which appears from the outside to be a minimalist cube – is composed of two underground floors and seven upper floors of varying heights, which are articulated only by thirteen irregularly arranged 'tubes.' These are bundles of steel tubes of varying diameters, diago-

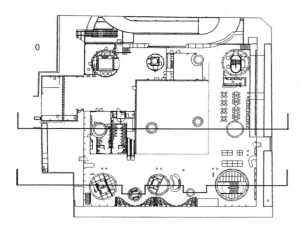

0

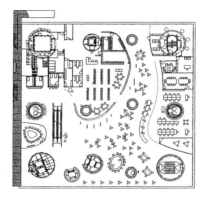

2

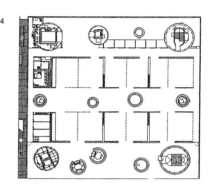

6

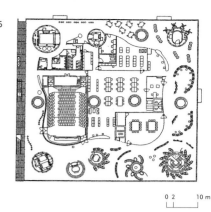

0 2   10 m

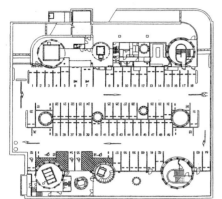

-1

1

4

Ground plans

nally crossing each other; their tree-like form is reminiscent of the "primeval hut" said to be the origin of architecture. Here, it is no longer surrounded by nature, but by the modern city conceived as second nature. The 'tubes' form not only an earthquake-proof supporting structure, but also contain the entire infrastructure, serve for vertical access and ventilation, and deflect daylight into the interior by means of concave glass prisms.

Between these towers, whose effect is both organic and expressive at the same time, and whose form changes from one floor to the next and thereby evokes analogies to nature – Toyo Ito described one design sketch as "seaweed dancing in water" – the

flowing spaces develop into wide open areas. The architect conceives of these and their transparent boundaries of glass of different materialities as the correlative of an open life form. The transparency of the façade skin defined as an organic membrane aims at flexibility and "equality of perspectives." This program developed out of Japanese culture and targeting the continual change in today's media society, forces one to question the certainty of one's own perspective. A quarter of a century ago, and under different premises, the Centre Pompidou had already demonstrated that this external transparency and open building organisation open up possibilities – in particular for exhibitions – that are as exciting as they are problematic.

Casabella 684-685/2000-2001, pp. 144-165 (Andrea Maffei) • ARCH+ 148, 10/1999, pp. 36-41 • Architectural Design 71/ 2001, pp. 104-108 (Jeremy Melvin) • Architectural Record 189/2001, pp. 191-201 (Naomi R. Pollock) • Archis 2/2001, pp. 104-124 (Tom Avermaete; Thomas Daniell) • Baumeister 6/2001, pp. 60-73 (Nikolaus Knebel; Mike Schlaich) • Detail 7/2001, pp. 1202-1212 (Andrea Wiegelmann) • Domus 835/ 2001, pp. 36-59 (Deyan Sudjic) • Japan Architect 41/2001, pp. 16-17 (Toyohiko Kobayashi) • Hubertus Adam/Jochen Paul (eds.), Höhepunkte der Weltarchitektur, Cologne, 2001, pp. 410-411 • Toyo Ito, Sendai Mediatheque, Miyagi, Japan, 1995-2000, Tokyo, 2001 • Ron Witte/Hiroto Kobayashi (eds.), Toyo Ito: Sendai Mediatheque, Munich/London, 2002 • Tomoko Sakamoto/Albert Ferre (eds.), Sendai Mediatheque, Barcelona, 2003 • Annette LeCuyer, Steel and Beyond, Basel/Berlin/ Boston, 2003, pp. 74-79

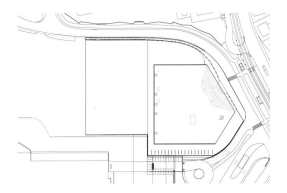

Site plan

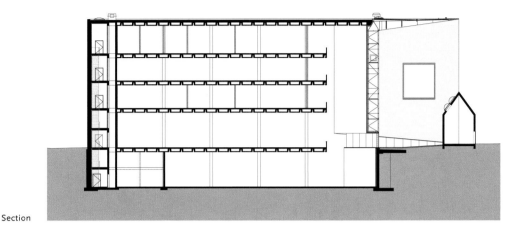

Section

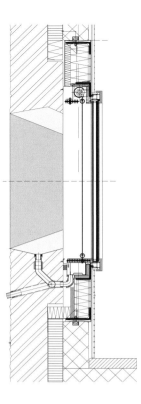

Detail section: first floor / south

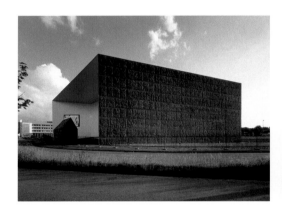

above and right
The compact, clay-brown volume is broken open only on the entrance side by a trapezoid white inversion and accentuated by a minimalist entrance | An enormous window slit at the foot of the entrance niche and one (of two) LED screens create links on different levels between inside and outside

Schaulager for the Emanuel Hoffmann-Foundation

Münchenstein/Basel, Switzerland

Client	Laurenz Foundation, Basel
Architects	Herzog & de Meuron, Basel
Total area	20,000 m²
Exhibition area	4,300 m²
Depot area	7,244 m²
Construction time	2000-2003 (award 1998)

In contrast to a traditional museum, as an accessible depot for the often extremely space-consuming and also very fragile works of contemporary art, the Schaulager (the architects had the name copyrighted) is to be seen as a new type of building. It redistributes the weighting of the museum tasks of collecting, conserving, and researching, by offering not only optimum curatorial conditions, but also making these objects permanently accessible to a limited circle of experts. In addition to this storage of art works according to archival principles, for which the majority of the floor space is destined, the building also provides the facilities for a restricted number of exhibitions to be put on every year.

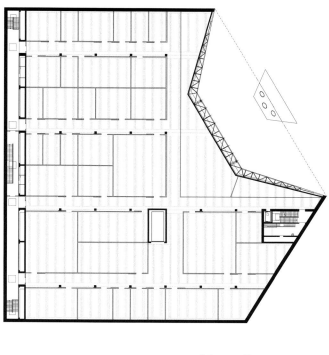

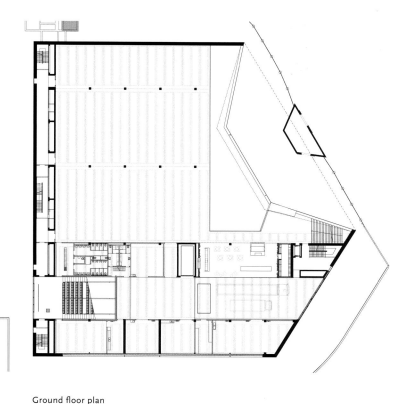

Ground floor plan

Ground plan of the third floor

0 2 10 m

from left to right
The depot levels stacked on top of each other open onto an interior the height of the building | "Warehouse berths" | Window-"clefts" for offices and workshops

The design of the building resulted out of the structure of the internal arrangement of the depot, the shape of the building site, and not least, out of the requirement for an optimum internal climate with a constant temperature of 21 degrees centigrade at 50 percent humidity. Above the ground plan, which is an irregular pentagon with two right angles, the five-storey volume rises as a compact block. The earth-like surface texture of its mud-brown walls of concrete and the gravel accumulated from the excavation is penetrated at only a few places by irregularly curving window bands that look like horizontal cracks in the walls. In an effective contrast to this, the trapeziformly recessing entrance side painted in dazzling white forms an inviting external space that is watched

over, as it were, by a little earth-coloured building at the eaves line. Two LED screens acting as huge eyes that transmit to the outside images from the exhibition currently running supplement the architectural gesture on a virtual plane.

When one comes into the entrance hall that takes up the entire height of the building, the interior – lit by a window slit the height of a man at the foot of the entrance niche – gives a magnificent view over the two exhibition levels and the three upper levels of the depot divided into cell-like units. These levels all open onto the atrium, and in the regular rhythm of the balconies stacked above each other and the linear arrangement of the strip lighting, clearly illus-

trate their function as a neutral series of storage rooms.

architektur aktuell 9/2003, pp. 66-75 (Andrea Nussbaum) • *Baumeister* 9/2003, pp. 70-77 (Hubertus Adam) • *Detail* 7-8/2003, pp. 766-767 (Frank Kaltenbach) • *Werk, Bauen & Wohnen* 7-8/2002, pp. 4-11 (Jacques Lucan)

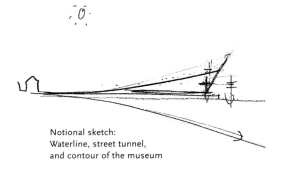

Notional sketch:
Waterline, street tunnel,
and contour of the museum

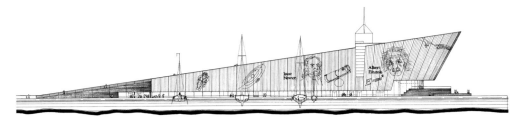

Eastern elevation

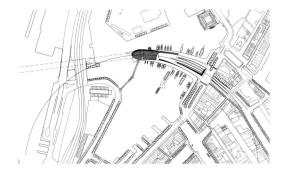

Site plan

Longitudinal section

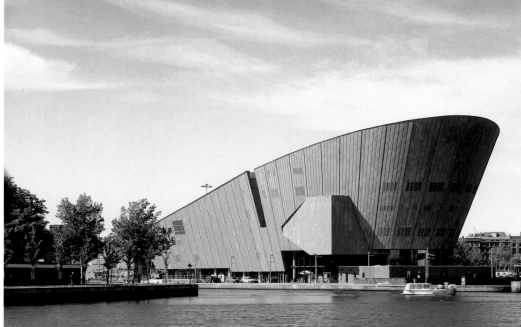

from left to right
View from the southeast; in the foreground, the footbridge
that serves as the main access | View from the northeast |
West façade with the main entrance (above the entrance to
the street tunnel) | The interior, seen from the third floor

newMetropolis. National Center for Science and Technology

Amsterdam, Netherlands

Client	NINT (Netherlands Institute for Industry and Technology)
Architect	Renzo Piano Building Workshop, Genoa
Enclosed space	64,212 m³
Total area	11,675 m²
Exhibition area	4,300 m²
Roof terrace	3,750 m²
Construction time	1994-1997 (commissioned in 1992)

The intention of newMetropolis – which is more a communications centre than a museum – is to enable visitors take part in a variety of events in and around science and technology through interactive media. Exhibition halls for temporary exhibitions, a cinema, a science theatre, and a learning laboratory were to be housed in a single building, the design for which the architect (who did not have to enter a competition to win the commission) developed primarily out of the unusual urban situation at the historical port of Amsterdam.

According to the architect, the dynamic form of the museum (covered with copper cladding that had already acquired a patina) was not based on

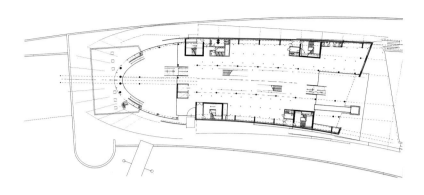

Ground plan of the first floor

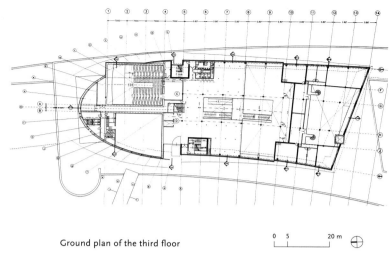

Ground plan of the third floor

0   5   20 m

the naïve metaphor of a ship at anchor as the optimum visualisation of the Dutch technology of wresting land from the sea. Instead, the design idea resulted out of the location exactly above the entrance of a curved traffic tunnel. The rising contour of this museum is therefore supposed to mirror the street leading under the sea at the waterline but at the same time it also results in the building (requiring complex static structures because it rests for the most part on the tunnel itself and is additionally supported by pilings) reaching a maximum height of 32 metres. In a way, the museum is the "three-dimensional answer to the two-dimensional appearance of the city." The dialectic relationship to the old part of the city – an unparalleled view of which

is to be had from the freely accessible roof terrace – is also expressed in the contrast between the bricks typical of the area on the lower parts of the museum and the metal cladding signalling another world on those parts that tower above the city's skyline.

Mostly artificially lit, in the museum's interior, whose design was arrived at in close co-operation with the Anglo-Canadian exhibition team of James Bradburne, the architecture keeps itself as much in the background as possible, providing fluid space for the exhibits (mostly destined for experimentation). In so far it exemplifies an open museum space totally subordinate to function. The space is distributed across four levels, and it opens toward the middle,

where unpretentiously designed stairways enable flexible circular tours.

architektur aktuell 209/1997, pp. 58-71 (Stefan Löffler) • *The Architectural Review* 1210/1997, pp. 54-58 (Peter Buchanan) • Contemporary Museums (Architectural Design Profile 130), 1997, II-V • The Renzo Piano Logbook, London, 1997, pp. 212-216 • Peter Buchanan, Renzo Piano Building Workshop. Complete Works, vol. 4, London, 2001, pp. 36-55

Henderson, pp. 182-187

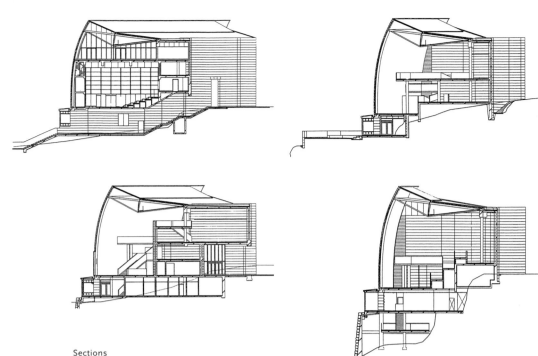

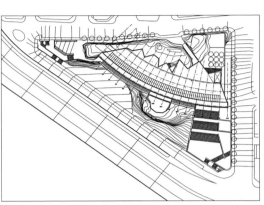

Site plan

Sections

from left to right
Wide steps lead from the embankment road to the entrance on the other side of the museum | View from the embankment road | At the tip of the corner, the two different façades meet | The fortress-like side of the museum faces the city | Main level of the interior with the stairway leading to the gallery | The interior, seen from the gallery

Domus

La Coruña, Spain

Client	City of La Coruña
Architects	Arata Isozaki, Tokyo César Portela, Pontevedra
Exhibition area	1,200 m²
Construction time	1993-1995

A modern science museum which has the aim of making mankind, the human body, and human culture comprehensible in an appealing fashion should also attract attention with an unusual architectural form. Of very different origins and persuasions, the two architects who were commissioned to design this museum so open to experimentation developed a building structure that started with the specific topography, letting the building appear as if it were a continuation of nature using its own means. It therefore presents a clear contrast to the conventional forms of the surrounding buildings. Above a bay on the seacoast, the dark, gently curving building sits upon the cliffs and cyclopean boulders of shimmering reddish granite. The double curve of

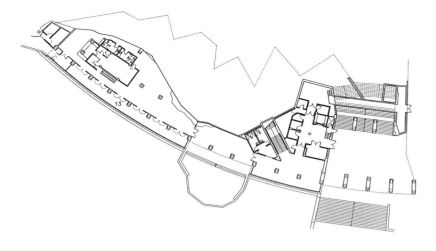

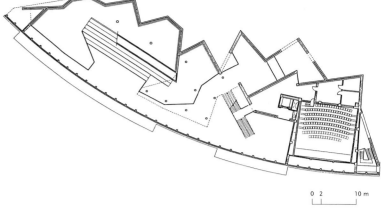

Ground plan of the lower floor

Ground plan of the main level

0 2 10 m

this façade of screwed down slate slabs awakens associations that are contradictory but nonetheless quite justified – of a sail bellying out in the wind or a paralysed tank, its interior shrouded in mystery. In contrast to this organically rounded form, the side of the museum facing the city, irregularly saw-toothed and of grey granite, thus continuing the structure of the cliff formation, functions like a demonstration of the anorganic principle. Or are the two so different façades supposed to be understood as metaphors for the antagonism between nature and culture?

The interior, lighted almost exclusively from above and bathed in an atmosphere of the experimental,

consists essentially of an extended room, 17 metres high, divided by an irregularly formed gallery into two levels on which the scenario of the interactive transfer of knowledge can unfold. Separated from this spatial continuum are only the service rooms on the bottom floor illuminated from the exterior by a narrow band of windows and an event auditorium above the wide stairway, which leads from the street paralleling the shore below the museum and through it to the cave-like entrance on the side facing the city.

The Architectural Review 1183/1995, pp. 58-62 (Carolyn Jarvitts) • *GA Document* 44/1995, pp. 74-83 • Isozaki & Domus, eds. Ayunamento de la Coruña-Domus-Cubiertas, La Coruña, 1995 • *Bauwelt* 40/1996, pp. 2306-2309 (David Cohn) • *Deutsche Bauzeitschrift* 1/1996, pp. 28-29 • *El Croquis* 76/1996, pp. 78-91

Cerver, pp. 60-71 • Mostaedi, pp. 156-165 • Peressut, pp. 112-119

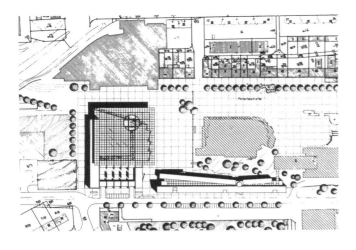

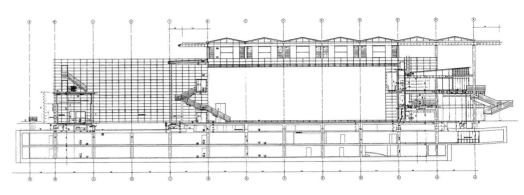

Site plan and sections

from left to right
General view from the southwest | General view from the
northwest (city side) | Central hall | North cabinet | Foyer

Kunstmuseum

Wolfsburg, Germany

Client	Kunststiftung Volkswagen
Architects	Schweger + Partner, Hamburg
Enclosed space	51,500 m³
Net floor area	8,510 m²
Exhibition area	3,500 m² (+ 670 m² sculpture courtyard)
Construction time	1990-1993 (competition 1989)

In sight of the theatre by Hans Scharoun and next to
the cultural centre by Alvar Aalto, the Kunstmuseum
was to define a new entrance to the city centre. The
Hamburg office of Schweger + Partner designed a
building that as a "city loggia" narrows the access
to the pedestrian zone and thereby creates an entrance situation that is still further emphasized by
the roof jutting far out. While the southern façade
appears to be a closed factory wall, the museum
opens toward the culture centre opposite in demon-
strative openness and turns out to be a largely
transparent cube surrounded by slender columns
more than 17 metres tall supporting the projecting
roof which appears to be filigree in spite of its size.
A glazed rotunda marks the entrance at the north-

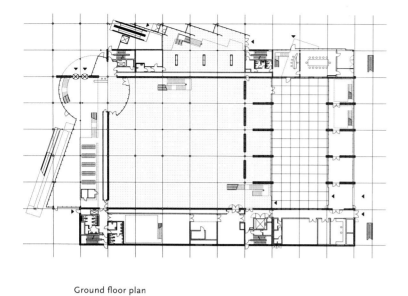

Ground floor plan

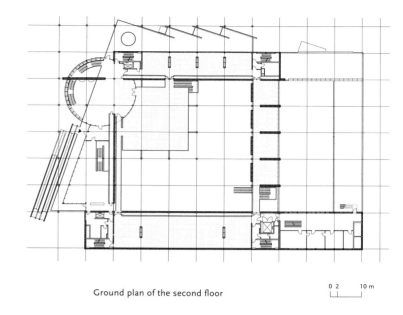

Ground plan of the second floor

0 2   10 m

western corner of the museum. Like the urbanistically sensible diagonally placed external ramp to the café, this rotunda also breaks the strict grid structure of the building.

The arrangement of the ground plan of the museum is clear and easy to grasp. Around a square hall (whose sides are five times as long as those of the basic 8.10 metre grid) that takes up the entire height of the building are grouped on two levels partly open, partly closed rooms that are flexibly adaptable, so that all the walls, for example, have interchangeable surfaces. From the surrounding gallery one recognizes the impressive spatial effect of the great hall, but also the technical difficulties associ-

ated with exhibiting in it. On the eastern side, across from the entrance, an open sculpture courtyard is attached, the same length and half the width of the central hall and surrounded by ateliers, depots, and administrative offices.

The high-tech appearance of this architecture consisting primarily of steel and glass corresponds to the technical refinement above all of the extraordinarily sophisticated lighting system. A micro-grid integrated in the laminated glass of the ceilings and the side walls filters the sunlight coming in that afterwards can still be broken by reflectors and selectively directed. Finally, in addition to a system for supplementing the daylight, there is also an artificial

lighting system for entirely closed rooms as well as for evenings and nights.

wettbewerbe aktuell, 6/1989, pp. 359-370 • *Bauwelt* 35/1993, pp. 1798-99 • Kunstmuseum Wolfsburg. Architekten Schweger + Partner, Berlin, 1994 • *Baukultur* 1-2/1995, pp. 15-17

Maier-Solgk, pp. 247-255

Site plan

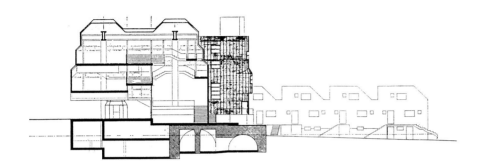

Section

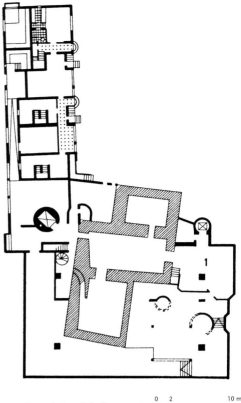

Ground plan of the basement

0 2   10 m

from left to right
General view from the marketplace with the cathedral in the background | The museum from the north, with the administration wing in the foreground | The interior of the museum (original state) | View from the main entrance into the interior (after it was redesigned)

Erzbischöfliches Diözesanmuseum

Paderborn, Germany

Client	Archiepiscopal Vicariate-General in Paderborn
Architects	Gottfried Böhm, Cologne Michael Brawne (alteration)
Enclosed space	13.000 m³
Net floor area	1,576 m²
Exhibition area	1,200 m²
Construction time	1971-1974 (restricted competition 1969) 1991-1992 (alteration/refurbishment)

The restoration of the area around Paderborn cathedral provided the opportunity to erect a diocesan museum. Gottfried Böhm's design adopts the proportions of the old urban structure.

The four-storey main building of the museum is situated on the northern side of the marketplace, right next to the main entrance of the cathedral. While this main building is as tall as the cathedral's nave, to the north a lower wing destined for offices is attached to it. This office wing is angled around the cathedral, ending precisely at the foot of the mighty western tower of the cathedral. Thus a dialectic relation comes into being between the mediaeval church building and the massively structured shape of the

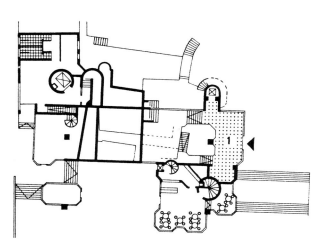

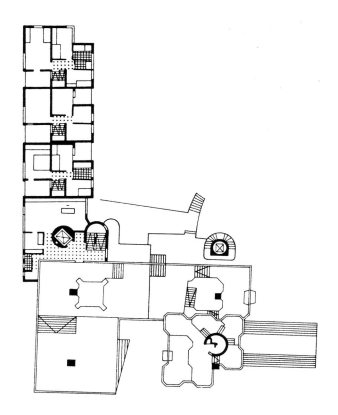

Ground floor plan (market level)

Ground plan of the mezzanine

museum, which makes it impossible to see the cathedral as a whole except from certain precisely calculated angles. The skin of grey lead that unites the façade and the roof of the museum, which is supported by four columns, into a three-dimensional unit matches the roofing of the cathedral in both size and colour. In contrast, the ground floor, which is set back somewhat, is glazed so that the marketplace seems to be incorporated into the museum.

Providing a counterpoint to the building's forbiddingly 'closed' external aspect, Gottfried Böhm designed the interior as an "open museum." Apart from a treasure chamber built into the mediaeval vault of the cellar, it consists of an undivided room

whose different levels – linked by a continuously climbing circuit – afford visitors views into all the other levels. The silver-grey colour of the interior space and its furnishings as well as the accumulation of rod-like elements on landings and plinths generated a high-tech atmosphere which took away the religious aura from the exhibits – mostly sculptural – thus virtually objectifying them.

Soon after the opening of the museum, building defects already started to appear, mainly in the HVAC system. Finally it was decided to set a new inner shell into the existing external skin of the building in accordance with a design by the English exhibition architect Michael Brawne. Although this

leaves the spatial structure of Böhms' architecture untouched to a great extent, it replaces its transparency marked by glass and metal with cream-coloured wall surfaces, creating an entirely different spatial effect. The result renders visible the dilemma between curatorial conditions that are unquestionably better and a loss of architectural stringency.

Bauwelt 2/1976, pp. 52-59 • Deutsche Bauzeitschrift 9/1977, pp. 1115-1118 • Ulrich S. von Altenstadt, "Zwiesprache zwischen Alt und Neu," in: Der Architekt 2/1979, pp. 105-107 • Bauwelt 34/1992, pp. 1883 (Karin Jansen) • Diözesanmuseum Paderborn 1913-1993. Commemorative volume on the occasion of the reopening on 18th June 1993, Paderborn, 1994 • Wolfgang Pehnt, Gottfried Böhm, Basel/Berlin/Boston, 1999, pp. 86-87

Schubert, pp. 104-105

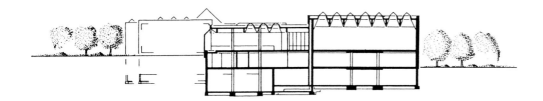

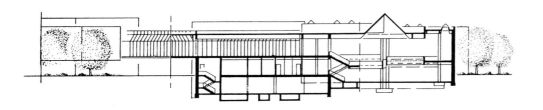

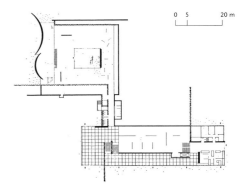

Ground plan of the lower floor
(first and second building phases)

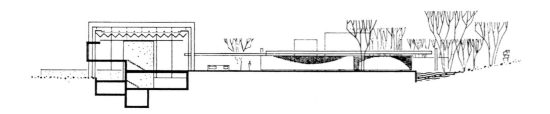

Sections from top to bottom
First and second phase of building | third building phase | third building phase

from left to right
The concrete building reserved for Wilhelm Lehmbruck's
sculptures (second building phase) | Glazed hall (first build-
ing phase) seen from the entrance side | Second building
phase, interior | Large exhibition hall (third building phase)

Wilhelm-Lehmbruck-Museum

Duisburg, Germany

Client	City of Duisburg
Architect	Manfred Lehmbruck, Stuttgart
Enclosed space	23,900 m³ (1ˢᵗ + 2ⁿᵈ building phases)
	21,290 m³ (3ʳᵈ building phase)
Net floor area	4,340 m² (1ˢᵗ + 2ⁿᵈ building phases)
	3,545 m² (3ʳᵈ building phase)
Exhibition area	1,890 m² (1ˢᵗ building phase),
	1,220 m² (2ⁿᵈ building phase)
	2,356 m² (3ʳᵈ building phase)
	1,300 m² (sculpture courtyard)
Construction time	1959-1964 (1ˢᵗ + 2ⁿᵈ building phases)
	1985-1986 (3ʳᵈ building phase)

Apart from Cologne's Wallraf-Richartz-Museum by
Rudolf Schwarz, this building that is devoted to
modern art – primarily the sculptural work of the
Duisburg artist Wihelm Lehmbruck (1881–1919) –
is one of the first important German museum buildings of the postwar era. Manfred Lehmbruck, the
artist's son, designed two entirely different building
segments linked to each other by a common entrance hall and a raised sculpture courtyard. For
the general collection, there is a glazed rectangular
volume suspended from five steel girders (first
building phase) that leaves all possibilities of light
incidence open, containing a large hall that can be
subdivided at will and a smaller picture gallery suspended within it.

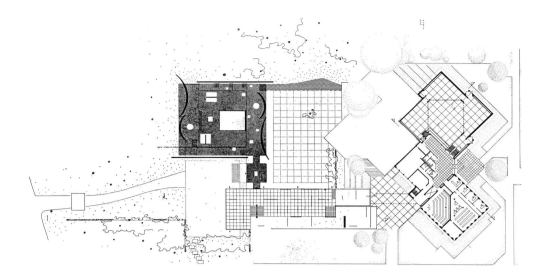

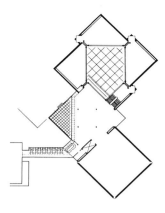

Ground floor plan (first to third building phases)

Ground plan of the upper floor
(third building phase)

In contrast to this open hall reminiscent of Mies van der Rohe, Manfred Lehmbruck designed for the presentation of his father's work a volume of concrete, experienced as more sculptural than otherwise (second building phase) which does not need to be flexible and is undoubtedly one of the most impressive achievements of more recent museum architecture. Around a rectangular sunken inner courtyard that functions as a central source of light is positioned a calm, almost square space whose external boundaries are formed by great, in part lightly curving, wall slabs of exposed concrete; inside it is articulated by slender, rectangular slices stood on end, piercing the ceiling. As these concrete walls neither touch each other nor are attached to the ceiling, the latter – pierced by very varied openings for light – appears to be floating in spite of its apparent weight. The incidence of light focused by the openings lends the sculptures three-dimensionality. By means of terraces and galleries, the architecture takes up the dialog with the sculptural works and, moreover, enables viewers to see above and below the sculptures, which is essential.

More than twenty years later, a third building phase doubled the spatial volume of the museum, both for the exhibition and the secondary areas. Based on the square and its rotation, the ground plan structure of the wing – which is roofed over by a glass pyramid and clearly set apart from the rest of the building – does not achieve the latter's strong concentration.

Deutsche Bauzeitung 11/1964, S. 881-894 (Manfred Lehmbruck/Hans Klinkhammer) • *Architektur und Wohnform* 72/1964, S. 347-356 (Manfred Lehmbruck) • Wilhelm-Lehmbruck-Museum Duisburg, Duisburg, 1964

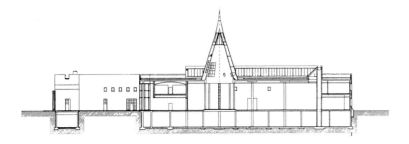

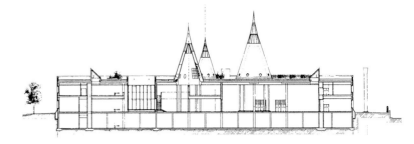

Sections

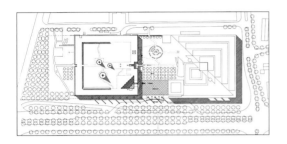

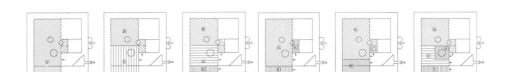

Plans for different exhibition areas

Site plan: to the left, the Bundeskunsthalle,
to the right, the Kunstmuseum (original design)

from left to right
The glass façade of the entrance foyer and the three light
cones at night | General view from the northwest (seen from
the Kunstmuseum) | East gallery | Atrium hall | Great Hall

Kunst- und Aus-
stellungshalle der
Bundesrepublik
Deutschland

Bonn, Germany

Client	Federal Republic of Germany (Bundesbaudirektion, Bonn)
Architect	Gustav Peichl, Vienna
Enclosed space	154,600 m³
Total area	32,000 m²
Exhibition area	5,412 m² (+ 8,000 m² roof garden)
Construction time	1989-1992 (invited competition 1985)

It was only after the decision was made to move the seat of government to Berlin in June 1992 that Bonn was able to fulfill the dream – cherished since 1949 – of an art and exhibition venue. The Vienna architect Gustav Peichl won the competition that was eventually separated from the municipal project of an art museum and specially initiated by the Federal Government.

The architect reacted to the existing urban situation – a square plot of land in faceless surroundings that was to function as a counterpart to the municipal art museum of approximately the same size – with the design of a compact block measuring 96 x 96 metres, whose severe austerity is not only relativized

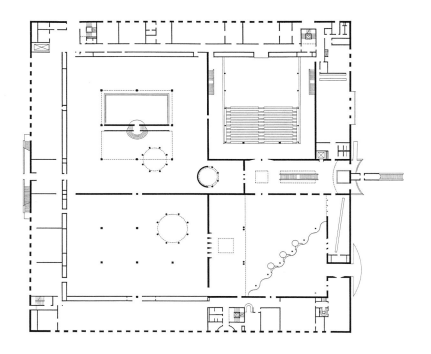

Ground floor plan

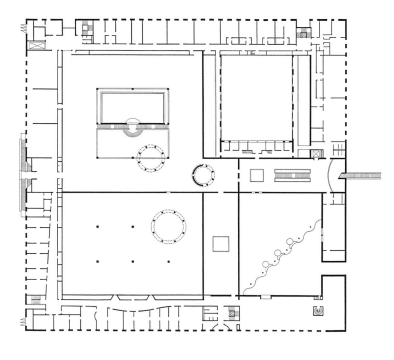

Ground plan of the upper floor

0   5   20 m

by three cones on the roof, but virtually subverted. These blue ceramic cones of different heights and with glass points function as sources of light for the interior, but above all, they signal something exceptional, directing attention – in particular when they are illuminated at night – to the 'fifth façade,' the roof, which is accessed via steep stairs, providing additional exhibition space primarily for sculptures.

The two-storey interior is laid out as a central area and a peripheral zone which contains all the service facilities and the administration, etc. on the ground floor, and on the upper floor, several gallery-like exhibition rooms. Visitors access in succession the entrance, a tall slit in the wall shifted to the corner –

the wiggly lines of the floor paving playfully direct one to this – and then an intimate triangular forecourt that is only separated from the spacious foyer by a fluted glass façade. From there, visitors access the large hall that occupies the entire height of the building, the open, two-storey atrium, and the auditorium. Creating the form of a tholos, slender columns that mark the position of the three light cones admittedly form exciting architectural accents within the otherwise entirely open rooms, but at the same time, they prevent the spaces from being really flexible, as is required for the presentation of very different exhibitions usually shown in parallel.

wettbewerbe aktuell 10/1986, pp. 587-598 and 7/1992, pp. 95-100 • *Transparent* 18/1987, pp. 4-16 • *Deutsche Bauzeitung* 8/1989, pp. 34-37 (Heinrich Schlüter) • *Baumeister* 9/1992, pp. 21-25 (Wolfgang Bachmann) • *Bauwelt* 26/1992, pp. 1528-1537 • Kunst- und Ausstellungshalle der Bundesrepublik Deutschland, ed. Bundesministerium für Raumordnung, Bauwesen und Städtebau, Bonn-Bad Godesberg, 1992 • Die Kunst- und Ausstellungshalle der Bundesrepublik Deutschland. Architekt Gustav Peichl, Stuttgart, 1992 • *Deutsche Bauzeitung* 4/1993, pp. 40-49 (Ingeborg Flagge) • *The Architectural Review* 1151/1993, pp. 58-64

Maier-Solgk, pp. 80-89

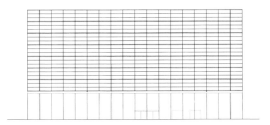

Elevation of the west façade (street façade)

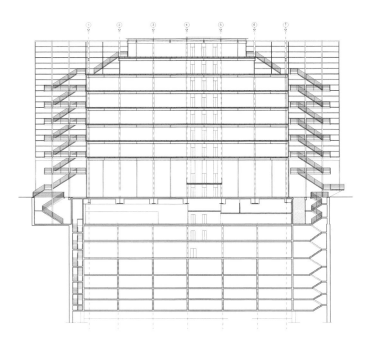

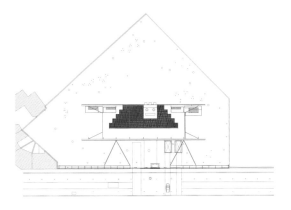

Site plan

Longitudinal section

from left to right
Glazed wall facing the street | General view from Boulevard
Raspail | Entrance situation (with Chateaubriand's cedar tree) |
View from the garden into the exhibition room on the ground
floor | Exhibition room on the ground floor

Fondation Cartier

Paris, France

Client	GAN Vie Insurance, Paris
Architects	Jean Nouvel, Emmanuel Cattani & Associés, Paris
Net floor area	ca. 6,200 m² (without underground garage)
Exhibition area	1,200 m²
Construction time	1991-1994

In accordance with the ideas of Cartier, the renowned
jewellers, an insurance company had a building
erected on the Boulevard Raspail in the Montpar-
nasse quarter of Paris by Jean Nouvel and Emmanuel
Cattani. It was to house Cartier's foundation for contemporary art in addition to the company's headquarters. The architects exploited the requirements
that they take into account existing building lines,
retain the surrounding park with its trees, and above
all, a cedar tree planted by Chateaubriand in the
early nineteenth century to design a clever creation.
They separated the plot of land from the street by
erecting two enormous, 8-metre high glass walls,
between which a paved path leads under the huge
umbrella of the cedar into the building, which is set

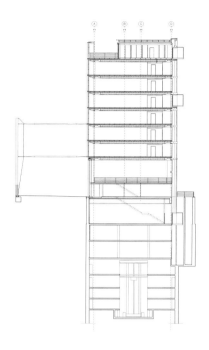

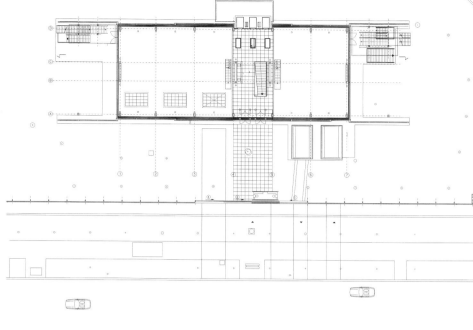

Cross section   Ground floor plan

back several metres. A transparent prism of glass, steel, and aluminium on a transversally laid out rectangular ground plan, the building towers over the external glass walls, twice as tall as these and crowned with the open frame structure of a belvedere. Of the sixteen storeys in total, the topmost serve as offices, while eight are below ground and are used for storage and service rooms as well as parking. The clever trick of letting the glass façade (which is overlaid with a fine-meshed grid of latticework) jut out above and laterally beyond the building volume has a determinative influence on the appearance of the entirely symmetric building. Therefore, by superimposing multiple views, reflections, and reflected light, an impression of haziness and contourlessness is

created that dematerializes the architecture, making it into a tangible illusion.

The ambiguity of this virtual reality is also characteristic of the almost entirely glazed exhibition hall on the ground floor which roller blinds can transform into a white or a black room. However, its 8-metre high glass walls along the long sides can also be slid away in order to generate a fluid transition from inside to outside, a unity between architecture, art, and nature. In contrast to this, the 6-metre high, whitewashed exhibition room on the first underground floor is without windows and receives what little daylight it gets only through three skylights.

Bauwelt 26/1994, pp. 1470-1476 • *ARCH+* 122 6/1994, pp. 56-59 • *Deutsche Bauzeitschrift* 9/1994, pp. 57-59 (Katrin Koch) • *Techniques et Architecture* 415/1994, pp. 26-31 • Olivier Boissière, Jean Nouvel, 3rd ed., Basel/Boston/Berlin, 1996, pp. 163-166 • Andrea Gleiniger/Gerhard Matzig/Sebastian Redecke, Paris. Contemporary Architecture, Munich/New York, 1997, pp. 76-81

Lampugnani/Sachs, pp. 146-153 (Sebastian Redecke)

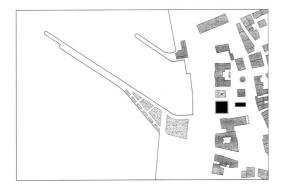

Site plan

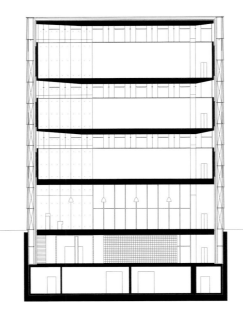

Section A

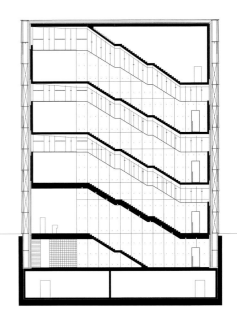

Section B

from left to right
The Kunsthaus, from the Seestraße | The Kunsthaus and the administration building from the city side | Entrance hall | Exhibition hall; on the right, the descending stairway | Exhibition hall

Kunsthaus

Bregenz, Austria

Client	State of Vorarlberg
Architect	Peter Zumthor, Haldenstein/ Switzerland
Enclosed space	28,000 m³
Net floor area	3,340 m²
Exhibition area	1,390 m²
Construction time	1994-1997 (Competition 1990)

For temporary exhibitions of contemporary art, Peter Zumthor developed a simple cube, the principal theme of which is light, out of the specific site situation on the outskirts of Bregenz' old city and on the shores of Lake Constance. Clad with more than 700 overlapping opaque glass shingles, their appearance changing dependent on the viewing angle and the lighting conditions, the plinthless solitaire without moulding of any kind appears to be a blinding cube when the sun is shining, while when it is foggy, it appears to almost literally melt away. As a weather skin, this glass skin, held at a distance from the walls by brackets of stainless steel and for that reason able to be lit from inside at night, also fulfils the functions of solar protection and insula-

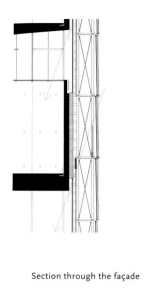

Section through the façade

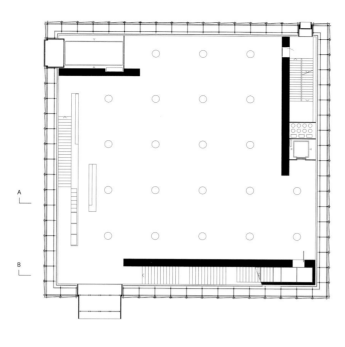

Ground floor plan

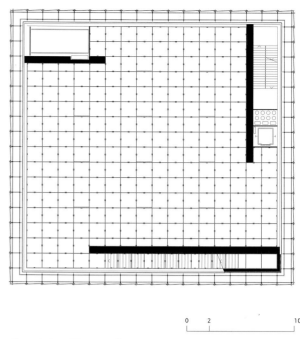

Ground plan of the upper floor

0   2   10 m

tion and not least, directs the light into the interior. Above each of the three exhibition levels, which are entirely surrounded by concrete walls, and slightly increasing in size to the top, is a light space, which is illuminated by daylight entering through the shell of the façade from all directions. It is deflected into the exhibition rooms below (supplemented as necessary by artificial light) through a light-dissipating ceiling of square, unframed matte glass plates. Below, the changing times of day are perceptible to visitors, to a lesser extent in the middle of the room, so that their attention is directed to the room boundaries. On the ground floor, the situation is reversed; light comes in only from the side through the glass walls while the ceiling remains dark. The building's

structure becomes clear here – it is supported by three walls of different length extending through all five storeys. The walls are positioned to each other in such a way that not only do they spatially separate out the access areas from the total square of the ground plan, but also generate a slight rotation corresponding to the circular route through the museum. Shielded like this, the terraced stairs lit from above are lent decided dynamics, while the exhibition rooms are lent a meditative character that is achieved not least through the subtle material composition of the exposed concrete of the walls and the terrazzo floor without joints, which subtly reflects the diffuse ceiling light. A factor that contributes significantly to Zumthor's cube achieving

this concentration is the shifting of the secondary areas into an administration building (kept all in black) that contrasts with the glass cube and adapts itself to the proportions of the small-scale development of the old city.

Paul Naredi-Rainer, "Zum Projekt 'Kunsthaus' in Bregenz", in: Bau-Handwerk-Kunst. Beiträge zur Architekturgeschichte Vorarlbergs im 20. Jahrhundert, Innsbruck, 1994, pp. 85-96 • Peter Zumthor, Kunsthaus Bregenz, Stuttgart, 1997 • architektur aktuell 207/1997, pp. 50-63 (Friedrich Achleitner) • The Architectural Review 1210/1997, pp. 46-53 • Archithese 4/1997, pp. 58-63 • Baumeister 9/1997, pp. 50-57 (Wolfgang Bachmann) • Bauwelt 12/1997, pp. 1910-1917 (Hubertus Adam)

kunst im bau, pp. 106-111 (Peter Zumthor) • Lampugnani/Sachs, pp. 116-123 (Friedrich Achleitner) • Mack, pp. 98-107 • Maier-Solgk, pp. 90-95 • Newhouse, pp. 56-60 • Peressut, pp. 190-197

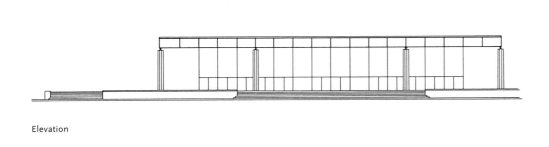

Elevation

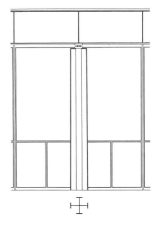

Support and roof, detail

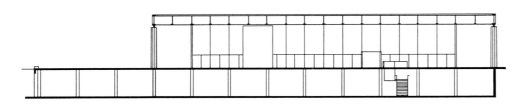

Section

from left to right
Exhibition hall, collage | View of the main entrance | Rear view
with sculpture courtyard | Exhibition hall during the OMA-
exhibition "Content", 2003/04

Neue
Nationalgalerie

Berlin, Germany

Client	Stiftung Preußischer Kulturbesitz
Architect	Ludwig Mies van der Rohe, Chicago
Enclosed space	79,500 m³
Net floor area	10,135 m²
Exhibition area	6,855 m² (+ 1,870 m² sculpture garden)
Construction time	1965-1968 (commission awarded 1962)

The burning desire to have a representative late
work by one of the most important architects of the
twentieth century was the prime motive for award-
ing the National Gallery project to Ludwig Mies van
der Rohe. Only afterward was the epoch-making
spatial enclosure fitted out with paintings from two
different collections. Mies van der Rohe, who was
less concerned with finding individual solutions than
he was with attaining a "higher unity of nature, man
and architecture" in general building types, fell back
on older, as yet unrealized plans for the Berlin project, which was encumbered with only a few requirements. On a granite plinth – an important motif
borrowed from Schinkel – sits a quadratic hall glazed
on all sides as the main storey with an entirely open

Free-form Spaces

The characteristic that is common to the museum buildings in this section, whose labelling ranges from "expressive" to "deconstructivist" to "plastic" and "organic" is the rejection of the prismatic form based on the axiom of the right angle. As the uniqueness of their appearance lies primarily in the extravagance (very differently motivated) of their architectural form, buildings such as the Jüdische Museum in Berlin, The Kiasma Museum in Helsinki, and the Neanderthal Museum in Mettmann are collected together here under the category of free-form spaces, although they also meet — and in this sequence — the criteria for "spatial interpenetration," "directed sequences of rooms" or "open plans." Even the Guggenheim Museum in Bilbao, which is considered to be the epitome of that 'plastic architecture' that breaks with all architectural conventions also has a sequence of rooms linked in enfilade on a square or rectangular ground plan. Yet the declared intention of all these buildings to underline the 'museum' purpose not least through their architecture understood as autonomous work of art justifies the appropriateness of the organizational category of "free-form spaces."

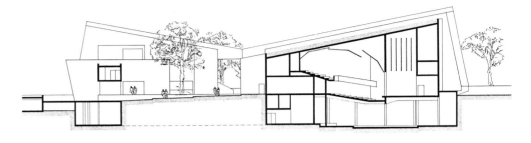

Longitudinal section

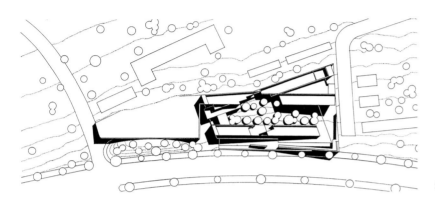

Site plan

from left to right
The narrow side reminds one of a fortress on a crag | The street side is characterized by the opposing movements of the ascending ramp and the descending wall, whose surface of dark kurkar (a calcareous sandstone) contrasts expressively with the light-coloured concrete of the ramp and the oriels | The shady courtyard opens onto a little open theatre | The access rooms too are characterized by plastic expressivity

Palmach Museum of History

Tel Aviv, Israel

Client	Palmach Veterans Association
Architects	Zvi Hecker and Ravi Segal, Tel Aviv
Built area	ca. 5,100 m²
Construction time	1992-1998 (competition 1992)

Although the building was programmatically intended as a multicultural facility with a theatre and a youth centre, etc., it is primarily a museum, commemorating Palmach, the Jewish underground organization (long since become a legend) that fought against British rule in Palestine and eventually, after the creation of the new sovereign state, was assimilated into the Israeli army. The expressive form of the museum, considered by architects to be a "portrait of Palmach," is developed as much out of the topographic conditions as it is out of the desire to make a symbolic statement. The different alignments of the ground plan figure, which consists of two extended parallel volumes, the one behind being diagonally cut through by a third, reacts to the

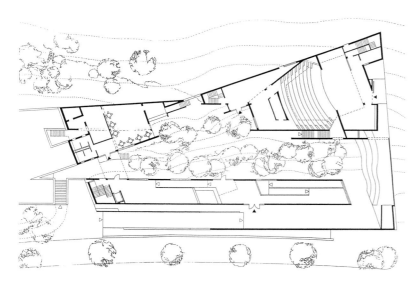

Ground floor plan

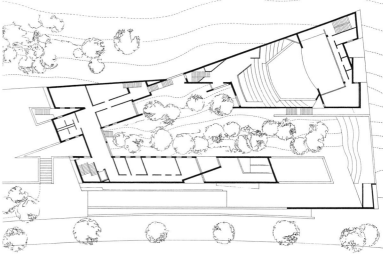

Ground plan of the first floor

0 2   10 m

immediate surroundings, while the elevation with its rising terraces and walls mirrors the character of the graduated site. Grouped around the approximately triangular inner courtyard containing a stand of old pines, which it was also a requirement to preserve, a system of concrete walls defines not only the three overlapping volumes, but also the exterior spaces. By partially cladding the mostly slanted and occasionally tilted walls (interrupted by cutouts and oriels) with kurkar, a crumbly, brownish stone quarried from the building site itself and pressed into the wet mortar in thin layers not only is the age-old idea of an oriental fortress evoked, but also a living image, which in Israel is strongly bound up with the Palmach myth. The Palmach pioneers see them-

selves as being rooted in the foundation of Israel in the same way as the building is tied into the topography. In this way, the topos of architecture as landscape also takes on a significant historical dimension.

The tour through the museum – whose main entrance is at the end of a long ramp leading upwards – begins as a descent, because the majority of the exhibition rooms are located on the lower floor. Their fluid design structured only by columns at the intersections of the alignments marking the ground plan is, however, barely perceptible, because the underground circuit in these artificially lighted rooms is staged as a multimedia show, for which the architects have no responsibility.

Architecture 10/1998, pp. 118-123 (Peter Cook) • *architektur aktuell* 232/1999, pp. 44-65 (Matthias Boeckl) • *Bauwelt* 22/1999, pp. 1196-1197 (Ulf Meyer) • *Blueprint* 165/1999, pp. 34-37 (David Baß) • *Baumeister* 5/2001, pp. 62-69 (Falk Jaeger)

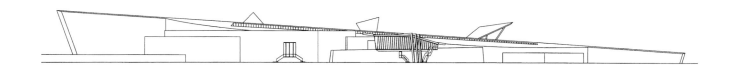

Elevation from the south

Elevation from the north

from left to right
View from the southwest with the dominant "ship's prow" |
View from the north, across Ishøj Beach | Main foyer | Central
"axis of art"

Arken. Museum
for Modern Art

Copenhagen-Ishøj, Denmark

Client	Administrative district of Copenhagen
Architect	Søren Robert Lund, Copenhagen
Total area	9,200 m²
Exhibition area	3,500 m²
Construction time	1994-1996 (competition 1988)

Created for a collection of contemporary art in the course of development, the new museum was at the same time to be a cultural landmark in northern Copenhagen, and in addition to form a counterpart to the Louisiana Museum not far away. Søren Robert Lund, who was still a student when he won the competition, describes the interaction between the building and the surrounding coastal landscape with its beaches, ports, and lakes as the focus of his planning. Although he uses the ship metaphor so often encountered in modern architecture, he does not use the image of a stranded ship "as a form element, but as a creative starting point for the design." Taking up and accentuating the linearity of the landscape with a collage of wall slices of various forms

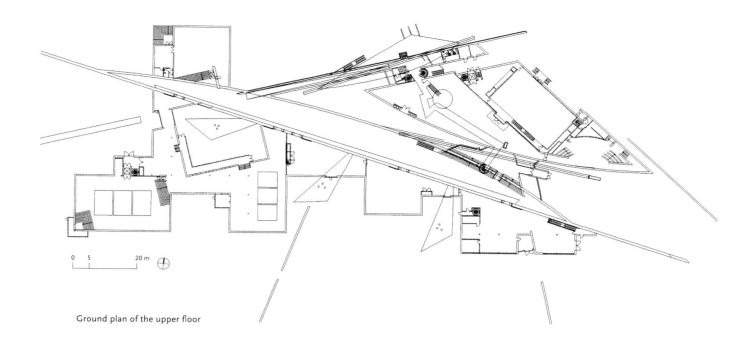

Ground plan of the upper floor

and sizes and extended metal sails, he tries to unite figurative and abstract tendencies.

The original plan called for the interior to be open to the exterior; now, however, it is shielded as much as possible from the exterior. Access is supplied via the main entrance to the west, from which one turns right to go into a main foyer spanned by a steel footbridge and illuminated by a domed skylight. From there, one goes into a theatre, a cinema, a restaurant or turns left into the central "art axis." This exhibition room, 150 metres long, runs tautly through the museum like a drawn bowstring. Illuminated evenly from above by a band of light along its straight wall, the dynamics of its dimensions un-

folds, swelling up and dying down as it progresses. It broadens out to a maximum width of 10 metres, and from a height of 12 metres at the entrance, diminishes to 3.5 metres at the other end – an impressive effect. This room also accesses the rectangular exhibition rooms laid out around a sculpture garden in the eastern part of the building. These rooms receive bright daylight through translucent skylights and planes of glass articulated by latticed forms. A sea view can only be had from the restaurant, whose form reminds one of the skeleton of a ship set on stilts and thus concretizes the ship metaphor once again.

Baumeister 10/1996, pp. 21-27 (Eric Messerschmidt) • *Bauwelt* 40/1996, pp. 2273 • *Deutsche Bauzeitschrift* 3/1997, pp. 57-62 • *Living Architecture* 15/1997, pp. 116-133 (Henrik Sten Moller) • Contemporary Museums (Architectural Design Profile 130), 1997, pp. 78-81

Cerver, pp. 84-95

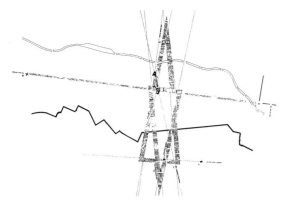

Daniel Libeskind: "matrix" of the Jewish Museum

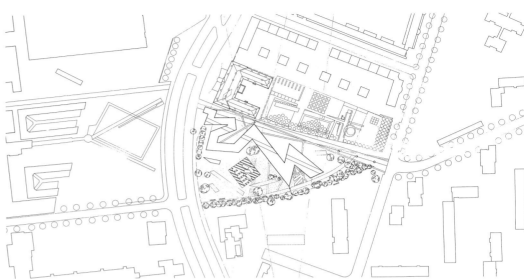

Site plan

from left to right
Exterior view | The entire complex of the Jewish Museum with the Baroque Berlin Museum | General view from the south; in the foreground, the Holocaust Tower and the Garden of Exile | Main stairway through all levels

Jüdisches Museum

Berlin, Germany

Client	Federal State of Berlin
Architect	Daniel Libeskind, Berlin
Total area	15,500 m²
Exhibition area	9,500 m²
Construction time	1992-1999 (competition won in 1989)

This unusual project, the first large building of Libeskind to be actually built, not only approaches the limits of architectural representation, but has also contributed significantly to the decisive change that this museum has undergone as far as its content is concerned. Originally planned as an extension for the Jewish section of the Berlin Museum, the semantically laden architecture soon became the crucial vehicle for the eventually successful claim of Berlin's Jewish community to an autonomous museum, even if it was bound up with the history of the city.

Libeskind's architecture, whose ground plan brings to mind a flash of lightning, is an extended volume multiply fragmented that is intended to describe

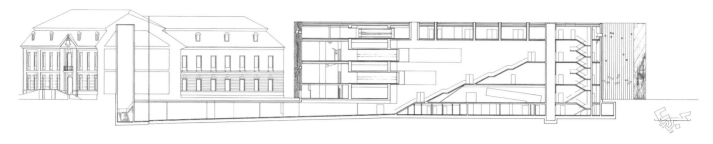

Longitudinal section

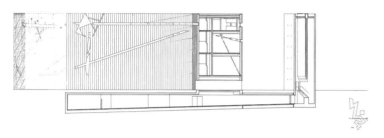

Cross sections

metaphorically the dense interpenetration of Berlin's history with the history of Berlin's Jewish population. The dialog between two lines, each doubled and multiply overlapping, is the artistic means of rendering visible that which is invisible and translating it into spatial sequences and movements. While one line, interpretable as the backbone of the building, runs straight but is fragmented in many places, the other one zigzags across it again and again, symbolizing the changing course of German and Jewish history, inseparably intertwined with each other. At the interfaces voids are created to focus the fundamental idea of this theoretically brilliantly founded architecture, "to build the museum around an empty space," in which the invisible manifests

itself as a sign of absent Jewish presence in Berlin.

The lightning metaphor that can be read in the ground plan – already implemented by Libeskind in 1988 in the "Fireline" project – is capable of expressing as spatial formula not only catastrophe and forgetting, but also memory, a central category in Jewish religion that is always linked to hope. The fact that visitors only experience this fractal ground plan figure as a labyrinthine interlinking of routes and spaces dramatically staged in an interplay of light and darkness does nothing to detract from the validity of this emblematic conception, whose unique, almost cabbalistic iconography is based on an extraordinarily complex matrix of meanings. An oblong hexa-

gram that can be seen as a compressed and distorted Star of David resulted out of the imaginary lines that connect the (literal) addresses of important Berlin intellectuals who are considered to be binding links between German and Jewish culture. A deliberately symbolic figure, the Star of David is called upon to explain the form of the ground plan, as is Walter Benjamin's "Einbahnstraße" [One-Way Street], interpreted by the architect as an "urban apocalypse," whose structure dictates the number of building sections. Libeskind's architecture reflects Benjamin's conception of history, which counters continuity with the dynamics of the dialectic, just as much as it does the boundary manifested in Arnold Schönberg's unfinished opera "Moses and Aaron"

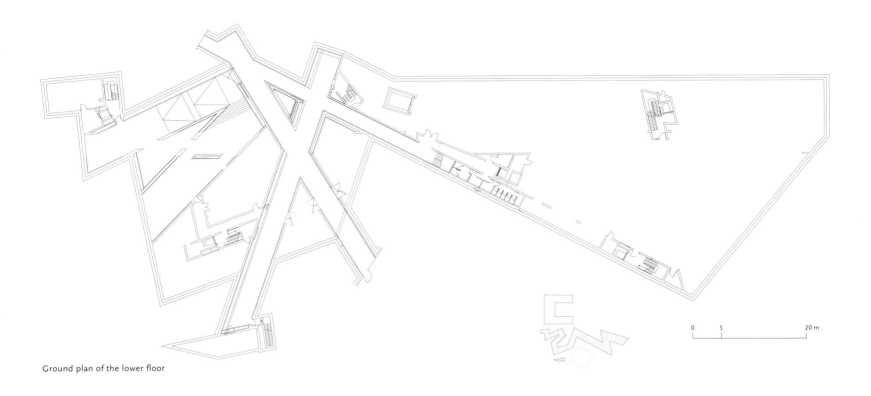

Ground plan of the lower floor

from left to right
The intersecting passages on the lower floor | The fifth and final
Void | Empty exhibition rooms | Exhibition room with exhibits

between that which can be sung and that which can only be said. For the architect – who has repeatedly grappled theoretically with the relationship between imagination and architectural space – the spatial equivalent for this lies in the relation between the visible and the invisible.

No matter how one answers the question as to whether it was the architecture that actually brought forth the complex concept for the museum's content or whether it was adapted from the specific formal language of the architect, in the circulation and staging of the spatial sequences, visitors have it impressed upon them that this architecture, whose exterior clad with zinc sheets is pierced by window

slits and openings in the form of splinters in analogy to the outlines of the ground plan is not simply a theoretical building, but instead an expressive experiential space. Connected underground with the Berlin Museum, an old triple-winged Baroque building, Libeskind's museum is accessible exclusively from the latter by means of a dimly lit ceremonial stairway, which is again to be understood metaphorically – it is to remind us of the degree to which Jewish and non-Jewish history are inseparably interwoven. Instead of a clear spatial orientation, one arrives at a point where three routes cut across each other at angles, of which one, called the Axis of Exile, leads out of the building and into the Garden of Exile and Emigration, a tilted surface populated

bizarrely by 49 not-quite-vertical concrete stones. This is meant to offer the corporeal correspondence to the disquiet and disorientation of emigration. A second route, the Holocaust Axis, ends as a cul-de-sac in a high, acutely angled tower – dramatically lit from above – with bare walls of exposed concrete. Its emptiness as the embodiment of absence leaves one speechless. The longest of these subterranean roads eventually leads to the narrow main stairway (implying hope for a continuity reaching into the future), which, cut through by diagonal concrete struts and rhythmicized effectively by narrow bands of light, links the three main floors with each other. Here, a circuit dramatised by narrowing, darkening, broadening, and lightening – again, pregnant with

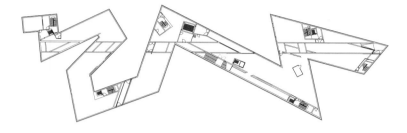

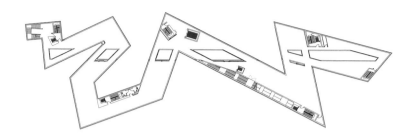

Ground floor plan   Ground plan of the upper floor

meaning – leads through the exhibition rooms. These are all laid out the same way on each level, and their numerous, mostly small-scale exhibits from daily life generate a unique atmosphere oscillating between pathos and banality, the result of this architecture's ambivalence between museum and memorial.

wettbewerbe aktuell 9/1989, pp. 535-548 and 9/1998, pp. 93-98 • *archithese* 5/1989, pp. 60-66 (Gerhard Ullmann; Daniel Libeskind) • *Bauwelt* 32/1989, pp. 1467-1473 • *Architectural Design* 3-4/1990, pp. 62-77 and 7-8/1990, pp. 26-29 • Kristin Feireiss (ed.), Daniel Libeskind. Erweiterung des Berlin Museums mit Abteilung Jüdisches Museum, Berlin, 1992 • *ARCH+* 131 4/1996, pp. 56-61 • *Deutsche Bauzeitung* 11/1996, pp. 52-107 (Reinhart Wustlich; François Burkhardt; Luis Fernández-Galiano; Ernst Hubeli; Bjørn Larsen) • *Techniques et Architecture* 431/1997, pp. 34-39 (Jean-François Pouisse) • Architektur Jahrbuch 1998, Frankfurt, 1998, pp. 114-121 (Volker Fischer) • Elke Dorner, Daniel Libeskind. Jüdisches Museum Berlin, Berlin, 1999 • Bernhard Schneider, Daniel Libeskind. Jewish Museum Berlin. Between the Lines, Munich/London/New York, 1999 • *Deutsche Bauzeitschrift* 6/1999, pp. 126-129 • Domus 820/1999, pp. 32-37 (Marco de Michelis) • Jüdisches Museum Berlin. Architekt Daniel Libeskind, Amsterdam/Dresden, 2000 • Rolf Schneider, Jüdisches Museum Berlin (Die Neuen Architekturführer No. 2), Berlin, 2002

Lampugnani/Sachs, pp. 100-107 (Angeli Sachs) • Newhouse, pp. 235-239 • Peressut, pp. 256-265 • Tzonis/Levaire, pp. 290-293

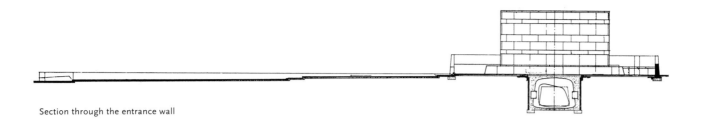

Section through the entrance wall

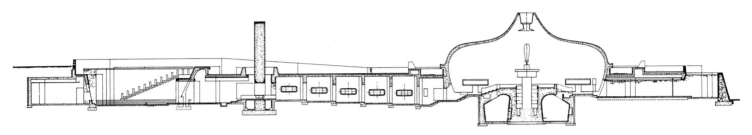

Longitudinal section

from left to right
One reaches the entrance courtyard via a stairway from above | The contrast between the black basalt wall and the white dome, sprayed by fountains, its lower diameter 24.38 metres, marks the appearance of the ensemble, carefully adapted to the land-scape | The entrance corridor, whose display cases along the sides also allow it to serve as an exhibition room, evokes mystery and increases the expectation which is finally fulfilled in the domed room that forms the real centre of the complex

Shrine of the Book

Jerusalem, Israel

Client	D.S. & J.H.Gottesman Centre for Rare Manuscripts, Jerusalem
Architects	Frederick J. Kiesler and Armand P. Bartos, New York
Construction time	1962-1965 (commissioned in 1957)

Not only because of the exceptional historical importance of the ancient scrolls found in 1947 in the caves of Qumran on the Dead Sea, but also because the date of this discovery (interpreted as constitutive of identity) coincided with the foundation of the state of Israel, it was decided that a building should be erected especially to house these scrolls and at the same time to embody their meaning aptly. Frederick Kiesler, who had countered the "superstition of the functional" with "the realities of a magical architecture" in his visionary writings, created a multi-part building complex in an elevated position designed to look monumental from a distance, one that is basically intended to be a "reliquary." It is the dome clad in white tiles that is dominant, a

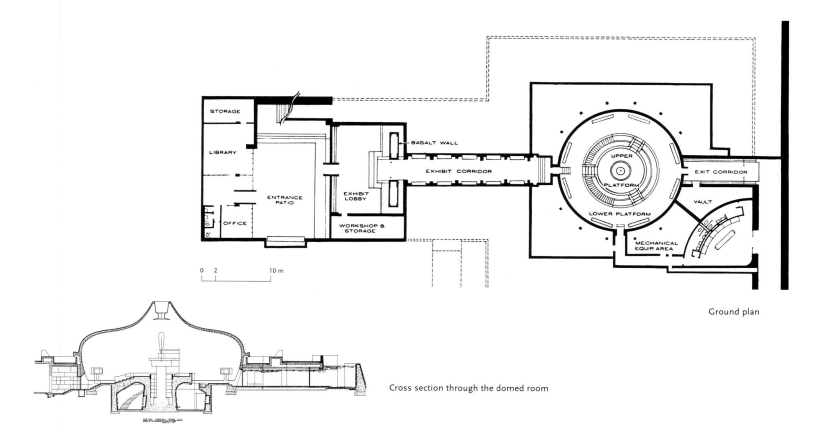

Ground plan

Cross section through the domed room

round shell structure of a double parabolic form that is supposed to remind one of the cover of the vessels in which the Qumran scrolls survived for centuries. Seemingly floating above a square pool of water, it forms a stark contrast to the strict prism of the functionless black basalt wall – a contrast that the architects want to be understood as a reference to the spiritual and cultural meaning of the scrolls in the "fight of light against darkness, good against evil, knowledge against ignorance."

The interior, programmatically staged by a varied graduation of darkness to light as a mystic spatial sequence and largely sunken below ground level, is accessed from an inner courtyard lying yet lower,

characterized by different sorts of stone and accessible via a sequence of steps. Grouped around this inner courtyard are service rooms and an exhibition hall. From here the visitors proceed through a bronze gridwork of pipes, into a corridor with several changes of level by means of steps and articulated by archways leaning away from each other. The corridor leads eventually into the cupola room lighted from above. In this two-storey "shrine," at the centre of which is an oversize Torah scroll and which holds display cases with handicrafts in ring-shaped rock caves, the most valuable scrolls are kept and put on show.

Progressive Architecture Sept.1965, pp. 126-133 • Dieter Bogner (ed.), Friedrich Kiesler, Vienna, 1988, pp. 249-255 • The Israel Museum, Jerusalem – The Shrine of the Book, Jerusalem, 1991 • *Architektur & Bauforum* 151/1992, pp. 72-73 (Helmut Weihsmann) • Hans Nevidal (ed.), The Book of the Shrine, Exhibition catalogue, Graz/Vienna, 1992 • Frederick Kiesler. Artiste – architecte, Exhibition catalogue, Paris, 1996, pp. 229-248 (Michael Sgan-Cohen, Bruno Zevi)

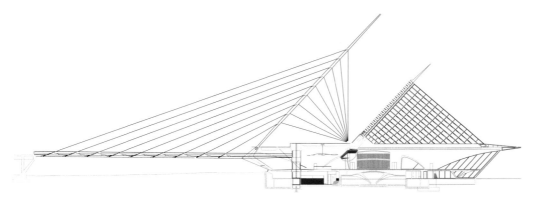

East-west section

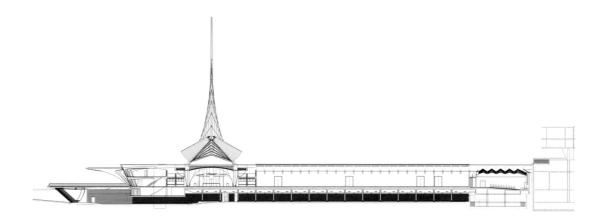

North-south section

from left to right
View from the southeast (with the awning closed) | View from
the southwest with the striking silhouette of the extended
awning against the background of Lake Michigan | Two views
of the entrance hall | One of the two "aisles" of the extension,
called "Galleria"

Milwaukee
Art Museum
Extension
Quadracci Pavilion

Milwaukee/Wisconsin, USA

Client	Trustees of Milwaukee Art Museum
Architect	Santiago Calatrava Valls, Zurich
Total area	ca. 13,200 m²
Exhibition area	1,500 m²
Construction time	1994–2001 (invited competition)

It was the client's wish that the addition to the existing museum also be an attraction in its own right as a spectacular architectural achievement, and not just an envelope for the expansion. The existing museum was initially only housed on the two lower floors of a building designed in 1957 by Eliel Saarinen as a war memorial, and David Kahler had given it a first, modest extension in 1976. Calatrava adapted the level of his wing extending off at right angles to that of the old building and shifted the entrance, with all the infrastructure that went with it, to the end of his wing, which concludes in the form of a triple apse – a solution that seems simple and achieves exceptional quality only by the new entrance from the city centre – across a footbridge elegantly

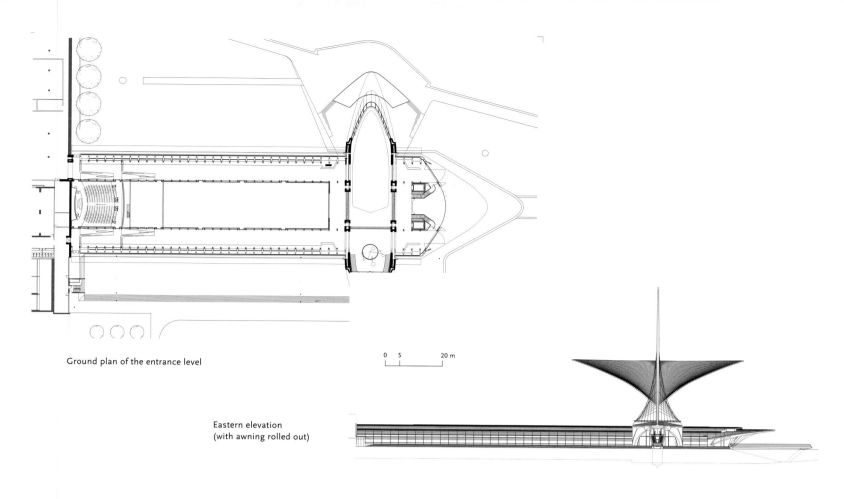

Ground plan of the entrance level

0 5 20 m

Eastern elevation
(with awning rolled out)

suspended from a slanting mast – and above all, the shimmering white structure of a moveable awning above the elliptical domed space of the entrance hall.

Although this soaring structure of 72 hydraulic-powered movable steel lamellas of different lengths arranged in pairs that can be opened and closed like the wings of an over-sized bird serves only to shade the glass foyer, as a striking landmark effectively staged against the backdrop of Lake Michigan, it achieves its real purpose which is to attract the identity-promoting attention that the museum had never had in the shadow of the war memorial. By linking a kinetic sculpture newly interpreted in bio-morphous forms with the abstraction of a nautical vocabulary – the silhouette of the entrance pavilion

reminds one of a yacht – Calatrava does justice as much to architecture's understanding of itself as art (which here indicates the contents of the museum at the same time) as he does to the topographic situation.

In view of this accentuation, it should hardly be surprising that only a small part of the three-naved new building is used as exhibition area. The side naves, rhythmicized by white reinforced concrete ribs, lead to the exhibition areas in the old building, while the spacious central nave holds in addition to a room for special exhibitions also the large museum shop and an auditorium.

Sergio Polano, Santiago Calatrava. Gesamtwerk, Stuttgart, 1997, pp. 296-301 • *Bauingenieur* 6/2001, pp. 293-294 (A. Jähning) • *Architectural Record* 3/2002, pp. 92-104 and pp. 224 (Blair Kamin, John E. Czarnecki) • *Architecture* 2/2002, pp. 52-61 (Joseph Giovannini) • *ARCH+* 159/160, 5/2002, pp. 100-107

Lampugnani/Sachs, pp. 162-167 (Luca Molinari)

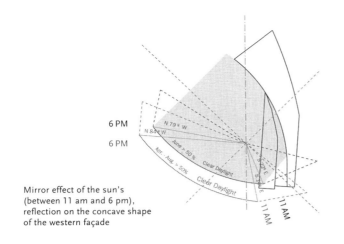

6 PM
6 PM

Mirror effect of the sun's
(between 11 am and 6 pm),
reflection on the concave shape
of the western façade

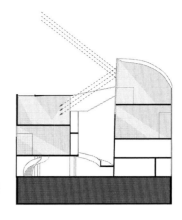

Sketch of directional lighting

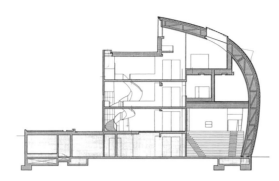

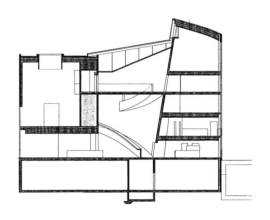

Cross sections A-A | B-B | C-C

Museum of Contemporary Art (Kiasma)

Helsinki, Finland

Client	Finnish Ministry of Education
Architect	Steven Holl, New York
Built area	70,000 m²
Total area	12,000 m²
Net floor area	9,100 m²
Exhibition area	3,600 m²
Construction time	1994-1998 (competition open to Scandinavian and Baltic architects and four foreign invitees 1993)

At a location as prominent as it was problematic from an urban-planning perspective, surrounded by important buildings but on a main street, the new art museum was to be a cultural and political monument as well as an architectural one. Steven Holl rose to this challenge by designing a building described by the jury as "enigmatically sculptural," whose high-tech skin (aluminium, titanium zinc, and shimmering green glass) sets it apart from its surroundings and allows it to shine even when the sky is overcast. According to Holl, its unusual form – provoking a wealth of associations (ranging from a cornucopia or a banana to a stranded whale) was the result of its mirroring the curve of the solar trajectory during the building's opening hours. The architect himself called

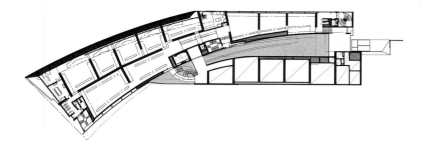

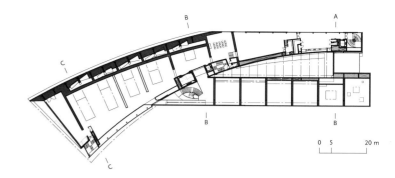

0 5 20 m

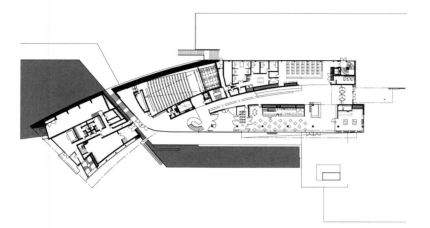

from below left to above right
Ground floor plan | Second floor | Fourth floor

from left to right
Transition from the eastern façade to the roof | General view from the south | Entrance hall | Exhibition room on the second floor | Exhibition room on the fourth floor

his project, whose form develops out of the intersection of a right-angled and a curved volume, Chiasma (in Finnish, Kiasma) – a term adopted from biology to denote the cross-over of two strands (optic nerves or chromosomes) which Holl uses here to refer not only to the form of his museum, but also to its function and its urban situation. The strikingly curved five-storey volume and the somewhat lower wing with an essentially orthogonal form meet exactly at the spot where a public passage leads through the complex.

The entrance into the museum building, 132 metres long and 28 metres wide, lies between the two wings on the southern side, where a ravine-like hall lit from above leads visitors downwards with an elegant sweep through a funnel-shaped form which then brings them to the upper levels via a gently climbing ramp. Of varying sizes, the exhibition rooms on the upper floors of the curving main wing – although arranged more or less in a sequence – have very unusual forms. They receive natural light coming in variously through ceiling openings and slits in the curving walls. The introverted atmosphere thus created, from time to time seeming almost religious, is relativized only by a few carefully staged views of the cityscape.

Architecture and Urbanism 277/1993, pp. 64-71 (Andrew Mac-Nair) and 335/1998, pp. 16-39 (Yehuda Safran) • *The Architectural Review* 1218/1998, pp. 46-53 (Annette LeCuyer) • *Baumeister* 9/1998, pp. 26-33 (Wolfgang Jean Stock) • *Bauwelt* 10/1998, pp. 476-483 (Mathias Remmele) • Sandro Marpillero, "Construction of Space", in: *Daidalos* 67/1998, pp. 18-25 • *Domus* 810/ 1998, pp. 12-25 (Dietmar Steiner) • *El Croquis* 93/1998, pp. 50-85 • Kiasma – Museum of Contemporary Art, Helsinki, 1998

Newhouse, pp. 52-55 • Peressut, pp. 248-255 • Trulove, pp. 40-49

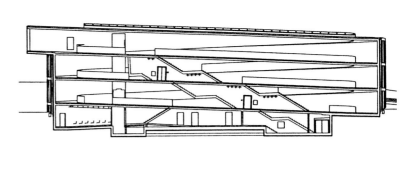

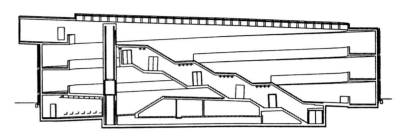

Sections

Site plan

above and right
View from the north | View from the south-west

Neanderthal Museum

Mettmann, Germany

Client	Foundation Neanderthal Museum, Mettmann
Architect	Günter Zamp Kelp, Düsseldorf
Built area	12,000 m²
Exhibition area	2,500 m²
Construction time	1995-1996 (competition 1994; 2ⁿᵈ prize)

An antiquated little museum not far from Feldhof Cave, where the remains of the skeleton of an ice age man were found in 1859, was to be replaced by a new building to display human evolution, focusing on the Neanderthal period in particular. Against the jury's recommendation, it was the project that was rated second in the competition that was executed, its form logically and consistently developed from the content of the museum. Günter Zamp Kelp, who, as a member of the Haus-Rucker-Co Group had become known in the sixties and seventies with "objects to expand consciousness," designed his museum as a climbing spiral-formed ramp rising out of the ground and into the air "as a synonym for infinity," and thereby, according to the

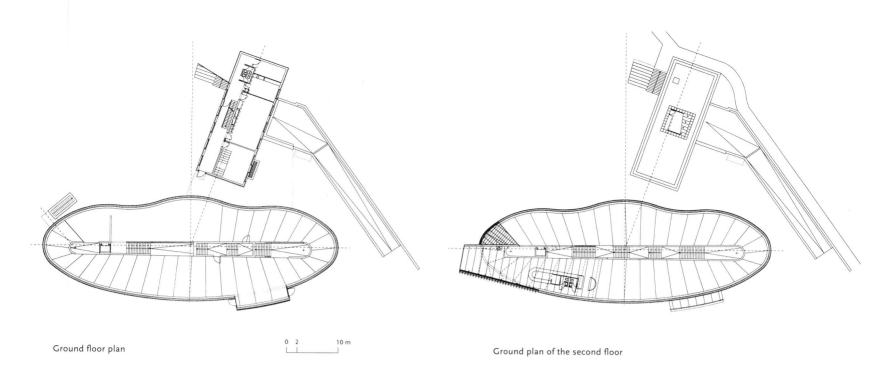

Ground floor plan

0 2   10 m

Ground plan of the second floor

from left to right
Central stairway | Exhibition room (without exhibits) | Café

architect, as a "spatial parable for the development of mankind, which after all is part of infinity."

The exterior of the exhibition building of cast reinforced concrete (the administrative and service rooms are housed in a modest building next to it) is entirely clad with narrow, storey-height double-glazed panes roughened on the inside, whose artificial green creates an allusive tension in relation to the natural greens of the surroundings. Narrow bands of moulding trace both the amoeba-like ground plan of the museum and the gentle rise of the spiral-shaped ramp inside it, on which unfolds the whole scenario of a multimedia presentation of the history of mankind. In the centre of the interior

space unencumbered by columns, a narrow stairway, illuminated by natural light coming through equally narrow openings in the ceiling, runs through the entire building. Experiencing the museum as a cave-like spatial continuum, visitors may use the ramp, the stairway (with several landings to pass over to the ramp) or a lift to reach the top floor, which finally opens into a tubular space that juts out above the building, ending in a glass wall high above the ground. This is an ambiguous architectural metaphor that cleverly illustrates the questions "where do we come from? where are we going?" – and makes an ironic comment, for at the spiral's glass end we find the café.

wettbewerbe aktuell 3/1994, pp. 53-64 • *architektur aktuell* 198/1996, pp. 48-61 (Lisbeth Wächter-Böhm) • *Bauwelt* 47/1996, pp. 2654-2657 (Michael Baumunk) • Neanderthal Museum, Exhibition Catalogue Aedes West, Berlin, 1996 • *Deutsche Bauzeitschrift* 2/1997, p. 38 • *Architektur-Jahrbuch* 1997, Frankfurt, 1997, pp. 136-141 (Axel Drieschner) • Contemporary Museums (Architectural Design Profile 130), London, 1997, pp. 26-29

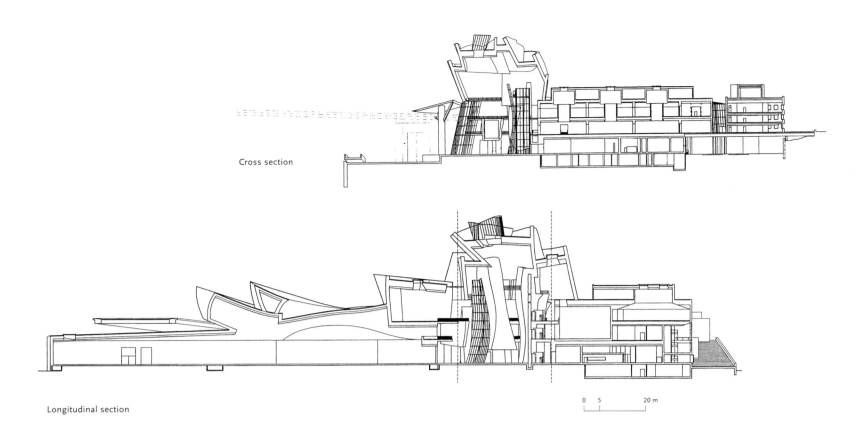

Cross section

Longitudinal section

0 5   20 m

from left to right
The museum as a ship mirrored in the waters of the Nervión |
The museum, a shining sculpture in front of the dark mountain, forms the ending point of the street leading from the city
to the river | The administration cube contrasts effectively
with the heterogeneous shape of the museum which reaches
its highest point in the central atrium while the otherwise
unused tower beyond the motorway only serves to neutralize
the latter's appearance

Guggenheim
Bilbao Museoa

Bilbao, Spain

Client	Guggenheim Bilbao Museoaren Fundazioa, Bilbao
Architects	Frank O. Gehry & Associates Inc., Santa Monica, CA
Total area	24,290 m²
Exhibition area	10,560 m²
Construction time	1993-1997 (invited competition 1991)

This ambitious project pursued the goal of creating
on one hand a spectacular new architectural landmark for Bilbao in order to give back to the Basque
metropolis the brilliance it had lost through economic decline and social unrest, and on the other,
an appropriate framework for the Guggenheim
Foundation's practice of lending and exhibiting
worldwide. As an expression of the underlying
museum concept both striking and functional at the
same time, it also had to measure up to Frank Lloyd
Wright's Guggenheim Museum in New York, coun-
tering this incunabulum of museum architecture
with a contemporary equivalent.

Between the late nineteenth century buildings of the

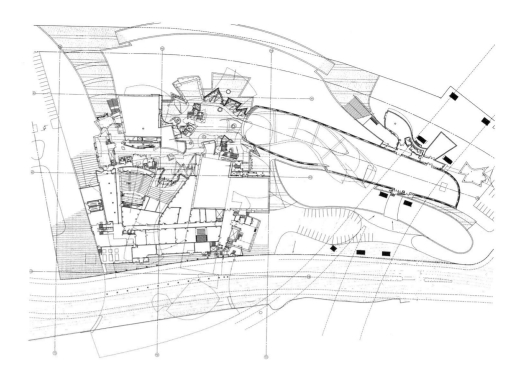

Ground floor plan

city centre and the river bank at the foot of a mountain, between a container terminal and a dominant motorway bridge, the architect favoured from the outset for this commission placed a variform structure that is almost indescribable. Its appearance seems to be continually changing and precisely because of that, it is able to focus the heterogeneous topography, apparently as a matter of course, without giving up its aesthetic distance. Like an elastic creature, the shining volume – either silver or gold depending on the weather – nestles into its surroundings in such a way as to evoke intentional associations that range from an enormous animal to the reflection of a ship in the water. At all events, they embody movement, dynamism, and growth. At

the same time, Gehry also wants the rampant stackings and inversions of his architecture – which does not seem to obey any recognizable rules – to be understood as a monument to his conviction that "the real order is disorder" and that in view of the social upheavals in our time, any demonstration of a stable order would be self-deception. However, the loss of semantic clarity that accompanies the enormously intensified rhetoric of this language of form also allows one to interpret – hardly less plausibly – the complexity of this building and its illusionist effects as an expression of a Baroque world view, in which the domination of international capital over local culture is manifest and aesthetic sensation is justified by its economic success.

The largely biomorphous form of this sculptural architecture, which Gehry gradually developed out of the cubist dismemberment of geometric bodies – put to the test in an exemplary fashion in the Vitra Design Museum in Weil am Rhein, for example – was only realizable with this consistency and perfection with the aid of a computer program used for aircraft construction (CATIA), which defines every three-dimensional form as an equation and can thereby determine every point on its surface. With this tool, the form developed in a long design process operating essentially with models could be translated into a supporting structure laid out as a basket-like network of steel sections. While a secondary supporting system for the curved walls and

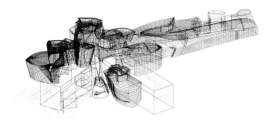

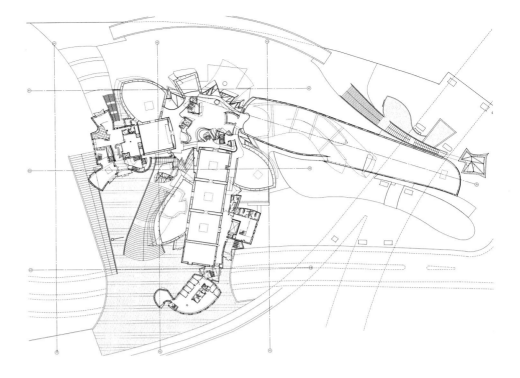

Steel skeleton

Ground plan of the first floor

ceilings was covered over with gypsum plasterboard inside, the volume's exterior – apart from the rectangular parts of the building, executed in Spanish limestone and the glazed curtain walls – was clad with scales of sheet titanium, each of a different size, which the architect selected after protracted experiments because of its special colour and its changing reflective capabilities, but above all, because of its extraordinary mechanical and chemical durability. The extreme thinness of the titanium sheets (measuring only 0.38 millimetres) lends the surfaces a rippling quality that makes the building seem alive.

The pivotal point and fulcrum of the museum is the atrium, more than 50 metres high, placed directly behind the main entrance. It was inspired by the expressionist spatial vision in Fritz Lang's movie Metropolis (1927). It is flooded with light pouring through the glazed curtain wall and a roof construction formed like a plant, which is Gehry's interpretation of the classic museum dome. Accessing the radially arranged exhibition rooms distributed over three levels are bridges of steel, suspended catwalks and glass elevators – which offer views of the city and the river, but above all, ever new and surprising perspectives onto this almost incomparable spatial form that blurs the boundaries between inside and outside and overcomes the restraints of gravity. "Fish," the architect's name for the 130-metre long tunnel-shaped hall with continually changing con-

tours that is by far the largest of these rooms – and whose ceiling devoid of columns is suspended by a flexible network of struts – extends eastwards up to and underneath the motorway bridge. The majority of the galleries, however, are almost quadratic rooms strung together in enfilade, on two levels, one on top of the other. Those on the third floor are illuminated conventionally with light from above that through an opening in the middle of the floor also reaches the galleries below. Apart from that, the rooms are illuminated by a special system of lighting bridges and wall spotlights that enables evenly distributed lighting at eye-level. Finally, as the third room-type, almond-shaped cave-like or free-form exhibition rooms, each with its own individual char-

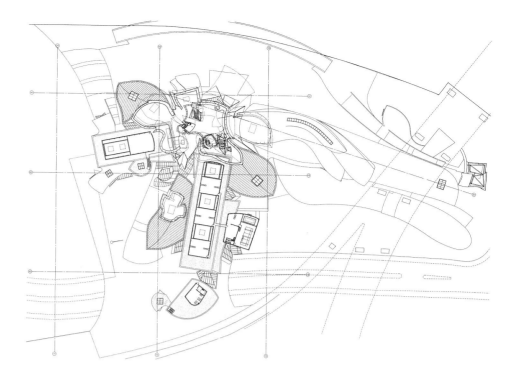

Ground plan of the third floor

from left to right
The entrance, like a ravine running into the building, provides direct access to the central atrium lit through the curtain wall façade and from above; bridges leading through it on several levels provide ever new perspectives | View from the balcony into the gallery on the ground floor resembling a ship's belly; even Richard Serra's steel snake, which is 31 metres long and 4 metres high, seems almost lost within it | The light from the skylights in the conventionally shaped orthogonal exhibition rooms on the third floor is led through floor openings (whose boundaries serve as picture hanging areas) down to the next level with similar shaped galleries

acter, complete the selection of different possibilities for presenting and observing art.

ARCH+ 128/1995, pp. 24-25 • *Werk, Bauen und Wohnen* 12/1995, pp. 40-44; 12/1996, pp. 22-25; 12/1997, pp. 56-57 (Jürg Senn) • *Architectural Record* 10/1997, pp. 74-87 (Karen D. Stein) • *The Architectural Review* 1210/1997, pp. 30-45 (Catherine Slessor; Annette LeCuyer) • *L'architecture d'aujourd'hui* 313/1997, pp. 43-73 (Jean-Paul Robert) • *Art in America* 7/1997, pp. 48-55, 105-106 (Kim Bradley) • *Domus* 798/1997, pp. 10-19 (Sebastiano Brandolini) • Coosje van Bruggen, Frank O. Gehry. Guggenheim Museum Bilbao, Ostfildern-Ruit, 1997 • *Bauwelt* 13/1997, pp. 682-693 (Antón Amann Murga/ Fernando Pérez Fraile/César Caicoya Gómez-Morán; Javier Mozas) • *Deutsche Bauzeitung* 12/1997, pp. 22-23 (David Cohn) • *Architecture and Urbanism* 334/1998, pp. 110-132 (Michael Webb) • *Der Architekt* 9/1998, pp. 506-508 (upw Nagel) • *El Croquis* 88-89/1998, pp. 22-63 • *Deutsche Bauzeitschrift* 1/1998, pp. 49-54 (Benedikt Kraft) • *GA document* 54/ 1998, pp. 6-93 • *Lotus* 98/1998, pp. 6-26 (Pierluigi Nicolin) • Francesco dal Co/Kurt Forster, Frank O. Gehry. Milan, 1998, pp. 480-487 • Kurt W. Forster, Frank O.Gehry. Guggenheim Bilbao Museoa, Stuttgart/London, 1998 • Annett LeCuyer, Stahl & Co., Basel, 2003, pp. 44-49

Francisco Asensio Cerver, The Architecture of Museums, New York, 1997, pp. 72-83 • Justin Henderson, Museum architecture, Gloucester/Mass., 1998, pp. 32-39 • Vittorio Magnago Lampugnani/Angeli Sachs (eds.), Museums for a New Millennium, München/London/New York, 1999, pp. 124-131 (Kurt W. Forster) • Gerhard Mack, Art Museums. Into the 21st Century Basel/Berlin/Boston, 1999, pp. 23-36 • Frank Maier-Solgk, Die neuen Museen, Cologne, 2002, pp. 71-79 • Victoria Newhouse, Towards a New Museum, Ostfildern-Ruit, 1998, pp. 245-259 • Luca Basso Peressut, musei. Architetture 1990-2000, Milan, 1999, pp. 208-221

Conversions and Extensions of Architectural Monuments

Although the organizational parameter of this category necessitates an additional change of perspective, it is justified not only by the fact that many of the oldest and at the same time most prominent buildings, such as the Louvre or the Uffizi, came into being as conversions of existing buildings, but also by the fact that the attempt to come to terms with existing structural fabric denotes a fundamental preconditioning of any planning that allows hardly any free choice between the typologies mentioned before. The scope of this category ranges from preservation to the highest degree with only very minor extension of the existing historical structure in the Centre for Art and Media Technology in Karlsruhe, to the extensions of the Korbach Regionalmuseum and the Kassel Museum für Sepulkralkultur, both of which used an entirely new formal language, but whose dimensions were oriented on those of the original buildings. Finally, in the Gipsoteca Canoviana, the completely autonomous extension provides a contrasting accent to the old building left in its original museum function, and from that perspective, represents a borderline case that leads back to the Neue Stuttgarter Staatsgalerie at the beginning of the project selection. That gallery could be classified as an extension, just as the Sainsbury Wing of the National Gallery in London or the East Wing of the National Gallery in Washington could as well.

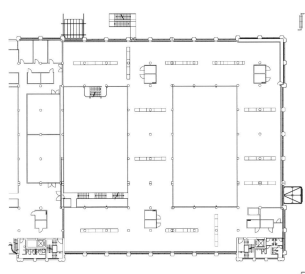

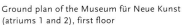
Ground plan of the Museum für Neue Kunst
(atriums 1 and 2), first floor

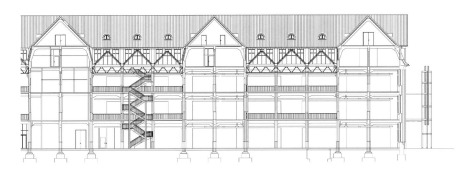

Longitudinal section through the Museum für Neue Kunst
(atriums 1 and 2)

from left to right
East façade with the Media cube | Aerial view of the entire com-
plex | Museum für Neue Kunst | ZKM, galleries and bridges

Zentrum für Kunst und Medientechnologie (ZKM)

Museum für Neue Kunst (MNK)

Karlsruhe, Germany

Client	City of Karlsruhe/Foundation ZKM
Architects	Schweger + Partner, Hamburg
Total area	70,905 m² (10 atria, each 18 x 32.4 m, height 18.56 m)
Net floor area ZKM	17,500 m²
Net floor area MNK	9,567 m²
Construction time	1994-1997 (ZKM)/1998-1999 (MNK) (restricted competition 1992)

Founded in 1988, the ZKM, a research and development centre at the interface between art and media, was originally supposed to be housed in a glass cube designed by Rem Koolhaas. Its electronically equipped façades were to function as supports for multimedia messages and thus would have perfectly exemplified media architecture.

However, for financial reasons, this spectacular project was shelved in favour of the solution eventually arrived at, to accommodate the ZKM, a museum of contemporary art, the Städtische Galerie, and the Hochschule für Gestaltung (also newly established) in a much larger building, a former munitions factory subsequently put under historical protection.

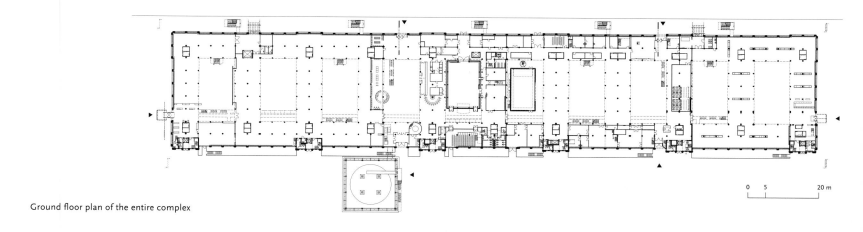

Ground floor plan of the entire complex

0 5   20 m

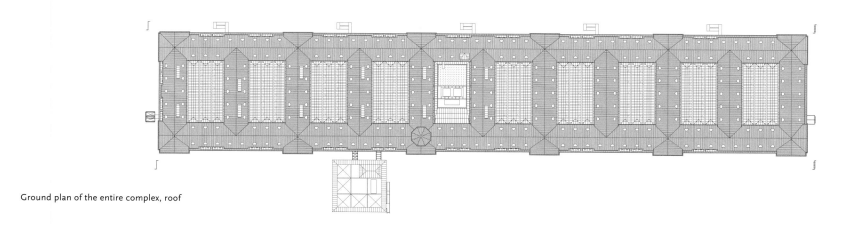

Ground plan of the entire complex, roof

Built during the First World War by Philipp Jakob Mantz, this concrete skeleton construction is 312 metres long and 56 metres wide; it has ten interior courtyards, and each of its long sides is sparsely articulated by six projections crowned by gables.

The Hamburg office Schweger + Partner wanted to retain as much as possible the open character of the three-storey atria spanned by glazed sawtooth roofs. For them, the appeal and the quality of this architecture was to be attributed to its spatial structure – which, due to the galleries running through the whole building on two levels not only allows varied uses but also, moreover, thematizes that transitory moment of movement relating to the contents of the

ZKM. The effect and practicability of the existing building was merely intensified and at the same time pragmatically interpreted by (consciously experimentally designed) light catwalks, bridges, and stairways. Unavoidable interventions such as the installation of self-contained rooms were kept to a minimum.

It is only in front of atrium 7, which serves as the entrance foyer and also fulfills an urban planning function as a connection between the eastern and western sides of the building, that the architects placed a high-tech structure referred to as a "media cube" inside which there is a state-of-the-art music studio. With every change in the lighting, the multi-

layered quality of its glass hull enveloping a blue core generates the subtle shifting of the levels of reality that is a distinguishing feature of the virtual world, which is what this museum attempts to portray.

Zentrum für Kunst und Medientechnologie. Architektur Wettbewerb, Munich, 1990 • Karlsruhes neues Kulturzentrum. Kunstfabrik im Hallenbau A, Karlsruhe, 1997 • *Bauwelt* 46/1997, pp. 2576-2583 (Uwe Hinkfoth) • *Werk, Bauen und Wohnen* 3/1998, pp. 22-25 (Gerhard Ullmann) • *Detail* 3/1998, pp. 373-377 • *The Architectural Review* 1214/1998, pp. 64-68 (Layla Dawson) • Andrea Gleiniger, Architekten Schweger + Partner. Zentrum für Kunst und Medientechnologie Karlsruhe, Stuttgart/London, 1999

Maier-Solgk, pp. 139-147

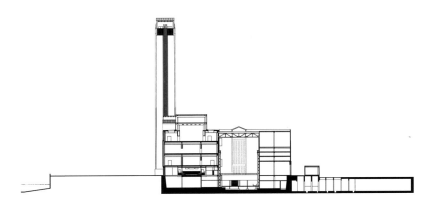

Section through auditorium

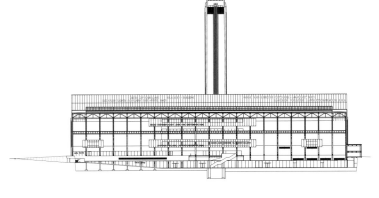

Section through turbine hall

from left to right
The old industrial monument dominated by the high brick tower is given a new accent by the glazed top | View over the Thames | The former turbine hall, now accessed by an enormous ramp | Exhibition rooms on the upper floors

Tate Modern

London, UK

Client	Tate Gallery, London
Architects	Herzog & de Meuron, Basel
Total area	34,547 m²
Construction time	1998-2000 (competition won in 1995)

The Bankside Power Station, an enormous building on the bank of the Thames that was erected in 1947-63 according to plans by Giles Gilbert Scott (the inventor of the red English telephone boxes) and shut down only two decades after it was put into operation, was to be converted into one of the largest museums of modern art. In addition, it was to fulfil an identity-promoting function in a rather neglected urban neighborhood. The architects left the exterior of the imposing brick building largely untouched, with the exception of the new main entrance marked by a spectacular ramp and above all, the two-storey glass 'lightbox' on the extended volume. Magically lighted up at night, this offers a formal equivalent to the tall brick tower that once

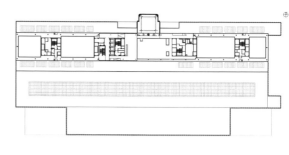

Level 6

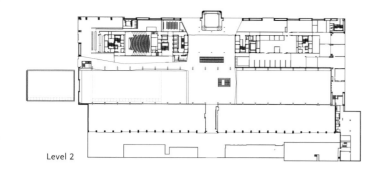

Level 2

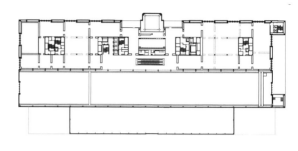

Level 4

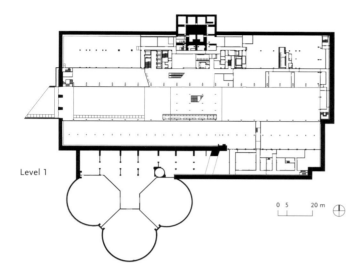

Level 1

0 5   20 m

served as a chimney; it also serves for the natural lighting of the uppermost exhibition rooms. Moreover, in addition to service rooms it contains a restaurant with a magnificent view of London's city centre.

In the interior, almost entirely gutted, leaving only its steel skeleton and brick hull, the original organisation was nonetheless conserved: three spatial layers arranged in parallel, although each has a different number of storeys. A broad ramp leads into what used to be the turbine room, whose floor lies below the water level of the Thames and which with its imposing dimensions (155 metres long, 23 metres wide and 35 metres high) is at the same time both entrance and public square. At the north side it is ac-

centuated by long light sources or open vitrines, apparently floating, jutting far out into the room. These are placed in carefully calculated contrast to the steel pillars of the supporting structure. These horizontal elements conceal some of the more than eighty exhibition rooms of different sizes and heights, which on three floors connect to the hall that has a central distribution function. The appearance of the exhibition rooms, which are lighted in a great variety of ways (and differently in each room) by vertical bands of windows, ceilings illuminated by artificial light or strip lighting recessed flush with the ceiling, is marked by a cleverly staged industrial aesthetics, which is reduced to simple but refined materials such as polished concrete and oak, stainless steel, and frosted glass.

Bauwelt 40-41/1998, pp. 2186-2291 and 23/2000, pp. 27-33 (Hubertus Adam) • *Casabella* 661/1998, pp. 13-19 (Nicholas Serota) and 684-685/2001, pp. 88-105 (Chiara Baglione) • *architektur aktuell* 243-244/2000, pp. 40-53 (Roman Hollenstein) • *Architectural Record* 6/2000, pp. 102-115 and p. 244 (William J.R. Curtis) • *Deutsche Bauzeitschrift* 6/1995, pp. 14-16 (Jochen Wittmann) and 6/2000, pp. 18-19 • *Deutsche Bauzeitung* 3/2000, p. 24 (Oliver Herwig) • *Detail* 7/2000, pp. 1251-1261 • *Schweizer Ingenieur & Architekt* 4/2000, pp. 9-14 (Inge Beckel) • Gerhard Mack, Herzog & de Meuron 1992-1996 (The Complete Works, vol. 3), Basel/Boston/Berlin 2000, pp. 90-109 • Rowan Moore/Raymund Ryan, Building Tate Modern, London, 2000

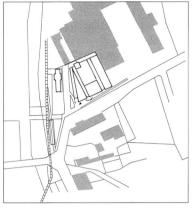

Site plan

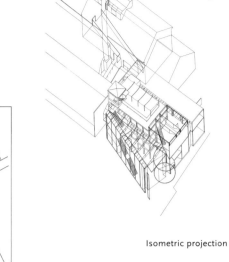

Isometric projection

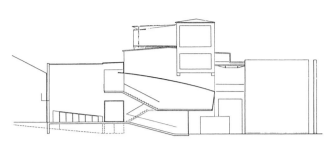

Longitudinal section

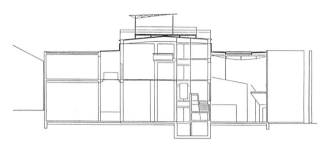

Cross section (parallel to the entrance façade)

from left to right
View from the south (entrance hall) | View from the south-west | Entrance hall | View over the cylinder of the museum shop into the entrance hall

Glass Museum

Bärnbach, Austria

Client	Cultural Affairs Department of the Styrian Provincial Government
Architect	Klaus Kada, Graz
Enclosed space	11,454 m³
Net floor area	8,510 m²
Exhibition area	1,649 m²
Construction time	1987–1988

A vacant building that had contained the generator for a glass factory in the town of Bärnbach in the western part of the province of Styria, a structure with a reinforced concrete skeleton dating back to the post-war period, is the nucleus of the Styrian Regional Exhibition of 1988, the theme of which was industrial culture characterized by opencast coal mining and glass production. The architect sheathed this industrial monument interpreted as an "objet trouvé" on three sides with new elements, large-format slabs attached to the core building by filigree structures. Illustrating the glass theme with a wealth of variation, these slabs – some transparent, some opaque, some translucent – contrast with the robust core building, whose grid-form structure is

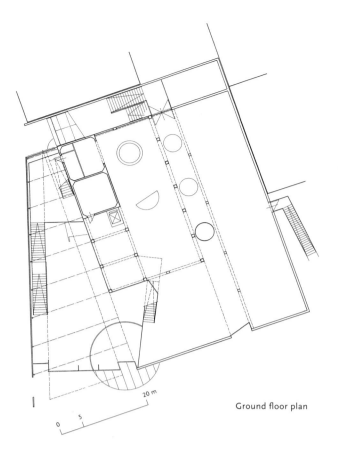

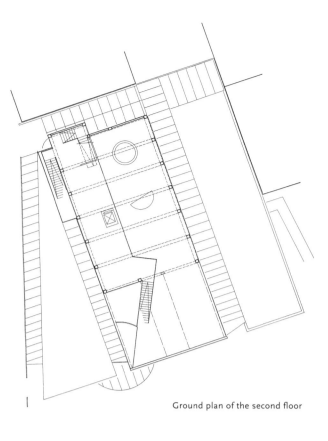

Ground floor plan

Ground plan of the second floor

20 m

0   5

clearly shown now that it is exposed, the partition walls having been removed.

This sheath dissolves the boundaries between inside and outside and generates sophisticated lighting effects. It also serves to integrate the building into its surroundings – having the frontage parallel the street, and placing the wall facing toward the river obliquely and thus parallel with the railway line running along its bank anchors the building in its urban environment. First and foremost, however, it creates space for the multi-storey entrance hall, an "unperspectivist space" that narrows toward the back like a funnel and leads via several levels into the exhibition rooms inside the core building, where

glass objects are mounted in glass display cases. The fragile-seeming corrugated iron ceiling of the entrance hall does not extend all the way to the walls, but appears to float between glass bands, elucidating the triangular ground plan of the entrance hall and emphasizing in a variety of ways the contrast to the cubic grid structure of the static old building.

A sculptural element at the entrance front endows the crosswise joining of polygonal basic forms – called the "axonometric explosion," but strikingly simple in the final analysis – with the crucial supplement that gives the building its unmistakable character. A cylinder of corrugated iron, diagonally capped (the museum shop is inside it) bulges into the

street, linking, jointlike, the main volume with the entrance hall, appearing to break through its glass wall, and almost literally sucking visitors into it.

The Architectural Review 113/1989, pp. 48-54 (Peter Blundell Jones) • *L'architecture d'aujourd'hui* 264/1989, pp. 153-157 • *Techniques et Architecture* 383/1989, pp. 95-99 • *Werk, Bauen + Wohnen* 1-2/1989, pp. 4-9 (Ernst Hubeli) • *Bauwelt* 32/1990, pp. 1580-1586 • *Deutsche Bauzeitung* 7/1991, pp. 46-50 • *Deutsche Bauzeitschrift* 1/1991, pp. 47-49 • Jan Tabor, "Steirisches Glaskunstzentrum und Glasmuseum Bärnbach", in: Architektur als Engagement. Architektur aus der Steiermark 1986-1992, Graz, 1993, pp. 20-21 • Otto Kapfinger et al, Klaus Kada (Portraits of Austrian Architects, vol. 4), Vienna, 2000, pp. 30-43

Allégret, pp. 12-17 • Tzonis/Levaire, pp. 208-209

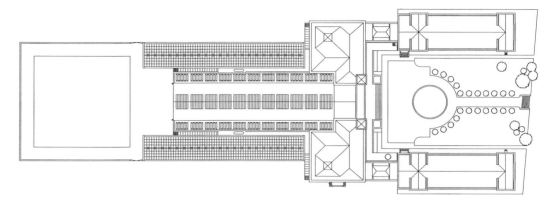

Site plan (including the western gallery and the sculpture courtyard, neither of which have yet been built)

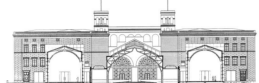

Cross section

from left to right
Entrance façade | Central exhibition hall | Large gallery | Exhibition rooms on the upper floor of the cour d'honneur wing

Hamburger Bahnhof – Museum für Gegenwart

Berlin, Germany

Client	State of Berlin
Architect	Josef Paul Kleihues, Berlin
Net floor area	ca. 17,900 m²
Exhibition area	ca. 9,000 m²
Construction time	1989-1996 (invited competition 1989)

In order to accommodate exhibitions of modern art that would not otherwise have found a venue, it was decided at the end of the eighties to adapt the Hamburger Bahnhof. The building had had an eventful history; built in 1846/47 by Georg Ernst Friedrich Neuhaus and Ferdinand Wilhelm Holz as the terminus of the Berlin-Hamburg railway line, it only fulfilled this function for a few decades, and then became a residential and administrative building before it was converted into a transportation and railway museum in 1906. For this, Ernst Schwartz replaced (among other things) what had been the structure containing the passenger platforms with the three-naved hall with a structural frame of iron that now – almost unchanged – forms the centre of

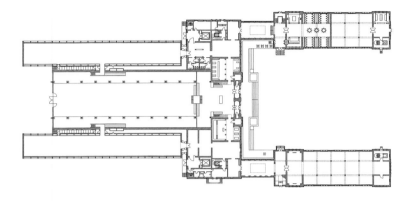

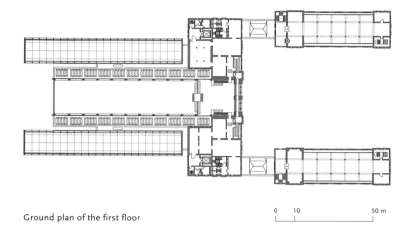

Ground floor plan

Ground plan of the first floor

0   10   50 m

the complex. The two wings were also erected in the early twentieth century; together with the historicizing entrance façade, they form a cour d'honneur whose round flowerbed reminds one of the locomotive turntable that used to be there.

The redesign of this building complex, badly damaged in 1943 and then allowed to fall into a state of disrepair in the postwar years, started with the meticulous restoration of the existing architecture, supplemented by two symmetrically arranged galleries on the sides of the central exhibition hall. As its extension, a square sculpture courtyard (still unrealized, like the westernmost of the two new gallery wings) is to conclude the ensemble's northern end.

In reaction to the disparate character of the individual elements accessed clearly by a few new stairways and ramps, the design tries to generate a unified architecture by geometric references between its elements and in so doing, at the same time to pick up the thread of Karl Friedrich Schinkel's design principles, considered exemplary. This becomes particularly apparent in the exhibition rooms of the entrance wings, whose autonomous existing dimensions are brought into relation to each other through the quadratic subdivided illuminated ceiling. In spite of its entirely independent character, the new gallery too – which gains its effect from the tension between the mild toplight of the ceiling vaulting and the lateral light in the depth of the room – obeys

strict geometric laws: completed into a circle, the daylight barrel vault – recognizable, by the way, as a quotation of the Grande Galerie of the Louvre – would exactly intersect with the outer edge of the floor of the 80-meter long room.

Bauwelt 47/1996, pp. 2664-2671 (Peter Rumpf) • *Deutsche Bauzeitung* 10/1996, pp. 20-24 (Falk Jaeger) • Walter Kambartel, "Zwischen geflügeltem Rad und Pegasus. Der Ausbau des Hamburger Bahnhofs zum Museum für zeitgenössische Kunst", in: Andrea Meseke/Thorsten Scheer (eds.), Josef Paul Kleihues, Basel/Boston/Berlin 1996, pp. 216-244 • Thorsten Scheer, Hamburger Bahnhof. Museum für Gegenwart Berlin, Cologne, 1996 • *Baumeister* 2/1997, pp. 52-59 (Wolfgang Bachmann) • *Detail* 6/1997, pp. 928-933 • *Werk, Bauen und Wohnen* 7-8/1997, pp. 49-51 (Gerhard Ullmann)

Maier-Solgk, pp. 58-64 • Peressut, pp. 131-139

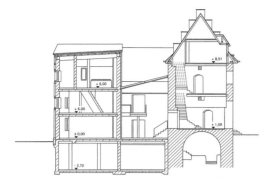

Cross section

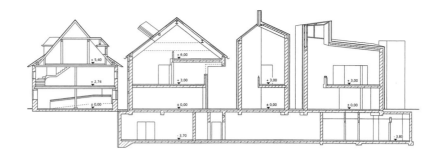

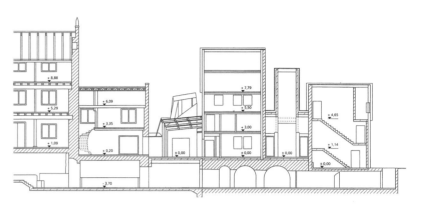

Longitudinal sections

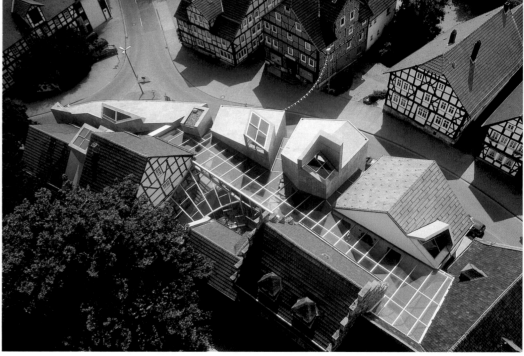

from left to right
Old and new buildings of the museum at the foot of the tower of St. Kilian's Church | The entire museum complex seen from the tower of St. Kilian's Church | Entrance building | The glass-clad access axis | View of the interior courtyard and the tower of St. Kilian's from the entrance hall

Regional museum

Korbach, Germany

Client	City of Korbach
Architect	Berthold H. Penkhues, Kassel
Enclosed space	11,527 m³
Net floor area	1,864 m²
Exhibition area	1,200 m²
Construction time	1995-1997 (competition 1991)

The regional museum in the heart of the small Hessian town of Korbach, housed in three little buildings at the foot of the Gothic tower of St. Kilian's church, was to be expanded. The architect fulfilled the requirement associated with the expansion, to renovate the dilapidated ensemble (heterogeneous due to empty sites) of stone and half-timbered buildings – some of them listed – without reconstructing a historical situation, by adopting the small-scale structure of the old development, but translating it into monolithic individual volumes. The sculptural form of these new buildings covered with local muschelkalk betrays the fact that for several years Berthold Penkhues worked with Frank O. Gehry, whose overloaded formal language is here,

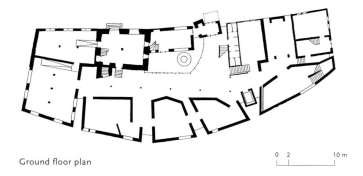

Ground floor plan

0 2   10 m

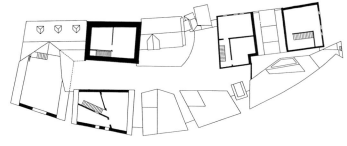

Ground plan of the second floor

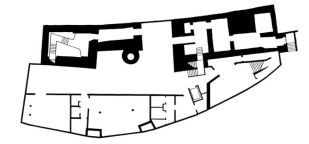

Ground plan of the basement

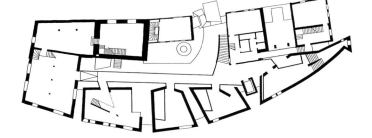

Ground plan of the first floor

however, subordinated to the local historical context and sensitively implemented. One aspect of this is that the individual building segments are not jumbled up against each other, but instead are separated by narrow lanes corresponding to the mediaeval fire lanes. Here, they serve as access ways and moreover, create numerous interconnecting views to facilitate orientation. These glazed interfaces linking old and new volumes into a sophisticatedly articulated whole on the scale of the original town structure also allow views into the interior of the museum. From the courtyard of the church, a new entrance building of stone leads between two old half-timbered buildings into the interior. Here, a glazed, two-storey hall interconnects all the museum rooms

via individual access ways, opening changing perspectives onto the old buildings, the small interior courtyard, and the church tower as well, from which the entire ensemble can be seen, resembling a small town staged deliberately so that not only can it be experienced as a dialectic interplay of old and new building elements, but also, the exhibition building itself is made into a display object.

wettbewerbe aktuell 10/1991, pp 695-704 and 10/1997, pp. 91-94 • *architektur aktuell* 207/1997, pp. 64-73 (Katja Behn) • *Deutsche Bauzeitschrift* 10/1997, pp. 51-56 • *Naturstein architektur* 1/1997, pp. 6-14 • *wettbewerbe aktuell* 10/1997, pp. 91-93 • *Detail* 6/1999, pp. 1002-1004

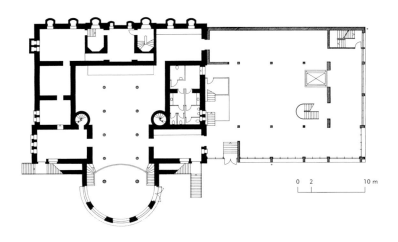

Ground plans, from left to right
Lower floor | Ground floor | Upper floor

0 2 10 m

View from the north (street side)

New building, spatial continuum

from left to right
The new building from the southeast, accentuated by a glazed half-cylinder | The entrance at the north side of the glazed hall between the old and the new building | The glass hall with a view of the city below | View of the suspended mezannine level of the new building from the bridge above the entrance into the glazed hall | Gallery on the upper floor | View from the lower floor of the new building toward the old building

Museum für Sepulkralkultur

Kassel, Germany

Client	Arbeitsgemeinschaft Friedhof und Denkmal e.V. – Stiftung Zentralinstitut and Museum für Sepulkralkultur, Kassel
Architect	Wilhelm Kücker, Munich/Berlin
Total area	3,014 m²
Net floor area	2,122 m²
Exhibition area	1,300 m²
Construction time	1989-1992 (invited competition 1987)

There were no models for a museum focusing on the cultural background and characteristics of death in all its forms throughout the ages. The starting point for the planning of this museum and a scientific institute attached to it was the remains of a villa complex in an exposed situation above the city centre, a two-storey triple-winged building in the neo-Renaissance style. The architect doubled the floor area of the old building and adopted its dimensions, but nevertheless made use of an uncompromisingly modern formal language. With lightweight concrete, steel, and glass, he created not only the greatest possible contrast to the old building's sandstone and clinker brick, but also an "open, light, intimate" atmosphere that is almost "cheer-

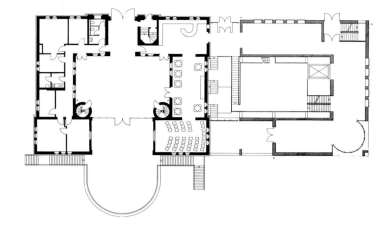
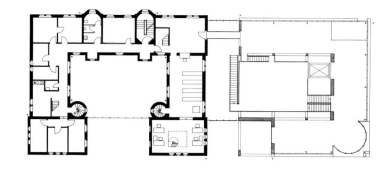

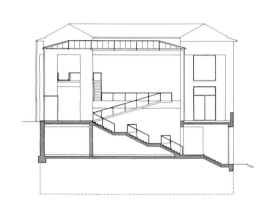

Longitudinal section through the old building and the new building and cross section through the new building

ful," not the least of its aims being to dissipate the public's fear of the subject matter presented here.

A narrow, building-height glass hall at the interface between the old and the new building serves as the entrance and access area. Not only does it open a glorious view over the city below, but above all, it reveals the multilayered but nevertheless transparent spatial structure of the new building. The shift in relation to the level of the old building by means of a suspended intermediate ceiling creates suspense and transforms the erstwhile external façade into an interior wall. In spite of the clarity of this spatial continuum, the exhibition levels linked to each other by open stairways differ distinctly from

each other in their spatial and lighting effects. This enables the very different objects to be presented appropriately and, in addition, quickens visitors' interest. While the lower storey, articulated only by slender pillars and bounded on two sides by room-height window walls, appears to be fluid space whose illumination is gradually reduced and continues into a dark exhibition room reminiscent of a crypt, the galleries above it are laid out around a light-flooded open space in the middle, shifted a half-storey, closed on the ground floor, but open to it on the upper floor.

wettbewerbe aktuell 5/1988, pp. 303-305 and 4/1992, pp. 4-5 • *Friedhof und Denkmal* 2/1988, pp. 21-25 (Hans-Kurt Boehlke) and 1-2/1992, pp. 1-32 • *Architektur Innenarchitektur Technischer Ausbau* (AIT) 7-8/1992, pp. 72-77 • *Architektur Jahrbuch* 1992, Frankfurt 1992, pp. 74-83 • *Bauwelt* 16/1992, pp. 900-909 (Klaus-Dieter Weiß) • *The Architectural Review* 1154/1993, pp. 44-48 (Anne Frey) • Wilhelm Kücker. Museum für Sepulkralkultur (Bau Werke 1, ed. Ingeborg Flagge), Berlin, 1993

Sectional isometric projection

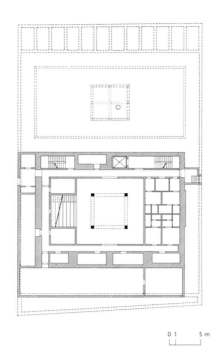

Ground plan of the first underground floor (level 1)

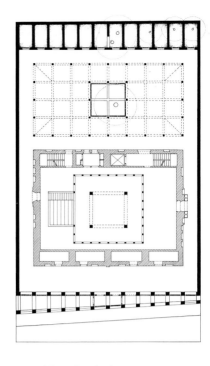

Ground floor plan (level 2)

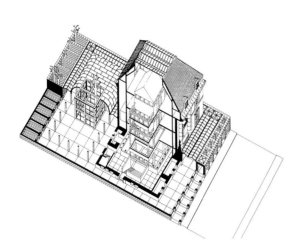

from left to right
General view from the banks of the Main | Exhibition pavilion (columned hall) on the garden side | Lecture hall on the lower floor (level 1) | Hall on the ground floor (level 2) | Consolidation of the supporting system (level 4) | "House" on the top floor (level 5)

Deutsches Architekturmuseum

Frankfurt on Main, Germany

Client	City of Frankfurt on Main
Architect	Oswald Mathias Ungers, Cologne
Enclosed space	12,597 m³
Net floor area	1,737 m²
Exhibition area	1,328 m²
Construction time	1981-1984 (commission 1979)

The first project on the Museumsufer in Frankfurt, initiated by Heinrich Klotz in 1979 as a documentation and exhibition centre for contemporary architecture, is not a new building, strictly speaking, but a conversion or more precisely, an installation. The plinth zone of a neo-classicist villa by Fritz Geldmacher that dates back to 1912/13 was surrounded by a columned hall of red sandstone with a glass roof; on one side, it condenses into a 'city wall' and on the garden side, it widens out into a glass-roofed pavilion. In every detail, right down to the floor surface, the structure of this pavilion – which encloses a tiny inner courtyard with a carefully conserved tree – demonstrates the omnipresence of the quadrate or rather the cube, which dominates the whole

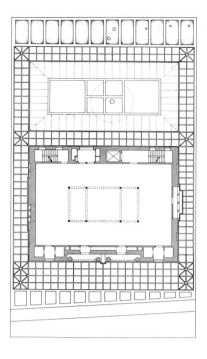

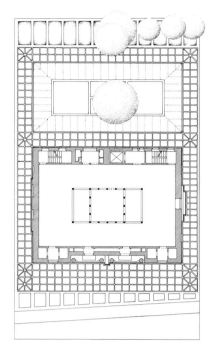

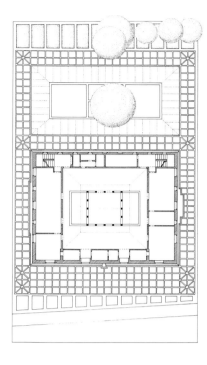

Ground plan of the first floor (level 3)

Ground plan of the second floor (level 4)

Ground plan of the third floor (level 5)

building as a modular system. (Glass roofing that had begun to leak, in the meantime replaced by lead roofs, disrupt the intended spatial impression considerably.)

Through this enclosure, the old villa itself is turned into an exhibition piece, whose gutted interior, top-lighted by a glass roof, in turn hides an entirely new volume with five exhibition levels. With absolute logical consequence, a dazzling white structure crowned by a gable roof is developed out of the most elementary form of a building, the house with four supporting pillars; it offers fascinating spatial experiences demonstrating by his own example what architecture can be. The architect and theore-

tician O. M. Ungers writes about this 'building within a building:' "this reversal from inside to outside, this entrance into a room and in so doing, being outside the next room, consciously exploits an opportunity to experience space. This is the theme of the architectural museum..."

As convincing as architecture has become here, as the "semantic support of a representable fiction," it can only fulfil to a limited extent its task as exhibition space for the museum's objects (drawings, plans, and models), because the artificial perfection of this spatial structure (that nonetheless cannot avoid undesired residual space such as the all-too-small hallways on the ground floor) makes any addi-

tion or change into a potential disturbance – unless it fits into the modular basic structure of the omnipresent quadrate.

Baumeister 8/1984, pp. 31-39 • *L'architecture d'aujourd'hui* 233/1984, pp. 10-13 • *Lotus international* 3/1984, pp. 7-22 (Heinrich Klotz) • *Architectural Record* August 1984, pp. 104-117 (Barry Bergdoll) • *Casabella* Sept. 1983, pp. 14-23 (Pierre-Alain Croset/Heinrich Klotz) • *The Architectural Review* 1050/1984, pp. 30-38 (Vittorio Magnago-Lampugnani) • Deutsches Architekturmuseum Frankfurt am Main. Festschrift zur Eröffnung am 1. Juni 1984, Frankfurt, 1984 • Oswald Mathias Ungers. Architektur 1951-1990, Stuttgart 1991, pp. 108-117 • Martin Kieren, Oswald Mathias Ungers, Zürich/Munich/London, 1994, pp. 114-119 • Gert Kähler, Ein Jahrhundert Bauten in Deutschland, Stuttgart/Munich, 2000, pp. 192-193

Lampugnani, pp. 138-151 (Heinrich Klotz) • Montaner/Oliveras, pp. 86-89 • Schubert, pp. 152-154

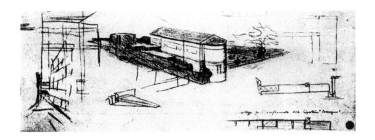

Carlo Scarpa: sketch of the entire complex

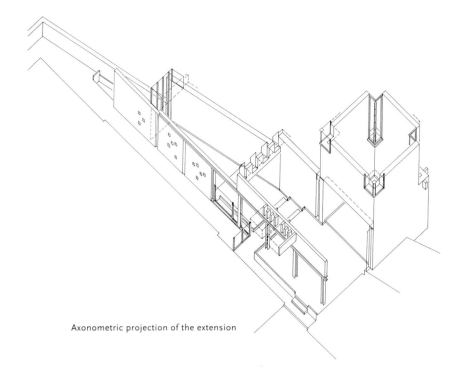

Axonometric projection of the extension

from left to right
Scarpa's conically-formed wing ending in a glass wall at the side of the old building | The exhibition hall with a coffered ceiling vault dating back to the nineteenth century | View from the lobby into the raised, funnel-shaped exhibition room and the light corridor that separates it from the old building | The view from the "articulation room" between the square tower and the funnel-shaped exhibition hall enables one to recognize the cascade-like graduation in room height used for the provision of light | The transparent prisms in the corners of the tower-like room create a unique incidence of light

Expansion of the Gipsoteca Canoviana

Possagno, Italy

Client	Soprintendenza di Belle Arte, Venice
Architect	Carlo Scarpa, Venice
Exhibition area	ca. 140 m²
Construction time	1956-1957

The two-hundredth birthday of the neo-classicist sculptor Antonio Canova (1757-1822) was the occasion for the expansion of the existing museum, a thermal baths hall, erected in 1834-36 by Guiseppe Segusini in the classical style and attached to the house in which Canova was born. Carlo Scarpa, who, due to his designs for exhibition rooms in Venice and Palermo, was already regarded at the time as one of the most sensitive museum architects, created a sophisticatedly articulated extension, whose filigree formal language contrasts radically with the nineteenth-century barrel-vaulted museum room opening onto an apse.

Scarpa's extension, which follows to a great extent

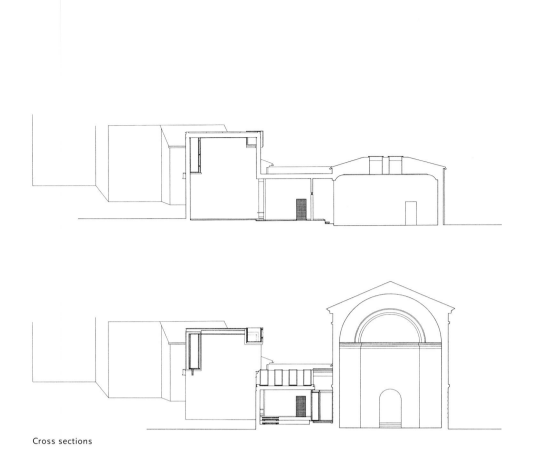

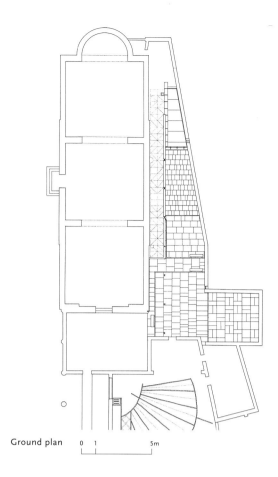

Cross sections

Ground plan   0 1   5m

the sharply-angled, tapering form of the slightly slop-ing site between the old Gipsoteca and a small street, consists of three spatial forms. Entered from the ves-tibule of the old museum is a room with a rectangu-lar ground plan that functions as an articulation and opens on one hand into a high cubic space, and on the other hand, into a low, extended trapezoid space that is separated from the old building by a corridor that alternates between exterior and interior space. While the funnel-shaped exhibition room descends in several sets of steps to open onto a glass wall that allows the sole view of the landscape across a pool of water, the cubic room that rises above the ensemble like a tower is raised above the normal level inside too by a carefully staged podium. The really decisive

design and connection element of the rooms – which also have a sophisticated variety of floorings – is introduced by the incidence of light coming through windows in unusual places and in unusual forms. Thus, for example, the transparent prisms cut into the corners of the cubic room allow light to come in without glare, the changes in natural light during the course of the day casting changing reflections on the walls. Together with the diffuse light generat-ed at other spots and indirect side lighting, the sculptural quality of the plaster models effectively mounted on special pedestals and in display cases designed especially for them is thus emphasized and at the same time, visitors are encouraged to walk round and observe them from different angles.

Casabella 222/1958, pp. 8-14 • Antonio Piva, La fabbrica di cul-tura. La questione dei musei in Italia dal 1945 ad oggi, Milan, 1978, pp. 17-23 • Carlo Fonatti, Elemente des Bauens bei Carlo Scarpa, Vienna, 1983 • Francesco dal Co/Giuseppe Mazzariol, Carlo Scarpa. Opera completa, Milan, 1984, p. 117 • Christine Hoh-Slodzyk, Carla Scarpa und das Museum, Berlin, 1987, pp. 15-22 and pp. 56-69 • Sergio Los, Architekturführer Carlo Scar-pa, Stuttgart, 1995, pp. 46-49 • Bianca Albertini/Sandro Bagno-li, Scarpa. Museen und Ausstellungen, Tübingen, 1992 • Carlo Scarpa Carlo Scapa Architect: Intervening with History, New York, 1999, pp. 60-65 • Carlo Scarpa. Mostre e musei 1944-1976. Case e paesaggi 1972-1978, Exhibition Catalogue, Verona, 2000, pp. 136-145 • Carlo Scarpa a Possagno. Disegni per l'am-pliamento della Gipsoteca Canoviana (1957), ed. Gianna Ghiz-zoni, Possagno, 2001 • Judith Carmel-Arthur/Stefan Buzas, Carlo Scarpa. Museo Canoviano, Possagno, Stuttgart, 2002

Aloi, pp. 343-348

Project Data

Arken. Museum for Modern Art
Copenhagen

Architect
Søren Robert Lund, Copenhagen
With
Helgi B. Thoroddson, Jørgen Erichsen, Mette B. Andersen, Finn Bøgsted, Hanne Hindsgavl, Michael Cederfeld, Klaus G. Jørgensen, Rita Kristensen, Christian Lund

Engineers
Structural engineering
Carl Bro A/S
Lighting design
Hansen of Henneberg A/S

Bonnefantenmuseum
Maastricht

Architect
Aldo Rossi, Milan
With
Umberto Barbieri, Giovanni da Pozzo, Marc Kocher

Engineers
Structural engineering
Grabowsky & Poort BV, Maastricht

Carré d'Art
Nîmes

Architects
Norman Foster and Partners, London
With
Wendy Foster, Robert Partington, Max Neal, Nic Bailey, Andrew Birds, Nicholas Eldridge, Martin Francis, Paul Jones, Serge Belet, Arnault de Bussière, Garnet Geissler, Michael Haste, Richard Hawkins, Edward Hutchinson, Huat Lim, David Morley, Hartwig Schneider, Martin Webler, Ken Shuttleworth, David Nelson, Graham Phillips, Rodney Uren, Paul Kalkhoven, Alex Reid, Chris Eisner, Max Neal, Tim Quick, John Small, Chris Abell, Ruth Conroy, Katherine Delpino, Pascal Desplanques, Shaun Earle, Bertrand Feinte, Lulie Fisher, Jean Pierre Genevois, Michael Jones, Alexander Lamboley, Eddie Lamptey, John McFarland, Sophie Mears, Jesper Neilson, Irene Pham, Victoria Pike, Etienne Renault, Joel Rutten, Kriti Siderakis, Ken Wai, Cindy Walters, Louisa Williams

Engineers
Structural engineering
Ove Arup and Partners / OTH, London
Lighting design
Claude Engle, Washington

Centre d'art contemporain
Vassivière-en-Limousin

Architect
Aldo Rossi, Milan
With
Xavier Fabre, Stefano Fera, Vincent Speller

Centre National d'Art et de Culture Georges Pompidou *Paris*

Architects
Renzo Piano and Richard Rogers, Milan/London
With
Laurie Abbott, Shundjiu Ishida, Hiroshi Naruse, Hiroyuki Takasaki, Bernard Plattner, Walter Zbinden, Hans Peter Bysaeth, Philippe Dupont, Johanna Lohse, Peter Merz, Eric Holt, Gianfranco Franchini, Allan Stanton, Michael Dowd, Rainer Verbizh, Mike Davies, Noriaki Okabe, Jan Sircus, Ken Rupard, Cuno Brullmann, William Logan, Marco Goldschmied, Flavio Marano, Claude Gallot, D. Leverd, Tom Barker, Marco Espinoza, Lennard Grut, Rob Peirce
Alteration 1985
Gae Aulenti
Alteration 1997-2000
Jean-François Bodin

Engineers
Structural engineering
Peter Rice, Edmund Happold (Ove Arup & Partners, London)

Galerie der Gegenwart
Hamburg

Architect
Oswald Mathias Ungers, Cologne
With
Joachim Sieber (project management), Ingo Schweers, Andreas Geitner, Volker Diekmann, Frank Wieschemann, Peter Pfertner

Engineers
Structural engineering
Polonyi + Partner, Cologne; Wenzel + von Seth, Hamburg
Lighting Design
Lichtdesign, Cologne

Gemäldegalerie
Berlin

Architects
Heinz Hilmer und Christoph Sattler, Munich
With
Thomas Albrecht, Peter Dörrie, Sigrid Brockstedt, Dieter Pichler, Johannes Modersohn, Ulrike Flacke

Engineers
Structural engineering
Ingenieurgesellschaft Höpfner, Berlin
Lighting design
Institut für Tageslichttechnik Dr. Hanns Freymuth, Stuttgart/ Lichtdesign Ingenieurgesellschaft mbH, Cologne

Gipsoteca Canoviana, Expansion
Possagno

Architect
Carlo Scarpa, Venice
With
Valeriano Pastor

Glass Museum
Bärnbach

Architect
Klaus Kada, Graz
With
Gerhard Mitterberger, Elisabeth Steiner, Dieter Feichtinger, Johann Reiterer, Josef Ebner, Günther Gebhardt

Engineers
Structural engineering
Manfred Petschnigg

Guggenheim Bilbao Museoa

Architects
Frank O. Gehry & Associates, Inc., Santa Monica, CA
With
Randy Jefferson (project manager), Vano Haritunians, Douglas Hanson, Edwin Chan, Bob Hale, Rich Barrett, Karl Blette, Tomaso Bradshaw, Matt Fineout, David Hardie, Michael Hootman, Grzegotz Kosmal, Naomi Langer, Mehran Mashyekh, Chris Mercier, Brent Miller, David Reddy, Marc Salette, Bruce Shepard, Rick Smith, Eva Sobesky, Derek Soltes, Todd Spiegel, Jeff Wauer, Kristin Woehl
Execution
IDOM, Bilbao: José Maria Asumendi (project director)

Engineers
Structural engineering
Skidmore, Owings and Merrill, Chicago
Service engineering
Consentini Associates, New York
Lighting design
Lam Partners, Boston

Hamburger Bahnhof – Museum für Gegenwart *Berlin*

Architect
Josef Paul Kleihues, Berlin
With
Roger Karbe (project manager), Dirk Blomeyer, Georg Heidenreich, Susanne Junker, Ralf Malter, Gerritt Vetter and others

Engineers
Structural engineering
GSE-Ing. Gemeinschaft Saar, Enseleit, Kropp & Partner
Lighting design
HL Technik, Munich; Se'Lux, Berlin

Kunsthaus
Bregenz

Architect
Peter Zumthor, Haldenstein/Schweiz
With
Daniel Bosshard (project management), Jürg Bumann, Roswitha Büsser, Katja Dambacher, Thomas Durisch, Marlene Gujan, Thomas Kämpfer

Engineers
Structural engineering
Robert Manahl, Bregenz
Daylighting
Hanns Freymuth, Stuttgart
Service engineering
Meierhans und Partner

Kunstmuseum
Bonn

Architect
Axel Schultes, Berlin
With
Jürgen Pleuser (project management), Georg Bumiller, Michael Bürger, Margret Kister, Enno Maass, Heike Nordmann, Volker Staab u.a.

Engineers
Structural engineering
Polonyi und Fink, Cologne and Berlin; Spitzlei und Jossen, Siegburg; Stettner und Wald, Bonn
Lighting design
Institut für Tageslichttechnik, Stuttgart; Büro Lichtdesign, Cologne

Kunstmuseum
Wolfsburg

Architects
Schweger + Partner, Hamburg (Peter P. Schweger, Franz Wöhler, Hartmut Reifensein, Bernhard Kohl, Wolfgang Schneider)
With
Philipp Kahl, Wilhelm Meyer, Alexander Mayr, Rolf Achilles, Ulrike Andreas, Ingeborg Biedermann, Michael Giebeler, Christiane Hansen, Hannelore Hedde, Dieter Heinrichs, Erika Kamprad, Rudolf Krebs, Frank Morgernstern, Peter Oschkinat, Bettina Peschka, Matthias Schmitz, Thomas Ventker, Arne Wellmann

Engineers
Structural engineering
Bendorf + Partner Ing.-GmbH, Wolfsburg
Lighting design
Christian Bartenbach GmbH, Aldrans

Kunstsammlung Nordrhein-Westfalen *Düsseldorf*

Architects
Hans Dissing and Otto Weitling, Copenhagen
With
Dieter Fremerey (project management), Reinhard Tölke, Jürgen Röschmann, Ulrike Christiansen, Helle Ingvarsen and others

Engineers
Structural engineering
Integral, Düsseldorf
Lighting design
Mogens Balslev, Rø dovre (Denmark)

Literature Museum
Himeji

Architects
Tadao Ando & Associates, Osaka

Engineers
Structural engineering
Ascorial Engineering Ass.

Louisiana Museum for moderne Kunst *Humlebæk*

Architects
Jørgen Bo and Vilhelm Wohlert
With
Svend Bruno Nielsen, Folmer Kristensen, Niels Halby, Niels Presskorn, Stg Løcke, Erik Mannik Sørensen, Henrik Sperling, Claus Wohlert

Engineers
Structural engineering
Johannes et Jørgensen A/S; Mogens Balslev A/S

Deutsches Architekturmuseum
Frankfort on Main

Architect
Oswald Mathias Ungers,
Cologne
With
K.L.Dietzsch, Barbara Taha,
Katrin Nagel

Engineers
Structural engineering
Stroh und Ernst
Lighting design
Alois Zitnik

Domus
La Coruña

Architects
Arata Isozaki, Tokyo/César
Portela, Pontevedra
With
Toshiaki Tange, Mashata Ori,
Naoki Ogawa, Igor Peraza, Fede-
rico Garrido, Amparo Casares,
Jose Luis Gahona, Paulino
Sánchez, Jose A. Suárez

Engineers
Structural engineering
Antonio Reboreda

**Erzbischöfliches Diözesan-
museum** *Paderborn*

Architect
Gottfried Böhm, Cologne
With
Hans Lindner, Franz Rolf Kilian
Alteration and refurbishment
Michael Brawne, Bath

Engineers
Structural engineering
Varwick, Cologne

Essl Collection
Klosterneuburg

Architect
Heinz Tesar, Vienna
With
Susanne Veit (project manage-
ment), Oliver Aschenbrenner,
Ruedi Bühlmann, Urs Geiger,
Kathrin Grumböck, Johann
Osterrieder, Franz Steinberger,
Marc Tesar

Engineers
Structural engineering
Konstruktion Aste, Martin
Gruber, Innsbruck
Lighting design
CH Design, Charles Keller, St.
Gallen

Fondation Beyeler
Basel

Architects
Renzo Piano Building Workshop,
Paris/Genoa
(Renzo Piano, Bernard Plattner,
Loic Couton)
Collaborating Architects
William Mathews, Ronnie Self,
Pascal Hendier; Burckhardt +
Partner AG, Basel

Engineers
Structural engineering
Ove Arup & Partners, London; C.
Burger & Partner, Basel

Fondation Cartier
Paris

Architects
Jean Nouvel, Emmanuel Cattani
& Associés, Paris
With
Didier Brault (project manage-
ment), Pierre André Brault,
Laurence Ininguez, Philippe
Mathieu, Viviane Morteau, Guil-
laume Potel, Steeve Ray, Arnaud
Villard, Stéphane Robert

Engineers
Structural engineering
Ove Arup & Partners, London

Jüdisches Museum
Berlin

Architect
Daniel Libeskind, Berlin/
New York
With
Matthias Reese, Jan Dinnebier
(project management); Stefan
Blach, David Hunter, Tarla
MacGabhann, Noel McCauley,
Claudia Reisenberger, Eric J.
Schall, Solveig Scheper, Ilkka
Tarkkanen

Engineers
Structural engineering
GSE Tragwerksplaner, Berlin;
IGW Ingenieurgruppe Wiese,
Berlin
Lighting design
Lichtplanung Dinnebier KG,
Wuppertal

Kimbell Art Museum
Fort Worth

Architect
Louis I. Kahn, Philadelphia
With
Marshall D. Meyers; Preston M.
Geren & Ass., Frank H.
Sherwood

Engineers
Structural engineering
August E. Komendant
Lighting design
Richard Kelly; Edison Price

Kirchner Museum
Davos

Architects
Annette Gigon and Mike Guyer,
Zurich
With
Urs Schneider (Building execu-
tion), Judith Brändle

Engineers
Structural engineering
Davoser Ingenieure AG (DIAG)
Lighting design
Institut für Tageslichttechnik,
Stuttgart; Alois Zitnik,
Ingenieurbüro für Kunstlicht,
Frankfurt

**Kunst- und Ausstellungshalle
der Bundesrepublik
Deutschland** *Bonn*

Architect
Gustav Peichl, Vienna
With
Martin Kohlbauer (project mana-
ger), Joachim Güth, Rudolf Weber

Engineers
Structural engineering
Polonyi und Fink, Cologne and
Berlin
Lighting design
Lichtdesign-Ingenieurges.mbH/
Lichtplan Cologne

Kunsthal
Rotterdam

Architects
Rem Koolhaas, Office for
Metropolitan Architecture,
Rotterdam
(Rem Koolhaas, Fuminori
Hoshino, Leo van Immerzeel,
Herman Jacobs, Jo Schippers,
Ron Steiner, Petra Blaisse)

Engineers
Structural engineering
Cecil Balmond, Ove Arup +
Partners, London

Kunsthalle
Bielefeld

Architect
Philip C. Johnson, New York
With
Cäsar Pinnau

Engineers
Structural engineering
Severud-Elstad-Krueger
Lighting design
Hans T. v. Malotki, Cologne

Mediatheque
Sendai

Architects
Toyo Ito & Associates, Tokyo

Engineers
Structural engineering
Sasaki Structural Consultants,
Tokyo
Lighting design
Urthec, Taihei Electricity, Tokyo;
Tozan Electricity, Tokyo

Miho Museum
Shigaraki

Architects
Ieoh Ming Pei & Partners,
New York
With
Kibowkan International Inc., Perry
Chin, Tim Culbert, Chris Rand,
Carol Averill, Price Harrison, Celia
Imrey, Hubert Poole

Engineers
Structural engineering
Leslie E. Robertson, Saw Teen
See, Katherine Hill
Lighting design
Paul Marantz, Alicia Kapheim,
Hank Forrest

**Milwaukee Art Museum,
Extension (Quadracci Pavilion)**

Architect
Santiago Calatrava Valls, Zurich
Collaborating Architects
Kahler Slater Architects,
Milwaukee

Engineers
Structural engineering
Graef Anhalt Schloemer
Mechanical and electrical systems
Ring & DuChateau

**Musée d'Art Moderne et
Contemporain** *Strasbourg*

Architect
Adrien Fainsilber, Paris

Engineers
Structural engineering
O.T.E. / R.F.R.

Musée de Grenoble

Architects
Groupe 6, Grenoble
(Olivier Félix-Faure, Antoine
Félix-Faure, Philippe Macary)
With
Yves Pervier, Jean-François
Treyve, Lorenzo Piqueiras

Engineers
Lighting design
Marc Fontoynont

Musée de l'Arles antique
Arles

Architect
Henri Ciriani, Paris
With
Jacques Bajolle, Jacky Nicholas

Engineers
Structural engineering
BET Scobat, Paris; Cesba, Aix-en-
Provence

Project Data

Museo Nacional de Arte Romano *Mérida*

Architect
José Rafael Moneo Vallés, Madrid
With
Francisco González Peiró and Rafael Luque (project management), Nieves de la Roche, Juan José Echeverría, Enrique de Teresa, Georges Meylan, Charles Meyer, Stanley Allen, Pedro Feducchi

Engineers
Structural engineering
Jesús Jiménez and Alfonso Garcia Pozuelo

Museu d'Art Contemporani *Barcelona*

Architects
Richard Meier & Partners, New York
With
Thomas Phifer, Reny Logan, Alfonso Pérez-Mendez, Daniel Brown, Steve Dayton, Patrick Flynn, Raphael Justewicz, Jonathan Marvel, Gilbert Rampy Jr., Madeline Sanchez, Thomas Savory, David Shilling, Fernando Ramos, Isabel Bachs

Engineers
Structural engineering
Obiol, Brufau, Moya
Lighting design
Fisher, Maranth, Renfro & Stone

Museu de Serralves *Porto*

Architect
Álvaro Siza Vieira, Porto
With
Clemente Menéres Semide (project management), Tiago Faria, Christian Gänshirt, Sofia Thenaisie Coelho, Edison Okomura, Abilio Mourão, Avelino Silva, João Sbugueiro, Cristina Ferreirinha, Taichi Tomuro, Daniela Antonucci, Francesca Montalto, Francisco Reina Guedes de Carvalho, Ulrich Krauss, Angela Princiotto

Engineers
Structural engineering
GOP-João Maria Sobreira, Porto

Museum Abteiberg *Mönchengladbach*

Architect
Hans Hollein, Vienna
With
Thomas van den Valentyn, Jürgen Bertisch

Engineers
Structural engineering
Karl-Heinz Grambuch, Martin Janhsen, Mönchengladbach
Lighting design
Hans T. von Malotki, Heinrich Kramer, Cologne

Museum für Kunsthandwerk *Frankfurt on Main*

Architects
Richard Meier & Partners, New York
With
Gunter R. Standtke, Michael Palladino, Hans Christopher Goedeking, John Eisler, Manfred Fischer, David Diamond, Margaret Bemiss, Geoffrey Wooding

Engineers
Structural engineering
G. Rosenboom, Frankfurt
Lighting design
Alois Zitnik, Frankfurt

Museum für Moderne Kunst *Frankfurt on Main*

Architect
Hans Hollein, Vienna
With
Franz Madl (project manager), Shinichi Eto, Walter Kripicsenco, Miroslaw Machnacz, Bernd Kretz, Hans Streitner, Rainer Pirker, Taro Abe, Haiko Achilles, Engelbert Auer, Sina Baniahmad, Finn Erschen, Thomas Herzog-Punzenberger, Toshiko Kawaguchi, Noboru Kimura, Stefan Maisch, Erich Pedevilla, Madeleine Jenewein, Dorit Pachler, Elisabeth Rahbari, Dorrit Korger

Engineers
Structural engineering
Ingenieurbüro für Bauwesen Gert Rosenboom, Frankfurt on Main
Lighting design
Institut für Tageslichttechnik Dr. Hanns Freymuth, Stuttgart

Museum of Eastern Asian Art *Cologne*

Architect
Kunio Mayekawa, Tokyo
Rock garden
Masayuki Nagare
Extension
Jochen Jacobs, Cologne

Engineers
Execution
Berner und Jacobs, Cologne
Structural engineering
Pechuel-Lösche
Lighting design
Hans T. von Malotki, Cologne

Museum of Modern Art *San Francisco*

Architect
Mario Botta, Lugano/Switzerland
With
Hellmuth, Obata & Kassabaum, Inc.

Engineers
Structural engineering
Forell and Esesser Inc.

National Gallery, Sainsbury Wing *London*

Architects
Robert Venturi, Denise Scott Brown and Associates, Philadelphia
With
David Vaughan (project manager), John Rauch, Steven Izenous, William Algie, Ed Barnhart, Britt Brewer, Andrew Erstad, Steve Glascock, James Kolker, Jeff Krieger, Perry Kulper, Brian LaBau, Robert Marker, Richard Mahler, Tom Purdy, Nancy Rogo Trainer, George Ross, Mark Schlenker, Carreth Schuh, David Singer, Rich Stokes, Maurice Weintraub, Mark Wieand, Sheppard Robson

Engineers
Structural engineering
Ove Arup & Partners, London
Lighting design
Jules Fisher and Paul Marantz Inc.

National Gallery of Art, East Wing *Washington DC*

Architects
Ieoh Ming Pei & Partners, New York
With
Leonard Jacobson (project architect), F. Thomas Schmitt, Yann Weymuth, William Pederson

Neanderthal Museum *Mettmann*

Architects
Günter Zamp Kelp, Düsseldorf and Julius Kraus, Arno Brandlhuber
With
Thomas Guitt, Astrid Becker, Marko Glashagen, Carlos Gonzales, Alex Kouzmine, Götz Leimkühler

Engineers
Structural engineering
Hochtief GmbH

Neue Nationalgalerie *Berlin*

Architect
Ludwig Mies van der Rohe, Chicago

Pinakothek der Moderne *Munich*

Architect
Stephan Braunfels, Munich
With
Gabriele Neidhardt, Helmut Peuker (competition team); Aika Schluchtmann (design team); Gabriele Neidhardt, Sven Krüger (project management); Dagmar Adams, Jutta Braun, Tanja Freiberg, Inge Hager, Nina Höhne, Uwe Koch, Birgit Lange, Alfons Lenz, Katharina Leutheußer, Michaela Lind, Karin Melcher, Jürgen Mrosko, Christian Müller, Michael Poplawski, Ulrich Rumstadt, Maureen Schäffner, Silke Staab, Reinhard Weiss, Matthias Wichmann

Engineers
Structural engineering
Seeberger, Friedl und Partner, Munich
Lighting design
Institut für Tageslichttechnik Dr. Hanns Freymuth, Stuttgart; Lichtdesign GmbH Cologne

Museum Quadrat and Josef Albers Museum *Bottrop*

Architect
Bernhard Küppers, Bottrop

Engineers
Structural engineering
Theo Alkemper, Bottrop
Service engineering
Gaidys und Worbs, Essen
Lighting design
Städt. Hochbauamt Bottrop

Regional museum *Korbach*

Architect
Berthold H. Penkhues, Kassel
With
Siegfried Wendker (project management), Johannes Wettengel, Peter Becker, Antje Nieberfall, Annika Saenger, Katharina Schneider

Engineers
Structural engineering
EHS Ingenieure, Lohfelden-Kassel / W. Slomski + K.-D.Schmidt-Hurtienne GmbH

Schaulager *Basel*

Architects
Jacques Herzog & Pierre de Meuron, Basel
With
Senta Adolf, Philippe Fürstenberger, Harry Gugger, Nicole Hatz, Ines Huber, Jürgen Lohner, Carmen Müller, Cornel Pfister, Katja Ritz, Marc Schmidt, Florian Stirnemann, Lukas Weber, Martin Zimmerli

Engineers
Structural engineering
Zachmann + Pauli Bauingenieure, Basel
Lighting design
Amstein & Walthert AG, Zurich

Shrine of the Book *Jerusalem*

Architects
Frederick J. Kiesler and Armand P. Bartos, New York

Engineers
Structural engineering
Strobel & Rongvec
Lighting design
Frank J. Sullivan & Associates

Sprengel Museum *Hanover*

Architects
Peter and Ursula Trint, Cologne/ Dieter Quast, Heidelberg

Engineers
Landscape architect
Georg Penker, Neuss
Structural engineering
Kohlhaas/Schaper/Bergmann, Hanover
Lighting design
Hans T. v. Malotki, Cologne (1st building phase) / Christian Bartenbach, Aldrans (2nd building phase)

Museum für Sepulkralkultur
Kassel

Architect
Wilhelm Kücker, Munich/Berlin
With
Klaus Freudenfeld, Hans-Joachim
Ewert (project manager), Kai
Abresch, Sebastian Berz, Andrea
Düchting; AIS Arbeitsgruppe
Kirchhoff, Möller, Rügemer und
Partner, Kassel

Engineers
Structural engineering
Seeberger + Friedl, Munich
Lighting design
Walter Bamberger, Pfünz

Museum Het Valkhof
Nijmegen

Architects
Ben van Berkel (UN studio van
berkel & bos), Amsterdam
With
Henri Snel, Rob Hootsmans,
Remco Bruggink, Hugo Beschtor
Plug, Walther Kloet, Marc Dijk-
man, Jacco van Wengerden, Luc
Veeger, Florian Fischer, Carsten
Kiselowsky

Engineers
Structural engineering
Adviesbureau voor Bouwtechniek,
Arnhem
Lighting design
Hans Wolff & Partners,
Amsterdam

Museum La Congiunta
Giornico

Architect
Peter Märkli, Zurich
With
Stefan Bellwalder, Naters

Museum Ludwig
Cologne

Architects
Peter Busmann and Godfrid
Haberer, Cologne
With
Alfred Bohl, Ulrich Kuhn (project
management), Gabriele Bartsch,
Wilfried Diercks, Hans-Jürgen-
Faust, Peter Hövels, Brigitte
Maresch, Bernhard Mörsch,
Zbiegniew Oksiuta, Susanne
Reichstein, Jost-Henner Schwedes,
Lütfi Sengül, Edith Simandi,
Heinz Stenzel, Knut Würfel

Engineers
Integrated artistic design
Dani Karavan, Paris (open air
spaces)
Structural engineering
Ingenieurgemeinschaft Varwick,
Horz, Ladewig, Naumann,
Tripler, Zilinski; Cologne
Lighting design
Institut für Tageslichttechnik
GmbH Hanns Freymuth, Stuttgart;
Hans T. von Malotki, Cologne

Museum of Contemporary Art
Chicago

Architect
Josef Paul Kleihues, Berlin
With
Johannes Rath (project mana-
ger), Greg Sherlock, Mark
Bastian, John de Salvo, Pablo
Diaz, Arden Freeman, Haukur
Hardason, Richard McLoughlin,
A.Epstein and Sons Int'l., Inc.

Engineers
Structural engineering
Ove Arup & Partners, London
Lighting design
Claude R. Engle

**Museum of Contemporary Art
(Kiasma)** *Helsinki*

Architect
Steven Holl, New York
With
Vesa Honkonen (project mana-
ger), Janet Cross, Justus Rüssli,
Chris McVoy, Pablo Castro-Esté-
vez, Justin Korthammer, Tim
Bade, Anderson Lee, Anna Müller,
Tapani Talo, Tomoaki Tanaka,
Molly Blieden, Juhani Pallasmaa,
Timo Kiukkola, Seppo Mäntylä,
Heikki Määttänen, Timo Ruusu-
vuori, Seppo Sivula

Engineers
Structural engineering
Insinööritoimisto Oy Matti Ollila
& Co., Helsinki
Lighting design
L'Observatoire International,
New York

Neue Pinakothek
Munich

Architect
Alexander Freiherr von Branca,
Munich
With
Christian Raupach, Klaus
Sprenger, Karin Blum

Engineers
Structural engineering
Rudolf Eibel, Taufkirchen
Lighting design
Institut für Tageslichttechnik,
Stuttgart

Neue Staatsgalerie
Stuttgart

Architects
James Stirling – Michael Wilford
& Ass., London
With
Russel Bevington, Ulrich Schaad,
Peter Ray, John Cannon, Alexis
Pontvik, John Cairns, Alfred Mun-
kenbeck, Shinchi Tomoe, John
Tuomey, Markus Geider, Paul
Keogh, Walter Nägeli, Peter
Schaad, Chris MacDonald, Sieg-
fried Wernik, Tommi Tafel, Rudolf
Schwarz, Pia Riegert, Laszlo Gla-
ser, Heribert Hamann, Christian
Ohm, John Rodgers, Jacques
Thorin, Jürgen Noris, Jochen Bub

Engineers
Structural engineering
Ingenieurgemeinschaft Boll-
Arup-EDN,
Stuttgart/London/Tamm
Lighting design
Ingenieurbüro Weidner, Wernau

Neues Museum
Nuremberg

Architect
Volker Staab, Berlin
With
Stefan Reik (project manage-
ment), Thomas Schmidt, Kathrin
Zimmermann, Alexander Böhme,
Peter Deluse, Martina Pongratz,
Stefan Matthey, Angelika Gaul,
Birgit Hübner, Klaus Gehrmann,
Mareike Krautheim, Barbara
Hubl, Carole Chuffart, Filiz Dogu

Engineers
Structural engineering
Ingenieurgemeinschaft H. Fink
GmbH, Berlin and A. Schöppler
+ D. Kästner, Nuremberg
Lighting design
Licht Design Ingenieurges. mbH,
Cologne, and Institut für
Tageslichttechnik, Stuttgart

**newMetropolis. National Center
for Science and Technology**
Amsterdam

Architects
Renzo Piano Building Workshop,
Genoa
With
Olaf De Nooyer (project mana-
ger), Massimo Alvisi, Jack Backus,
Mario Bassignani, Dante Cavagna,
Ivan Corte, Junya Fhjita, Antonio
Gallo, Domenico Guirrisi, Adam
Hayes, Shunji Ishida, Hembert
Peneranda, Enrico Piazze, Anto-
nella Recagno, Kelly Shannon,
Florian Wenz, Hiroshi Yamagucchi

Engineers
Structural engineering
D3BN (J. Kraus); Ove Arup &
Partners, London
Lighting design
IGuzzini; Philips

Nordjyllands Kunstmuseum
Ålborg

Architects
Elissa & Alvar Aalto,
Jean-Jacques Baruël
With
Ola Viskum, Martin Rubow, Ole
Mortensen, Hans Burkart, Hans
Rohr, Ulrich Hoerni, Peter Gerber

Engineers
Structural engineering
Adam Christensen
Lighting design
Sophus Frandsen

Palmach Museum of History
Tel Aviv

Architects
Zvi Hecker and Ravi Segal,
Tel Aviv

Engineers
Structural engineering
Waintraub-Naginski-Zeldin

Tate Modern
London

Architects
Jacques Herzog & Pierre de
Meuron, Basel
With
Thomas Baldauf, Christine Bins-
wanger, Ed Burton, Michael Casey,
Victoria Castro, Peter Cookson,
Irina Davidovici, Liam Dear,
Catherine Fierens, Hernan Fierro,
Adam Firth, Matthias Gnehm,
Nik Graber, Harry Gugger, Kons-
tantin Karagiannis, Angelika
Krestas, Patrik Linggi, José Ojeda
Martos, Mario Meier, Filipa
Mourao, Yvonne Rudolf, Juan
Salgado, Vicky Thornton, Kristen
Whittle, Camillo Zanardini;
Sheppard Robson + Partners,
London

Engineers
Structural engineering
Ove Arup & Partners, London
Lighting design
Ove Arup & Partners, London

Van Gogh Museum
Amsterdam

Architects
Gerrit Rietveld, J. van Dillen, J.
van Tricht
Extension
Kisho Kurokawa, Tokyo

Engineers
Structural engineering
Bureau Bouwkunde, Rotterdam

Wallraf-Richartz-Museum
Cologne

Architect
Rudolf Schwarz, Cologne
With
Josef Bernard
Redesign
Walter von Lom, Cologne

Wilhelm-Lehmbruck-Museum
Duisburg

Architect
Manfred Lehmbruck, Stuttgart
With
Klaus Hänsch (3ʳᵈ building
phase)

Engineers
Structural engineering
Lewenton (1ˢᵗ – 3ʳᵈ building
phase),
Werner, Schwarz (3rd building
phase)
Lighting design
Manfred Lehmbruck and Philips
(1ˢᵗ and 2ⁿᵈ building phase)
Christian Bartenbach (3ʳᵈ building
phase)

Yale Center for British Art
New Haven

Architect
Louis I. Kahn, Philadelphia
Completed by
Anthony Pellecchia and Marshall
D. Meyers

**Zentrum für Kunst und
Medientechnologie (ZKM) /
Museum für Neue Kunst (MNK)**
Karlsruhe

Architects
Schweger + Partner, Hamburg
(Peter P. Schweger, Hartmut H.
Reifenstein, Bernhard Kohl,
Wolfgang Schneider, Wilhelm
Meyer)
With
Chris Ambrosius, Matthias Boger-
ding, Matthias Borsch, Yvonne
Daum, Frank Finkenrath, Nadja
Herrmann, Ilona Kopp, Roland
Linsenmeyer, Peter Neideck,
Maria Neigel, Thomas Peschel,
Udo Schröder, Henning Stiess,
Michael Windbiel

Engineers
Structural engineering
Janssen und Rieger,
Karlsruhe/Rastatt
Lighting design
Bartenbach LichtLabor GmbH,
Munich

Bibliography

The following publications are cited in the bibliographies of the project selection

LITERATURE ON MUSEUM ARCHITECTURE
(without monographs)

Laurence Allégret
Musées
Paris 1987

Laurence Allégret
Musées, vol. 2
Paris 1992

Roberto Aloi
Musei. Architettura – Tecnica
Milano 1962

Stephan Barthelmeß
Das postmoderne Museum als
Erscheinungsform von
Architektur
Munich 1988

Michael Brawne
The Museum Interior:
Temporary and Permanent
Display Techniques
Stuttgart 1982

Michael Brawne
The New Museum
New York/Washington 1965

Francisco Asensio Cerver
The Architecture of Museums
New York 1997

Pippo Ciorra
Botta, Eisenman, Gregotti
Hollein: musei
Milan 1991

Joan Darragh/James S. Snyder
Museum Design. Planning and
Building for Art
New York/Oxford 1993

*Dortmunder
Architekturausstellung 1979*
Museumsbauten:
Musentempel, Lernorte,
Jahrmärkte (= 15. Dortmunder
Architekturheft)
Dortmund 1979

Douglas Davis
The Museum Transformed
New York 1990

Ingeborg Flagge (ed.)
Museumsarchitektur 1985.
Entwicklung und Innovation im
Museumsbau der jüngsten Zeit
Heidelberg 1985

France musées récents
(le moniteur architecture amc)
Paris 1999

Elke Harten
Museen und Museumsprojekte
der französischen Revolution
Münster 1989

Justin Henderson
Museum Architecture
London 1998

Oliver Herwig
Sechs neue Museen in Bayern
Tübingen/Berlin 2002

Heinrich Klotz / Waltraud Krase
New Museums
London 1986

*Kunst- und Ausstellungshalle der
Bundesrepublik Deutschland (ed.)*
kunst im bau
Göttingen 1994

Jean Lacouture
Les musées en chantier
Paris 1991

*Vittorio Magnago Lampugnani
(ed.)*
Museumsarchitektur in
Frankfurt 1980-1990
Munich 1990

*Vittorio Magnago Lampugnani /
Angeli Sachs (eds.)*
Museums for a New
Millennium
Munich/London/New York 1999

Michael D. Levin
The Modern Museum. Temple
or Showroom
Jerusalem/Tel Aviv 1983

Wolfgang Liebenwein
Studiolo. Die Entstehung eines
Raumtypus und seine
Entwicklung bis um 1600
Berlin 1977

*Lluisa López Moreno/José Ramon
López Rodríguez/ Fernando
Mendoza Castells (eds.)*
El Architecto y el Museo
Jerez 1990

*Gail Dexter Lord and Barry Lord
(eds.)*
The Manual of Museum
Planning, 2ⁿᵈ ed.
Walnut Creek/CA, 2001

Gerhard Mack
Art Museums into the
21ˢᵗ Century
Basel/Berlin/Boston 1999

Frank Maier-Solgk
Die neuen Museen
Cologne 2002

Otto Martin
Zur Ikonologie der deutschen
Museumsarchitektur zu Beginn
des zweiten Kaiserreiches.
Bauformen und Bildprogramme
der kunst- und kulturgeschicht-
lichen Museen in den siebziger
und achtziger Jahren des 19.
Jahrhunderts, Dissertation,
Mainz 1983

Josep Maria Montaner
New Museums
New York 1990

Josep M. Montaner/Jordi Oliveras
Museums for a New Century
Barcelona 1995

Arian Mostaedi
museums and art facilities
Barcelona 2001

Alessandra Mottola Molfino
Il libro dei musei
Torino 1998

Museo d'arte e architettura,
exhibition catalogue
Lugano 1992

Victoria Newhouse
Towards a New Museum
New York 1998

Luca Basso Peressut
musei. architetture 1990-2000
Milan 1999

Nikolaus Pevsner
A History of Building Types
London 1976

Volker Plagemann
Das deutsche Kunstmuseum
1790-1870
Munich 1967

Achim Preiß
Das Museum und seine
Architektur. Wilhelm Kreis und
der Museumsbau in der ersten
Hälfte des 20. Jahrhunderts
Alfter 1993

Wolfram Prinz
Die Entstehung der Galerie
in Frankreich und Italien
Berlin 1970

Räume für Kunst, exhibition
catalogue
Graz 1993

Arthur Rosenblat
Building Type Basics
for Museums
New York/Toronto 2001

Jost Schilgen
Neue Häuser für die Kunst
Dortmund 1990

Hannelore Schubert
Moderner Museumsbau
Stuttgart 1986

Helen Searing
New American Museums
New York 1982

Helmut Seling
Die Entstehung des
Kunstmuseums als Aufgabe
der Architektur, Dissertation
Freiburg 1952

James Steele (ed.)
Museum Builders
Berlin 1994

Suzanne Stephens (ed.)
Building the New Museum
New York 1986

Susan A. Sternau
Museums. Masterpieces
of Architecture
New York 1999

James Grayson Trulove
Designing the new museum.
Building a new destination
Gloucester/Mass. 2000

Twentieth-Century Museum I
London 1999

*Cornelis van de Ven and Bob
Martens (eds.)*
Museumarchitectuur
Rotterdam 1989

Heinrich Wagner
"Museen. Neu bearbeitet von
Heinrich Wagner jun.", in:
Handbuch der Architektur,
4. part, 6. half-volume,
4. issue, 2. ed.
Stuttgart 1906

Alma S. Wittlin
Museums. In Search of
a Usable Future
Cambridge/Mass. 1970

**ADDITIONAL LITERATURE
ON 20ᵀᴴ CENTURY ARCHI-
TECTURE**

Architektur Jahrbuch 1984
Frankfurt on Main 1984

Architektur Jahrbuch 1985/86
Frankfurt on Main 1986

Architektur Jahrbuch 1992
Frankfurt on Main 1992

Architektur Jahrbuch 1997
Frankfurt on Main 1997

Architektur Jahrbuch 1998
Frankfurt on Main 1998

Architektur Jahrbuch 2000
Frankfurt on Main 2000

*Andrea Gleiniger/Gerhard
Matzig/Sebastian Redecke*
Paris.
Contemporary Architecture
Munich/New York 1997

Falk Jaeger
Architektur für das neue
Jahrtausend. Baukunst der
neunziger Jahre in Berlin
Stuttgart/Munich 2001

Gert Kähler
Ein Jahrhundert Bauten
in Deutschland
Stuttgart/Munich 2000

*Friedbert Kind-Barkauskas/
Bruno Kauhsen/Stefan Polónyi/
Jörg Brandt*
Concrete Construction Manual,
2. ed.
Basel/Boston/Berlin 2002

Heinrich Klotz
Moderne und Postmoderne
Braunschweig/Wiesbaden 1984

Heinrich Klotz
Revision of the Modern
Munich 1984

*Anna Meseure/Martin Tschanz/
Wilfried Wang (eds.)*
Architektur im 20. Jahrhundert.
Schweiz, Munich/London/
New York – DAM
Frankfurt on Main 1998

Winfried Nerdinger (ed.)
Konstruktion und Raum
in der Architektur des
20. Jahrhunderts
Munich/Berlin/London/
New York 2002

Mathias Schreiber (ed.)
40 Jahre Moderne in
der Bundesrepublik
Stuttgart 1986

Alexander Tzonis/Liane Lefaivre
Architecture in Europe
Since 1968
London 1992

*Alexander Tzonis/Liane
Lefaivre/Richard Diamond*
Architecture in North America
Since 1960
London 1995

Wilfried Wang (ed.)
World Architecture 1900-2000:
A Critical Mosaic, vol. 3
Vienna/New York 2000

Authors

Prof. Dr. Paul von Naredi-Rainer
Born 1950 in Knittelfeld/Steiermark, Austria

Studied art history, musicology, archaeology, and philosophy at the University of Graz and the University of Bonn.

1975
Awarded Ph.D.

1976 to 1988
Director of the Rheinisches Bildarchiv (Museen der Stadt Köln)

1982
Post-doctoral qualification (habilitation)

1985/86
Interim chairman of the department of architectural history at the University of Cologne

since 1988
Professor of art history
at the University of Innsbruck

Most important publications:
Architektur und Harmonie. Zahl, Maß und Proportion in der abendländischen Baukunst (DuMont: Cologne, 1982), 7th edition 2001 • "Musiktheorie und Architektur," in: Ideen zu einer Geschichte der Musiktheorie (vol. 1 of Geschichte der Musikforschung, ed. Frieder Zaminer), (Darmstadt, 1985), 149-175 • Salomos Tempel und das Abendland. Monumentale Folgen historischer Irrtümer (with an essay by Cornelia Limpricht), (Cologne: DuMont, 1994) • "La bellezza numerabile. L'estetica architettonica di Leon Battista Alberti," in: Leon Battista Alberti (exhibition catalogue), ed. Joseph Rykwert and Anne Engel (Mantua, 1994), 292-299 • Grundriß der abendländischen Kunstgeschichte, initiated by Leonie von Wilckens, continued with Dagmar von Naredi-Rainer (Stuttgart, 2000) • Imitatio. Von der Produktivität künstlerischer Anspielungen und Mißverständnisse (Editor), (Reimer: Berlin, 2001)

On the subject of museum architecture:
Neue Museumsbauten in der Bundesrepublik Deutschland (slide series with accompanying text), (Cologne, 1986) • "Zur Ikonologie moderner Museumsarchitektur," in: Wiener Jahrbuch für Kunstgeschichte 44/1991, 191-204, 291-302 • "Zum Projekt 'Kunsthaus' in Bregenz," in: Bau Handwerk Kunst. Beiträge zur Architekturgeschichte Vorarlbergs im 20. Jahrhundert (exhibition catalogue No. 5, Institut für Kunstgeschichte der Universität Innsbruck), (Innsbruck, 1994), 85-96 • "Der Traum von der Stadt. Zeitgenössische Museumsbauten als summa architectonica," in: Kunsthistoriker 13-14/1997-98 (9ᵗʰ Österreichischer Kunsthistorikertag), 145-154 • "Alvaro Siza. Wege, Licht und Linien. Fondacao Serralves: Museu de Arte Contemporanea in Porto," in: architektur aktuell 237-238/Jan.-Feb. 2000, 144-156 • "Konsum im Musentempel – Musen im Konsumtempel. Zu Hans Holleins Museums- und Kaufhausarchitektur," in: Museum und Kaufhaus. Warenwelten im Vergleich, ed. Bärbel Kleindörfer-Marx and Klara Löffler (vol. 15 of Regensburger Schriften zur Volkskunde), (Regensburg, 2000), 119-146 • "Le miracle du miroir. Reflexionen über den Erweiterungsbau des Palais des Beaux-Arts in Lille," (with Dagmar von Naredi-Rainer) in: Form und Stil. Festschrift für Günther Binding zum 65. Geburtstag, ed. Stefanie Lieb, (Darmstadt 2001), 378-386 • "Zwischen Stadt und Kult. Die Sprache der modernen Museumsarchitektur," (Siebente Sigurd Greven-Vorlesung, held on 15ᵗʰ May 2003 at Museum Schnütgen, Cologne), (Cologne, 2003)

Dipl.-Ing. Oliver Hilger
Born 1967

1992
Graduated from the Cologne Fachhochschule

Since 1993
Has had his own engineering firm, Ingenieurbüro Hilger

Since 1996
Ingenieurgesellschaft Hilger in Aachen

Since 1999
Managing partner of Ingenieurgesellschaft Hilger (whose scope of activity encompasses the entire field of technical building services)

Gerhard Kahlert

Studied architecture

Since1976
Has had his own engineering office as an civil engineer for climate control systems in museum buildings. Numerous commissions and competitions as designer and expert

Since 1996
He teaches Preservation of Historic Buildings and Monuments in the department of architecture at the Fachhochschule Trier

Prof. Dipl.-Ing. Herbert Pfeiffer
Born 1935

1961
Graduated from the Technische Hochschule Stuttgart

From 1961 to 1964
On the staff of Professor W. Lutz, Stuttgart-Bad Cannstatt

From 1964 to 1969
Assistant to Professor. H. Deilmann at the University of Stuttgart

From 1969 to 1974
Chief engineer at the University of Dortmund, department of Land Use Planning

Since 1974
Professor of planning theory in the department of civil engineering and architecture at the University of Dortmund

Since 1979
Has had his own office in Lüdinghausen (since 1986, in partnership with Christoph Ellermann, since 1996, in partnership with Jörg Preckel). Numerous buildings, projects, competitions, prizes and participation in exhibitions

Since 1996
Member of the board of the Architektenkammer NRW (Architectural Association of North Rhine-Westphalia). Since 2000, member of the Deutsches Nationalkomitee für Denkmalschutz (German National Committee for the Protection of Historic Buildings and Monuments)

Prof. Dr.-Ing. Helmut F. O. Müller
Born 1943

From 1966 to 1972
Studied architecture at the University of Hannover and the University of Stuttgart – graduating from the latter – as well as at the Bartlett School, London University College

From 1972 to 1982
Design and research activity in the building industry, in an consulting office, and at the University of Stuttgart, which awarded his PhD

From 1982 to 1993
Professor in the department of architecture at the Cologne Fachhochschule

In 1991
Founder and general manager of the Institut für Licht- and Gebäudetechnologie at the Cologne Fachhochschule (researching light that directs holograms)

Since 1993
Professor in the newly-established department of environmental architecture and building physics at the University of Dortmund (researching energy-efficient façade technology)

Since 1997
General manager and stockholder of GLB, Gesellschaft für Licht- und Bautechnologie in Cologne (development and production of holographic optical elements for building applications)

Dr.- Ing. Hans Jürgen Schmitz
Born 1964

Studied architecture at the Technische Hochschule in Aachen

2002
Ph.D. awarded in by the University of Dortmund, thesis on user acceptance of daylighting conditions in offices. Lighting planner at LICHTDESIGN, Cologne/Frechen

Since 1997
Project manager for integral planning and building simulation at the Gesellschaft für Licht- und Bautechnik Dortmund. Co-author of diverse publications

Index of Names

*Of all persons in texts, captions and notes
(except of authors of secondary literature)*

Index of Places

Illustration Credits

The Author and the publisher thank the following photographers, architects and organizations for the kind permission to reproduce the photographs in this book.

8
Ruedi Walti, Basel

12
Paul v. Naredi-Rainer, Matrei

13
1 Paul v. Naredi-Rainer
2-4 Kunsthistorisches Institut der Universität Innsbruck

14
5-10 Kunsthistorisches Institut der Universität Innsbruck

15
11 Paul v. Naredi-Rainer

16
12-14 Bildarchiv Preußischer Kulturbesitz, Berlin

17
15-17 Rheinisches Bildarchiv, Cologne

19
19, 20 Paul v. Naredi-Rainer
21, 22 Kunsthistorisches Institut der Universität Innsbruck

20
18, 23, 24 Kunsthistorisches Institut der Universität Innsbruck
30, 31 Paul v. Naredi-Rainer

21
25-29 Kunsthistorisches Institut der Universität Innsbruck

22
Kunsthistorisches Institut der Universität Innsbruck

23
36 Paul v. Naredi-Rainer
37, 38 Kunsthistorisches Institut der Universität Innsbruck
39 Kölnisches Stadtmuseum

24
40, 41, 43, 44 Kunsthistorisches Institut der Universität Innsbruck
42 Paul v. Naredi-Rainer

25
46, 111 Kunsthistorisches Institut der Universität Innsbruck

26
45, 47-50 Paul v. Naredi-Rainer
51 Kunsthistorisches Institut der Universität Innsbruck

27
52, 53, 55 Kunsthistorisches Institut der Universität Innsbruck
54 Franz Ebner, Knittelfeld

28
56-58 Paul v. Naredi-Rainer

29
59-64 Paul v. Naredi-Rainer

30
65-68, 73 Paul v. Naredi-Rainer

31
69-71 Paul v. Naredi-Rainer
72 Kadu Niemeyer, Rio de Janeiro

32
75-77 Paul v. Naredi-Rainer

33
74 Enrico Cano
(Studio Mario Botta, Lugano)

34
78-80 Paul v. Naredi-Rainer
82 Angelika Schnell, Berlin

35
83, 86 Kunsthistorisches Institut der Universität Innsbruck
84, 85, 87 Paul v. Naredi-Rainer

36
88-91 Paul v. Naredi-Rainer

37
92 (arial photo) Scott Frances/Esto (Richard Meier & Partners, New York)

93-96 Angelika Schnell

38
97-100 Paul v. Naredi-Rainer

39
101-103 Paul v. Naredi-Rainer

40
104 Rheinisches Bildarchiv, Cologne
105-109 Paul v. Naredi-Rainer

41
109, 110 Paul v. Naredi-Rainer
112 Manfred Lehmbruck, from:
deutsche bauzeitung 8/1980, p.12

42
115, 117, 118 Paul v. Naredi-Rainer
119 Herbert Bayer, from: *ARCH*+
156/2000, p. 97

43
113, 114, 116, 120
Paul v. Naredi-Rainer

45
Oliver Hilger, Aachen

48
Gerhard Kahlert, Haltern

49
Gerhard Kahlert

50
Gerhard Kahlert

51
Gerhard Kahlert

53
132 Helmut Müller, Dortmund
133 Renzo Piano Building Workshop, Genoa
138 Paul v. Naredi-Rainer

54
135 Paul v. Naredi-Rainer

55
136, 139 Hans Jürgen Schmitz, Dortmund
137 Peter Zumthor, Haldern

56
140 Hans Jürgen Schmitz
142 Paul v. Naredi-Rainer

57
134 P. Hester (Renzo Piano Building Workshop)

58
143 Hans Jürgen Schmitz

59
141, 144 Hans Jürgen Schmitz

61
145, 146 Paul v. Naredi-Rainer

70-73
Paul v. Naredi-Rainer

74-75
Stefan Müller, Berlin
76-77
Paul v. Naredi-Rainer

78-79
Paul v. Naredi-Rainer

80-81
Hélène Binet, London
(Josef Paul Kleihues, Berlin)

82-83
Paul v. Naredi-Rainer

84-85
Paul v. Naredi-Rainer

86 right
Robert Canfield
(Studio Mario Botta, Lugano)
86 left, 87
Pino Musi
(Studio Mario Botta)

88 left, 89 left
Rheinisches Bildarchiv
88 centre right, 89 right
Artur Pfau, Mannheim

90-93
Paul v. Naredi-Rainer

94-95
Paul v. Naredi-Rainer

96 left, 97 left
Lluís Casals, Barcelona
96 right, 97 right
José Rafael Moneo, Madrid

98 left
Paul v. Naredi-Rainer
98 right, 99
Margherita Spiluttini, Vienna
(Heinz Tesar, Vienna)

100 left, 101 right
Paul v. Naredi-Rainer
100 right, 101 left
Maija Holma
(Alvar Aalto Museum, Jyväskylä)

102 left and right, 103 left
Paul v. Naredi-Rainer
102 centre, 103 right
Scott Frances/Esto
(Richard Meier & Partners)

104-105
Paul v. Naredi-Rainer

106, 107 left and right
Paul v. Naredi-Rainer
107 centre
Wolfgang Zurborn, Cologne

108-109
Paul v. Naredi-Rainer

110, 111 left
Stefan Müller
111 centre and right
Paul v. Naredi-Rainer

112 left, 113 centre and right
Matt Wargo (Venturi, Scott Brown and Assoc., Philadelphia)
112 right
Paul v. Naredi-Rainer
113 left
Phil Starling (Venturi, Scott Brown and Assoc.)

116-117
Paul v. Naredi-Rainer

118 left, 119 right, 121 left
Michel Denancé (Renzo Piano Building Workshop)
118 right, 119 left, 120, 121 right
Paul v. Naredi-Rainer

122-123
Paul v. Naredi-Rainer

124 left
Paul v. Naredi-Rainer
124 right, 125
Margherita Spiluttini

126-127
Paul v. Naredi-Rainer

128-129
Paul v. Naredi-Rainer

130-133
Paul v. Naredi-Rainer

134 left, 135 right
Pei Cobb Freed & Partners, New York
134 right, 135 left
Ezra Stoller ©Esto

136-137
Paul v. Naredi-Rainer

138-141
Paul v. Naredi-Rainer

144, 145 left
Mitsuo Matsuoka (Tadao Ando Arch. & Assoc., Osaka)
145 right
Shigeo Ogawa
(Tadao Ando Arch. & Assoc.)

146 left
Rheinisches Bildarchiv
146 right, 147
Paul v. Naredi-Rainer

148, 149 left
Paul v. Naredi-Rainer
149 right
Kunsthalle Bielefeld

150 left, 151 left
Paul v. Naredi-Rainer
150 right, 151 right
Bernhard Küppers, Bottrop

152
Paul v. Naredi-Rainer
153
Bernadette Clerbout-Sels, Lest

154-155
Paul v. Naredi-Rainer

156-157
Thomas Brown
(Yale Center for British Art)

158-159
Michael Bodycomb
(Kimbell Art Museum)

160-161
Paul v. Naredi-Rainer

162 left
Paul v. Naredi-Rainer
162 right, 163
Hans Werlemann/Hectic Pictures

164 left
Kiyohiko Higashide, Osaka
164 right, 165
Timothy Hursley, Little Rock/AR

166-167
Paul v. Naredi-Rainer

168-169
Paul v. Naredi-Rainer

170 left, 171 left
Heinrich Helfenstein, Zurich
(Gigon + Guyer, Zurich)
170 right, 171 above right and below
Paul v. Naredi-Rainer

174
Gianni Berengo Gardin
(Renzo Piano Building Workshop)
175, 177
Paul v. Naredi-Rainer
176 left
Michel Denancé (Renzo Piano Building Workshop)
176 right
Angelika Schnell, Berlin

178-179
Nacàsa & Partners, Inc.

180-181
Ruedi Walti

182, 183 right
Michel Denancé (Renzo Piano Building Workshop)
183 left
Paul v. Naredi-Rainer

184-185
Paul v. Naredi-Rainer

186, 187 left
Paul v. Naredi-Rainer
187 above right and below
Bernhard Kroll
(Schweger + Partner, Hamburg)

188-189
Paul v. Naredi-Rainer

190-191
Paul v. Naredi-Rainer

192 left, 193
Atelier Prof. Gustav Peichl, Vienna
192 right
Paul v. Naredi-Rainer

194-195
Paul v. Naredi-Rainer

196-197
Paul v. Naredi-Rainer

198 left
Museum of Modern Art, New York
198 right, 199 above left and below
Paul v. Naredi-Rainer

199 right
Angelika Schnell

202 left, 203 right
Yael Pincus, Tel Aviv
202 right, 203 left
Michael Krüger, Berlin

204-205
Søren Robert Lund arkitekter, Copenhagen

206-207
Stefan Müller
208 left and centre
Stefan Müller
208 right, 209
Jüdisches Museum, Berlin

210 left, 211 left
Ezra Stoller ©Esto
210 right, 211 right
Paul v. Naredi-Rainer

212-213
Santiago Calatrava Valls AG, Zurich

214-215
Steven Holl Architects, New York

216 left, 217 right
Paul v. Naredi-Rainer
216 right, 217 left and centre
Michael Reisch
(Zamp Kelp, Düsseldorf)

218-221
Paul v. Naredi-Rainer

224 left, 225 right
Paul v. Naredi-Rainer
224 right, 225 left
Bernhard Kroll
(Schweger + Partner)

226-227
Margherita Spiluttini

228 left
Paul v. Naredi-Rainer
228 right, 229
Michael Schuster
(Klaus Kada, Graz)

230 left
Oliver Kleinschmidt, Berlin
230 right, 231 left
Atelier Schneider
(Josef Paul Kleihues)
231 right
Paul v. Naredi-Rainer

232-233
Paul v. Naredi-Rainer

234-235
Paul v. Naredi-Rainer

236, 237 centre and right
Paul v. Naredi-Rainer
237 left
Dagmar v. Naredi-Rainer, Matrei

238-239
Paul v. Naredi-Rainer

Every effort has been made to trace the copyright holders, architects and designers and we apologise in advance for any unintentional omission and would be pleased to insert the appropriate acknowledgement in any subsequent edition.